THE
Litigation
MANUAL

Depositions

THE
Litigation
MANUAL

Depositions

Priscilla Anne Schwab and Lawrence J. Vilardo, Editors

SECTION *of* LITIGATION
AMERICAN BAR ASSOCIATION

AMERICAN BAR ASSOCIATION
Defending Liberty
Pursuing Justice

Cover design by ABA Publishing.
Cover art by W.B. Park.

Printed in the United States of America.

Cataloging-in-Publication Data is on file with the Library of Congress

The Litigation Manual: Depositons / Priscilla Schwab, editor
ISBN 1-59031-678-9

Discounts are available for books ordered in bulk. Special consideration is given to state bars, CLE programs, and other bar-related organizations. Inquire at Book Publishing, ABA Publishing, American Bar Association, 321 N. Clark, Chicago, Illinois 60610-4714.

www.ababooks.org

CONTENTS

FOREWORD

Every litigator must prepare for depositions at some point in the life of a lawsuit, even if the case doesn't end up in a courtroom and a trial. Over the years, federal and state court rules governing depositions have changed, but the fundamentals of preparation have not. A wise practitioner recognizes the importance of the deposition of an adverse witness to her case; not only will the deposition help her "discover" facts, it will also lock the deponent into a story, and provide clues to the witness's credibility and demeanor. The preparation of one's own witness for a deposition is, for the same reasons, equally vital.

The articles in this book originally appeared in LITIGATION, the quarterly journal of the Section of Litigation, and like all LITIGATION's articles, these are written by active practitioners who are writing practical advice for other practitioners. Some of these articles appeared before the recent update to the Federal Rules of Civil Procedure, but the advice in them stands apart from references to the rules, and reflects the timeless skills necessary for deposition preparation.

LITIGATION seeks to be "practical and concrete, not abstract and theoretical; lively and readable." It has been so since LITIGATION first appeared, in the early 1970s. These articles fulfill the journal's mission to instruct and to help, without ever being dull.

Janet S. Kole
Philadelphia
August 2006

PART I

Preparation

CHAPTER 1

Documents and Depositions: The Basics

Arthur H. Aufses III*

In commercial litigation, documents usually are at the heart of depositions. Some depositions are taken solely to get documents and to establish their admissibility. More often, the examiner seeks substantive testimony from an adverse witness and uses documents to shape, organize, or impeach testimony. Because documents are important, both examining and defending lawyers at depositions must become fluid in handling documents and fluent in the rules governing their use.

Deposition preparation in commercial cases begins with the documents that are produced by and about the witness. Under the federal rules, such documents may be sought from both party and nonparty witnesses before the deposition. Unless a deposition must be expedited, it should not be held until the documents have been received, reviewed, and organized. If it appears that key documents have not been produced and that a motion to compel production will be required, do not conduct the deposition until the motion has been resolved.

*Arthur H. Aufses III is a partner with Kramer, Levin, Naftalis & Frankel in New York City. This article originally appeared in the Winter 1994 issue of LITIGATION.

How you organize documents for use at a deposition varies with the size and demands of the suit. Computers are all the rage now as document organizers, but, even in an era of advanced technology, some of the old rules remain valid.

First, the lawyer who will take the deposition should read every document herself; paralegals and supporting lawyers cannot be relied upon to decide what is significant. Documents invariably contain nuances and clues that the examiner must be prepared to explore.

Second, when reviewing documents, work with a copy—never an original—and use pens or highlighters of different colors. Mark the documents, highlight what seems critical or interesting, write questions for you and your colleagues to pursue. Note the little things—the persons who received carbon copies; the time, date, and origin of telecopy transmissions; the initials of the typist; the handwriting in the margins; the descriptions of any enclosures.

Next, organize the documents chronologically in a "key documents" folder; as new documents are produced, add them to that file. Although computers now let lawyers maintain such files electronically, there still is no substitute for the immediacy of tangible copies in a file near your desk.

Begin by collecting in chronological order all documents that refer to, or were authored or received by, the witness. If a number of depositions will involve the same documents, it is best to perform this "witness pull" only once. If this is done manually, clip to each document a slip of paper that lists all persons whose names appear on the document. As the deposition of any one of those people approaches, a set of the relevant documents can be compiled easily.

The Augmented Chronological Collection

To the chronological collection of documents for each witness, add any other documents on which you plan to ask questions. These may include documents that do not mention the witness, but that are significant in the suit—contracts or deeds, for example. Other possibilities are documents that the witness can authenticate or establish as being business records. In combing through your growing compilation, you will begin to know how much deposition time will be required with the witness. Select the documents that you will want to mark as exhibits at the deposition; that choice will depend on, among other things, the importance of the document, the probable familiarity of the witness with it, and the likelihood that another witness can provide similar testimony concerning it. Obviously (though this sometimes seems to be forgotten by questioning lawyers) you must understand the case before you do this kind of document sorting.

Once you have plucked deposition documents from the chronological master set, you must put them in order for questioning. The examination will proceed either chronologically or by subject matter, or through a combination of the two formats. Choosing an approach involves weighing the interests of simplicity and coherence (which favor a chronological approach) against the value of surprising the witness or exhausting a given topic all at once (which favors the subject matter approach). Some lawyers prefer not to make that decision in advance; they will organize the documents chronologically and by subject matter and then select them as the deposition proceeds. In general, though, you should make up your mind before the deposition starts.

When this decision has been made, ready the documents for use. When I take a deposition, I prefer to work with copies from my "key document" file. By the time of the deposition, these copies have become old friends; many of the questions that I will ask already have been written in the margins. I organize my copies in the order I plan to use them, following my outline of the issues and questions that I expect to pursue.

If a document is to be marked as an exhibit at the deposition, it must be copied. At a minimum, there must be one copy for the stenographer to mark and give to the witness. It is good practice to make another copy to be marked and placed in your office file, as well as copies for the witness's lawyer and for other parties who may be represented at the deposition. In a case with more than four or five parties and a deposition with more than 20 documents, this can result in a formidable stack of paper. The logistics become even more difficult if the deposition is out of town and you must get the copies there in advance. Plan ahead.

I place a set of the copies of each potential exhibit in a separate folder, and I keep the folders in accordion files for easy access during the deposition. The folders are organized in the order I plan to use the documents during the deposition.

It takes time to identify and mark the exhibits at the deposition; thus it often is useful—especially in the dawning era of presumptive deposition time limits—to do that work with the stenographer *before* the deposition and during recesses. Examining lawyers sometimes don't do this because they are reluctant to let the witness and her lawyer see the documents on which the examination will be based. The idea is that surprise will be lost or a documentary trap disarmed. But be realistic; how often can such surprise be achieved? How often does it yield anything but obstructionist blustering? Even if surprise is a concern, the examiner can save time by using a recess to mark at least a few of the documents that will be used after the break.

Pick a Marking System

When the documents are marked, *how* are they marked? What sequence of numbers or letters will be used for identifying documents? Numbers are generally better than letters, because numbers can continue in a single sequence forever, while letters must be repeated. For example, it usually is easier to work with "Exhibit 30" than with "Exhibit DD." When the examiner takes a series of depositions, she can either mark all of the exhibits in a single sequence or start a new sequence at each deposition.

The advantage of a single sequence is that it avoids having many separately marked copies of the same exhibit. The advantage of separate sequences is that the examiner need not worry about bringing to each deposition all of the previously marked exhibits or about remembering where the sequence left off and whether a document has been marked in earlier depositions. If numbers are used, the parties can avoid possible confusion at trial by not using the same numbers for plaintiff's and defendant's exhibits. Plaintiff's exhibits, for example, can begin with 1001, and defendant's exhibits can begin with 3001.

Another common technique is to include the witness's name in the designation—so a document may be Smith 7 or Jones 2. This eliminates the confusion possible from numeral-only separate numbering. Unfortunately, it creates the possibility of another sort of confusion: Jones 2 and Smith 7 (and Brown 301 for that matter) may be the same document. In addition, name and numeral designators are not as easily sorted and searched by computer as numbers alone.

In these matters, there is no perfect answer. Lawyers tend to number documents as they learned to number them in their first few depositions—and they have trouble understanding why anyone would do it any other way.

6

Besides the anticipated exhibits, an examiner should bring to the deposition copies of other documents that refer to the witness or are otherwise significant. These include key pleadings, interrogatory answers, and responses to requests for admissions; discovery orders and confidentiality stipulations; and notable exhibits from prior depositions. You never know when you will need them. If the litigation will involve a series of depositions in the same law office, it often is advisable to arrange for file space to store these sorts of materials.

At the beginning of many depositions—and *all* "document" depositions held under Rule 30(b)(6) or a subpoena *duces tecum*— it often is useful to examine the witness about his search for and production of relevant documents. Many examiners mark the notice, document request, or subpoena as their first exhibit, and take the witness through the categories of requested items. The aim is twofold: to ensure that the witness has searched diligently for documents and produced them or provided them to his lawyer; and to determine whether any documents have been withheld on improper or debatable grounds. Some witnesses try to block this inquiry by saying that they gave "everything" to their lawyer. Push on beyond this response: What kinds of files did the witness (or corporation) have on the events the suit concerns? What was in them? Who maintained them and where? Did the witness make any notes or memoranda? Did he find them when he searched the files? If not, what happened to them? Did he destroy any relevant files? If so, when and why? If the defendant is a corporation, how many offices, divisions, or affiliates were searched? What about document storage facilities? Archives? Microfilm? Did the witness tell someone else to do the document search? Who? What were the instructions?

If such questions reveal that the witness has not searched his files and that relevant documents exist, consider delaying the start of the deposition until the documents are produced. If you traveled a long way to the deposition, proceed with the prepared questioning, press for prompt production, and consider an application to the court for sanctions if the witness's failure to make timely production has caused additional expense to the examiner's side.

Last-Minute Production

Even when document requests have called for production long before the deposition, documents often are produced for the first

7

time by a witness at the deposition. These may be the documents in what is sometimes conveniently called the witness's "personal" file—the one that he kept in his desk or took with him when he left the company. (For that reason, document requests should ask for all such "personal" files of the likely deposition witness.) Or the opponent may have found the documents after the first production. He then produces them at the deposition to avoid a claim that the examiner was prejudiced by not having timely access to all documents.

Such late production of documents presents special problems. The examiner must review the documents—often many of them—quickly at the first available recess. If the documents are produced before the deposition is scheduled to begin, the examiner may choose not to start until he has read the new documents. Unless it is clear that the new documents would add nothing to the examination, the examiner should not agree that the deposition has been concluded until after a full, careful review of all the documents—sometimes on a later day.

The production of documents at a deposition is governed by Rule 30(f) of the Federal Rules of Civil Procedure. Under that rule, the person producing the documents may provide either originals or copies. If copies are produced, the examiner is entitled to a "fair opportunity to verify the copies by comparison with the originals." Although the examiner does not have a right to retain the originals, he "may move for an order that the original be annexed to and returned with the deposition to the court, pending final disposition of the case."

Before asking any questions about the content of documents, try to establish the practices and procedures by which they were created. Who authored documents? Who helped? Where did the information in the documents come from? How much time was spent on drafting? How many drafts were usually made? Were the drafts retained? Who reviewed drafts before a document became final? Whom was it sent to? Who else read it after it became final? Were any special steps taken to ensure its accuracy?

There is a reason to ask these questions early, apart from orderliness. Most people, when questioned about documents or business in general, will want to make themselves look good. The emphasis will be on how accurately and carefully things were done. If that testimony is gotten in first, it will be harder to back away from difficult individual documents. If the witness is first shown a document that is damaging to him, he may be tempted to disavow it by saying record-keeping was shoddy.

The examiner also should explore the witness's procedures for keeping and discarding documents. How were documents filed? What happened to extra copies? Did the witness's organization have written guidelines governing the retention and destruction of documents? Did the witness follow the guidelines? The purpose is as before: by locking the witness into responses to these sorts of questions, it will later be more difficult to justify the disappearance of a document.

Any documents that will be marked at the deposition should be described on the record first. Remember, however, that under Rule 30(c) of the Federal Rules of Civil Procedure, deposition examinations may proceed only "as permitted at the trial under the Federal Rules of Evidence." When the examiner describes the document, the rule is that it is not yet in evidence, and its contents cannot be published to the jury. Thus, to be perfectly scrupulous, the examiner should be careful to describe the document only by date, author, recipient, number of pages, and production numbers. The examiner may say, for example, "We have marked for identification plaintiff's deposition exhibit 15, which appears to be a four-page memorandum carrying production numbers 00020 through 00023, dated January 15, 1999, from Mr. Jones to Ms. Smith." The substance should be developed through testimony, not a predocument speech.

In a deposition, as in any examination, a document may be used as substantive evidence, to impeach, or to refresh recollection. The purpose for which a document is used affects how it is handled by the examiner. Consider each purpose in turn.

Substantive Evidence: A document often contains a record of events that the examiner ultimately will want to place before the fact-finder. A deposition lawyer's principal task is to ensure that such a document will be admissible when the time comes. If the document was created by an adverse party, its substance will be the admission of a party opponent, and thus will not be hearsay (assuming it meets all other party admission requirements). The examiner need only authenticate the document by showing that it is what it purports to be. The examiner should use leading questions to elicit the usual facts from the witness: the witness recognizes the document, the document was created when it appears to have been, and the witness can identify it.

Remember Hearsay Exceptions

If the document was created by someone *other* than the adverse party, it will be admissible for the truth of its substance only if it satisfies an exception to the rule against hearsay. In such cases, the examiner must elicit testimony that both authenticates the document *and* attempts to establish the existence of a hearsay exception.

In commercial suits, by far the most common documentary hearsay exception is the "business records" exception, as codified in Rule 803(6) of the Federal Rules of Evidence. An examining lawyer must know the series of questions used to establish the business records exception: The witness must be a "custodian or other qualified witness"; the document must have been created at or near the time of the events; it must have been created by or from information transmitted by a person with knowledge of those events; it must have been the regular practice of the witness's business activity to make such documents; and the document must have been kept in the course of a regularly conducted business activity. These points are straightforward; their application to the infinity of facts surrounding documents is not. Think ahead for each document you plan to use, and consult the cases if need be.

After establishing the admissibility of a document, the examiner must decide whether to ask other questions about it. This decision turns on the purposes of the deposition and the significance of the document to the examiner's case theory. Some documents are significant only because they were created and delivered; a letter accepting an offer or a memo providing notice of an event or claim are examples. In those cases, the examiner may not need any other testimony about the document.

Less Can Be More

Sometimes, you may not *want* the witness to explain the contents of the document. Suppose, for example, the witness is not a party and is outside the trial subpoena power of the court. The deposition will be the only examination of that witness; he will not show his face in the courtroom. The examiner may not know what the witness will say about the substance of the document and—if the document is good by itself—may prefer not to give the witness an opportunity to confuse or disavow its contents. In those situations, the examiner may choose to do nothing but establish the admissibility of the document. Sometimes, of course, the opposing party will try to elicit such muddying testimony during its deposition cross-examination, and the examiner must use redirect to try to establish that the document should stand on its own.

Evidence Gathering: If the purpose of a deposition is principally to obtain facts and leads for further discovery, the examiner surely will probe the key portions of documents. Who took part in preparing the document? What other documents were used in preparing it? How many drafts of the document existed? What happened to them? How did the drafts differ from the final version? Who received the document? What discussion was there concerning the document? Can you tell us more about the events described in the document?

If the document contains an admission useful to the side taking the deposition, the opposing party may try at trial to attack the accuracy of the document. For the examiner, the deposition is the time to smoke out the nature of this attack. After authenticating the document, determine whether the witness will adopt the statements in it as accurate. If the witness tries to disavow the document, pepper him with questions about the disavowal: If the document is not accurate, why does it say what it does? Was a correction—written or otherwise—ever prepared? Did anyone tell the author that it was inaccurate? If so, is there written evidence of that communication? When were the statements "corrected"—before or after the parties were in dispute? Was the author reprimanded for his "mistake"? If so, where is the written evidence of that reprimand? If the document is inaccurate, in precisely what ways does it go wrong? How does that compare with other facts and evidence in the case?

In trying to *prevent* questioning about the contents of a document, defending lawyers sometimes object on the ground that the "document speaks for itself." Ignore this objection. It is meritless. You are entitled to determine if the document accurately describes events. If the witness authored the document, ask the witness why he wrote the document and what he meant by particular passages. Similarly, if the witness had seen the document, you are entitled to know, for example, what the witness understood the document to mean and whether the witness did anything in response to it. If the "speaks for itself" objection continues or, even worse, the witness is instructed not to answer on that basis, go to the court for help.

11

Impeachment or Refreshment: Before using a document to impeach a witness's deposition testimony or to refresh his recollection, the examiner usually questions the witness on the events without referring to the document. The aim is to exhaust the witness's recollection and to pin down his version of the event.

If the defending lawyer knows that there is a document that describes the events covered by the questions, he may start to play games: He may try to keep the witness from contradicting the document by pressing to have the document placed before him during testimony. The usual argument on this point is that the deposition should not become a "memory test" and that the examiner is somehow not interested in the facts, but instead is trying to "trick" the witness. This argument often is made as part of a long-winded speaking objection so that, even if the examiner decides not to let the witness see the document, the witness will be forewarned and reminded of what the document says. And, miraculously, some witnesses, after being instructed by such an objection, will say they are likely to get confused or make mistakes if they can't see the document.

The examiner should resist this gambit. In one sense, the deposition *is* a "memory test." One of its appropriate purposes is to establish what the witness remembers and how well, without the help of documents. You are never obligated to show the witness any documents. When the examiner does use documents, she is entitled to use them after questioning concerning the events described in the documents.

Whenever there is an inconsistency between the testimony and a document, the examiner must decide whether to confront the witness with the document. If the oral testimony is more favorable for the examiner's side, she undoubtedly will leave the document in her file. But if the document contains a more favorable version of the event, the decision becomes more difficult. Again, choice is guided by the purposes of the deposition. If the witness is not likely to testify at trial, and the deposition will be the only questioning of that witness, then the examiner probably will be forced to try to impeach the witness with the document.

Should the Witness See It?

But, if the witness is expected to testify again at trial, and the deposition testimony is not admissible in the opposing party's case in chief (as, for example, when the deposition witness is the

12

opposing party himself), then the examiner's decision is still more difficult. If the examiner confronts the witness with the document in the deposition, the witness may be able, right there, to reconcile the testimony with the document. The informality of a deposition makes that easier. Even if the deposition explanation is halting, the witness may come up with something better in the time between deposition and trial. In the end, the examiner may choose to save the document for use during cross-examination at trial.

When using a document to impeach deposition testimony, a lawyer must try to convince the witness that the version contained in the document is more credible than the deposition testimony—so that the witness retracts the deposition testimony and adopts the document. To accomplish this, several considerations can be stressed in questioning. The date of the document will be nearer to that of the events than is the deposition. The recollections and observations contained in the document should therefore have been more fresh than the witness's memory in the deposition. Also, the witness's practices and procedures undoubtedly were intended to ensure the accuracy of the document. The document probably was written before a dispute arose (or at least before the lawsuit was begun) and thus before the time the witness might be influenced by its impact on the case. (If the document was created *after* the dispute arose and it still is helpful, it will be that much more powerful before the jury.) And between the date of the document and the day of the deposition, the witness surely has prepared with a lawyer and probably even reviewed the particular document with the lawyer.

Showing that a witness has been primed with pat testimony or selected documents can be part of successful impeachment, but it is factually and legally tricky. It always is useful to ask whether key documents were shown to the witness in preparation for the deposition. The defending lawyer, however, often invokes attorney-client privilege and the lawyer work product doctrine to block an answer. The examiner has several tools with which to overcome that objection. Rule 612 of the Federal Rules of Evidence allows the court, in the interests of justice, to order production of, and permit cross-examination on, any writing that a witness used "to refresh memory" before testifying. On this authority, when the conditions of the rule were satisfied, courts have ordered the production of documents that counsel provided to witnesses before their depositions, even when those compilations comprised lawyer work product ordinarily immune from discovery. *See, e.g., James Julian, Inc. v. Raytheon Co.,* 93 F.R.D. 138, 144–46 (D. Del. 1982); *Wheeling-Pittsburgh Steel Corp. v. Underwriters Laboratories, Inc.,* 81 F.R.D. 8, 9–11 (N.D. Ill. 1978). Some more recent cases, however, have declined to order the production of such documents where it has not been shown that the witness "relied upon the requested documents for his testimony and that those documents impacted on his testimony." *See Sporck v. Peil,* 759 F.2d 312, 318 (3d Cir. 1985); Applegate, "Preparing for Rule 612," 19 *Litigation,* No. 3, at 17 (Spring 1993).

Drawing on these cases, your questions must track Rule 612. Ask whether the witness was shown any documents in preparation for the deposition and whether that review refreshed the witness's memory. If the witness admits to having had his memory refreshed in any way by the documents, the examiner will have a basis to press for production. It will remain for the defending lawyer to contend that the examiner must show that exposure to particular documents both refreshed the witness's memory and caused a change in the witness's testimony.

After exhausting a witness's recollection on a subject (with or without using a document to refresh), an examining lawyer should ask whether the witness knows of other documents that would help him to remember more. If he identifies such documents and they have been produced, the examiner should question the witness about them until the witness's memory has been exhausted. If the witness describes documents that have not been produced, they should be requested on the record. At the deposition, defending lawyers rarely agree to produce those documents; instead, they "note the request" or take it "under advisement." Whether or not the defending lawyer agrees to produce the documents, the examiner should follow up immediately after the deposition: Send a written request, either in a letter or a formal request for the production of documents under applicable rules.

In questioning a witness about a document, assume that the transcript will be read to the jury at trial. Try to visualize the scene at trial and frame the questions so that the transcript will be coherent for the jury. If you get too relaxed and conversational, what seemed like free, easy, and useful testimony may come out awkward and ineffective (at best) when read, flat and

14

cold, in court two years later. Therefore, observe certain formalities. Unless there is a compelling reason to do it differently, begin questions with the first page of the document and proceed toward the end. When referring to a "key passage," make clear where in the document (by page and paragraph number) that passage is. Read the passage into the record, and then question the witness about it. Have the witness identify any handwriting and define any technical terms or jargon. Use page and paragraph numbers. Avoid pronouns and indefinite articles. "This," "that paragraph," or "the earlier sentence" may mean something in the deposition, but they won't later.

Reorganize the Documents

When the deposition ends, the examiner must again organize the documents. Ensure that none of the original, marked exhibits is missing. Prepare a set of copies of those exhibits for the office. Restore all documents to the "key documents" file. Make a list of the exhibits that were marked, and have it printed both according to the order in which the exhibits were marked and in chronological order by the dates of the exhibits. Note the documents that were requested orally at the deposition, and immediately prepare a written request. If the witness produced documents at the deposition, and some of them were marked as exhibits, make copies so that the production set is kept intact. Such follow-up work is critical.

What are the document-related duties of a lawyer *defending* a deposition? The preparation of the defending lawyer will mirror that of the examiner. The defender will compile his own set of documents that refer or relate to the witness and will try to anticipate all the questions that the examiner is likely to base on those documents.

Documents can be central to the defender's preparation sessions with the witness. In addition to the customary instructions to answer only the question posed and not to guess or volunteer, the defender will focus on special problems in responding to documents.

A witness must be taught to resist the pressures that documents can create in a deposition. For example, a witness may feel he will appear incredible, untruthful, or inept if he testifies that he does not recall sending a letter he authored or receiving a letter that was sent to him. The witness must be helped to understand such a lack of memory may be entirely credible—anyway, if it is true, it should be the testimony. If the witness says he remembers a document when he actually does not, a questioning lawyer may have a field day pressuring the witness into making harmful admissions concerning the circumstances and contents of the document about which he knows little. In such instances, the witness must be shown that he can truthfully say, for example, that while he has no reason to doubt that the document was sent or received, he has no memory of it.

Similarly, the witness must be helped to understand that documents are not always accurate. They are tangible. They seem more real than mere memory. For that reason, documents can have a formidable presence. They don't change and may intimidate uncertain witnesses. But documents too have flaws, most embedded at their creation. They may contain shorthand descriptions that are not complete, plus estimates and predictions that proved inaccurate. In fact, memoranda may not have been intended to provide an exhaustive or even accurate account of events. The best way to train the witness on these points is through a mock cross-examination, using the documents that the defender expects the examiner to use in the deposition.

In preparing the witness, the defender, like the examiner, must be sensitive to the potential impact of Rule 612. In fact, though she may fight it, the defender should assume that all documents she shows the witness will be discoverable. As a consequence, the defender should try to avoid showing the witness any document that has not already been produced in discovery. Lawyer work product, such as internal memoranda and draft briefs, should not be shown to the witness at all. A chronology can be useful in helping the witness to reconstruct key events, but the defender will have to weigh that benefit against any costs of possibly having to produce the chronology. Consider acquainting the witness with the chronology orally. Similarly, if binders or other compilations of documents may reveal the defense's case theories, don't present the documents to the witness in that form.

At the deposition, the defender must work to protect the witness within the increasingly strict limits imposed by the rules. Be sure that the witness carefully reviews all documents that are shown to him. Do not allow him to answer any questions concerning a document until he has reviewed it. If the document is long, the witness should focus on the sections of concern to the examiner. The defender should try to have the witness review each document in the same deliberate way so that the examiner cannot tell whether the witness has been surprised by any of them.

The defender must keep the witness from being misled. The witness may be shown only part of a document, or a document without its exhibits or enclosures. If such additional material is necessary to provide the witness with a context for the questioning, the defender should insist that it be presented to the witness. If the examiner declines, the defender will have to decide between an instruction not to answer (which may not be permissible under practice or rules in many courts) or just objecting (perhaps pointing out in the process that such ill-informed testimony is pointless and misleading) and allowing the questioning to proceed.

A witness sometimes may be shown a document that he neither authored nor received. If the examiner then asks the witness about the contents of the document, the line of questioning may be objectionable. The examiner certainly may inquire about the witness's own communications or actions concerning the contents of the document or the events it recounts, but questions about the witness's understanding of those contents may improperly assume that the witness actually had such an understanding. Questions about what the document "means" are likely to be objectionable on the ground that they call for the witness to speculate. Although, in response to such questions, the defender will be free to object, an instruction not to answer may not be appropriate. The witness is the party mostly responsible for coming up with a proper answer. With documents, as with other aspects of the deposition, the success of the defense depends principally on the quality of the preparation.

CHAPTER 2

Reconstructing Reality: Preparing the Deponent to Testify

Dennis R. Suplee and Diana S. Donaldson*

Rader and I had a dozen similar conferences over the next five months. "Preparing testimony," it was called. . . . I was fascinated by the testimony that was produced by our Socratic Dialogues. . . . There were qualifying phrases here and there . . . but there wasn't a single lie in it. And yet it wasn't the truth.

P. Caputo, A Rumor of War, pp. 329–330 (1977).

You place the two documents side by side, one apparently contradicting the other. The police report describes 20 feet of skid marks from the tires of Harry Sweeney's car leading to the point of impact. Next to the police report is the statement Harry made to the investigator. In it, Harry says flatly, "I never saw the other car before the crash."

---

*Dennis R. Suplee and Diana S. Donaldson are partners in the Philadelphia office of Schnader Harrison Segal & Lewis LLP. They are coauthors of The Deposition Handbook: Strategies, Tactics and Mechanics. This article originally appeared in the Fall 1988 issue of LITIGATION.

What is the truth? Are trial lawyers charged with finding it? These questions confront you when you first encounter your own witnesses, usually with a deposition on the horizon.

You depend on the witness's memory. But human memory is frail. The typical deponent does not have a clear and specific recollection of all the important events. If there was an accident, he saw a thousand details in the blink of an eye. Months, or even years, later he will remember them selectively. Sometimes, he will unconsciously substitute inference or desire for memory. In a business case, the problem may be reversed. Not a thousand dramatic details in a flash, but a thousand unremarkable details in slow motion, diluted by millions of mundane daily events.

Is It True?

Preparing a witness for a deposition means fashioning a reality from what the witness remembers (or thinks he remembers) and can testify to with conviction (or at least with a modicum of assurance). Your job, and that of every trial lawyer, is to help the deponent reconstruct his memory even though you do not know whether that restored memory is the truth. In a way, the process is truth neutral.

This aspect of witness preparation has produced familiar, faintly cynical guidelines. Some experienced litigators say you should strive for a reconstruction that helps your client's position, regardless of your own view of the truth. In fact, you have been told that your notion of the truth is irrelevant to preparing the witness (unless, of course, you believe that the witness is lying). But this is troubling advice. Even if you accept it, you still face the hard question: How eagerly do you invite the witness to adopt a version of the facts you yourself do not believe?

These are not idle exercises in moral philosophy. You are a lawyer (an ethical one, you tell yourself), alone in your office, struggling with an intensely practical question: Can you sell the fact finder a story you do not buy?

The answer for most of us is no. A central challenge of witness preparation is therefore this: You must prepare the witness to tell a coherent, credible story in a way that does not compromise his view of the truth but still helps your case.

Each time you prepare a witness for a deposition you remind yourself of the goal: effective reconstruction of reality. Each time, you should review a handful of rules that prepare you to prepare the deponent to undertake such reconstruction:

Rule 1: Preparing a deponent is harder than taking a deposition. To take a deposition, you need only develop *an* approach and questions to elicit the desired testimony. But to prepare a deponent, you must anticipate *every* plausible line of attack, sometimes even anticipating how individual questions may be worded.

When you take a deposition, you control the questions. But no matter how well you prepare your witness, your control of the answers will be indirect at best. There is little room for corrective action once the deposition starts. Your only weapons are objections and instructions (rarely given) not to answer. Neither helps much in a surprise attack.

You need to remind yourself periodically how much more difficult it is to prepare a witness for a deposition than it is to take a deposition. Otherwise, you may succumb to the feeling that being onstage—being the dogged inquisitor in the limelight—is more important than being behind the scenes. Experienced litigators know better. That is why younger lawyers usually get to take depositions of the other side's witnesses long before they get to prepare their side's important witnesses.

Maintaining good client relations is another reason for giving top priority to preparing and representing the deponent. If a client's employee performs badly at his deposition, the senior litigator will not enjoy the questions he will get about where he was and why he let a less experienced lawyer handle the deposition. From the client's viewpoint, there can never be satisfactory answers to such questions. The presence of a senior counsel may have made no difference, but you cannot prove it. The lesson is clear: If you are lead lawyer on a case and your witness may be bloodied at a deposition, be sure you are near enough to be splattered.

Rule 2: Determine whether the witness is your client. Before ever meeting the deponent, carefully examine whether a lawyer-client relationship exists between you and him. If it does not, decide whether efforts should be made to create one. The benefits are, of course, substantial. Only if a lawyer-client relationship exists is the witness preparation session protected from discovery. And, only if you represent the witness can you instruct him not to answer at the deposition.

Fortunately, it is usually clear whether you represent a particular corporation or individual in a lawsuit. *Former* employees of a corporate client are the principal problem. Some courts have held that predeposition sessions between former employees of a company and counsel for that company are protected by the attorney-client privilege. *In re Coordinated Pretrial Proceedings in Petroleum Antitrust Litigation*, 658 F.2d 1355 (9th Cir. 1981). That is not a universal view, however. *See, e.g., Henderson v. National R. R. Passenger Corp.* 113 F.R.D. 502, 510 (N.D. Ill. 1986). Blithely assuming that someone who used to work for your client is still covered by the lawyer-client relationship can be a major mistake.

Even though a lawyer-client relationship is normally useful, remember that you can sacrifice potential benefits by representing a former employee. For example, in a dispute about insurance coverage, counsel for the defendant insurer in his opening statement portrayed a former employee of the company as a disinterested witness. The gambit failed badly. Opposing counsel called the witness as part of her own case; the former employee conceded that he had retained the insurance company's lawyer at no fee to represent him at his deposition. He had followed several instructions by that lawyer not to answer questions. The plaintiff's lawyer then was granted leave to ask leading questions on the ground that the former employee had become "a witness identified with an adverse party." Fed. R. Evid. 611(c).

A particularly difficult case is the so-called disgruntled former employee who, you believe, is inclined to "get even" by giving deposition testimony harmful to his prior employer, your client. Even if he is willing to meet to prepare and to be represented by you at the deposition, it may be best not to do so. The more closely identified he is with you in the pretrial stage of the case, the harder it will be at trial to convince the jury that his harmful testimony is the product of vindictiveness. Of course, if you meet with the witness in advance of the deposition, you then have a chance to persuade him to put aside his personal animus toward the employer and to live up to his oath by telling his facts truthfully at the deposition. But if you choose that option yet sense that he is still determined to torpedo the employer's case, don't undertake to represent him at the deposition.

At the beginning of a deposition, your opponent may attack your attorney-client relationship with the former employee-witness. There are steps you can take to lessen the effectiveness of such an assault. Try, for example, not to initiate the representation at the last minute. If an offer of representation is to be made, it should be made by your client, not by you. Avoid being in the awkward position of having to offer your services when you and the former employee first meet. And before anyone offers anything, consider whether dual representation could create conflicts.

Do Your Homework

Rule 3: Do your homework before meeting with the deponent. Too often an inexperienced (or careless) lawyer will begin an initial fact-gathering session with a witness by rummaging through the file for a quick reminder of what the case is about. He may simultaneously ask the witness where he fits into things. Such an approach is inexcusable. You must prepare.

The first thing to do is review the file. Get a firm grasp on the contentions of the parties and the facts (agreed and disputed) revealed in answers to interrogatories, interviews, depositions, and the underlying documents. Have at hand a chronology of the significant underlying events, documents relevant to the witness (including those written by, addressed to, or received by the witness), the most important documents in the case (even if the witness did not write or receive them), and a list of words and actions attributed to the witness by others at their depositions.

Find out as much about the witness as you can. Learn what he is likely to know. What is he like? Bright? A good listener? Likely to follow instructions? Naturally confident? Taciturn? Too eager to please? Garrulous? Reasonable? Opinionated? Likely to panic under pressure? In an accident case, look for hints in an investigator's report. In a business case, ask house counsel for insights and the story behind internal memoranda.

Try to identify those subjects where painstaking fact reconstruction is likely to be important. In a business case, for example, the deposition could turn on whether a deponent's memory of what was said at a key meeting is consistent with that of others who were there. In any kind of case, the deposition could turn on two contradictory—or apparently contradictory—documents.

Rule 4: Before meeting, plan your strategy for refreshing memory with documents. Decide which documents you will show the deponent. This decision can be crucial: Federal Rule of Evidence 612 (and its state analogues) may require you to produce to opposing counsel any document used to refresh a deponent's memory, even if it has not been requested or produced. Even if the documents *have* been provided, this production requirement may be troublesome. Think about whether you want to let opposing counsel learn which documents you considered important enough for the deponent to review. Your opponent may take a closer look at such key documents and see new significance in them.

Decide before you meet with the deponent how you will avoid or minimize these risks of refreshing memory. If you decide not to show the document to the witness, be careful not to describe it in detail; this would arguably bring it within the production rule. If you do use the document, and it does not refresh his memory, prepare him to say that at the deposition.

There are other ways to deal with the problem of Rule 612. If the witness was only shown documents that have already been produced, you can say that at the deposition, and assert that a second, repeat production is not, as Rule 612 requires, "necessary in the interests of justice." Another approach is to have the deponent review many documents beforehand, all of which have been produced to the other side. That way, if production is required under Rule 612, opposing counsel will not learn what you think are the most important documents: The important will be masked by the unimportant. Finally, look at *Sporck v. Peil*, 759 F.2d 312 (3d Cir.) *cert. denied*, 474 U.S. 903 (1985). It holds that a lawyer's selection and compilation of documents to prepare a witness for a deposition is work product; it further holds that Rule 612 will override this work product protection for documents the witness relied on in his testimony only if opposing counsel shows that the witness used those documents to refresh his memory and to answer specific, relevant deposition questions. Courts have disagreed with *Sporck*'s extension of opinion work product protection to counsel's selection of documents. *See In re San Juan DuPont Plaza Hotel Fire Litigation*, 859 F.2d 1007, 1018 (1st Cir. 1988); *Pepsi-Cola Bottling Co. v. Pepsico, Inc.*, 2001 U.S. Dist. LEXIS 19935 (D. Kan. 2001). Some courts that have agreed with *Sporck* have confined it to situations in which there was a real concern that a lawyer's thought processes concerning strategy would be disclosed. *See In re Grand Jury Subpoenas*, 959 F.2d 1158, 1167 (2d Cir. 1992); *Gould Inc. v. Mitsui Mining & Smelting*, 825 F.2d 676, 680 (2d Cir. 1987). *See also Hambarian v. Comm'r*, 118 T.C. 565, 2002 U.S. Tax Ct. LEXIS 35 (2002).

Rule 5: Plan fact gathering and witness preparation as two stages. Fact gathering and witness preparation are different. Many lawyers confuse the two. As a result, they do neither well.

In gathering the facts, you want the deponent to be expansive, to volunteer possibly relevant information even if you have not specifically asked for it. Reconstruction of reality begins with such memory dredging. But deposition preparation is entirely different; you want the deponent to answer questions as he would at the deposition itself—briefly and to the point, providing no information beyond what the question requires.

It can be difficult for you and disorienting for the deponent to switch back and forth from fact gathering to witness preparation. Worse yet, such confusion can cause the deponent—convinced by your witness preparation advice—not to tell you all the important facts you need to know. That happened to a lawyer representing the manufacturer of a new surgical device that supposedly malfunctioned during surgery. The lawyer, who had conscientiously prepared the manufacturer's salesman, was not fazed by a deposition inquiry about where the salesman was during the operation. But he was astonished by the answer: "In the operating room. This was a new device and I wanted to see personally how well it performed." Asked later why he had not mentioned this in the preparation session, the witness said, "You never asked me directly about it, and you told me not to volunteer."

To avoid such unhappy results, have two separate sessions: one for facts and another for preparation. If you cannot do that, split your meeting with the witness into two clearly defined stages.

Rule 6: Carefully control how and when the witness will first recount crucial events. Despite your best efforts, it is not always easy to separate fact gathering from witness preparation, so remember this: The first discussion of events, whatever it is called, is likely to be critical. The deponent will likely stick to his version of the facts from the first session.

Therefore, before you have the witness say anything, be sure you know where the trouble spots are in the case and in his view of events. With that knowledge firmly in mind, be sure you ask questions the first time around that do not invite, or stampede, the witness into an unhelpful narrative. The bad story may prove to be both the witness's reality and the truth—but it may not. So, when you first meet, work around the problem to see if what actually happened may have been something else.

25

Rule 7: Give the deponent the big picture first. Start your fact-gathering session by giving the deponent a context. If he is anxious about what a deposition is and why his testimony is important, he may be distracted. His concentration may suffer. Explain that a deposition is questioning under oath in advance of trial. Tell him that courts allow depositions so each side can learn the facts to improve the chances of settlement or, if the case is tried, to produce a just result.

Describe the physical setting of the deposition, including where it will be taken, who will probably be present, and what the court reporter does. Assure the witness that you will be there to represent him. After this, tell him you will focus later on rules of thumb for answering deposition questions, but that you now want to move to the facts.

Some lawyers like to save time by sending the deponent a letter covering these points before their first meeting. But, even if you send a letter, review the points. Many witnesses will not read your missive. Some who do may not understand.

Do not assume that a witness—even a main actor—knows the contentions of the parties or recalls the key facts in dispute. Months or years may have elapsed since the events leading to the lawsuit. Unlike you, the deponent probably has not lived with the case all that time. Furthermore, he is probably not trained to organize his experience into the pigeonholes of the law. Even if the witness says he understands the dispute and remembers well his relevant experiences, insist on being sure you are both on the same wavelength. Outline the major contentions of each side and the most important facts each relies on to support its position.

Next, confirm with the witness the dates of the pivotal events in the case. In a contract case, for example, these might include the date that the contract was entered into, the date on which the deponent first learned that scarcity of raw materials would make it hard to perform, and the date of the alleged breach. Especially where the timing is important, it may help to have the witness consult a chronology of the most important events. (Assume that opposing counsel will ultimately discover this chronology.)

Rule 8: First review the facts chronologically. Learn what the deponent knows of the relevant facts. Skipping randomly from event to event increases the risk that you will miss something. A chronological review is easy to follow and reduces the chance of oversight. Take each key event in order, and ask what, if anything, the deponent knows about it. Ask appropriate follow-up questions, and then ask whether anything important happened between that event and the next one on the list.

A case loaded with documents requires more. While there is much to be said for also presenting documents in chronological order, it is time-consuming and tedious to review the facts and documents at the same time during the first pass through. Worse, the big picture may be obscured by a mass of detail.

Instead, review the facts first, including perhaps the five or six most important documents. At the end of that exercise, review the main points with the deponent to be sure that nothing has been overlooked. Then, review all of the documents separately. That way, the deponent will begin his review of the documents with a good hold on the facts, which will be reinforced by the document review.

Rule 9: Try to get at the facts from different angles. A chronological review is only the beginning. Follow that with questions about various topics or allegations. Suppose, for example, plaintiff claims defendant's employees fraudulently misrepresented the capabilities of defendant's software. You are defendant's lawyer and review with your client's employees the conversations that took place at four meetings between the parties. Do not stop there. Take a different tack and ask about misrepresentations as a thematic unit: Do you personally know any facts that might support the claim that plaintiff was misled? Anything an employee of defendant might have said or done? Or failed to say or do? Maybe unintentionally? Anything that might have been misunderstood? Have you heard anything from anyone else that could support the claim?

Explore even remote possibilities. Suppose now that you represent plaintiff in the software case. Counsel for defendant notices the deposition of plaintiff's controller, presumably to learn about plaintiff's damage claim. When you prepare the controller for his deposition, be sure to ask whether he knows anything about the principal liability facts. Even if he did not participate in the meetings at which the misrepresentations were allegedly made, has he heard from others what was said there?

Few things will make you feel more uncomfortable than failing to cover a significant question in a preparation session and then having it asked at the deposition. Remorse will wash over you as you hear it, and watch the witness, unprepared, flounder around. He could have testified confidently and effectively if you had prepared him properly.

Rule 10: Structure your questions carefully. Reconstruction is the hardest part of fact gathering. The most important thing about it may be the order in which you ask questions. How you do this varies with the case. Many suits will present reconstruction challenges that become apparent only when you meet the witness.

Faulty Sprinklers

Take, for example, a case in which your client's building has burned down. Whether insurance covers the loss depends on reconstruction of a telephone conversation between the insurance company's agent and the employee in charge of insurance for your client. The agent said he was issuing a property insurance binder on the building, but that the policy would contain a sprinkler clause (i.e., no coverage if sprinklers are not operational). After the binder was issued, but before the policy itself was delivered, fire destroyed the building. The sprinklers did not operate. The insurance agent claims he told your man that if there were a fire and the sprinklers were not in operating order, there would be no coverage.

In the first fact-gathering session, your client's employee is candid: His recollection of the telephone conversation is hazy. He thinks he remembers the agent's saying that the sprinkler clause affected only rate, not coverage. But he is hesitant to deny the agent's story.

How do you reconstruct this reality? Do not focus on the deponent's doubt. That will reinforce it. Instead, recount the scene described by the agent and press your witness on what he would have done if the agent is right. It might go this way:

> You're sitting in your office. You've asked the insurance company to cover this warehouse. The phone rings. The insurer's agent tells you that he will issue the binder, but that it will be made subject to a sprinkler clause. He says that means that if the warehouse burns down because the sprinklers are not operational, you have no insurance.
>
> What do you do? Say "Thank you," hang up, and go back to your paperwork?
>
> Did you know whether the sprinklers in the warehouse worked?

Who did?

Well, if the conversation really had gone the way the agent says, what would you have done?

Do you remember saying to yourself, "I should call Charlie Johnson to check if the sprinklers are operational," or anything like that?

What was the amount of this policy?

Do you recall deciding not to bother calling Johnson even though this was a $5 million policy?

Did you just decide to take a chance and hope for the best? What possible reason would there be to do that?

How about when you first found out about the fire? Did the thought go through your mind, "My Lord! I wonder if we don't have any insurance because the sprinklers weren't operational"?

Now think back to the original conversation about the binder. Is this other guy right about what he says he told you?

If the deponent then says he is sure the agent did not say the sprinkler clause would affect coverage, follow up with, "Do you feel comfortable with that? Is it the truth?"

Then try various alternative formulations to find the most positive one the deponent agrees with. He might prefer "To the best of my recollection, Mr. X mentioned only rate, not coverage, in telling me about the clause." Or he might like, "Although I do not recall the conversation verbatim, Mr. X said something to the effect that the clause concerned rate. I feel certain that if Mr. X had mentioned that we would not have coverage if the sprinklers were not operational, I would remember that." And so on.

Rule 11: Take the deponent through formal practice sessions. There are a few basic, well-worn rules of thumb about how to answer the other side's questions at a deposition. They boil down to this:

1. Listen to the question.
2. Be sure you hear the question.
3. Be sure you understand the question.
4. Answer the question, nothing more. Don't volunteer. If you don't know the answer to the question, say that. If you don't remember, say that.
5. Stick to your first answer (if it was truthful and accurate).
6. Tell the truth.

Such rules are like a lecture on how to swim. A pupil may understand the words, but have trouble applying them in deep water with a storm coming up.

After you give the deponent the traditional preliminary instructions, turn to the substance of the testimony. Take him through some dry runs. But be certain that you both know when you are simply lawyer and client consulting about the deposition, and when you are "playing" opposing counsel interrogating the deponent in deposition.

Say something like, "You're on the stand, Mr. Segal," before you question him for real. To end the mock deposition, say "You're off the stand, Mr. Segal." Then switch to the deponent's first name. Those cues should let the deponent know at any moment whether he is on stage and should follow the testimony rules, or is off stage, conferring with his own lawyer, and should speak freely.

Even when the witness is not giving mock testimony, always avoid shorthand references that could be dangerous. In one case, a deponent wrote a letter that ended by inviting questions about enclosed specifications. The other side had never responded to that invitation, but still later claimed the specifications were ambiguous. The invitation was a big help to deponent's side of the case.

When his lawyer first asked about the closing line of the letter, the deponent flippantly said the invitation was "sales garbage." Then, more seriously, he said he would have been glad to field any questions. The deponent and his lawyer continued to banter about "sales garbage," though they both knew better than to use that language at the deposition. Unfortunately . . . You know the rest: When the letter was mentioned at the deposition, the deponent, like Pavlov's dog, blurted out, "That was just sales garbage."

Rule 12: Adapt the "don't volunteer" rule to the individual. The most troublesome rule for a deponent is, "Answer the question, nothing more. Don't volunteer." Lawyers say it to keep deponents from rambling on—which is important—but they do not mean it. At least not all the time. For example, if defendant's design engineer in a product liability case were faithfully following the rule, he might testify this way:

Q: Isn't it a fact that three years before the manufacture of this product you thought about relocating the on-off switch?
A: Yes.

30

Q: Isn't it a fact that if it had been relocated to the place you were considering, this accident would not have happened?

A: Yes.

Q: Back when you were considering making this change, did you determine the additional cost of relocating this switch?

A: Yes.

Religiously following the instruction to answer the question and say nothing more, the deponent would not volunteer the reason the switch was not relocated: He and others concluded that relocation presented an even greater risk that an employee would accidentally trip the switch. Nor would he say that the added cost was so slight that it was not considered in deciding whether to make the change.

Of course, you may ask your own questions at the end of the interrogation to develop this helpful information. But the fact finder will suspect this delayed explanation is a fabrication, particularly if it follows a break when the deponent may have conferred with you. The explanation may seem even more suspect if it is presented for the first time at trial.

How do you let the deponent know when to follow the "don't volunteer" rule and when to answer aggressively? The best you can do is to tell the deponent to follow the general rule when in doubt, but to remember there are exceptions. Then try to give the exceptions life. An abstract discussion of the problem will not help. Go "on the stand" and use some examples of anticipated lines of inquiry to which the deponent should respond aggressively.

Types of Witnesses

Some witnesses never seem to get it. You want to crawl into their skins and answer for them. But most will find your examples useful, and some may develop an instinct for sensing questions that call for aggressive testimony.

Above all, consider the deponent's personality. That will dramatically affect the application of the "don't volunteer" rule. The compulsive technician, the arrogant businessman, the taciturn bookkeeper, the angry doctor—each will hear and follow your instructions in a different way. And each will respond differently to the personality and style of the real interrogator.

Rule 13: Be tough, but build the deponent's confidence. Prepare the deponent by being harder on him than the interrogator will be.

Experiment with different approaches to the same subject, though the interrogator may use only one. But think twice about playing the hard-nosed interrogator when the deponent gives a wrong answer to a tough question. At the deposition, of course, the interrogator will ruthlessly pursue any opening. But one of your objectives is to give the deponent confidence. Repeatedly forcing him to the wall will not do that.

Do not deflate your witness. Give him a taste of hard reality, then show him how to cope with it. Immediately after the deponent gives a bad answer, tell him he is "off the stand" and then explain the implications of his answer. Rattle off the next six or seven questions that opposing counsel would ask, but do not force the deponent to answer them. Leave him whole and give him a chance to do it right.

Rule 14: Keep preparing the deponent until the deposition is over. Continuity is the key. Be in touch with and attuned to the deponent, a living, changing person. Ideally, meet the deponent five to 10 days before the deposition and then again for a brush-up session on the morning of the deposition. The timing of the initial meeting (or meetings, if the fact-gathering session will be separate) is important. It should be early enough to let the fact reconstruction settle in. If the deposition starts too soon after the fact-reconstruction session, the deponent still may be tentative about the truth of the reconstructed facts.

In the interval between the fact-reconstruction session and the deposition, the deponent can test the accuracy of the recon-structed facts. He may recall additional details which will con-firm—or cast doubt on—the reconstructed facts. In business liti-gation, the deponent may speak with others who know about the events or consult other documents to verify the reconstructed facts.

Anticipate these possibilities. Tell him whether you want him to consult anyone or anything else. Recognize that by informing himself on new subjects, he may be forced to answer substantive deposition questions instead of saying he does not know. Worse yet, he may consult with, and be tainted by, unreliable sources.

If you tell the deponent it is all right to check other sources to confirm his recollection, ask him to keep you posted on what he is learning. Otherwise, on the morning of the deposition, he may arrive and tell you, "I've figured it all out, and what I told you the other day is wrong."

Witness preparation does not end even when the deposition starts. Without being unduly instructive or obstructive, you can remind the deponent of the rules of thumb and even encourage him to be more forthcoming. If the deponent is asked and gives the date of a meeting, you may cut off his impulse to tell what was said at the meeting by reminding him not to volunteer. If you have to, be tougher, saying, "You've answered the question. Keep quiet and wait for the next one."

On the other hand, if the deponent's terse answers may be misleading, protect the record and prompt the deponent by saying to the interrogator, "Well, there's a lot more to it than that, as you will find if you ask a few follow-up questions." While such a verbal nudge to the witness is arguably at odds with Rule 30(d)(1)'s requirement that objections be made in a "non-suggestive manner," if the defending lawyer's conduct is otherwise unobjectionable, it is unlikely that the interrogator will make an issue of it, particularly if the suggestion is made in a neutral tone of voice.

Rule 15: Use fact reconstruction to free the deponent's memory from emotional blind spots and to clarify his intent. You do not need a psychologist to tell you that people remember things to fit their own needs. Before Harry Sweeney enters your office for the first time, you glance again at his statement to the investigator about his car. You remind yourself that a person's needs may differ from one time to another and that people use language carelessly. Even something that sounds as unequivocal as "I never saw the guy's car before the crash" may contain imprecision.

The police report shows skid marks from the car to the point of the collision. But if Harry testifies that he saw the other car before the accident and put on his brakes, his contrary statement to the investigator makes him a natural for impeachment. You must help him reconstruct the facts. Why did he say those words to the investigator? What might he really have meant?

In the sea of questions you have asked yourself, one thing is clear: If you ask him without preamble whether he saw the other car before the collision, he is likely to say no. After all, that is what he told the investigator. If he answers your question the same way, he may then refuse to budge from that position—

even though the physical evidence suggests he saw the car and braked, and even though the liability picture is worse for him if he failed to see the car.

Here he is. Harry nervously enters your office. You are—or can be—in control because you know the rules. You put him at ease on your terms. You establish the context, structure your questions, and finally approach the big moment—but cautiously. You start with the skid marks:

Q: Let me show you the diagram from the police report. (Review a number of factually correct items on the report, then turn to the skid marks.) It shows 20 feet of skid marks from your car leading to the point of impact. Does that agree with your recollection of how things looked at the scene after the accident?

A: Yes.

Q: The police report shows the skid marks starting about 12 feet west of the west curb line and continuing about 8 feet into the intersection. Does that look about right to you?

A: Yes.

Q: Why did your car leave skid marks?

A: Because I slammed on my brakes.

Q: Why did you slam on your brakes?

A: To try to avoid hitting the other guy.

Q: Where were you when you slammed on the brakes?

A: I guess about 12 feet away from the intersection.

Q: Where were you when you first saw the plaintiff's car?

A: A little more than 12 feet from the intersection.

Only then should you refer to his statement about not seeing the other car before the crash. Harry explains that he meant he did not see the other car until the accident started to happen. He hit the brakes as soon as he saw danger.

Yes, that's about what you thought he meant. Because you followed the rules, Harry Sweeney was not bound by his hasty words. It is one of those good days; the deponent's reconstructed reality converges with your own sense of truth.

CHAPTER 3

Preparing a Witness for Deposition

Janeen Kerper*

A junior partner (J.P.) decided to teach a young associate how to prepare a witness for a deposition. He introduced the associate to their client, Jack, a businessman, who sat anxiously.

"Well, Jack, tomorrow's the big day. Are you ready to kick butt?"

"To tell you the truth, J.P., I'm a little nervous."

"Don't be. There's nothing to worry about as long as you follow a few simple rules. Remember that although the attorney taking the deposition may seem friendly, her only goal is to get ammunition for her case. No matter how nice she seems, don't be too comfortable. Always remember that she's out to get you, so don't let her charm you. You got that?"

"Yeah."

"Listen closely to every question and try to figure out what she's driving at before you answer. Waiting before you answer will give me time to object. Listen closely to my objections. I

*Janeen Kerper taught ethics and trial advocacy at California Western School of Law in San Diego. This article originally appeared in the Summer 1998 issue of LITIGATION.

may object that there is a 'lack of foundation' or that the question 'calls for speculation.' If you hear either of those objections, you should stop and ask yourself whether you really know the answer to the question from personal knowledge or whether you are drawing inferences based on other facts that you know. So will you listen to my objections?"

"I'll listen."

"But the most important rule is: Don't go beyond the scope of the question. Don't volunteer! By the way, do you know what time it is?"

"It's ten minutes to three."

"Wrong! That's just what I mean by not volunteering. That question—'Do you know what time it is?'—called for a yes or no answer. I didn't ask you, 'What time is it?' You volunteered that answer. Now do you see the importance of listening closely to the question and not volunteering?"

"Yeah, I'm sorry."

"Look, I figure this deal came down in one of two ways: either you were too busy worrying about your own promotion to check the files, or when you got Mr. Lubell's letter saying he wanted the goods shipped as 'per our usual agreement,' you naturally assumed he meant the usual practice in the industry. Of course, I wasn't there and only you know what happened. So I'll leave it to you to say which version is the truth. OK?"

"I gotcha, J.P."

And so it went. J.P. talked virtually nonstop, lecturing Jack on the do's and don'ts of depositions. Then there was a "rehearsal" in which Jack was brutally cross-examined on sensitive areas and shamed into shading his testimony in a manner more favorable to the case.

Jack performed poorly at his deposition. He was belligerent and evasive, he talked far too much, and was easily trapped in inconsistencies. Why? What went wrong in the preparation?

The worst error is an ethical violation. By "leaving it" to Jack "to say which version is the truth," J.P. coached Jack to shade his testimony. At a minimum, this is unprofessional. Some say it may even be grounds for discipline.

ABA Model Rule 3.4(b) states that a lawyer shall not "falsify evidence, counsel or assist a witness to testify falsely, or offer an inducement to a witness that is prohibited by law." Comment 1 to the rule notes that "[f]air competition in the adversary system is secured by prohibitions against destruction or concealment of evidence, improperly influencing witnesses, obstructive tactics in discovery procedure, and the like." In Great Britain, barristers may not "rehearse, practice, or coach a witness in relation to his evidence or the way in which he should give it." Code of Conduct of the Bar of England and Wales 607(b)(1995). The American rule is far more permissive, but even in this country, it is both unprofessional and unethical to coach a witness, as J.P. did, to shade or alter testimony.

Experienced litigators may be shocked to hear this. Witness preparation of this sort is time-honored in the United States—it even was immortalized in the lecture scene in "Anatomy of a Murder." Jimmy Stewart plays the lawyer, Biegler, who is defending Manion against the charge of murdering a man who allegedly raped Manion's wife. At the start of the interview, Manion tells Biegler that he killed the victim about an hour after learning of the rape.

Biegler interrupts Manion and gives "The Lecture," a step-by-step explanation of the law of murder and the available defenses. "The Lecture" makes clear to Manion that his only possible defense is temporary insanity. Manion then describes his mental state in a way that suggests the defense of irresistible impulse.

Lawyers who believe that "The Lecture" is ethical are kidding themselves. Either they are forgetting how malleable witnesses are or they are ignoring the "hidden messages" that "The Lecture" conveys. In a series of studies, Elizabeth Loftus and her colleagues have shown that witnesses are highly suggestible. Just one of their findings illustrates the point. To study the effect of leading questions on perception and memory, Loftus asked two comparable groups of people about headaches. One group was asked, "Do you get headaches frequently, and, if so, how often?" The second group was asked, "Do you get headaches occasionally, and, if so, how often?" Group One reported an average of 2.2 headaches per week. Group Two reported an average of 0.7 headaches per week.

These results will not surprise experienced litigators, who appreciate the power of the leading question, both to cross-examine and to suggest testimony to witnesses. Although Loftus's studies have not been universally accepted, her underlying premise remains unchallenged: Witnesses are extremely susceptible to suggestion.

In a brilliant article on "The Ethics of Witness Coaching," 17 *Cardozo L. Rev.* 1 (1995), Richard Wydick suggests that there are three levels of witness coaching. In Grade One the lawyer overtly induces a witness to testify to something the lawyer knows is false. When it is detected, Grade One witness coaching is punishable under the present lawyer disciplinary rules and perjury statutes.

Never Suggest Inaccurate Testimony

In Grade Two, the witness coaching is done covertly, through implication. Wydick argues that Grade Two witness coaching is as morally corrosive, as harmful to the court's truth-seeking function, and as much in breach of the disciplinary rules and perjury statutes as is Grade One coaching. But it is much less likely to be detected and punished. Wydick suggests that Grade Two witness coaching cannot be effectively controlled by disciplinary rules or criminal laws and that it must be governed by each lawyer's conscience.

In Grade Three witness coaching, the lawyer does not try to induce the witness to testify to something the lawyer knows is false, but the lawyer's conversation alters the witness's story. I recall a painful example. At issue was my client's business acumen. The opposition had called for the deposition of the client's former business partner. In an interview, I had learned that the former partner would resist saying anything bad about my client. But it also was clear from the partner's shrugs and discomfort that he didn't think much of my client. Stupidly, I concluded our interview by summarizing the unspoken message as follows: "Oh, I see. You thought that Bob just didn't give it the old college try!"

At the deposition, the witness was asked about my client's performance as a businessman. To my horror, the witness paused, looked directly at me, and answered: "Well, I've always thought that Bob just didn't give the business the old college try"—something he never would have said if I had not unwittingly suggested it. This was a nonparty deposition in the days before video. Had I kept my mouth shut, the shrugs and discomfort never would have come out at trial—nor would the damning phrase ever have been uttered. The lesson: Because witnesses are so suggestible, the lawyer must never suggest inaccurate testimony.

On Wydick's principles, both J.P.'s ploy of "So I'll leave it to you to say which version is the truth" and Jimmy Stewart's lecture are examples of Grade Two witness coaching. The problem is not what is said, but what is implied. Actors have long recognized the difference between text and subtext. The text is the script; the subtext is its meaning, which can be changed entirely through emphasis and inflection. British philosopher Paul Grice called this "conversational implicature," the difference between the conventional meaning of the speaker's words and the message the speaker wants to send. Even without inflection or emphasis, J.P.'s message to his client is clear. J.P. "says" that only the client knows what happened, but the clear suggestion or "implicature" is that the client would be an idiot to adopt the first version of events, *even if it is the version that comes closer to the truth.*

The bitter fruits of Grade Two coaching are revealed at the end of "Anatomy of a Murder." Jimmy Stewart learns that he has succeeded in defending Manion only because he was suckered into believing the false version of events that he had suggested to the client. He has lost both his self-respect and the respect of his client. As a final irony, Manion skips town, stiffing his lawyer for the fee and leaving behind a note: "Dear Mr. Biegler: Sorry I had to go, but I was seized by an 'irresistible impulse.'"

Even if Grade Two witness coaching avoids detection and a formal sanction, it often draws a more practical penalty. It produces witnesses who are easily led because they are no longer sure of the truth and have been taught to respond to the suggestions of counsel. These witnesses are easily caught in inconsistencies: Their desire to "improve" the evidence to please their lawyer makes it easy to trap them on details. Having been taught that it is acceptable to shade testimony, they engage in wishful thinking, only to find themselves contradicted by incontrovertible evidence—a document, an exhibit, or even a tape recording, as in the highly publicized impeachment of Mark Fuhrman in the O.J. Simpson trial. Smooth and over-rehearsed in his initial testimony, Fuhrman appeared to perform well and was embraced by the prosecution. When his seemingly professional presentation was shown to be riddled with lies, the cost was the credibility of both the witness and the prosecution.

Even without the ethical violation, J.P.'s witness preparation was badly flawed. The witness was shamed and discounted. The reasons for his nervousness were never heard. Instead, he was told that he had no right to be nervous. This only made him more nervous. Then he was fed a list of do's and don'ts without examples or explanations of the reason behind the rules. He could not possibly absorb all of this. The "laundry list" only made the witness more fearful. Finally, he was tricked and shamed into erring again. The lesson learned was not the one intended. Instead, Jack came away from the "Do you know what time it is?" exercise convinced that he is pretty stupid and will be tricked easily by the examining lawyer. The "don't volunteer" message was lost on him. In addition to flaunting the rules of ethics, J.P.'s suggestion that his objections might coach the witness encouraged an unhealthy dependence on the lawyer for the "right" answer. The witness was taught to see the deposition as a competitive sport and not as a search for truth or as a means to achieve justice. There was no way that J.P.'s preparation could have taught anyone to be a good witness.

How can J.P. do a better job? He could learn some basic precepts of stress management and adult learning theory. J.P. must see himself as an educator. He is, after all, trying to teach the witness about depositions and how to respond to questions. Students do not learn well when they are fearful or when their learning is blocked by stress. Adults are not good passive learners; they learn best by doing—through experience. Unlike children who can memorize long lists of facts or spelling words, adults retain information best when it is presented to them in small parcels, in context. Lists do not work for adults.

J.P. also needs to know the concept of opportunistic teaching and learning. And to become more self-critical. He is far too enamored of the sound of his own voice. He needs to learn the "relative air time" test for judging how well the witness preparation is going. If the lawyer is talking more than the witness, the session is going poorly. The witness is not learning, and the teacher is missing opportunities to teach.

Lessons from the Zen

Opportunistic teaching is best expressed in the ancient Zen saying, "When the student is ready, the teacher will appear." In deposition preparation, the lawyer should not give the witness a list of do's and don'ts; she should wait for the opportunity to teach the witness a rule when that rule will solve an immediate problem. Present the rule when the witness states a concern, or when critiquing a segment of examination, or when the witness is struggling with a portion of the testimony. If the rule cures the dilemma, it will be remembered. In opportunistic teaching, each do and don't is taught in a context and in an easily digestible piece.

At this point J.P. may be ready to quit. "I didn't train to be a psychologist or a teacher," he may be thinking. "I'll just buy one of those videotapes, like the one from the ABA, and use that to train my witnesses." Good idea. The videotape is helpful, but it never takes the place of preparation. Adults are not good passive learners. Children can watch a film and imitate it almost immediately, but adults tend not to absorb material until they have experienced it. They will claim to understand the lessons illustrated by the videotape, but they will have difficulty putting them into practice. If they are shown the video without other preparation, they will learn nothing from it. To help them gain self-confidence, you must first calm their fears and then take them through the material. Thus the lawyer must be part psychologist and part teacher if she is to be effective.

Before preparing the witness, the attorney must be prepared. There are several steps.

Determine whether the witness is a client. If the witness is an employee of a corporate client, then unless you have entered into a special agreement, the witness is not your client—only the corporation is. Local evidentiary rules on the scope of the attorney-client privilege will be important. If your jurisdiction follows the "control-group" approach, the scope of the privilege will be narrow. If your jurisdiction uses the so-called UpJohn approach, the scope of the privilege will be broader. If both the witness and the corporation are clients, the preparation session will be covered by the attorney-client privilege.

But more serious conflicts of interest may be lurking. Do not agree to represent a corporate employee for the deposition unless you have carefully considered all potential conflicts of interest and obtained all required consents in writing. A cavalier decision to make the witness your client solely for the deposition may keep the preparation confidential, but may also result in your ultimate disqualification as counsel because of an overlooked conflict of interest.

If the witness is not a client or the employee of a client, there may be ethical constraints on talking to the witness. Rule 4.2 of the ABA Model Rules of Professional Conduct bars a lawyer

41

from communicating "about the subject of the representation with a person the lawyer knows to be represented by another lawyer in the matter, unless the lawyer has the consent of the other lawyer or is authorized by law to do so."

The most difficult problems under Rule 4.2 are presented by communications with corporate employees of an adverse party. Comment 4 to the Rule makes clear that when the opponent is an organization, the lawyer may not communicate with persons "having a managerial responsibility on behalf of the organization," or with any other person "whose act or omission . . . may be imputed to the organization . . . or whose statement may constitute an admission [by] the organization."

The authorities differ on whether Rule 4.2 permits former corporate employees to be contacted. If the witness is or was an employee of a corporate adversary, counsel should consult local rules concerning the scope of the attorney-client privilege and local ethical requirements.

Even if it is proper to conduct the interview, there may be ethical constraints on the content of the interview. The lawyer should not give legal advice to a witness whom the attorney does not represent. Comment 1 to Rule 4.3 of the ABA Model Rules of Professional Conduct states that "[d]uring the course of a lawyer's representation of a client, the lawyer should not give advice to an unrepresented person other than the advice to obtain counsel." Because of Rule 4.3, several jurisdictions require the lawyer conducting the interview to disclose fully to unrepresented corporate employees the fact that she represents only the corporation. Some jurisdictions also require counsel to inform employees of their right to refuse the interview and to have their own counsel present at the interview.

The attorney must determine if there are any special representation and confidentiality issues. Can the witness become a client for the purpose of the deposition or will that create conflicts of interest with an existing client? If the witness is not a client, the preparation session is not confidential. Opposing counsel will be entitled to discover everything that is said during any meetings between the attorney and the witness. The attorney must then inform the witness that it is proper for the two of them to meet, and that the attorney seeks only the truth. Without these admonitions, nonparty witnesses may believe that their meeting with the attorney is improper. A lawyer who fails to give a nonparty witness these two basic admonitions may be astonished when the nonparty witness lies or evades questions about the pre-deposition meeting.

The attorney also should thoroughly review the file, particularly as it relates to the witness. Be sure of the legal and factual theories of the case. Review all prior statements, correspondence, and diaries of the witness to avoid later impeachment with inconsistent statements.

Crawl inside the head of the opposing lawyer. What are the opponent's themes and theories? Where is the opponent likely to want information or concessions? If I were the opponent, what would I ask?

Fear Is a Universal Problem

Carefully consider the documents to be used to refresh the witness's recollection. Rule 612 of the Federal Rules of Evidence and similar state rules provide that documents that are used to refresh a witness's memory for purposes of testimony must be produced. A few courts even have held that this rule overrides protections of work product and attorney-client privilege. Learn the law of the applicable jurisdiction, and be most cautious about showing attorney-client or work product documents to the witness.

Expect that the witness will be under stress. Witnesses have all kinds of fears, preconceptions and personal agendas. Parties, in particular, see the deposition as their chance to tell "the judge" their story. Unless these issues are addressed early, they will impede the witness's learning.

Fear is a universal problem for witnesses, although it often will masquerade as anger, hostility, or competitiveness. Strong emotions like these are never calmed by discounting them, as J.P. did. Perhaps the worst thing to tell someone who is afraid or hostile is that there is no reason for him to feel that way. Before it can be reduced, the fear or hostility must be fully expressed, acknowledged, and validated. Only then can a joint strategy be formulated for coping with the stress.

There are other reasons for allowing a witness to air any concerns she may have. If the lawyer tries to learn all of the witness's concerns, he may discover previously unknown facts. New strengths and weaknesses may be revealed, and it is better to learn them now, rather than in the deposition.

43

Personal agendas can be remarkably varied. One witness may worry that he put only enough change in the parking meter for one hour, and you are saying that the preparation could take longer. Another witness may have problems with child care, or a physical handicap that limits his ability to sit for a long time. These individual concerns usually present themselves in response to the simple question: "Before we begin, do you have any concerns you would like us to address?" Most witnesses have similar concerns:

- How long will this take?
- Am I a good, valuable, and important person in your eyes?
- Can I do this? (Will I embarrass myself, disappoint you or my employer?)
- Will I have a chance to tell my whole story?
- Can they ask me anything they want?
- What if the opposing lawyer is belligerent?
- What if I don't want to answer a question?
- What if I'm asked a question about documents I've never seen or have forgotten?
- Will I have any control over the process? Can I take a break if I need one?
- Do you have a plan?
- Will you protect me?
- Will this be private or can anyone attend? What about hostile spectators or the press?
- Will you be better, smarter, tougher, stronger than the other attorney?
- Will I have the opportunity to correct any mistakes?

The attorney should expect and plan how to answer these questions. Some of the concerns provide the opportunity to explain a "do" or a "don't." The question "Will I have a chance to tell my whole story?" invites the lawyer to explain the rule against volunteering information. Most lay witnesses associate the term "volunteer" with charity work. The admonition "don't volunteer" doesn't make sense to them and should be avoided. It is more effective to explain that they will have the opportunity to tell their whole story at the trial, and that it is your obligation to help them do that.

Frank Rothschild, who trains lawyers in taking and defending depositions, explains it this way: "I tell my clients that depositions are like the childhood card game *Go Fish*. The other side wants to take your cards. If they get all your cards, you lose. If they say, 'Do you have any tens?' and you don't, the truthful answer is 'No.' The last thing on earth you want to say is 'No, but I've got some sixes and jacks.' You don't want to show your full hand until we get to trial."

Make clear to the witness that in the deposition, it is important to make the other side do their job to discover information. "If they ask a 5-cent question, give them a 5-cent answer. If they ask a 25-cent question, give them a 25-cent answer." To most lay witnesses, the concept of proportionality is much more understandable, and much more comfortable from an ethical standpoint, than the concept of withholding information.

When discussing proportionality, the witness may ask, "What happens if I don't want to answer a question?" The witness should be told that there are two possibilities: One will be the response to a question the other side has a right to know, and the other will be a response to a question they have no right to know. Many attorneys forget to instruct witnesses about the purposes of objections made during the deposition—that most objections are made solely for the record, and the judge will decide later whether the objections are correct or not. Without this instruction, the witness may be baffled when his counsel objects and then tells him to answer the question. Tell the witness that you will not allow him to answer questions that the other side has no right to ask, and at those points you will instruct him not to answer. But you will encourage him to answer proportionally all proper questions, even if the answer makes him uncomfortable, and even though you may make an objection for the record. It helps to reassure the witness that you will ask probing questions of the other side, and that even though he may sometimes feel uncomfortable in the deposition, the other side will have the same feeling when you ask the questions.

The question: "Will you be better or stronger than the other attorney?" is most often asked of younger attorneys, especially young women. But all attorneys face it, and young attorneys should not be offended by it. The client's concern usually can be answered by a thoughtful and candid assessment of the strengths and weaknesses of the opposition, a candid assessment of your own strengths and weaknesses, and an outline of your strategy. Relative inexperience can often be compensated for by more thorough preparation, stronger facts, and passion for the cause. Remember Gerry Spence's observation that he has no fear of the most experienced Wall Street lawyer, but he does fear the young lawyer who cares passionately about her case.

A good witness preparation usually has an introduction, a listening phase, and role play. In the introduction, the attorney describes what will happen in the meeting, and anticipates some of the usual witness concerns. At the outset, the attorney might say something like: "I expect that our preparation session will take about two and a half hours. I'd like to start by listening to any questions, concerns, or thoughts you might have, and let me explain to you some of the do's and don'ts of depositions. Then, I'd like to spend much of our time role playing some questions and answers so you can feel comfortable and confident about your ability to handle the questions that will be asked at the deposition. Is that OK with you?"

Once the witness assents, the attorney might begin the listening phase by saying, "Tell me what you know about depositions, and tell me any concerns you have." Finding out what the witness already knows about the process and building upon that knowledge are more efficient than lecturing about depositions. Most witnesses have a surprising amount of information about depositions, much of it wrong. The attorney must identify and clear up any misconceptions. As concerns surface during the listening phase, the attorney should understand them fully. This is best done through active listening. Demonstrate understanding by paraphrasing what the witness says and reflecting back to the witness the emotional content of his statements. When the attorney demonstrates complete understanding of the concern, the witness will be receptive to the attorney's advice. Now is the time for opportunistic teaching, to teach the rules about depositions that best answer the witness's concerns.

In the role play, the witness gets a preview of the deposition. A word of caution: Unless it is done skillfully, it can quickly degenerate into Grade Two witness coaching. Gary Stuart, an Arizona attorney, says that when he sees a witness who has gone through a role playing session with an unskilled and unethical lawyer, he is reminded of the TV admonition: "Do Not

Try This at Home." If the role play is clumsy or unduly suggestive, the witness picks up all the wrong cues from the lawyer's
amateur direction. The dangers of role playing include making
your client think it is all an act, causing the client to distrust
your ethics, and disruption of the loyalty and trust that is the
core of the client-lawyer relation. Worst of all, Grade Two coaching corrodes truth finding.

This raises the question whether role play should be done at
all. If it should, what are the ethical limits of the role play? Most
American ethicists agree that role play is appropriate for some
purposes. Ethically permissible objectives of the role play are to
refresh the witness's memory, put the witness at ease, encourage
the witness not to guess or speculate, and to listen carefully to
questions. Information can be obtained, clarified, and organized
through the role play. It can call the witness's attention to gestures and mannerisms that may distract from their testimony.
This is also a proper time to expose and resolve any mispercep-
tions the witness may have. It is not ethical to use the role play
to "script," "polish," "suggest wording," or repeatedly "rehearse"
the witness's testimony.

A goal in the role play is to subject the witness to vigorous
cross-examination without destroying her confidence in herself
or in her attorney. Try to separate the roles of the "adverse" and
defending attorneys. It is best for someone other than the
defending lawyer to play the role of the opposing lawyer. If you
do not have the luxury of a cooperating colleague, then make
clear to the client when you are "in role" as the opposing counsel. Sometimes it will be enough to change seats when you are in
role. Some lawyers even wear a hat when they are playing the
role of opposing counsel. Whatever method is selected, clarity is
critical. Otherwise the witness will feel anxious and confused
about her own role. The anxiety is easily spotted in questions
like: "Are you talking to me now as my attorney?" or "Can I tell
you this now, as my attorney?" These kinds of questions are a
warning. The witness's confusion can spill over into the deposition, with the witness unsure of how to respond to questions
and tending to volunteer more than is needed to respond to the
question posed.

The role play presents chances for opportunistic teaching and it
boosts the confidence of the witness. Since adults learn best by
doing, there is no better way to teach them deposition techniques.

To lose their fear of it, they must experience it. When they experience it, they understand it. No amount of videotape can replace the role play.

Reverse Role Play and Positive Objectives

Joshua Karton, a national trial consultant and expert on witness preparation, uses two interesting techniques in preparing witnesses for deposition. One is the reverse role play in which the witness asks the questions he expects to be asked in the deposition. The aim is not to give the answers to the witness, but to uncover concerns the witness might not raise on her own. Karton finds that the witness's tone of voice, demeanor, and topic selection can reveal issues the witness may not have admitted to himself.

Karton also recommends using positive instructions. Unlike most lawyers, he never says to a witness, "Don't volunteer," or "Don't guess." Karton also notes that a witness can become demoralized by giving repeated negative responses such as "I don't know" or "I don't remember." From time to time, a witness can become so embarrassed by her apparent lack of knowledge, she may begin volunteering what she does know, or even worse, presuming knowledge she doesn't have. In preparation sessions, Karton reminds the witness that she does know and recalls a lot, but this knowledge is only part of a whole. Therefore, he suggests an appropriate answer is: "That's not part of what I know" or "that's not part of what I remember." Although attorneys are often uncomfortable with this unfamiliar response, witnesses love it. In fact, a layperson listening to a series of these responses would ultimately become exasperated with the questioning attorney and wonder when the attorney was going to ask something the witness did know.

The phases of preparation overlap. Issues that merit active listening may surface during the role play. A mini–role play may answer a concern that surfaces during the listening phase. The key to an effective preparation is flexibility. The lawyer must control, but not over-control. The lawyer must seize all opportunities for teaching, while covering the necessary rules and substantive material.

In recent years, court decisions, coupled with amendments to court rules, codes of civil procedure, and rules of professional ethics, have transformed the landscape of depositions. The trend is to conclude that zealous advocacy cannot justify improper coaching tactics or overly aggressive deposition conduct.

The growing view is that the lawyer has a duty to learn the truth and to protect the integrity of the court. In an article on "Rediscovering Discovery Ethics," 79 *Marq. L. Rev.* 895 (1996), W. Bradley Wendel summed up this trend:

> Lawyers have an obligation to be advocates for their clients . . . but this duty does not apply with full force to discovery. The function of discovery within the litigation system requires that lawyers assist the court in adjudicating the dispute on the merits by disclosing the facts necessary for the court to make an informed decision. With limited exceptions, advocacy comes into play only after the facts are fully disclosed. . . . Courts are beginning to recognize that the discovery system is designed to facilitate truth-finding, and they are involving lawyers in this search for the truth. They are imposing public duties upon lawyers in discovery that are not merely rhetorical fluff, but have content and carry severe sanctions for their violation.

When the client has finished the preparation, she should feel confident that she will be able to tell the truth without fear of being "wrong" or humiliated by her own counsel. She should understand that, despite what J.P. believes, the deposition is not about "kicking butt." It is not even about winning or losing. It is not about zealous advocacy. It is about exchanging relevant information before the trial starts. It should not be competitive or adverse. There is plenty of time to do that in the courtroom when the facts, having been fairly exchanged, are presented to the factfinder competitively and yes—zealously.

CHAPTER 4

Talking Green, Showing Red— Why Most Deposition Preparation Fails, and What to Do About It

David M. Malone*

Like many of the lessons I've learned as a lawyer, this one was too long in coming. Most of what attorneys tell witnesses preparing for depositions is simply wrong-headed. By increasing a witness's anxieties, it makes him less confident, less effective. The testimony is confused and inconsistent, a story told in fits

*David M. Malone is the founding partner of Trial Run Inc., a trial consulting and advocacy training firm. This article originally appeared in the Summer 1998 issue of LITIGATION.

and starts, without coherence or confidence, I'm not talking about preparation on what happened or what was said. Lawyers do not make the facts. I am talking about the areas where a lawyer can realistically affect the outcome, when we talk about the deposition experience and its goals.

Take the books or videotapes some attorneys give their witnesses on "Preparing for Your Deposition," or "How to Give a Deposition." I don't do this and won't, and will not allow it to be done with any of my witnesses. This tells the witness: "This deposition business cannot be very important, if I can prepare myself with a book." There are lots of these books and tapes out there, though, so someone must be buying them. I believe they sell for two reasons: attorneys are not quite sure what the non-substantive portion of the witness's preparation session is all about; and witness preparation does not seem like much fun. So they give the witness a book.

Deposition preparation isn't fun like Broadway musicals are fun. But witness preparation on the deposition process is essential, and doing it well is a challenge. Witnesses have potential—they can perform at an A level or a B level. My job is to help them reach their potential. If a B witness performs at a B level, I have probably done a good job. If I get a B+ performance from him, I have done a really good job. And vice versa, of course.

Keep in mind what a "good job" means here. Among other things, let's stop measuring deposition success by whether your witness blocks discovery of harmful facts, or for that matter, whether you can keep your adversary's witness in the room for three days and "show the other side how good we are." Generations of young attorneys have viewed witness preparation as an exercise in finding ways to have them avoid acknowledging bad facts. But attorneys are not responsible for the facts, good or bad. Instead, we should rate the examining attorney "successful" if she discovers new information efficiently. The defending attorney is successful if the witness provides information in a coherent, articulate way without divulging privileged or confidential information. Both sides are successful if the deposition is conducted in a courteous manner in a reasonable amount of time.

We should also teach our new attorneys the difference between preparation and coaching. Preparation is helping the witness say what she actually wants to say, by providing word choices or assisting with organization or refreshing recollection. Coaching is improperly adding content to the witness's testimony, attempting to make it more useful to one's side. A simple rule of thumb: If the substantive content of the testimony comes from the attorney, it's coaching; if it comes from the witness, it's preparation.

So, how do we help witnesses perform to their potential in the deposition room? Not with a book. Many of these are chock full of sound analysis, good advice, and pithy examples involving deposition problems. An attorney could find here much of the information she needs to know to take and defend depositions well. Unfortunately, these books weren't written for lawyers, but for witnesses, and not professional, witnesses, like experts or hospital document custodians, but amateur witnesses like the car shop mechanic or the secretary. Here are people who have never testified before, do not want to testify now, and hope to God they never have to testify again. And their attorney is handing them a book. A thick book with a table of contents, an index and, worst of all, no pictures. A book that makes it seem likely that the attorney will not even be at the deposition. Not comforting. Not helpful. Not anxiety reducing.

There's the rub. The key to deposition preparation is reducing the witness's anxieties, letting her focus on the specific task at hand, and telling her that the specific task is simple, narrow, and well within her ability to accomplish. What is the witness's job? Telling the truth in response to questions, and keeping her statements brief. That's all. No more, no less, just that. I want to be certain that this is clear. I recommend that attorneys actually say to the witness, before the deposition, something like this:

> "You have only one job at the deposition next week: tell the truth, and keep your answers short. That's all. I'll worry about everything else that might come up. If something happens that you don't understand, ask me. I'll take care of it. You don't have to worry about it."

This brief speech should set the tone for the entire preparation session. No long discussions about hypothetical situations, no discussions about attorneys who lead or mislead or misstate or restate or review or recapitulate or summarize or speculate. The witness shouldn't worry about what the deposing attorney is doing, or why. All she has to remember is to tell the truth and do it briefly. "Everything else," I say, "is my responsibility, and I am going to be sitting right alongside you, just like I am now."

In preparation sessions, I do sit right alongside my witness, right at her elbow. I want her to get comfortable knowing I'm there. I even try to sit on the same side of her at the deposition as I did during the preparation sessions. Forget the folklore that the witness must sit next to the reporter, or across from the questioner, or at the end of the table, or, for that matter, next to her counsel. The witness and her attorney can sit wherever they want during the deposition. I like to sit next to the reporter, with the witness on my other side. That way I can put a hand up between the witness and the reporter if I need a second to make an objection or to think about a question. I know what you're thinking. What about the reporter who says, "I'll need the witness to sit here, next to me, so that I can hear her testimony." Short answer: "Thank you, but I am sure you will have no problem hearing her if she sits to my right. If you do, let me know, and we'll work it out. Counsel, you may proceed."

But don't talk to the witness about this either before the deposition. Just tell her that you will be sitting right next to her (or wherever you plan to sit). She does not have to worry about the seating arrangements, or the relationship with the reporter, or opposing counsel, so why put it in her mind? Just take care of it yourself, when the time is right. Leave her mind free to focus on her task: tell the truth, briefly.

The medium needs to parallel the message, as a simple example will show. In my classes on improving deposition skills, I often ask half the audience to close their eyes while I show the other half a computer slide with the words "red," "green" and "blue" repeated across and down. I ask the participants to tell me the color the words are printed in, not what they say. Like a conductor, I lead them through the slide, left to right, top to bottom, faster and faster. The first slide presents the names of the colors printed in their proper color, "red" in red, "green" in green and so on. The class has little problem calling out the colors of the print, and they gather speed and stay coordinated as we go through the page.

Next, I have that first half of the class close their eyes, and I ask the other half to look at the slides. But now I have switched slides. The words are not printed in their proper color. It says "red," but it is written in green. Sometimes "blue" is in red, sometimes "blue" is green. As we go left to right, top to bottom, trying to increase speed, more and more of this half of the class gets its wrong, reading the word instead of saying the color, then correcting themselves, then slipping again.

What accounts for this? In a class divided up arbitrarily, did we really wind up with all of the smart people in the first group? The real explanation lies in what the psychologists call cognitive dissonance. The brain in this exercise has to process two different streams of information—the color that is seen, and the word that is being read. There are two information streams processed by two different portions of the brain. In one, probably the limbic system or brain stem, we have color recognition. When we were small, furry mammals, this function was essential for spotting that part of our surroundings that did not belong and was probably dangerous. Colored predators moving against a green background, perhaps. Color recognition is a very basic function, carried on at almost an involuntary level. Directly related to survival, it was handled as a reflex, and still is.

Another portion of the participants' brain, maybe the frontal lobes, gives us the ability to read. Or rather a collection of abilities, like letter-shape recognition, pattern recognition, phonogram recognition, and so forth. Although this brain function may have developed late, skill at reading is now critical to human life and is deeply ingrained in adults, especially educated adults. It is difficult for them to see a word without reading that word.

Two different brain portions, both trying to send their messages through the speech center, bring conflict. The conflict must be resolved, the rule of decision ("say the color in which the word is printed") applied. The word-reading portion has to be blocked, the color-sensing portion allowed to proceed. Color must then be converted to speech and spoken in coordination with the speech of the other members of the class. It all sounds complex enough even when the signals are consistent, when "red" is printed in red. When the signals are inconsistent, and when a single mistake throws off everyone's timing, watch out!! *Cognitive dissonance.*

This is more than a parlor trick. It is essential to have in mind when your witness comes in the week or the day before his deposition for that final preparation session. This is the session where you want to make him comfortable with the process, rather than review the facts. Nine times out of ten it is done wrong. You say:

Well, I hope you are not nervous about this deposition. I don't see any serious problems. We've gone over the documents and you should do just fine. We'll get there early, so we can take care of any problems with seating, and then we'll get started. I've been in depositions with this attorney before, and I don't think she'll try to trick you or browbeat you, and of course I'll be right there if something comes up. The deposition will probably take all day, say until four-thirty or five in the afternoon, but I suppose it could run over until the next day.

Just remember that you'll be under oath, so you have to be careful to tell the truth. If you do make any mistakes, we'll have a chance to read the transcript of the deposition over and make corrections before the trial. Of course, you and I will prepare your trial testimony so they won't have much chance to impeach you when you testify in court.

And so forth. Talk about cognitive dissonance. The goal of this session is to put the witness at ease, to remove anxieties so that he can focus on his substantive responses. But almost your first word is "nervous." The witness thinks, "Nervous? Why should I be nervous? Is there something to be nervous about? What don't I understand?"

You don't see any "serious problems"? The witness thinks, "Oh, just some problems that you don't consider serious? What problems? What does serious mean? What do you mean by non-serious? Will I consider them nonserious? Problems for whom? Me? The case? You?"

You say, "You should do just fine." He thinks, "I should? Does that mean you think I might not? Why didn't you say, 'You *will* do just fine'?"

The rest of your speech is a witness's nightmare. "Problems with seating . . . trick . . . browbeat . . . if something comes up . . . could run over . . . be careful . . . mistakes . . . impeach . . ." All of this language make the witness think of difficulties, problems, things to worry about. And yet the message is supposed to be: "Don't worry. Relax. Focus on the facts of the case." The words may say they are a relaxing green, but they are written in red, worry-colored ink. Cognitive dissonance.

Remember my alternative speech, "All you have to think about at the deposition is telling the facts truthfully and briefly.

This is a routine process, it is common and usual, and I will take care of all the arrangements, all the legal procedures, before and during the deposition. If anything comes up that you don't understand, talk to me, because I'll be sitting right alongside you, just like I am now."

Here the words match the message. The witness should not worry, because you are there. Everything will go smoothly, because you will be sitting right next to her to handle anything that does not go smoothly. No cognitive dissonance. Follow the rule at every step. You want to conduct a bit of mock deposition, perhaps cross-examination style? Fine, but when you play the role of opposing counsel, go sit where opposing counsel sits. Don't cross-examine from the witness's elbow, the spot for friendly, supportive counsel, for you. Better yet, if your client can afford it, have a colleague do the mock examination—from the other side of the table—while you stay where you belong.

Friendly support, then, is crucial. But it isn't enough. Sure, we may avoid filling the witness's mind with shadowy and amorphous fears, but we haven't cleared his mind of whatever other concerns he is bringing with him to the deposition. Witnesses come to us not because they are deponents, but because they are people, with normal lives. They have families, jobs, schedules, expenses. They have obligations outside the deposition room, on the day of the deposition and every other day. You must help them handle the rest of their lives on the deposition day, so that they can focus on what for you (and probably you alone) is their most important job that day. Testifying.

Ask your witness if he has meetings or travel planned around the deposition day. Assure him that you will protect his schedule. Find out if he has family responsibilities, like children to pick up, that might distract him all afternoon if not handled in advance. Advise him to take a cab to your office on the deposition morning, or pick him up yourself. Never let a simple matter like parking be a problem. Make certain there is no possibility of a last-minute rush on the deposition morning.

Eliminate surprises. Tell him explicitly that there is no need for him to bring documents to the deposition. Even with a subpoena duces tecum, documents should be turned over to you in advance, for copying, for analysis, for privilege review. The witness should not be worrying about them. And the last thing you want at a deposition is for him, and you, to get thrown off stride with a new document popping out of a briefcase, a purse, an inside coat pocket or a day-timer. Sure, you can handle that with "We'll take a break now" but, who needs it? Not you. Not the witness.

OK. You've done your best to avoid creating new fears for the witness. And you've worked out whatever responsibilities the witness has as a person on the deposition day. Now you are ready to prepare the witness to answer truthfully, and briefly. It's time to tell him the seven most common answers to deposition questions.

Seven? When I worked as a federal antitrust and consumer fraud prosecutor, field attorneys would always ask our office, "How many consumer affidavits do we need for a preliminary injunction hearing?" It was useless to point out that it all depended on the strength of the case, the severity of the fraud, the danger of asset removal, and so forth. They wanted a number. We always said, "Seven." I always liked the number seven, but it turns out that the most common answers to deposition questions really do number seven. They are:

1. Yes.
2. No.
3. Green.
4. I don't know.
5. I don't remember.
6. I don't understand the question.
7. I need a break.

1. & 2. Yes and No: The typical witness has not been through a deposition and doesn't know what is expected of her. Often, in preparation sessions, we talk generally about the process, but we do not specifically approve or endorse common answers. The witness remains uncertain whether such answers are sufficient or more is expected. Tell her: "If the shortest, truthful answer is 'yes' or 'no,' that is what you should say, and it is perfectly fine. If the attorney asking the questions wants to know more, he can ask for more."

3. Green: The witness may believe that the best way to get this whole deposition thing over with is by telling his story straight out. He wants none of these "lawyer games" like "shortest, truthful answers" (or "don't volunteer," as is typically advised). So, the deposing attorney asks, "What color is your car?" and the witness answers, "It's a dark green Buick sedan." Or, "What did you have for lunch that day?" "I had half an apple, because I didn't want to eat too much while I was nervous about the exam."

How to convince your witness that short answers are best? Try this mid-nineteenth-century example. Sir Richard Francis Burton and John Speke, British explorers, sometimes rivals and sometimes colleagues, set out together to discover the source of the great Nile River. The river had been explored for a substantial portion of its 3,400 miles southwest, from the delta, but the source had not yet been found. Burton and Speke took their expedition overland to meet the river at the beginning of its unexplored portion, and then proceeded upriver. Wherever they encountered a fork in the river, they would establish a base camp and send some of their party ahead up one branch until it could be determined that it did not represent the main river, flowing from the source. The expedition would then reunite and proceed up the other fork, the main river, until another fork was encountered and the process had to be repeated. Fork by fork, stream by stream, the explorers continued, until the Nile was traced past the Blue Nile, through Lake Albert, to Lake Victoria. It took forever.

I tell my witnesses this story so that they understand that responding with all they know, instead of "green," will not shorten the deposition. Every word they add, every adjective, adverb or extra noun or verb, creates a fork that the opposing attorney will feel compelled to explore. Maybe the truth is just behind "sedan" in "green sedan," or the exam that the witness was nervous about. The questioning will probe each of these possibilities until the attorney believes he can safely abandon it as a backwater or dead-end. The answer "green," all by itself, is not only sufficient, it is superior.

4. I don't know: Witnesses often come to depositions believing that they have an obligation to be omniscient, to know everything that reasonably relates to the case that someone in their position could know. When they do not know something, they get uncomfortable and start creating information to fill in the blank. They are not lying; they are just trying to be helpful and responsive. But they are also trying to be perfect in their knowledge, because they think that is expected. Tell them it is not expected. "I don't know," is perfectly acceptable wherever it is, in fact, the truth. It is better than acceptable: It's the best answer of all. Tell your witness: "You cannot know everything that happened in your department during the four years this lawsuit covers. Not even everything that happened in your office. If you don't know, the short, truthful answer is, 'I don't know.' Don't try to figure out what was probably the fact, or likely to have happened. Say, 'I don't know.'"

5. I don't remember: Closely related to "I don't know," the answer "I don't remember" is equally hard for witnesses. They assume it makes them look and sound like a dummy, or an evasive dummy. Again, reassure them that it is appropriate, and sometimes preferred. Also, distinguish the two answers for the witness. In contrast to "I don't know," "I don't remember" suggests that the witness knew the answer at one time. It invites attempts at refreshing memory. Remind the witness that we sometimes create memories when we think we should know something but cannot quite recall it. The best advice to the witness: "If you do not have a clear and specific recollection of the event, or the conversation, or the thing in question, say, 'I don't remember.' The other attorney may follow up or attempt to remind you of something, or even ask for a guess. But you are entitled to say, 'I don't remember' if that best describes your state of mind."

6. I don't understand the question: The witness does not have to answer any question that he does not understand. Most defending attorneys tell their witnesses this in preparation; in fact, most deposing attorneys instruct the witness on this during their preliminary remarks, although they do it to set the witness up for later impeachment at trial. ("I told you that you didn't have to answer if you didn't understand my questions, didn't I? And you never said you didn't understand this question, did you?") The problem is we often forget to tell the witness the second half, what they should do in that situation, in place of answering. Tell him: "If you don't understand the question, say, 'I'm sorry. I don't understand your question.' Leave it to the attorney to ask a better question, or to try to fix his question, or to ask what it is that you don't understand. If you can tell him, fine, tell him about the word or phrase or other problem. Then it is up to him to decide whether to ask you more or simply move on."

7. I need a break: By local rule or standing order in some jurisdictions and courtrooms, there are supposed to be no breaks between questions and answers in a deposition. Some judges even bar the defending attorney and the witness from talking with one another once the deposition begins—before answers, after answers, during breaks, whenever. These rules focus on the abuses of coaching and outright interference with legitimate opportunities to obtain discovery. Clearly, however, they are not absolute proscriptions. Suppose a witness thinks that an answer will reveal privileged information, but the defending attorney has not seen the problem. The witness needs to talk to the attorney or the privileged information may be revealed, the privilege lost. Or the witness may be tired and confused, and realizes he cannot properly continue, perhaps until after a break or lunch. The witness needs to talk to his attorney and should be allowed to take a break. Sure, the witness may ask for a break for the wrong reason, to ask for substantive or tactical guidance on an answer. The ethical obligation on the defending attorney is then to encourage the witness to answer truthfully, and to avoid giving direction that would interfere with legitimate discovery. But such cases should not preclude all counsel from talking with all witnesses during all breaks.

I tell my witnesses in preparation sessions that, if they ask me for a break, I will get them a break. I am not omniscient. There is no way that I can anticipate every problem that may come up, or that a witness may perceive has come up. Unless I am available to talk with a witness, to help her resolve problems, to help her protect privileged information, I'm no better than the "potted plant" that Ollie North's counsel rightly refused to be during North's congressional hearings.

I promise the witness that we will take a break if she says that she needs one. I also get a promise in return:

> If I say, "Let's take a break," or "Let's have lunch now," or "That's enough for today," don't argue with me. Don't tell me that you'd like to finish this topic, or you can do another 15 minutes, or perhaps if we do another hour we can finish today and not come back tomorrow. Just stand up and leave the room with me.

Witnesses get tired, and after a while they make mistakes. Those mistakes always seem to come right before lunch, then again at four in the afternoon, or when people are rushing to finish to catch a flight and get home. Nor are lawyers immune.

They get tired and make mistakes, often failing to recognize the witness's mistake. The solution? Do not tell the witness to be especially cautious at this time or that time. This is not anxiety reducing. Instead, just be more cautious yourself. Take breaks to refresh the witness and yourself. Resist the temptation to stretch the day out a little bit to save another night on the road. If the witness says, during the break, "Why not stay another hour and finish up, so we don't have to come back?" your answer should be,

> Margaret, you have worked hard enough today to give a good deposition. We don't want to risk spoiling all of that good work by pressing on when we are both tired, when one of us might make a mistake that we will have to correct later, just to save a few hours. We'll stop now, I'll take you to a good dinner, we'll talk about political scandals and Hollywood movies, and tomorrow we can wrap it up when we're both fresh and ready to go.

One final note. Opposing counsel always lie about how much more they have left to do. They say they can finish in an hour, and they have two hours. They say two hours, and they go over to the next day. Few are so foolish as to guarantee that they will wrap up in sixty minutes. They will "try," or they "think," or "it looks like." Don't expose your tired witness (or your tired mind) to more questioning on hollow promises.

Finally, in preparing a witness to be deposed, tell the witness explicitly that she will have several opportunities to clarify or correct any matters that she believes require it. Do not say she can "correct mistakes" because that just raises that old cognitive dissonance problem again. Instead, talk about "matters that need clarification" or "things that you want to add." Tell the witness that if she thinks of something she wants to add to an answer, she can do it right then, by saying, "Let me go back and add something to my answers a moment ago about the patient's status on that Monday." Tell her that she can also add to the answer later on, if that is when the need occurs to her. She can say, "This morning we talked about the effects of deep anesthesia. There is something I want to add to that." She can also make additions or clarifications after the questioning by opposing counsel is complete, and you and the witness have had a chance to talk about matters to be addressed in the follow-up questioning. "Ms. Faber, yesterday afternoon you were asked about experience with the

Rheinsolt heart valve in 1993. Is there anything you would like to add to your answer?" And, finally, the witness can make any changes that she thinks are appropriate after you and she have reviewed the transcript (an opportunity that you must expressly reserve under the Federal Rules of Civil Procedure).

Contrary to popular belief, the witness's right to make changes to the transcript is not limited to correcting the reporter's errors. She can change a "yes" answer to a "no"; a "certainly" to a "maybe"; and an "I don't know" to a "14.7 percent." She can even change questions, if she believes that the change will more accurately reflect what occurred at the deposition. Of course, extensive changes may lead to a reopening of the deposition or even, in extreme cases, a striking of the changes and a direction that the deposition will stand as originally reported. There seems little reason to tell this to the witness in advance of the deposition, or to let her know that the court or jury can compare her original answer with any changes and decide for itself which to believe. There is time enough for that discussion after the deposition, during the review. Such talk during preparation will only undo all the other hard work you have done to reduce the witness's anxieties.

CHAPTER 5

130 Rules for Every Deponent

Stuart M. Israel*

Editor's Note: Paul Simon brought us "50 Ways to Leave Your Lover." Irving Younger made the "Ten Commandments of Cross-Examination" almost as famous as the "Twelve Days of Christmas." But you are probably asking: "How many rules are there for a witness in a deposition?" The answer is 130. Compliments of Stuart Israel, we present the list that no lawyer should forget to bring to the woodshed the next time she is preparing a client.

1. Tell the truth.
2. Listen to the question. Pause. Think as long as necessary before answering.
3. Don't pause too long before answering.
4. Make sure you understand the question. Don't answer unless and until you do.
5. If you don't understand the question, say so. Ask the questioner to explain, repeat, or rephrase the question.
6. Answer clearly and directly.
7. If you don't know the answer, say "I don't know."
8. If you don't remember the answer, say "I don't remember."
9. Don't confuse "I don't know" with "I don't remember."

*Stuart M. Israel is a partner with Martens, Ice, Klass, Legghio & Israel, P.C. in Royal Oak, Michigan. This article, which originally appeared in the Summer 2001 issue of LITIGATION, grew into his book, Taking and Defending Depositions, published by ALI-ABA in 2004.

10. Where appropriate, qualify your "I don't remember" answer. Say something like, "I don't remember at this moment" or "I don't remember without looking at" the document in question.

11. Answer "yes" or "no" if appropriate.

12. Don't answer "yes" or "no" to a yes-or-no question if the question cannot be answered accurately with yes or no.

13. Where appropriate, ask for documents that will aid your memory, saying something like, "I don't remember at this moment what I wrote, but if you show me the document it may help me to answer your question" or "If you'd like me to tell you what the document says, please show it to me."

14. Don't speculate or guess.

15. Speculate or guess if you are asked to speculate or guess, but qualify your answer by identifying it as speculation or a guess.

16. If you are unable to speculate or guess, say so. Where appropriate, explain why, saying something like, "I am unable to speculate on that because I don't have sufficient information."

17. Don't feel obligated to speculate or guess because the questioner suggests, and tries to make you believe, that you "should" know the answer.

18. Don't be embarrassed if you can't answer a question because you feel you "should" know the answer. If you don't know the answer, say so. If you can't remember the answer, say so.

19. Don't assume.

20. Assume if you are directed to make assumptions. Then, make sure the assumptions are clearly stated. Qualify as appropriate, e.g., "At your direction, I am assuming that the car was traveling at 60 mph even though I have no knowledge of the speed. Based on the assumption you want me to make, my answer is . . ." or "What you're asking me to assume is an impossibility."

21. Be positive, assertive, confident, certain, strong, and precise.

22. Or be quiet.

23. Don't give wishy-washy, equivocal answers like "possibly," "probably," and "maybe" when you should be positive, assertive, confident, certain, strong, and precise.

24. Beware of imprecise questions that contain vague, equivocal words like "possibly," "probably," "maybe."

25. If you cannot be precise, and you must approximate, say so: "It was around 3 p.m." or "It was about 50 feet."

26. Answer narrowly.

27. Answer only the question asked.

28. Don't volunteer.

29. Where appropriate, volunteer.

30. Don't help the questioner by answering the question that should have been asked.

31. Don't help the questioner by supplying information to fix the question.

32. Where appropriate, don't answer the question as asked. Rephrase the question as part of your answer. For example:

    Q. Isn't it true the car was blue?

    A. It was blue, but it wasn't a car. It was a pickup truck.

33. Don't let the questioner put words in your mouth. For example:

    Q. Isn't it true the car was blue?

    A. No.

    Q. What color was it?

    A. I would call it aquamarine.

34. Don't agree with the cross-examiner unless you are satisfied that the leading question is 100 percent accurate. Your simple yes or no answer to a leading question makes the premise and phrasing of that question your sworn testimony.

35. Don't be evasive. If you are worried about being cross-examined on some subject, tell me now. Tell me what you are worried about and why. I will help.

36. Don't ask the questioner questions about the questioner's questions. If you don't understand the question asked, say you don't understand.

37. Be comfortable with the questioner's pauses and silences. Don't feel obligated to fill silences. Answer the question, stop, and wait for the next question.

38. Don't answer a question with a question, rhetorical or otherwise. If you can answer, answer. If you don't understand the question, say so.

39. Don't think out loud.

40. Don't be apologetic or self-deprecating. ("Oh, I should know the answer. My memory is going.")

41. Answer questions; don't offer editorial comment. ("That's a good question." "That's an interesting question." "I'm glad you asked me that question.") If you need time to think about your answer, pause and think. When you are ready to answer, answer.

42. Don't exaggerate or overstate.

43. Answer from your personal knowledge, based on what you experienced with your senses—what you saw, heard, touched, tasted, and smelled.

44. Give short, succinct, concise answers.

45. Remember the transcript. Enunciate. "Uh-huh" can be erroneously recorded as "un-unh" and vice versa. Nonverbal communication—body language, gestures, tone of voice—does not make it into the transcript.

46. Don't use formulations that dilute your credibility. If you preface your answer with a term like "frankly," you are suggesting that you may be other than frank when giving answers not labeled as being frank. The same is true of formulations like "the truth is . . ." or "to be totally honest. . . ."

47. Don't go off on tangents. Stick to the point. Don't ramble. Don't respond with extraneous details and irrelevancies.

48. Don't offer information that was not requested. You are not obligated to provide all details and relevant information if not asked for these.

49. Give complete answers. Don't omit important details and relevant information.

50. Don't engage in "mind reading" by testifying to what others thought or felt. Instead, testify to what you saw and heard; the fact finder can draw the proper conclusions about what the others thought or felt, if relevant.

51. Pay attention. Focus. Concentrate.

52. Listen to every objection. Stop talking when an objection is made. Think about the objection. It may call your attention to a flaw in the question. If I object, it usually means the question and answer are important. Don't answer until I direct you to answer, after the objection is completed.

53. If I instruct you not to answer, follow my instruction. Don't answer.

54. If I instruct you to answer, answer, but follow the rules, i.e., listen to the question, pause, think before you answer.

55. After an objection, wait for my instruction. Don't follow the questioner's instruction. Wait to hear from *me*.

56. I will instruct you not to answer only if we have a sound legal basis for refusing to answer and we have a reason to keep the testimony out. Generally, this will occur when the question asks for privileged information or the inquiry is abusive or oth-

erwise grossly improper. If we are at trial, the judge will generally rule immediately, either sustaining (granting) the objection or overruling (rejecting) it and directing you to answer. At deposition, however, generally you have to answer all questions, even if they ask for irrelevant information.

57. Be calm. Don't get angry.

58. Be controlled. Don't ventilate.

59. Don't argue with the questioner. Leave the arguing to the lawyers. Your job is to answer questions.

60. Be polite and courteous.

61. Be serious. Your testimony is no place for humor, sarcasm, or irony.

62. Beware of unfamiliar terminology and expressions in questions.

63. Use words and terminology that are comfortable for you. Answer "in your own words."

64. Don't use offensive language. Don't use profanity, except as appropriate.

65. Don't let the questioner interrupt your answer. Say something like, "I haven't completed my answer. May I complete my answer?"

66. Don't interrupt the questioner. Listen to the entire question.

67. Look the questioner in the eye while being questioned.

68. Look the questioner in the eye while answering.

69. Remember the transcript. You are dictating. Watch the court reporter while answering. Make sure the court reporter hears your answer. Help the court reporter with spellings or unusual words.

70. Don't look at me as if you need help answering.

71. Correct mistakes. If you realize you have been inaccurate or incomplete, say so. ("Excuse me. A few minutes ago you asked me how many times I requested my personnel file, and I said three. I just remembered that I asked a fourth time, too.")

72. Request recesses: bathroom breaks or time for stretching, a cigarette, a cup of coffee.

73. Don't get wired on coffee.

74. Don't smoke, chew tobacco, or use snuff while testifying.

75. Don't drink alcohol before (or during) your testimony. Don't use drugs, prescription or otherwise, that will affect your performance.

76. Don't smell like alcohol.

77. Don't chew gum while testifying.

78. Don't eat candy, or anything else, while testifying.

79. Turn off your cell phone. Turn off your pager.

80. Be on your best behavior.

81. Don't cop an attitude. Don't be arrogant, flippant, hostile, evasive, uncooperative, nasty, or superior.

82. Be yourself.

83. Dress appropriately and comfortably.

84. Don't wear inappropriate jewelry or other paraphernalia.

85. Keep in mind that no matter how pleasant the cross-examiner is, she has interests different from, and likely hostile to, your interests.

86. The cross-examiner is not your friend. Be civil, but don't chat, socialize, or explore common acquaintances. Business is business.

87. If appropriate and useful, write notes outlining your answer before you give it, to make sure it is complete and organized. Don't write anything you don't want the cross-examiner to see.

88. Beware of questions that assume facts, as in, "Have you stopped beating your spouse?"

89. Beware of questions that require a choice between alternatives selected by the questioner, such as, "Was the light red or green?" If appropriate, answer "neither" and wait for the next question.

90. Beware of questions that purport to summarize your earlier testimony.

91. Beware of questions that rephrase your earlier testimony.

92. Beware of compound and multiple questions.

93. Beware of vague or ambiguous questions.

94. Beware of questions about what "might have," "could have," "must have," or "possibly" happened.

95. Beware of questions that use absolutes like "never" and "always."

96. Be careful of answering with absolutes like "never" or "always" unless you are *absolutely* sure.

97. Answer the question first, then add explanations: "Yes, except that . . ." or "No, but. . . ."

98. Speak up.

99. Sit up straight.

100. Nothing is "off the record," even if the court reporter is not recording.

101. Don't object. Be the witness, and let me be the lawyer.

102. Beware of questions that foreclose later recollection, like "Have you told me everything about the events of March 15?" Answer something like, "I have told you everything that I can recall right now."

103. Be assured that it is proper that you prepared for your testimony.

104. Be assured that it is proper that you discussed your testimony with me.

105. Acknowledge what you did to prepare your testimony, including review of documents, interrogatories, deposition testimony, or notes, unless I instruct you not to answer because the question calls for privileged information.

106. Review everything in advance.

107. Don't review anything in advance that you don't want to have to acknowledge having reviewed.

108. Review only what I tell you to review.

109. Don't bring anything that you don't want to be questioned about.

110. Bring what you need: checklists, key documents, notes.

111. Bring only what I tell you to bring.

112. Show me everything you have brought *before* the deposition starts.

113. Don't answer questions about a document until you have read the document. ("If you'd like me to answer that question, I'll need to review the document.")

114. Take your time and read any document that you are questioned about. Take as much time as necessary. Let the cross-examiner wait for you.

115. Don't assume anything about the authenticity of a document. Check it. Look at the dates and the signature. Make sure all the pages are there. Don't identify it unless you are positive.

116. State appropriate qualifications regarding your review of a document, like "This is a 57-page document. I've only had time to skim a few pages. If you want me to review it thoroughly so I can answer your questions definitively, we should go off the record for a few hours."

117. Tell me about all the skeletons in your closet now, so we can prepare for cross-examination. No surprises. Our discussion is privileged.

118. Admit what you have to admit.

119. Don't admit what is not true.

120. Don't worry about hearsay. Some hearsay is admissible, some is not. Some hearsay is favorable to us, some is not. If a question calls for inadmissible hearsay that is unfavorable, I will object.

121. Keep in mind the difference between what you know, what you have inferred, what you have assumed, and what you have been told. Keep in mind, too, when you learned what you now know.

122. Don't volunteer to do anything later. Don't promise to do anything later. If the cross-examiner wants you to search for documents or provide a name, the request should be directed to me. Respond: "Why don't you make that request to my lawyer? That's why he gets the big bucks."

123. Don't discuss confidential business in the hall, the elevator, the stairwell, the cafeteria, the restroom, or anywhere else that you might be overheard.

124. Relax, but keep that edge.

125. Don't relax. Stay wary and vigilant. Keep those critical faculties in high gear.

126. Beware of the midafternoon doldrums. Don't lose your concentration because of fatigue or boredom. Take a break to regain focus.

127. Don't be overwhelmed by the fact that I'm giving you 130 rules, some of which contradict others.

128. Break the rules if you have a good reason.

129. It is not just you. Testifying at a deposition is an unusual, artificial, disconcerting experience for everyone, and preparing for a deposition is hard work.

130. Don't screw up.

PART II

At the Table

CHAPTER 6

Taking Depositions

Jerome P. Facher*

In preparing for trial, depositions play an important and often crucial role. Tactics and strategy in planning, taking, and using depositions frequently determine the outcome of litigation, and the trial lawyer cannot neglect or indiscriminately delegate this vital phase of his case. If he does so, he may discover to his regret that he has lost or wasted a valuable tactical opportunity which he may never regain.

Preparation of a case rarely fails to benefit from a deposition, and in general a decision to depose at least the adverse party should be the rule. Even in uncomplicated litigation, knowing the adversary's testimony, his legal contentions, his witnesses,

*Jerome P. Facher is a senior partner in the Boston firm of Wilmer Cutler Pickering Hale & Dorr LLP and a lecturer in trial practice at Harvard Law School. This chapter is abridged from a comprehensive treatment of deposition practice and tactics written for members of the Massachusetts Bar upon the Supreme Judicial Court's adoption of rules permitting discovery depositions in civil cases. References in the original text to the Massachusetts rules have been omitted or, where applicable, changed to the comparable Federal Rules of Civil Procedure. The article first appeared in the Massachusetts Law Quarterly ("Deposition Practice and Tactics," 52 Mass. L.Q. 5) and was reprinted in the Fall 1997 issue of LITIGATION; it is excerpted here with permission. Further, this article was first written in 1967 and, since that time, there have been numerous changes to the Federal Rules of Civil Procedure which are not reflected in the article.

and his documents and records is an incalculable advantage far superior to written interrogatories or private investigation on the same subjects. In addition, a deposition affords an early opportunity to evaluate the opposing party as a witness and to appraise the overall strengths and weaknesses of his case. Finally, depositions often include or are followed by settlement discussions, and settlements are frequently reached at an earlier time than would ordinarily be the case.

Occasionally the argument is made that a deposition "educates" the adverse party, and should therefore be avoided. This is rarely, if ever, a sound tactical justification for not deposing a party who has information susceptible to oral discovery. While such a deponent may be exposed to some adverse facts and legal contentions, the usefulness of the information obtained by the examiner vastly outweighs this slight, and often illusory, disadvantage. Invariably, the "education" received will be far greater than any "education" given and the deposition will thus be worth taking. Moreover, in a skillfully conducted deposition, the adverse party may receive no "education" whatever, except a general awareness of the complexities of litigation and some familiarity with the examination process.

Tactically, the decision to depose a witness depends on the nature of his expected testimony, his availability, and his willingness to testify at trial. Generally, a friendly or neutral witness is not deposed if he will be available to testify at the trial since, in this instance, the educational value to the opposing party outweighs the risk of not preserving the witness's testimony. With a hostile witness, counsel must decide (a) whether his adverse testimony at the trial will be sufficiently important to warrant preparing to refute it in advance or (b) independently of any adverse testimony, whether he has evidence or documents essential to counsel's affirmative case which may not otherwise be obtainable.

Practical Considerations

Frequently, practical considerations will dominate the decision to depose. If the testimony of the deponent—whether he is a witness or a party—is needed, and illness, age, or distance indicate that he will not be available at the trial, there is little alternative but to take his deposition.

76

Since deposition testimony can affect the outcome of the trial, no competent trial counsel should consider taking or attending a deposition without thorough preparation. Not only examining counsel but deponent's counsel have important preparatory tasks if they are to represent their clients properly. If the examiner is unprepared, the deposition will likely be a tedious waste of time, effort, and expense with little information to show for it. If deponent's counsel is unprepared, the consequences can be more serious since the deponent may unnecessarily provide or volunteer much damaging information.

Counsel should never permit his client or a witness over whom he has control to be deposed without adequate advance preparation. Not only must the deponent's testimony and documents be reviewed, but equally important, he must be prepared for the deposition process itself. A full explanation by counsel of the nature and mechanics of the forthcoming deposition is essential if the deponent is to understand his role.

Perhaps the most important consideration that counsel must emphasize is the difference between a deposition and a trial. He should explain the one-sided nature of a deposition, its broad scope, the absence of any judge to settle disputes, the purpose and type of objections, the general obligation to answer all questions, and the circumstances under which the deposition is usable at trial.

Above all, a party deponent must fully realize that the deposition is designed to obtain as much information from him as possible, and that he cannot help his case by volunteering information, arguing with the examiner, or explaining his answers. In simple terms he should be told that his deposition can be used against him but that, unless he dies, it is not likely to do him much good at trial. He must be instructed that the time for explanation and further testimony is in the courtroom and not the deposition room, and that when that time comes, his side of the case will be fully presented. In short, he must fully understand the nature of the deposition proceeding and the substantial dangers it may present for his case.

The limited role of deponent's counsel must also be explained and understood so that the deponent does not mistake a proper lack of active participation by his counsel for failure of representation. Without such understanding and explanation, deponent's counsel may tend to become active vocally for what appears to be no other purpose than to demonstrate his diligence to his client, perhaps on the theory that the client may mistake movement for action.

Once the nature of the deposition process is understood, the deponent's preparation on the merits should begin. A few general guidelines about deposition procedures and a short lecture on the virtues of brevity, responsiveness, and truth are not adequate preparation for what may be a long and important examination. The client's testimony should be elicited in detail, the areas of possible examination reviewed, and the documents scrutinized. In addition, he should be tested by cross-examination and asked the hard questions that are to be anticipated from opposing counsel.

The examiner's preparation for the deposition is no less essential or extensive than the deponent's. He not only must know his client's case but must learn as much as possible about his adversary's. Whether the deponent is a party or a witness, counsel should carefully investigate what part he has played in the case and the specific information, knowledge, and evidence he possesses. At the same time counsel should review the existing documents and ascertain whether further documents are likely to be in existence and in the deponent's possession.

After obtaining the facts and documents, counsel should study the applicable law to learn what facts should be elicited at the deposition to support his overall legal theory or such specific legal conclusions as "waiver," "estoppel," "wilful," "knowingly." Thereafter, counsel should prepare a broad written outline of the general subjects to be covered as well as an event-by-event chronology of the case, noting each conversation, communication, or incident. He should also prepare a detailed outline of his examination as a checklist to assure continuity, perspective, and complete coverage. Without such a detailed guide, a deposition, which is peculiarly a proceeding where the subject matter can change frequently and fast, may tend to become disjointed and disorganized and its usefulness diminished.

Obtaining Stipulations

When the deposition convenes, the first practical and tactical situation generally facing counsel is that of stipulations. The most common stipulation waives the filing of the transcript and other related formalities and preserves to the time of trial all objections except as to form. Frequently signature is also waived and if they wish, the parties may broaden the stipulation to preserve all objections, even those of form, to the time of trial.

Without a stipulation, the deposition must be signed before the notary who took the testimony and the transcript must be sealed and filed in court. Objections as to form are waived unless made at the deposition, and no objections whose grounds could have been obviated at the deposition are preserved for trial. Rule 30(e)(6); Rule 32(d)(3)(A).

In considering a stipulation the tactical choices differ for each counsel. The examiner may prefer to have deponent's counsel make the required objections or lose them at trial. At the same tune, he may wish to preserve until trial his own objections to the witness's answers. He may also want to avoid filing the transcript in court but may be unwilling to waive the necessity of the deponent's signing the deposition.

On the other hand, deponent's counsel may wish to waive signature on the theory that the deposition thereby becomes slightly less impeaching, but may insist on the transcript's being filed in court, based in part on the dubious ground of additional expense to the opposing party. He may also wish to preserve all objections to the time of trial so that he loses no rights in failing to object at the deposition.

Obviation Clause

Apart from the trouble-making obviation clause, which does not preserve objections whose grounds are "obviable" [Rule 32(d)(3)(A)], Rule 32 itself would preserve to the time of trial all objections except as to form. The usual stipulation has the additional effect of rendering inoperative the obviation clause and thereby eliminating uncertainty at the deposition and controversy at trial. If counsel wishes to take the further step of eliminating any disputes about the distinction between form and substance, he may stipulate that *all* objections (not only those as to form) are preserved to the time of trial.

Where the deponent is a witness not represented by counsel the parties should be certain that he has been given a full and adequate explanation of the content and effect of any stipulation. Generally, the witness will have no objections to a stipulation in the usual form, including waiver of signature. It may be wise, however, for one party or the other to insist on signature, especially if the witness will not be available at trial and the deposition is to be offered in evidence.

Another preliminary matter which frequently arises concerns the attendance at the deposition of other witnesses, parties, or potential deponents. Rule 26(c)(5) provides that the court may make an order "that discovery be conducted with no one present except persons designated by the court." [Although parties and counsel appear to have an absolute right to attend the deposition, *see* 8 Wright and Miller, Federal Practice and Procedure [S]2041, it is not altogether clear who is entitled to attend a deposition in the absence of a protective order limiting attendance. One court has held that neither the public nor the press has a right to attend a deposition, but that only "the principals" do. *Times Newspaper Ltd. (of Great Britain) v. McDonnell Douglas Corp.,* 387 F. Supp. 189 (CD. Cal. 1974).—*Ed.*] Therefore, if counsel wish to exclude other witnesses, application for such protection should be made in advance of the deposition.

Once the preliminary skirmishes about stipulations, attendance of spectators, and other matters have concluded, the witness can be sworn and the deposition begun. However, there are some depositions when long speeches of counsel "for the record" precede the commencement of testimony. These will denounce the scope of the notice or subpoena, challenge the designation of the deponent as managing agent, or expound on some purported irregularity in the proceedings to that point. Most of such speeches accomplish no useful purpose, clutter the record, and enrich the reporter. If counsel were genuinely concerned about such matters, some action prior to the deposition (or a simple objection noted for the record as to certain matters of procedure or form) would be the more meaningful and appropriate practice.

Although examining counsel will have his outlines, chronology, and documents to guide his examination, perhaps the most important factors in the success of the deposition are his recognition and understanding of its purpose and an interrogation which reflects such purpose. Knowing the purposes of the deposition tells the examiner how to conduct the deposition. Unless counsel appreciates why and to what end he is interrogating, the examination may be not only meaningless, but harmful. Thus, his knowledge should include not merely a familiarity with the deponent's expected testimony, but how such testimony and the likely presence or absence of the deponent at trial affects his deposition tactics and fits into his overall trial strategy.

Examining counsel must first decide whether the deposition is primarily for discovery, for use as evidence at the trial, for later impeachment or contradiction at trial, for perpetuation as tactical insurance against age, illness, or death, for securing admissions, narrowing issues, or for some combination of these or other reasons. Usually there will be more than one purpose for the deposition, especially if the deponent is a party from whom both broad discovery and specific admissions will be sought and whom counsel may wish to impeach and contradict at trial.

The purpose of the deposition in general and of any specific question in particular largely dictates the form of question asked, and in turn, the form and substance of the answer received. If the purpose of the deposition is primarily for discovery, the examiner's questions will tend to be broad, the subjects far-reaching, and the answers rambling and discursive. Such an examination is basically devoted to information-gathering, with the examiner trying to discover what the deponent knows, without serious concern for the form in which the information is received or its later admissibility.

If the deposition is being conducted for the purpose of producing admissible evidence—whether documentary or testimonial—the form and substance of the questions and answers are crucially different since they must be admissible at trial in order to fulfill the examiner's purpose. Thus, the questions must be as sharp and precise, and the answers as complete and responsive, as if the deposition were in fact the trial. The examiner is primarily interested in usable evidence and not in gathering information. If the questions and answers are not in admissible form, the testimony becomes useless, the deposition will be excluded when offered at the trial, and the necessary evidence will be lost.

When the purpose of the deposition is largely evidentiary, objections to the form of the question and answer become more significant. If not made at the deposition, such objections are waived both under Rule 32(d)(3)(B) and the usual stipulation. When they are made at the deposition, the examiner must decide whether to rephrase the question to meet the objection or allow the question to stand and thereby run the risk that it will be excluded at trial.

81

If the purpose of the deposition or of a line of questioning is to freeze the deponent's testimony so that it will not change at the time of trial, the questions must be directed to, and accomplish, that purpose. The subject matter must be sufficiently broad and the questions sufficiently specific so that the deponent is fairly committed to a version of the facts which he cannot change at trial.

Make Full Record

An examiner may be completely prepared for a deposition and fully understand its purposes and yet not achieve such purposes because of a lack of thoroughness in his interrogation, and a failure to make a full and complete record of the deponent's knowledge and information.

Attention to detail, in depositions as in other affairs, is the hallmark of a craftsman skilled in his art. Since the federal and many state rules permit, and indeed encourage, a latitude of questions in detail far wider than would be permitted at trial, the examiner should take full advantage of the opportunity. For each important conversation or transaction about which he inquires, he should be certain that he has obtained all that the deponent's memory can provide. When the deponent's memory is exhausted, the examiner should attempt to evoke further testimony by refreshing his recollection or should establish for the record that it cannot be refreshed. The record should thus be clear that the deponent's version of a particular incident or conversation is complete so that at the trial the deponent will not be able to make changes or additions without risking impeachment. Frequently, an examiner fails to ask a deponent if he has given the substance of an entire conversation or conference. Thereafter, at trial the witness may give damaging testimony as to further conversation which would have been elicited on deposition if the examiner had pressed the point and insisted on complete information. Similarly, unless all of the witnesses to a given event are named, or all of the documents in a particular transaction identified, surprise witnesses and surprise documents may turn up to plague counsel at trial.

As to documents produced at the deposition, the examiner should make sure not only that they are made part of the record, but more importantly, that the questions and answers relating to them clearly identify the document or to words or phrases

82

within a document, the examiner should make it clear precisely what language he is asking about and where it is to be found in the document. Vague references to "this letter," "that agreement," or "the report" may be clear to those attending the deposition but will be meaningless in the typed transcript.

Mark as Exhibit

Before the examiner asks any questions about a document, he should have it marked as an exhibit for identification so that he can then refer to it by exhibit number and make sure that the witness does the same. Assuming the usual stipulation is in effect, no objection need be made to a document's being marked as a deposition exhibit since the question of its admissibility is reserved by Rule 32(d)(3) until trial. However, if the obviation clause is operative, other objections such as lack of foundation or best evidence may be required in order to void the possibility of waiver.

Thoroughness in examination and attention to detail also include such basic and often crucial procedures as authenticating documents or photographs, laying a proper foundation for testimony, qualifying an expert, identifying and describing physical objects, and other preliminary burdens required by the law of evidence before testimony or documents become admissible. Unless such matters are handled competently at the deposition, important evidence may be later excluded and the case seriously affected.

Once the purpose of the deposition and of a particular line of inquiry is fixed, the examiner should adopt the manner and method of examination which best serves that purpose. If the deposition is being taken to gather information, the witness should be encouraged to talk since the more he testifies the more the examiner knows. Counsel who takes a deposition for discovery and then prevents the witness from volunteering, bristles at self-serving statements, cuts off explanations, and continually demands only yes-or-no answers is neither hurting the witness nor helping the case.

Since the most important product of a discovery deposition is raw information, the examiner who prevents its emergence by such tactics not only defeats his own purpose, but may create a hostile atmosphere in which the witness is not likely to continue to be informative or cooperative.

Similarly, an examiner should never be reluctant to elicit unfavorable information at a discovery deposition. He should be as anxious to receive this information as the deponent will be to provide it. Although it should be the essence of the discovery procedure to learn adverse information early at a deposition rather than being surprised later at the trial, inexperienced examiners, allegedly seeking discovery, nonetheless avoid deposing on subjects which may yield statements and information damaging to their case. The damaging information will not disappear merely because counsel has not asked about it and sound tactics indicate that knowing the worst and preparing for it are far preferable to pretending that it does not exist.

If the purpose of the deposition is basically evidentiary, that is, for later introduction into evidence, the examiner's method and technique should closely resemble that used at trial. His questions should be in proper form and directed toward eliciting testimony which would be unobjectionable when offered at the trial. With this objective in mind he must carefully evaluate the answers received to assure himself that they are responsive and in proper form. An answer which is informative but inadmissible in form or substance serves no evidentiary purpose at the trial. Conversely, an answer improper in form may be admissible at the trial if the objection to form has not been made or preserved.

Some or all of the above considerations apply in varying degrees at every deposition. With a party, the examiner will ordinarily seek the broadest possible discovery, yet will also be concerned with obtaining usable admissions, laying the groundwork for possible later impeachment, and obtaining any evidence necessary to his affirmative case. He must also consider that while the party deponent is limited to using his own deposition to rebut portions offered in evidence, his unavailability at trial may make the deposition usable as part of his affirmative case. As to a witness, the examiner may have less interest in broad discovery and more in fixing the witness's version of events or in putting the testimony in admissible form for use at trial.

With such considerations clearly in mind, the examiner must frequently switch the form and format of his questions depending on his purpose and whether the deponent is a party or a witness. Where the examiner wishes discovery, his questions will be broad, occasionally open-ended, and may call for explanations or encourage the deponent to talk. For example, the "why" question which is usually avoided at trial by most cross-examiners as a foolhardy practice with an articulate hostile witness, may be a proper and logical question at a discovery deposition where information is the basic purpose served by the question. However, when the examiner comes upon a subject matter as to which he wishes to "freeze" the deponent's story, elicit an admission, or put the testimony in admissible form for the trial, he must change both his tactics and his questions. To accomplish these purposes, he will switch from what has been essentially information-gathering by direct examination to the specifics of cross-examination, paying careful attention to the completeness of his examination and to the form and substance of both question and answer.

In short, a good examiner will, for part of his interrogation, sound as if he were conducting a direct examination of his own client and at other times, as if he were cross-examining the adverse party. Both techniques are dictated by the purposes which the deposition is to serve and by the constantly changing nature of information sought and the testimony received.

The examiner who habitually conducts his deposition as if he were in the courtroom overlooks the fact that he is not. The examiner who conducts his deposition without any thought of the courtroom is equally shortsighted and his results will be as haphazard and as limited. The "art" of deposing is the right mixture of discovery and cross-examination, information and evidence, broad inquiry and pointed question, useful knowledge and usable testimony, and of knowing when and how to get the information required in the form best suited to the needs of the case.

Not only can a deposition be rendered unproductive by lack of preparation or by a failure to understand its purposes, but the examiner's style and attitude can cause similar results. Particularly is this the case in examining the adverse party where discovery is usually part of the purpose to be served.

Unsound Attitude

Some examiners, long accustomed to flamboyant courtroom cross-examination, bring the same manner and mannerisms to the deposition without fully realizing that courtroom tactics differ substantially from deposition tactics. Their cross-examination is often marked by petty tests of credibility carried out in an atmosphere of open hostility and accompanied by insinuations of disbelief or expressions of incredulity. Such an attitude is usually unsound and impractical. Cross-examination designed to impress a jury should be saved for the jury. At a deposition no one is impressed by such tactics, except possibly the client, and contentiousness for his benefit is not a sound tactical justification for wasting valuable deposition time and money. Secondly, a hostile and overly aggressive attitude generally tends to defeat the examiner's purpose, by resulting in less, not more, information and by indoctrinating the witness early in the type of examination to expect in court. Such conduct can also create resentments and antagonism which will diminish the effectiveness of the examiner and thereafter plague the case, possibly preventing an early settlement.

As far as the examiner is concerned, there is little reason why the deposition should not be conducted in a friendly or at least civil atmosphere. When cross-examination becomes necessary, a firm but polite manner is far superior to the slashing attack and will accomplish more. To be effective it need not degenerate into the quibbling and quarrelsomeness that often accompanies what passes for fierce courtroom cross-examination. The absence of any jury is precisely the reason why the examiner can concentrate on the major issues of the case, and on developing a broad base of discovery information which, by appropriate and selected examination techniques, he can narrow into admissible evidence when and if he chooses to do so.

For discovery purposes, there well may be much to gain and little to lose in the examiner's allowing the witness to volunteer information or make self-serving statements. However, at some point the examiner may need for the record a responsive answer in a form suitable for admission into evidence at the trial. A certain degree of tenacity is therefore required in rephrasing or repeating the question until a responsive answer is given.

While occasionally the deponent's answer remains wholly unresponsive, more frequently the examiner is faced with an answer part of which is responsive and part of which is not. In order to preserve his right to object at trial to the wholly nonresponsive answer, or to have stricken the nonresponsive portion of the otherwise responsive answer, the examiner may fear that he must do something further at the deposition—a fear based on the assumption that a nonresponsive answer is either an obviable defect or one of form. The fear is illusory and the assumption is unsound since neither category is applicable.

Clearly, it is not within the examiner's control to obviate a nonresponsive answer. Neither constant repetition of the question, long colloquies, or the threat of sanctions can force a deponent to be responsive or produce an answer the deponent does not wish to give. To argue that such a result is an obviable defect is contrary to common sense and inconsistent with experience.

Nor is a plainly nonresponsive answer or a nonresponsive portion of an answer (which in most disputed cases includes self-serving assertions) a matter of form, but rather goes to the substance of the question and often to the merits of the case. If a witness were asked to identify his signature, and replied that the signature was his, but that his adversary had tricked him into signing, or if he were asked whether he knew the plaintiff and replied affirmatively, adding that the plaintiff was an alcoholic, the defects of such answers hardly go only to form. Such improper answers no more require that the examiner immediately echo the meaningless phrase "move to strike" than an irrelevant or immaterial deposition question requires an objection. If such were not the result, the jury, in the absence of such a "motion" in the transcript, would be entitled to consider the entire answer and give such evidentiary weight and effect as they wished to the plainly prejudicial material. This consequence would be highly unfair to the examiner and in turn would oblige him to clutter the record with repeated motions to strike, admonitions and suggestion of sanctions, although in the last analysis, he could do nothing to change the answer.

While the problem, if any, can be dealt with by broadening the stipulation to preserve all objections (both to the question and answer) to the time of trial, examining counsel should not be forced to seek such a stipulation at the risk that a clever deponent may create admissible evidence out of nonresponsive and self-serving answers.

Best of Both Worlds

Although nonresponsiveness is a matter of substance, there are defects in the form of answers to which the examiner should voice objections at the deposition. A familiar example would be the deponent's testifying with characterizations rather than facts.

Subjective conclusions that the speaker "agreed," "pleaded," or "demanded" rather than testimony as to what he said are defects in the form of answer. Unless the matter has been covered by stipulation, counsel should note his objection and then either attempt to secure an answer in proper form or not as his tactics dictate.

In such a situation, the examiner has the best of both worlds. He has not only the information but the power to strike the defective answer at the trial should deponent's counsel attempt to offer it. On the other hand, deponent's counsel, recognizing this, may wish the testimony in admissible form and may seek to have the witness correct his testimony immediately or on cross-examination.

Although the deponent's counsel has a less vocal role to play at a deposition, it is no less important than the examiner's. At every stage of the examination, deponent's counsel must be alert for questions improper in form or considered outside the scope of the deposition, and must be prepared for any situation in which he is called upon to protect his client's interests. He may be obliged to make the hard decision instructing his client not to answer or to refuse production of documents, and ultimately he must decide whether to cross-examine and to what extent.

If the obviation clause has been rendered ineffective by stipulation and all objections except as to form have been preserved until the time of trial, deponent's counsel's principal concern will be identifying defects of form. Examples of such defects would be questions which are argumentative, ambiguous, multiple, or leading, all of which can be cured by the examiner's rephrasing the question. When such a defect appears in a question, deponent's counsel need do no more than state his objection as to form. If he wishes, he may state the ground for his objection, which may be of some aid to the examiner (who may then decide to reframe his question) and perhaps to the witness. Often the examiner will suggest that deponent's counsel state the ground of objection so that the question can be rephrased.

Ambiguous Question

Occasionally, in lieu of making a formal objection, deponent's counsel will merely request a clarification to prevent the witness's being confused by an ambiguous question. Such participation, if not overdone, can be helpful in maintaining an accurate and non-misleading record. Occasionally, however, whether a request for "clarification" more accurately represents advice to the witness than a genuine misunderstanding of the question becomes a matter of some debate.

Since the rules permit a broad scope of examination and generally require that all questions should be answered (with objections preserved until trial), counsel should rarely instruct his client to refuse to answer. *See* Rule 30(c). However, situations will arise when deponent's counsel must consider whether the examination so exceeds the permissible bounds that he is justified in running the risk of instructing his witness not to answer. His initial instinct should be against such an instruction if any other course is open, including asking that the question be reframed if its language is the source of difficulty. When all else fails and the subject is sufficiently important to the case (as opposed merely to a test of wills with opposing counsel), resort to a refusal to answer is not precluded by the rules. *But see Ralston Purina Co. v. McFarland*, 550 F.2d 967 (4th Cir. 1977).

Deponent's counsel should be aware that a refusal to answer gives the examiner the option to adjourn the deposition in order to obtain a court ruling. Rule 37(a)(2). Thus, the deposition may be halted and valuable time, effort, and expense consumed in motion proceedings while the client awaits the result, often unable to attend to his business or to complete his deposition. When the motion is finally disposed of, the deposition will continue and the client may find that his inconvenience and expense were substantially increased by his own counsel.

Matters which are privileged are outside the scope of examination permitted under Rule 26(b) and questions concerning such matters need not be answered on appropriate objection and instruction by counsel. Occasionally, however, the privilege is prematurely asserted, since an examiner is entitled to know when, where, and to whom the deponent made the privileged communication in order to determine if the privilege applies.

Similarly, matters not relevant to the subject matter of the litigation are not within the scope of examination. However, since the broad concept of relevance as stated in Rule 26(b)(1) and in the decided cases clearly permits fishing expeditions, counsel takes some risk in using irrelevancy as a basis for a refusal to answer. Although the scope of relevant examination is not without limit, he may often have difficulty justifying the refusal if the question has any connection with the proceedings or can lead to any admissible evidence.

While disagreements as to relevancy are a common source of colloquy at depositions, a request of the examiner as to the relevance of his question will often elicit a satisfactory explanation that will eliminate a possible refusal to answer. Similarly, the examiner should not be reluctant to state the relevance of the question, not only to avoid controversy and obtain the information but also to make a clear record if, despite the explanation, the refusal to answer nonetheless persists.

While misleading, argumentative, or ambiguous questions present, as a technical matter, only defects of form, often any response will provide misleading, argumentative, or ambiguous information, or start the examiner on an improper and time-wasting line of examination. Since the examiner is presumably not deposing either to mislead or to argue with the witness, refusals to answer are probably easier to justify under these circumstances than others. Once again, however, counsel can avoid friction, controversy, and eventual judicial intervention by seeking to reach agreement on the phraseology of the disputed question.

The form of interrogation, including endless repetition, over-long examination, overbearing behavior, unjustified preoccupation with minor matters for inordinate periods, and constant argumentativeness frequently result in refusals to answer. Such infringements by the examiner are matters of degree, and tactical judgments will differ as to whether it is simpler, faster, and less wasteful for counsel to permit an answer than to advise a refusal.

Longer Than at Trial

As to length of examination, the rules contemplate that a deposition examination, by its nature, will be longer than an examination at trial on the same subjects. Full discovery is one purpose of the rules and one of their chief benefits. Nonetheless there may well be a point at which a particular subject matter or the deponent's knowledge has been thoroughly exhausted or where the line between permissible and impermissible inquiry has been overstepped. At this point deponent's counsel may conclude that a refusal to answer is justified, although in so concluding, he must constantly be aware that the court may later draw the line differently and apply sanctions accordingly. *See* Rule 37(a).

In dealing with refusals to answer, both counsel should exercise restraint before taking rigid positions. Frequently, before giving any instruction not to answer, deponent's counsel should indicate his nonobjection to a certain line of questions if limited or clarified, or his willingness to continue with other areas of inquiry. If he finally decides to instruct the witness not to answer, it should be done with a minimum of speech-making, rancor, or colloquy and, if possible, without encouraging a suspension of the deposition by the examiner.

Similarly, the examiner should usually not waste time and money in pointless argument and long "for the record" speeches since the relevance and propriety of a well-phrased question ought to be apparent from the question itself and from the prior record. However, the examiner may occasionally wish to explain such relevance and propriety in order either to resolve the objection and obtain the information or to call such matters to the court's attention when the transcript is read.

Although the examining party can suspend as of right when he is faced with a refusal, he should rarely do so but should try to complete the deposition on all other matters. Frequently, he will obtain the information with other questions and in connection with other subjects. If, on rare occasions, the attitude of deponent's counsel or the importance of the subject matter make it impossible for the deposition to continue, a judicial determination should be sought immediately and an effort made to see the nearest available judge as soon as possible.

In general, however, neither the examiner nor the deponent's counsel benefits greatly from refusals to answer. Much time can be consumed in colloquies and by motions concerning refusals on matters which later events prove irrelevant or unimportant or which were originally based on exaggerated fears. Further, in many instances, resort to judicial intervention never materializes either because other evidence provides the information or hindsight indicates it was not worth the effort. Finally, the information sought is often inadmissible in any event and its expected usefulness greatly overestimated. For such reasons, advising refusals to answer should be a last-resort measure for unusual situations and not a standard tactical procedure.

Unfortunately there are counsel who, far from seeking to avoid refusals to answer and infrequent resort to judicial intervention, appear to welcome, if not to precipitate, such circumstances.

91

Thinking such conduct to be good tactics, they disrupt the continuity of the examination with constant objections and refusals together with challenges to the examiner to take up the matter with the court. Either these tactics mask an insecurity based on ignorance of the rules or their purpose is to prevent or hinder discovery.

Since the party deponent does not wish to provide his adversary with any more information than necessary consistent with giving responsive truthful answers, his counsel usually will not cross-examine him (or a favorable witness) if he will be available to testify at the trial. Exceptions to this general practice are often made to correct errors or to clarify misleading or ambiguous portions of the record in order to avoid the suspicion which attaches to last-minute changes or modifications of testimony at the trial.

Even if the party will be available to testify at trial, some counsel conduct a short cross-examination eliciting favorable testimony in general terms or denying the principal charges. It is argued that the possibility of the deponent's death or the possible introduction at trial of the cross-examination, if part of the deposition testimony is offered by opposing counsel, justifies this practice. The client's desire for equal time in order to present, in self-serving measure, his "side" of the case is also added as a minor justification. Although mortality is a fact of life, none of these considerations usually justifies more than a cursory cross-examination, if any. Such examination should probably do little more than indicate in broad outline that the party has a valid claim or has denied the allegations of the complaint.

The temptation to engage in extensive cross-examination, especially if the examiner has elicited some apparently damaging (but explainable) testimony, should be firmly resisted. Although the natural inclination of counsel and client may be to refute and rebut the examiner's case and to assert the righteousness of their own, the time for such presentation is normally not at the deposition but at trial. Counsel should ask himself what useful purpose will be served by trying to demonstrate to the examiner the worthlessness of his case and the validity of his adversary's. The examiner is not likely to be convinced, and the attempt will provide him with valuable information and education. Absent some overriding consideration, deponent's counsel should save his efforts for the trial, but he should also make sure that his client understands why the deposition is not the appropriate place to explain and narrate his version of the facts.

A Warning Sign

If deponent's counsel embarks on extensive cross-examination of his own client or a favorable witness, it generally indicates that (1) the deponent's counsel is misinformed on deposition tactics (and is about to educate his adversary); (2) counsel is excessively concerned about the possibility of death or unavailability; or (3) the deponent is likely to be unavailable at trial and thus must have his testimony perpetuated.

If the party taking the deposition concludes that the deponent's counsel is cross-examining in order to use the client's deposition at the trial, he must adjust his tactics accordingly. This will mean careful attention to the cross-examination to preserve objections of form and those which are obviable, and if necessary, conducting a redirect examination to obtain contradictions, admissions, or further testimony which can be introduced at the trial.

Counsel's judgment intuition, and experience and the form and substance of the questions are guides by which he can determine the purpose of cross-examination. If there is doubt, he should err on the side of assuming that the deponent's testimony is being preserved for use at trial and thereafter act accordingly.

CHAPTER 7

Medium v. Tedium: Video Depositions Come of Age

David M. Balabanian*

The medium has finally come to the courtroom. A lawyer can now record any deposition on videotape, if the other side agrees. In 1970 the Federal Rules of Civil Procedure were amended to permit electronic recording of depositions by stipulation. The change eliminates the requirement of a court order. FED. R. CIV. P. 30(b)(4). Even the criminal lawyer can now offer a videotaped defense. FED. R. CRIM. P. 15(d).

But you may want to check an impulse to record all your testimony for playback to the jury in color. Video depositions are a mixed bag, expensive and possibly misleading. And an alert opponent may not stipulate when the video deposition would do you the most good. Consider the following before you smear yourself with makeup.

A video record carries greater impact to a jury, and even a judge, than a cold transcript. A video deposition avoids the

---

Mr. Balabanian is a member of Bingham McCutchen LLP in San Francisco. This article originally appeared in the Fall 1980 issue of LITIGATION.

tedium that benumbs the mind on hearing large quantities of deposition transcripts. A video record may even entice judges in bench trials to watch rather than require that deposition testimony be submitted in writing.

A video record can capture the attention better than a transcript read by relays of dispirited lawyers. The new generation of jurors who receive their truth from the tube may prefer video to live testimony. But even for the print generation, video can be powerful.

- Video can show a witness's personal injuries in a manner that surpasses still photographs. Video can show limited motion or impaired function. Of course movies can also do this, but video can allow a distant witness to re-enact events or conduct experiments or demonstrations. But prepare yourself for disputes over the conditions under which the deposition is taken, the nature of the demonstration or experiment, or even the camera angle.
- Video can record a terminally ill witness. Testimony from "beyond the grave" at trial could prove highly effective. In one recent case the court allowed a plaintiff to take his own deposition at the point of death despite the defendants' opposition. *Carson v. Burlington Northern, Inc.,* 52 F.R.D. 492 (D. Neb. 1971).
- Video can liberate doctors and other experts from the rigors of trial scheduling for their testimony.
- Video can yield an immediate record, unlike the reporter. In a fast-moving injunctive situation, this alone may dictate use of video. Of course, the necessary equipment and technical personnel must be easily available and the tape should not require editing or you may lose this advantage.
- Video can suppress obstreperous counsel. Lawyers on camera may forego their more obstructive practices. But they may also replace bombast with ham.
- Video can bring home to a nonchalant witness the seriousness of the proceeding.

There are many things that video cannot do. Video will not save money, despite the hopes of the Advisory Committee in the Notes to Rule 30(b)(4). If you want to save money, use an audio cassette recorder. Parties can stipulate that a deposition or interview will be recorded on tape and then use the tape or the transcript as the deposition. You will need no sophisticated equipment, although be sure to use an external microphone (usually provided with any cassette recorder) rather than the internal mike. Each party should bring its own recorder to the deposition and make simultaneous copies of the tape. This reproduces the tape and guards against doctoring.

Surreptitious Recording

Because of the unpleasant consequences of surreptitious recording under certain state laws (ranging from inadmissibility to felony penalties, for example, CAL. PENAL CODE § 632), have the witness acknowledge on the tape that he is aware of the recording. The questioner might also make occasional statements *on* the record that the conversation is being taped.

The cost of video will vary greatly with the number and type of cameras used, auxiliary equipment, and whether it is in color or black and white. Stenographic recording will almost always be cheaper. A hidden problem may be that the case will demand both methods of reporting. Counsel will rarely be able to do without a written transcript and will often require a certified transcript prepared by a reporter present at the deposition.

You will need a transcript (probably certified) if the witness's testimony is used in pretrial motions. You will need a transcript (probably not certified) for pretrial review of the testimony and preparation of the witness because reviewing a videotape is woefully inefficient. For example, comparison of different portions of testimony will be impossible without a transcript. You will need a transcript for presenting objections to the court in advance of trial. You will need a certified transcript if the deposition is used for impeachment.

Of course, a stenographer in your office can prepare a written transcript from the videotape (or a simultaneous audio tape), but this course may lead to inaccuracies. Extensive use of a written transcript, along with the inevitable disputes, suggests that you should obtain simultaneous official reporting and videotape.

Most courts concern themselves with preventing alterations in the video record. In fact, it is difficult to doctor a videotape. If the recorder uses a digital time-and-date generator, alteration becomes almost impossible. This device creates a digital record on the taped image, identifying date and time by minutes and seconds. This permits more accurate location of specific portions of testimony than does the footage meter. However, the video-tape is invariably edited before trial. The tape played for the jury will have distracting gaps in the digital record. While the possibility of doctored tapes exists, it will not occur if the video operator is as qualified and respected as a court reporter.

Other video problems are not so easily solved.

People do not necessarily appear true to life propped in front of a television camera. A natural appearance can be achieved only with considerable effort. With some witnesses, it can never be achieved.

Counsel should not begin a video deposition without a rehearsal to check the appearance of the witness. During the deposition, a lawyer should look at a monitor from time to time while the camera rolls and check the tape during breaks in the deposition.

Where the appearance of the witness is particularly important, employ a professional consultant. Differences in camera angle, lighting, and other technical variables can change the entire effect of a deposition.

Pointers

Some practical considerations:

- Proper lighting is essential. Modern cameras can work with available light, but it must be properly balanced. Be alert for shadows that alter the witness's appearance. Light can turn a genial soul sinister.
- Color cameras are worth the extra expense. A natural look is hard to achieve in black and white.
- The best dress for a man will be a solid gray suit with a blue shirt. White "blooms" on television and black appears too dead. Checks and stripes are distracting.
- With women, prefer solid darker colors; avoid prints and checks.
- Women should use make-up and men a little talc or handkerchief action to keep down glow.
- Men should shave immediately before the deposition or at least use flesh-colored talc to cover stubble.
- Train the witness to look into the camera while testifying. Likewise, the witness should look at the questioner during accusatory questions or he will appear evasive.

- You must alter the conventional wisdom regarding witness behavior at depositions. A lawyer generally advises deponents to take all the time they need to formulate answers. But in a video deposition the camera grinds on through the delay and records expressions of confusion or dismay on the part of the witness. A witness must respond as promptly and confidently at a video deposition as at trial.
- The concentrated focus of the camera intensifies eccentricities or peculiarities of speech or manner. The witness's accents become more noticeable and mannerisms more distracting or offensive.
- Take care to muffle noise in the deposition room. Background noises such as air conditioning or traffic and the noises of shuffling documents or movements are intensified on television and will be distracting.
- Do not overlook camera angle. High shots produce pygmies. Low shots yield monoliths of the Citizen Kane type.

There are certain questions that frequently recur.

Do You Use Zoom Lenses?   A zoom lens enables the cameraman to achieve close-ups of the witness or a particular anatomical feature. A witness who is having trouble with a question appears evasive and his discomfort more devious with zooming. We all remember the televised grilling. Some courts have required that the cameraman be independent or that the camera be aimed and then not moved. The use of independent operators may be an unnecessary expense, though a reasonable precaution, given the increasing availability of video equipment.

The model stipulation at the end of this article presents alternate solutions to the problem of camera control. Selection among them will depend on the trust between counsel and the funds available.

How Many Cameras?   Both questioner and deponent should appear on camera when they speak. Otherwise the audience may ignore or downplay the unseen lawyer asking the questions. Panning the camera among the speakers will cure the problem but leaves viewers dizzy. Two cameras—the technique of television news reporting—will offer more relaxed shifting but is expensive. You will also have to rent mixing equipment and have an operator to switch back and forth from camera to camera to capture the current speaker. This will require great skill or it will become ragged. You could use a split-screen somewhat like the instant replay of a quarterback and receiver. But the audience will be frazzled after a few minutes of this technique.

Who "Notarizes" the Tape? In the usual deposition, the reporter, a notary, swears the witness. The Federal Rules suggest that the video operator should be the deposition officer.

But Rule 28(a) provides that "depositions shall be taken before an officer authorized to administer oaths by the laws of the United States or the place where the examination is held, or before a person appointed by the court in which the action is pending." This might require the presence of both a notary and the cameraman, unless you stumble across a video notary. The problem can be solved easily: Rule 29 authorizes the parties to provide by written stipulation that "depositions may be taken before any person. . . ."

Who Pays for the Deposition? Given the costs of video, disputes will arise over allocation of costs for creating the original tape, for taping cross-examination, for duplicate tapes, for blanking out objections, and for preparation of a transcript or stenographic record. Rule 30(b)(4) provides that even if there is a stipulation or order for the use of video, "a party may arrange to have a stenographic transcription made at his own expense." Think carefully about this problem before agreeing to a video deposition, especially if your client has limited means.

How Do You "Sign" a Video Deposition? As revised, Rule 30(b)(4) requires that a nonstenographic deposition be accompanied by a "writing" that sets forth any changes made by the witness and his signature identifying the deposition as his own or the statement of the officer if the witness does not sign. Presumably the witness will identify a videotape as containing his deposition and sign a writing to that effect before depositing it with the court. The suggested stipulation waives signature after an opportunity to review.

How Do You Handle Objections? One method for handling objections is to submit to the court before trial a written transcript of the testimony together with objections. After the court has ruled, an edited tape can be prepared. This is time-consuming and costly.

Another method, the "McCrystal Method," requires the court—equipped with a log that identifies the location on the tape of material to which objection has been made—to view the tape in advance of trial and note its rulings on objections. This technique may burden the court's time. Afterwards, an edited tape can be prepared.

Alternately, the technician who plays the tape at trial can suppress the audio during objectionable testimony. Although several authors recommend this latter practice, it sounds bizarre. How will a jury react to a videotape on which the witness mouths in silence? Jurors may become restive and annoyed with the party who shut off the sound.

One author suggests that jurors might lip-read and proposes that voir dire eliminate lip readers. *See* Kornblum & Short, *The Use of Videotape in Civil Trial Preparation and Discovery,* 23 Am. Jur. Trials 95 (1976). That, too, seems bizarre. A better solution would be to suppress both audio and video during objectionable sequences.

Given the variety of questions and problems in a video deposition, the best results may be achieved by a stipulation rather than a court order. A number of courts have considered the cost and accuracy of video recording and issued widely varying orders covering techniques and procedures. *E.g., Continental Federal Savings & Loan Ass'n v. Delta Corporation of America,* 71 F.R.D. 697 (W.D. Okla. 1976); *Matter of Daniels,* 69 F.R.D. 579 (N.D. Ga. 1975); *Wescott v. Neeman,* 55 F.R.D. 257 (D. Neb. 1972); *Kallen v. Nexus Corp.,* 54 F.R.D. 610 (N.D. Ill. 1972). The stipulation below represents an attempt to distill the best of these often conflicting rulings.

If agreement on a stipulation is not possible, video may still be available by court order. In *Colonial Times, Inc. v. Gasch,* 509 F.2d 517, 522 (D.C. Cir. 1975), the court ordered the trial court to grant a request for non-stenographic recordation. A different result was reached in *UAW v. National Caucus of Labor Committees,* 525 F.2d 323, 326 (2d Cir. 1975).

A number of states have adopted or are considering statutes or rules governing video depositions. Many of them follow Rule 30(b)(4) as it read before this current amendment. Read these rules before using this stipulation.

Televised testimony may bring life to the courtroom, but make sure you know what you are about before agreeing to try it. Video depositions could turn your client's tragedy into a soap opera and the opposing lawyer into Howard Cosell.

APPENDIX: Stipulation for a Video Deposition

It is hereby stipulated by and between _____ that the deposition of _____ (hereafter "deponent") in the above action shall be recorded on videotape in the following manner and upon the following conditions:

Time and Place

1. The deposition shall be taken at _____ on _____ commencing at _____. It shall continue thereafter from day to day, excluding weekends and holidays, until concluded.

Deposition Officer

2. The deposition shall be taken before_____, who is an employee of _____. He/she shall serve as deposition officer.

Video Equipment and Its Control

3. Except as otherwise provided herein, the deposition officer shall select and supply all equipment required to videotape the deposition and shall determine all matters of staging and technique, such as number and placement of cameras and microphones, lighting, camera angle, and background. He/she shall determine these matters in a manner that accurately reproduces the appearance of the deponent and assures clear reproduction of both the deponent's testimony and the statements of counsel. The deponent, or any party to the action, may place upon the record any objection to the deposition officer's handling of any of these matters. Such objections shall be considered by the court in ruling on the admissibility of the video record. All such objections shall be deemed waived unless made promptly after the objector knows, or has reasonable grounds to know, of the basis of such objection.

Use of Day/Time Generator

4. There shall be employed at the deposition a day/time generator to create on the videotape a continuous record of the day and time.

Commencing the Deposition

5. The deposition officer shall commence the deposition by stating on the video record his/her name and business address; the name and business address of the offi-

cer's employer; the date, time and place; the name of deponent and the caption of the action; the identity of the party on whose behalf the deposition is being taken; and the names of all persons present in the deposition room. The deposition officer shall also swear, on the video record, that he/she will record the deposition accurately and in confidence and abide by all provisions of this stipulation. The deposition officer shall then swear the deponent on the video record. Such oath shall be effective without regard to whether the officer is otherwise authorized to administer oaths.

Going "Off Camera"

6. The deposition officer shall not stop the video recorder after the deposition commences until it concludes, except, however, that any party may request such cessation, which request will be honored unless another party objects. Each time the tape is stopped or started, the deposition officer shall announce the time on the record.

Changing Tapes

7. If the deposition requires the use of more than one tape, the end of each tape and the beginning of the next shall be announced orally on the video record by the deposition officer.

Availability of Monitor

8. There shall be available to counsel throughout the deposition a monitor on which they can view the video record as it is being made.

Camera on Speaker

9. The deposition officer shall endeavor, to the extent possible without creating undue distraction, to focus the camera (or the live camera if there is more than one) on the person who is currently speaking, whether it be the deponent or counsel.

Exhibitions and Demonstrations

10. Except by agreement of the parties or order of the court, the deponent shall not be required or permitted to exhibit personal injuries or limitation of movement, conduct demonstrations or experiments, or re-enact physical events.

Allocation of Costs

11. The costs of videotaping the depositions shall be borne [by the party who noticed the deposition] or [by all parties equally] or [by all parties who interrogate the deponent, in proportion to the length of their direct examination]. Such costs shall [not] be taxable costs in this proceeding. Any party may obtain at its own expense, a copy of the videotape or any portion thereof from the deposition officer.

Stenographic Reporting

12. [Any party may, at its own expense, have the deposition reported by stenographic means.] or

   [The deposition shall be reported by stenographic means in addition to video. The allocation and taxability of the costs of such stenographic reporting shall be governed by the provisions of paragraph 11, *supra*.]

Discrepancies between Video and Stenographic Records [If the latter is used]

13. In the event of any material discrepancy between the video record and the stenographic transcript, the parties shall stipulate or, if they are unable to agree, the court shall determine which record shall be submitted to the trier of fact.

Examination and Correction of Deposition Record

14. After completion of the deposition the deponent and all parties shall be given reasonable opportunity to review the videotape [and any stenographic transcript] of the deposition and to request in writing (or on the video record if it is still open) any changes or corrections in such record[s].

Waiver of Execution

15. Thirty days after notice to the deponent and all parties that the videotape is available for inspection as provided in paragraph 14, *supra*, the original of the videotape (together with all requests for changes or corrections theretofore received) may be filed with the court where it shall have the same force and effect as a duly executed stenographic transcript of the deponent's testimony.

Certification of the Video Record
    16. [As soon as possible after expiration of the period pre-
        scribed in paragraph 15, *supra*] or [No later than ten
        days before trial] the deposition officer shall file the
        original videotape with the above court in a sealed
        envelope which shall identify the action, the deponent,
        and the date[s] of the deposition. To that envelope the
        deposition officer shall attach his/her sworn statement
        that the videotape is an accurate and complete record of
        the deposition and that he/she has complied with all
        provisions of this stipulation applicable to said officer.

Custody of the Tape
    17. The deposition officer shall maintain custody of the
        original tape until it is filed with the court. Parties may
        view the tape while it is in the officer's custody, but
        only under conditions that make impossible the erasure
        or alteration of the tape.

Editing the Tape
    18. A party who desires to offer any portion of the video
        record at trial for any purpose shall, no later than 60
        days before trial, advise all other parties of the portions
        of the tape it wishes to offer. Any party who believes
        that the portions so designated contain objectionable
        material may, by motion, seek that court's ruling on its
        objections in advance of trial. An edited tape, eliminat-
        ing material found by the court to be objectionable,
        shall be prepared (at the expense of the party responsi-
        ble for the original inclusion of that material) unless the
        parties provide, or the court orders, another method, for
        the suppression of the objectionable material.

Effect of Stipulation
    19. This stipulation shall supplement and, to the extent per-
        mitted, supersede the provisions of any statute, rule, or
        regulation otherwise applicable to the taking of video
        depositions in this jurisdiction.

CHAPTER 8

Conducting the Oral Deposition

Stuart A. Summit*

The oral deposition can be the litigator's most useful tool when he enters the discovery phase of the big case. It is perhaps the most effective discovery device for developing the facts critical to the litigation. Properly conducted, depositions can affect the whole complexion of the action. Finally, oral depositions can play a significant role in settling the case. Since most civil actions are settled, the face-to-face confrontation of an important witness through the deposition can determine the extent and nature of the ultimate settlement.

Generalized advice for the conduct of a particular deposition is, of course, difficult to provide. However, one type of deposition—that of an important witness in a case where the facts are complex and the documents numerous—illustrates the many problems that are likely to arise in this form of discovery. Such depositions, which generally consume several days and can last for weeks, also require careful advance analysis and planning if they are to serve their intended purpose. It is that type of deposition that will be the model for my observations in this article.

Too many depositions are approached casually and conducted routinely. The examiner will ask the obvious questions suggested

*Stuart A. Summit is a member of the New York City firm of Phillips Nizer L.L.P. This article originally appeared in the Spring 1975 issue of LITIGATION.

by the pleadings, perhaps pursuing some areas of inquiry in some depth, and he will consider that he has done his job. Too often the deposition is not preceded by careful planning, including a clear identification of the goals the examiner hopes to achieve through the deposition.

Is the deposition to be conducted simply to uncover facts? Are you honestly ignorant about certain areas of your case and will this witness supply the relevant information? Do you have serious doubts about the witness's view of the facts? If the deposition is needed principally to develop facts, you will want to isolate carefully the precise areas of factual inquiry for the witness.

However, oral depositions can serve other purposes. Would it be useful to have a full record of the witness's view of all possibly relevant facts, for example, to support a motion? Is it reasonable to expect that major factual disputes can be precluded by a careful examination of this witness on the entire case?

Or, perhaps the witness is in a position to encourage a settlement. Are there telling lines of inquiry that will suggest to the witness that settlement of the case should become a priority matter? Will a lengthy and exhaustive examination bring home to him the rigors of litigation and will he seek to avoid those rigors through settlement?

Perhaps the issues in the case have not yet been fully developed. The oral deposition can help you develop the issues favorable to your position. Can you emphasize certain lines of inquiry in a manner that will influence your adversary's thinking and thus influence the issues on which the case will be tried or settled? Particularly if the deposition will last for several days or weeks, the matters that assume importance during the deposition may be treated as important during the remainder of the action.

Setting Goals

If the examiner is fully conversant with the known facts of the case, and understands the witness and his role, he should be able to predict the reasonable result of the examination. There will be things that you cannot know in advance, but the likelihood that the witness has the missing information and the attitude he will probably take toward the relevant areas of inquiry should be predictable. Set your goals in advance and make them reasonable in light of what you do know.

It is also important that you know the witness as well as you can prior to the deposition. You should obtain as much background information on the witness as you can. The success of the oral deposition may depend on the extent to which the examiner understands the character, personality, and temperament of the witness.

Is the witness a quick thinker? Is he accustomed to working in the early morning? In the evening? Is he controlled in speech or is he loquacious? Is he cheerful and composed? Is he used to pressure and does he accept pressure well? Will his composure suffer from long periods of questioning? Will he be substantially less controlled in the early morning or in the late afternoon? Does he have any personal or business problems that may affect his composure?

Personal background is helpful even when not directly related to the witness's probable conduct during the examination. You should attempt to learn the nature of his family life, and his community, church, recreation, and social activities, and so forth.

Is he good at his job, respected by his fellow workers, subordinates, and superiors? How does he prefer to be addressed? Does he resent any particular form of address? What is his attitude toward his work and his employer?

Such information enables you to visualize and understand the witness as a person as you prepare for his examination and will give added meaning to his answers at the deposition. Your sensitivity to him as a person when you are planning the deposition and when you are taking it will be invaluable.

Some may believe this kind of investigation is offensive, or interferes with the witness's "right of privacy," or constitutes gamesmanship. I disagree. If a particular witness may play an important role in the outcome of significant litigation, a careful review of his background and personal qualities is necessary and inevitable.

Next, you should identify precisely the witness's relationship to the case. You should not rely on your general knowledge of the witness's role. It is not enough to know that he is president of the adversary or that he had general responsibility for an activity at issue in the case. You should review all documents which he is known to have authored, all documents he is known to have received, and all documents that he may have authored or received. You should also identify all documents which, in your understanding of his role, he logically should have authored or received but concerning which his role is not clear. Try to visualize what documents should exist, but apparently do not, which might affect his role. The documents frequently assume a pattern of their own, and you can spot events or subjects that should have been the subject of a writing, but apparently are not. Finally, you should attempt to distinguish between the "record" role and the actual role of the witness. There are instances of chief executives who insist on taking full responsibility but who, in fact, have little involvement in a given matter. Conversely, there are persons who prefer to remain in the background but who play a crucial role in a matter in dispute.

You should consider the possibility that the witness's attitude or motivations with respect to the case may not be the obvious ones. Ask yourself what his real attitudes or motivations might be. Try to think of him in relation to all of the other persons involved in the transaction. Was his role the natural one for him, given all the circumstances? Was he subordinate to persons he would resent? Was his role likely to have been resented by others? Might he have been overruled on some critical questions?

Getting Organized

Your next step should be to organize your materials. Your files should be well organized before you attempt to develop your actual method of questioning. Several methods of organization should be considered.

First, a full chronological memorandum is probably indispensable. Such a memorandum should list, by date, every possibly relevant occurrence or communication. Each entry should be described sufficiently to enable you to recall quickly the witness's role in each transaction listed. The chronological memorandum must be updated as discovery progresses.

Second, you should isolate every topic you believe the witness can testify about and prepare a "fact sheet" for each of those topics. The fact sheet should contain itemized summaries of everything you know of the important facts relating to that topic and the witness's role with respect to it. Document references will be very helpful. For example:

January 23, 1973—

Smith was present at lengthy meeting—pricing structure discussed—see Jones' transcript, 11, 35; docs. # 23, 27, 29.

Important documents related to the witness's role can be annexed to the fact sheet.

Third, if you have a great deal of information available, you should compile a list of every "mention" of the witness by any person or in any document. If feasible, use actual quotations. Such a compilation may be of no help at all, but occasionally it will enable you to spot a pattern or otherwise give you a new insight into the witness's role or how he was viewed by others.

Finally, the relevant documents should be organized in as many different ways as you can conceive. A complete chronological file is indispensable. Each document should be related to as many topics as are at issue in the litigation and a copy of the document should be filed under each of those topics. Have a separate document file consisting only of documents the witness authored or which are addressed to him. The more places a relevant document can be found, the more likely it is that it will not be overlooked. Different juxtapositions of documents suggest different possible patterns of thought or conduct. You should read each different file in sequence, even though you are reading the same documents over and over.

The final step before the deposition is to prepare for the questioning. In most instances, you will want to avoid prepared questions. No matter how much you have prepared, you will not fully understand the witness and be able to predict how he will react until you are well into the deposition. Set patterns of questioning, which are usually the result of advance question preparation, make the examiner predictable and the witness comfortable. While this result may be desirable, you will not know in advance. It is simple to develop patterns that make the witness comfortable during the course of the examination if that turns out to be desirable.

The advantages of spontaneous questioning are overwhelming. If you compose your questions as you go, you will be much more alert to the nuances of each answer. You will not overlook a follow-up question. You will be able to determine on a continuing basis whether your method of questioning is producing the result you hope to achieve.

Most importantly, spontaneous questioning enables you to carry on a dialogue with the witness. The atmosphere that is created through that dialogue will necessarily affect the witness's answers. A question that is read invites greater care in the answer. It creates a cautious mood. Conversely, spontaneous questions, which demonstrate that you have total command of the facts, permit a fast pace. You want the witness to forget that he is in an adverse position to you, that he has a lawyer present, and that a reporter is taking down every word he says. The witness must feel that he exists in a world in which there are only the two of you. Achieving this goal requires very hard work, good facility with questioning, and a very fast pace.

Prepared Questions

There are occasions when you will have to prepare questions in advance. It may be that a particular line of questioning, with each question carefully worded, is necessary to force either an admission or the realization that evasion is futile. Also, where a number of documents must be referred to in the course of a single line of questions, some degree of advance question preparation may be necessary. Even so, your preparation should permit you to avoid the appearance of reading a line of questions. Prepare the questions in advance, review them thoroughly, and keep the prepared questions in front of you. But you should attempt to maintain constant eye contact with the witness.

The extent to which questions are prepared in advance may also depend on your understanding of the witness. If he is a very controlled person who is likely to answer questions precisely and tersely, the questioning process will be slower, and a greater degree of advance question preparation may be necessary.

One instance in which advance preparation of questions may be essential is when you anticipate an evasive or dishonest witness. You will want to prepare questions that will take advantage of the witness's dishonest and evasive tendencies and will lead him in a direction he is trying to avoid. An obvious example is where the witness wants to establish his ignorance of certain facts. If you attempt to establish that he is ignorant of certain insignificant facts, he may defend himself and show his total command of those facts. Having demonstrated that he is an astute perfectionist on these matters, he will be reluctant to claim

112

ignorance of critical facts. Achieving this result requires careful advance wording of each successive question.

Whether you decide to make the entire examination spontaneous or prepare specific questions for certain areas of inquiry, you will need a checklist of the topics you intend to cover in the deposition. Such a checklist, combined with the "fact sheets" you have prepared for each topic, should assure a thorough and comprehensive inquiry.

With your preparation completed, you are ready to confront an important witness in the case. In such a deposition, as little as possible should be left to chance. Consider the room it will be held in. Consider how you want your papers arranged. Consider whether you want a colleague present to study the witness and advise you of the witness's reactions. Consider the timing of breaks and the lunch hour, and how such breaks will affect lines of inquiry. Consider whether you want to end the examination day with a dramatic flourish and whether you want to leave important lines of questioning open for consideration by the witness overnight.

You should have a reporter with whom you are familiar. There is nothing more frustrating than conducting an examination that has served your client well, only to find many days later that you have a garbled transcript. There is no sense in getting admissions that will never appear in print, and you cannot count on your adversary's good will when his choice is between a record of serious admissions or a garbled transcript.

You should face the witness directly. Put the reporter at the head of the table, with you and the witness occupying the seats adjacent to the reporter and across from each other. This forces adversary counsel to be out of the witness's line of sight and permits you to have direct eye contact with the witness.

Making a Record

In your preliminary questions, the witness should be made aware on the record of why he is being deposed and the nature of the litigation. You should also ask him how much notice he had of the examination. If the witness provides testimony favorable to your case which your adversary may wish to mitigate later, making a record of the extent of the witness's preparation may be important. You should determine what specific documents the witness reviewed in preparing for the examination. Objections of privilege may be raised to this line of inquiry. But you should be entitled to learn what the witness did, what the witness reviewed, and how much time the witness spent in preparation, even if some of that time was spent in the company of counsel.

During your initial questions, you will want to determine the witness's role in the litigation process itself. Did he have a role in determining to sue? Did he assist in the drafting or review of a pleading? Was he instrumental in organizing information or documents after the transaction in issue was completed? Did he participate in interviews with others who may be witnesses? If he is familiar with the pleadings or other litigation documents, the first substantive line of questioning might be based on those documents. If he assisted in organizing documents for production or preparing answers to interrogatories, those activities will be fruitful areas for inquiry.

Depending on what you determine to be the extent of his preparation, you may wish to ease into substantive questioning. If the witness seems to be very well prepared, you may have nothing to lose by starting at the beginning and taking him through the entire transaction chronologically. Some witnesses have a prepared story to tell and provide no useful testimony until they are permitted to tell that story. So you might as well get it out of the way promptly. If, however, you think the witness has not prepared adequately for the examination, he may need time to get comfortable and you may wish to plunge into a critical line of questioning before he relaxes. Properly done, nothing is more startling to an otherwise nervous witness than being asked a critical and difficult question just after he has given his name and address. If that method produces the answers you want, stay with it—jumping around from subject to subject to keep control of the witness.

In the important oral deposition, you can never obtain enough background information from the witness. You will frequently be unable to judge the candor of his answers unless you know a great deal of background. Do not hesitate to pursue lengthy lines of inquiry not directed to the immediate facts in dispute, if such inquiry will provide you with insight into the organization or persons who oppose you. This information should be obtained early, before your adversary's patience is strained.

You must at some point determine whether it is to your advantage to make the witness feel at ease. If the witness gives you the impression that he is trying to be candid and complete in his answers, you have nothing to gain by making him nervous. Indeed, if obtaining full and accurate testimony is your goal, you should make a deliberate effort to make the witness feel comfortable. If he is stumbling and you know of a document that will help him, offer it to him. Establish as much rapport as you can with the witness, in the hope that he will feel that he cannot in fairness be evasive or dishonest with you. If you are gratuitously nasty, the witness will view the deposition as a game in which his objective is to beat you out of whatever information you want.

A witness, however, must be taught to respect the examiner and to understand the dangers of being evasive. If you have treated the witness with courtesy and respect and he reciprocates with incomplete or evasive answers, you must quickly assert control and convince the witness his tactics are self-defeating. How you achieve that result necessarily varies with the circumstances. However, if justified by the witness's conduct, your questions should become sharper in tone and substance, and your manner with him should become peremptory. You should ask and re-ask the same questions until the answers are satisfactory or until you are precluded from doing so. Your objective must be to convey to the witness that he is making his own job much more difficult.

Obtaining Admissions

If the deposition lasts more than one day, you should ask the witness at the beginning of the next day or next session what preparation he has done in the interval. The documents he will have reviewed or the persons, other than counsel, he has talked to between deposition sessions may be very meaningful. Presumably he has concentrated on areas that troubled him. If the witness has been candid with you, it may be advisable to ask whether he wishes to change or comment upon any testimony previously given. If he should make any such change or comment, you will want to know what has prompted it. Has someone pointed out to him that he made an error, or did something else indicate that his initial testimony was in error?

There can be no general advice for getting a witness to make admissions he does not want to make. The informality of the oral deposition generally works against you. But the witness will find it difficult to avoid admissions if he is confronted by objective facts or documents that he must concede. The pace of the examination also is critical to the possibility of procuring admissions. People will not knowingly and willingly make damaging admissions. The witness must become disoriented, losing all sense of the context of the questions, or he must feel that he has no choice but to make the admission. It is difficult to envision a slow-paced examination that will produce either result.

A witness whom you believe is lying presents a very different problem from the witness who is merely evasive. Often, it is best not to pursue the apparent lie immediately. You should first take stock. Analyze what led you to believe that the witness lied. If you have objective evidence, particularly documents, which virtually establish that the witness lied, you must decide first whether it is to your benefit to demonstrate promptly that he has lied or whether it would be better to save that demonstration for settlement discussions or the trial. If you conclude that the better course is to demonstrate the untruth during the course of the examination, be certain that your materials are well organized so that the attempt will not fall flat.

If, however, you find that you cannot establish the falsity objectively, you will have to expose, through your questions, the thought processes by which you concluded the witness had not been truthful. This frequently requires extensive questioning, and you will have to decide whether such an approach will accomplish anything. In the absence of objective evidence that the witness will have to accept, you may be able to do little more than embarrass him and you may not have a usable record for trial. Your appraisal of the degree to which the witness can control himself under tension should also be an important factor in determining whether you should attempt to demonstrate that he has lied during the deposition.

If you do decide to attempt to establish the untruth, you should wait until unrelated subjects have been covered. A witness who has lied will often have a strong consciousness of having done so and will be relieved when you move on to other subjects. He will also be all the more chagrined when you return to the critical subject. The witness's surprise and chagrin may assist you in demonstrating that he has perjured himself.

A common phenomenon is the witness who cannot recall matters of importance. The methods for dealing with that situation are not much different from those you use at trial, but the oral deposition offers you the opportunity to be more painstaking. You should first cover other matters that either took place within the same time period or are similar in nature. Then, in a single question if possible, accumulate all that he can recall during that period and ask him to explain the lapses in his recollection. Show him in rapid succession all of the documents that relate to the matter, or refer to events that took place at the same time, and ask him if these refresh his recollection. The object is to force him either to state his actual recollection (on the assumption that he has one) or to make his failure to recollect conspicuous and an embarrassment to him. He will then have an incentive to give an honest recollection, at least on other matters. If the witness persists in his inability to recall, and you do not believe him, move on. Come back to the subject later, from another direction, and use a different kind of question.

You should, however, keep clearly in mind your ultimate objectives. The witness's faulty memory might help you by limiting his testimonial usefulness at trial. If so, you will want to be sure that his failures of recollection are as many in number and importance as possible, and you will want to preclude the possibility of a credible recapture of recollection between the deposition and the trial. You should ask the witness whether he knows of any document or person that might assist his recollection. If he identifies a document, you should insist that he examine it immediately. If he identifies a person who may be able to assist his recollection, probe why he believes that person can help. When did he last see that person? When did they last discuss the matter involved? If the matter involved is critical, you may wish to take that person's deposition.

Under the practice in many states and in the federal courts, objections except as to the form of a question are reserved for trial. Lawyers, however, frequently object to the substance of questions and, indeed, instruct the witness not to answer. Your approach when this occurs must be guided by your assessment of the judge who will decide such disputes. You should at least attempt to force your adversary to state the grounds of his objection and remind him that objections as to substance are reserved. If he states the reasons for his objection, discuss them with him. Depending on the circumstances, you may be able at least to head off similar objections. You may also be able to imply to the witness that his lawyer is preventing a full and candid airing of the facts. If you have been able to engage the witness in a dialogue with you, he might resent the intervention and believe that his lawyer does not respect him.

If the objection is that the question is misleading, point out that the witness does not seem to be easily misled. Ask the witness whether he understands the question as it was asked. Force his lawyer to acknowledge that he is not even allowing his witness to state whether he understands the question. Your specific approach should be governed by whether objections and instructions not to answer are being abused by your adversary.

In any event, you should not fight on weak ground. If you cannot adequately defend the question or its subject matter, why spread that fact on the record? But, if your adversary is truly obstreperous, develop an unambiguous record of his obstructive behavior and terminate the examination pending instructions from the court. There is little point to continuing an examination that is dominated by your adversary.

Rephrase the Question

You will not always want to rephrase a question when its form is objected to. First, you should determine if it matters to you that the answer will not be admissible at a trial. Often it is more important to keep the dialogue moving than it is to have an admissible answer to a particular question. Then determine whether the question is truly objectionable. While it is, of course, better to rephrase a question than to run the risk of nonadmissibility (if you care about admissibility), it is as important that your adversary come to realize that he cannot dominate or interfere with your examination. Your approach will often depend on the attitude your adversary is taking. It would be pointless to have a confrontation with a courteous and cooperative adversary over an occasional objection.

Witnesses occasionally will answer a question with a question. The examiner should not become involved with an explanation of the facts or of points he is trying to make. He should explain

118

to the witness that it is not appropriate for the examiner to answer questions during the deposition and then re-ask or, if necessary, rephrase the question. Similarly, do not permit your adversary, through the device of objections or requests for qualification, to force you to state the point of significant questions. Any hope of an uncontrolled answer from the witness is lost the moment you are put on the defensive and forced to explain precisely what you are up to. If your adversary insists on an explanation of relevancy and you do not want to carry the argument further, discuss your question out of the hearing of the witness.

The measure of your success in the deposition of an important witness is, in the final analysis, whether it achieved your predetermined goals. That result will elude you, however, unless you engage in careful and painstaking preparation, keep your predetermined goals in mind as the deposition proceeds, and maintain full control and initiative throughout the examination.

CHAPTER 9

The Four-Hour Deposition

Kenneth R. Berman*

Four hours. Four hours to find out how the project engineer mishandled the design and construction of a bridge that collapsed and killed five people. Four hours to commit the movie producer to a version of the events surrounding the formation, performance, and breach of a multi-million dollar film contract. Four hours to unravel the maze of financial transactions and property transfers that a CEO masterminded to deprive the minority shareholders of a meaningful return on their investment. Four short hours.

Limiting the time for depositions is a major goal of cost-cutting reformers. Under the Civil Justice Reform Act of 1990, federal district courts were commissioned to develop new rules to reduce the time and expense of litigation. State courts have been doing the same. Among the changes popping up are rules that—absent a stipulation or court order—limit the time for taking depositions. In the Northern District of Georgia, Northern District of Oklahoma, Middle District of Pennsylvania, and Eastern District of Wisconsin, depositions are now limited to six hours. In state courts, Arizona limits deposition time to four hours. Illinois allows three hours. Montana gives eight. Judges and lawyers are discussing and debating this trend elsewhere.

*Kenneth R. Berman is a partner in Nutter McClennen & Fish LLP, Boston, Massachusetts. This article originally appeared in the Spring 1993 issue of LITIGATION.

Even if a jurisdiction does not adopt such a rule, courts are more often entering discovery orders on a case-by-case basis that do the same thing. And, regardless of new rules or court orders, cost-conscious clients will naturally be drawn to trial lawyers who can take an effective four-hour deposition.

Like it or not, litigators must master the art of gathering lots of evidence without spending a lot of time doing it. Whatever their basis—rule, stipulation, order, or self-discipline—such constraints will limit lawyers who have never known time limits before. The challenge thus is learning to take an effective deposition in less time than what most lawyers have thought a good job requires.

Being effective with rationed time may not be easy. We have been taught to be thorough. We fear leaving the winning testimonial gem behind. Our relentless quest for every detail is a natural enemy to the forces that would—at the end of day one—have the final word in the transcript read "concluded" rather than "continued."

But it can be done. Lawyers can eliminate much of what now consumes time in a deposition without sacrificing the needs of the case. What some attempt to justify as thoroughness is more likely produced by inexperience or insecurity. Others waste time in a deposition because of poor planning.

In most instances, a good lawyer should be able to take an effective deposition within tight time limits. What is needed is discipline plus an introduction to concepts new for some in discovery—notions such as triage, segmentation, and time budgeting. Also required are careful planning and focused questioning.

Triage is a technique adapted from battlefield medicine. The idea is to sort cases by severity, giving priority to those with the most grievous ailments or injuries. When time is short, a lawyer needs to sort the issues in a similar way.

This is not the usual approach. By instinct, training, or observation, many lawyers take a deposition by first asking for the deponent's vital statistics (name, address, date of birth, marital status, children, social security number), then asking about the deponent's education (in needlessly numbing detail), then asking about the deponent's military status and employment history (in more numbing detail), then asking for general background information about the suit, and then asking about events leading up to (but not including) the specific matters in controversy (usually in chronological order). Then, and only then, do they ask about the specific matters in controversy. Finally (sometimes days later) comes the denouement, a potpourri of questions without any theme, but designed to exhaust every arguably relevant topic not previously covered.

Time-Wasting Preliminaries

Such an approach is probably what inspired the movement to limit deposition time. It has no place in a time-restricted world. When you finally reach the meat of the matter, you will have burned up valuable time (and your client's and adversary's money) on matters of little or no importance. As an added bonus, you will have left yourself with inadequate time and energy to interrogate the witness on the important subjects.

Why, for example, is it important to know what the witness's responsibilities and duties were in a job held five years before the events at issue? Perhaps there is some marginal utility in the information, but surely it is not as important as the events surrounding the utterance of the defamatory remark upon which suit is based.

So here is the first step in using deposition time well: Recognize that some topics are more important than others. Learn how to spend the best time—i.e., when lots of time still remains—on the most important issues. This means you may need to sacrifice some topics. It also means not structuring a deposition in chronological order. In the era of time limits, taking a chronological order deposition makes as little sense as treating emergency room patients in the order they arrive, rather than based on who needs the fastest treatment.

A successful four-hour deposition will therefore start almost immediately with the most important issue in the suit. You must, of course, ask a few preliminary questions to establish who the witness is. Once the preliminaries are out of the way, however, get right to the heart of the matter:

Q: Would you tell us your name and address?
A: Jane Smith, 80 Barnett Street, Needham.
Q: If at any time I ask you a question that you do not understand, will you tell me?
A: Yes.
Q: How are you employed?
A: I am the production manager at Acme Corporation.

Q: How were you employed on November 1, 1997, when John Plaintiff was injured at the plant?
A: I was the fabrication specialist at Acme.
Q: Do you know what time of day John got injured?
A: Yes, it was about 2:30 that afternoon.
Q: What were you doing at that time?
A: I was on break.
Q: Immediately before you went on break, what were you doing?
A: I was operating the fiber shredder.
Q: Was that the same fiber shredder that caught John's hand?
A: Yes.

In this example, after eight questions and about 30 seconds, the witness has begun her testimony about the injury in dispute. Once you have asked the witness everything you want to know about the machine, the injury, and what the witness did or did not do that caused or contributed to the injury—remember, that is why you are taking the deposition in the first place—you can use the remaining time to ask about significant, but less central matters: the company's training programs and safety manuals, the witness's own training and experience, previous problems with the machine, the witness's education, and any other topic you feel is worth covering before four hours expire. When time runs out, you may not have touched, say, the reasons the witness left her previous employment, but at least you will have done what you needed to do.

Beginning the deposition by covering the most important issue first does not mean that you should ask the ultimate question immediately after establishing the witness's name and address. Thus, if your objective is to establish that in violation of company safety rules, the witness left the machine running while taking a break, you should not feel pressured into conducting an examination such as:

Question 1: What is your name and address?

Question 2: On November 1, 1997, you took a coffee break and left the fiber shredder machine running, didn't you?

Strategy and skillful examination should not be overwhelmed by expediency. Instead, the idea is to segment a deposition into a number of topic groups. Ask about the most important groups first. Within a given grouping, you can be methodical: Set up questions and lay whatever clever traps you would otherwise have done had you not been under time constraints.

Before the four-hour era, the buzzword in deposition practice was preparation. "Preparing" for a deposition in what is becoming the old days usually meant drafting an exhaustive outline on every imaginable and marginally relevant topic. The more topics or questions in your outline, the better prepared you thought you were. After you bled a witness dry at deposition, at your leisure you could pick and choose what portions of the transcript to use for your summary judgment motion or trial.

In the four-hour era, the buzzword is planning. You should view depositions as a limited resource: Every hour spent in a deposition where nothing helpful occurs is time during which, with better planning, you might have gotten profitable testimony. The wasted hour cannot be repeated, reclaimed, or recycled.

Planning for a deposition means establishing objectives and drafting an outline that will meet those objectives. Planning begins at the earliest stages. It starts with having a theory of the case and an idea of how to prove that theory. It requires careful decisions about the most efficient way to obtain needed evidence. The well-prepared deposition will not be a mind dump; it will be a focused inquiry, one that searches not merely for any helpful evidence, but for the most meaningful evidence.

Keep It All Coordinated

Careful deposition planning demands coordination with other discovery tools. If you have gotten certain evidence through a document request, do not waste time getting the same evidence in a deposition. If you already have an admission from your opponent—whether in a document, an interrogatory answer, a pleading, or otherwise—do not depose someone to establish the admitted fact. If your opponent has admitted the authenticity of documents in a Rule 36 request, do not ask a deponent whether they are what they purport to be.

Depending on the case, there may be a variety of ways to plan a deposition. Here is a reasonable way to plan: First, confer with your client and review your client's documents; get a firm understanding of the events, the key players, and the issues. This will give you a general idea of what you need to prove and what evidence you already have. You can also use this information to prepare a chronology, which you can embellish at every step before the first deposition.

Second, serve a Rule 34 request to get your opponent's relevant documents. Review them carefully. They will add to your knowledge of the case and give you a better idea of what you need to prove. This added knowledge will also shape your thinking about the universe of potential deponents and what you might expect to accomplish with each.

Third, based on what you have learned from your client's and your opponent's documents, serve Rule 45 subpoenas to obtain relevant documents from third parties. Under the Rule 45 amendments that went into effect in December 1991, third-party documents can be subpoenaed for inspection and copying without conducting a deposition. Your review of the third-party documents will give you an even better idea of what you need to prove and whom you need to prove it.

Fourth, after reviewing all documents from all sources, serve a Rule 36 request for admissions as to both the authenticity of documents and the truth of important facts. The responses to your Rule 36 request could significantly narrow the issues and obviate the need for much of your deposition program.

Once you have obtained, reviewed, and organized the documents, and once your opponent has answered your Rule 36 request, you can make intelligent choices about which depositions to take and what to ask. You will know, for example, by reading an internal memo, that the decision to terminate your client's product line was made by the defendant's vice-president of purchasing, and not by the field buyer who gave your client the bad news. If you need to establish that the defendant terminated your client's product line because of an agreement between the defendant and your client's largest competitor, the vice-president of purchasing will be one of your deponents; you will first ask about dealings between the defendant and your client's competitor before the date of termination. The field buyer's deposition might be avoided altogether.

With time limits on depositions, you must avoid common time wasters. One obvious time waster is argument with opposing counsel. On a slightly less contentious level, do not let opposing counsel lure you into on-the-record colloquies. That will do nothing but eat up your four-hour allowance. To avoid such aimless discourse, try to establish the ground rules at the beginning. If your opponent has an objection, he can state it without windy speeches. If your opponent wants to instruct the witness not to answer, the grounds for the instruction should be stated without elaboration. Indeed, since December 1993, Federal Rule 30(d) has sought to end the type of colloquy that eats up time.

If you must engage in a long discussion to resolve a dispute, do it off the record, and have the reporter note the time you went off and the time you went back on. (Failing to get the time noted may prevent you from determining how much time you have left.) If you cannot resolve the problem off the record, then, when you come back on, briefly summarize (but do not debate) the conflicting positions and move on.

In extreme cases, you may find your adversary insists on giving speeches. She may refuse to go off the record for colloquy or do other things that unfairly chew up your limited time. If that happens, suspend the deposition after you have gotten as far and as much as you can, and then apply to the court for more time and for a protective order.

Bickering with the witness is another less obvious form of time wasting. You may not realize that you are doing it. You may even mistakenly think you are making progress. Witness bickering might start, for instance, when a witness gives a generally helpful answer but not in the exact words you would have preferred:

> Q: Mr. Broker, did you help the defendant sell the Tainted-corp stock to the plaintiff?
> A: I was the broker on that transaction.
> Q: So you did help the defendant sell Taintedcorp to the plaintiff?
> A: Well, I told the plaintiff that the stock was on the market, if that's what you mean.
> Q: And would you say that by telling the plaintiff about that stock, you assisted the defendant in making that sale?
> A: I'm not sure that I know what you mean by assisted. Most private sales of this type are done through a broker.
> Q: So in order to sell stock of this type, it's important to have a broker?
> A: That's what brokers do for a living but it's possible to sell stock without a broker.

Q: But would you say that you helped the defendant make this sale?

A: I can't really say how much of a help I was. I certainly hope that my services were useful but sometimes it's just luck, you know.

The first answer was the best, and that is where this line of questioning probably should have stopped. A listener would have inferred that it was the witness's way of answering yes. If something about the answer was genuinely inadequate for the case, the follow-up questions should have moved in another direction. Instead of trying to force the witness to characterize his involvement as "help," the questioner simply should have asked the witness for details of what he did in connection with the stock sale. The extra effort to muscle the witness into saying that he "helped" the defendant did nothing but waste time and diminish the force of the original answer. Unfortunately, this sort of witness bickering occurs too often; it can consume page after page in a transcript.

You also waste time when you apply the right techniques at the wrong times. For example, when a conversation is relevant, it is generally effective to exhaust the witness's memory as follows:

Q: When did the conversation take place?

Q: What time of day was the conversation?

Q: Where was the conversation?

Q: How long was it?

Q: Who was present at the conversation?

Q: Who said what to whom?

Q: Did anybody say anything else?

Q: Have you now exhausted your memory and told me as much as you can recall about who said what to whom?

Q: Did you make any notes of the conversation?

Q: Is there anything else you can do to refresh your memory about anything else that was said and by whom?

But, in limited-time deposition, this routine should be saved only for the important conversations. If you went through this drill every time the witness mentioned a conversation, as many lawyers do, the deposition would be a major investment with a small return.

Fumbling for documents at depositions also wastes time. Sometimes a witness will mention a document or will give testimony that suggests the need for one. A questioning lawyer should have such documents at his fingertips. It is frustrating to the witness and the witness's counsel when the questioner starts fishing through stacks of unorganized papers or cartons in a long and sometimes unsuccessful search.

To use deposition time wisely, you must budget it, especially where there are a number of important areas for questioning. If you were managing a business and had a fixed amount of money to spend, you would decide in advance how much money should be devoted to each expense item. Time is to a deposition what money is to a business.

Always note the starting time of a deposition. If you budget an hour for the first topic, go on to the second topic after the hour is over. By following a time budget, you will force yourself to complete a topic to your reasonable satisfaction before the time is up and ensure that you will cover other important topics.

If you find yourself running out of budgeted time before adequately covering a topic, you must make quick decisions about borrowing time from other topics. Perhaps you will stay with your original time budget and return to earlier topics if time permits. Or you may rearrange your time budget to adjust to the importance of the remaining issues.

Sometimes you will know in advance that a case is too complex, or witness's knowledge too extensive, for a deposition to be completed in four hours. Under most rules and proposals for deposition time limits, parties are supposed to stipulate to lengthen the time of depositions in cases where the need is apparent. To minimize court involvement in the process, parties who unreasonably refuse to stipulate may be sanctioned. If both parties can identify a need for longer depositions, cross-stipulations for more time ought not to be a problem.

Not all cases can be resolved so easily. Your adversary may insist on keeping things short. Or you might be surprised; a deposition that seemed certain to take three hours may look like an all-day affair when a talkative witness goes in surprising directions.

No matter how carefully you plan and take the deposition, inevitably there will be depositions when the witness will be long-winded, slow-speaking, or evasive, when the answers will suggest the need for further inquiry, or when things just do not go as well as planned. Four hours will go by, and the job may not be done. You will need more time. There are only two places you can get it: from your adversary or from the court.

Unless your adversary is in a stipulating mood, you will have to buy more time. This may require some bartering. If you need a few extra hours, be prepared to add a few extra hours to the depositions your adversary will take. Or, offer to shave off time from depositions you have yet to take.

Do not barter for time unless it is absolutely necessary, however, and only do it when the need for more time arises from circumstances beyond your control. It would defeat the purpose of time-and-expense reduction plans—and your clients would not be happy—if you had to sacrifice elsewhere in order to get additional time that, with better planning, you would not have needed. In addition, if you let your opponent know at an early stage that you will barter for more time, your opponent will have an incentive to waste your future deposition time, knowing that you will yield up something to get it back.

Other times, of course, bartering may cost nothing. For example, if among your deponents were a witness whose testimony you know can be brief, you may want to work out an agreement to trade some allowable time from that deposition and tack it onto another deposition. Be sure, however, that the agreement is reasonable, because third-party witnesses, like parties and counsel, might also complain about lengthy depositions.

If bartering for time is not possible, you must get more time from the court. To justify the request, build a good record. You will need to show that you have used your time wisely and that, despite your best efforts, four hours is insufficient. If the transcript teems with repetitive questions, prolonged colloquy, or patent disorganization, the other side will surely highlight it. If the witness has been unduly wordy or non-responsive, you should periodically and politely ask during the deposition for the witness to provide a responsive answer. You can highlight these repeated requests later in your motion for more time. And be sure you say something if there are repeated examples of time wasters that do not show up in a transcript: slow delivery of answers and long pauses between questions and responses. Similarly, a witness can waste your time with private whispering with opposing counsel; this too will not show upon in a transcript. In aggravated situations, you may want to consider suspending the deposition and resuming it on videotape. If the videotape does not keep the witness in line, at least it will enable you to show the judge why you need more time.

CHAPTER 10

Multilevel Depositions

Christopher T. Lutz*

One of John McPhee's early books is an essay on tennis called *Levels of the Game.* In it, he described the contests contained within a single match at the U.S. Open. What seemed to be three hours of two men beating a ball back and forth across a net was much more. It was a multi-faceted contest of mind games, personality, and psychology. The match was played on many levels.

Few would confuse a civil discovery deposition with a championship tennis match. Depositions are longer, less graceful, and, usually, not as sweaty. But depositions too can be contested on many levels. Besides the asking and answering of questions, information is gathered and judgments are made in many ways. The transcript of a deposition is merely topsoil: it obscures many strata of gamesmanship.

Notice that the preceding paragraph says depositions "can" have such layers. The word is not "must" or "should" or "do." What is described here is optional. Many lawyers do not conduct a deposition on many levels—and they should not. If you cannot ask questions crisply and keep track of your purpose; if you fumble with documents; if you are thrown off by an obstreperous opponent—in short, if you have not taken many

---

*Christopher T. Lutz, a former editor-in-chief of LITIGATION, is a partner with Steptoe & Johnson L.L.P. in Washington, D. C. This article originally appeared in the Spring 1990 issue of LITIGATION.

depositions—read this article for amusement but not (now anyway) for guidance.

For those who want to brush up on deposition basics, there is a seemingly endless supply of articles and books. Among the best guides is Suplee and Donaldson, *The Deposition Handbook* (4th ed. 2002).

Another cautionary note: Even if you are a pro, never forget the principal purpose of a deposition: discovery. You must not let the secondary levels of a deposition dominate fact gathering. Such efforts are no excuse for extending the length of questioning, much less making it abusive or offensive. The trick is to play the game on many levels simultaneously.

Doing anything right requires the proper attitude. With depositions, you must begin with an appreciation of the advantages and opportunities they offer. On points like this, I am what an investment analyst might call a contrarian. Many litigation practices that receive abundant praise—"fast track" court procedures or alternative dispute resolution—I find often oversold or ineffective, and sometimes harmful.

On the other hand, I like depositions. Yes, depositions. Nowadays, the word "deposition" rarely appears without one of these words before it: endless, excessive, expensive, unnecessary, abusive, boring, rambling, multitrack, repetitive. A distinguished judge once decried the fact that in many lawsuits "deposition notices drop like autumn leaves." Schwarzer, "Mistakes Lawyers Make in Discovery," 15 *Litigation*, No. 2, at 31 (Winter 1989). And, of course, there are war stories; when lawyers complain about litigation, they talk mostly about reviewing mountains of documents or sitting glassy eyed through depositions.

Someone needs to speak up for depositions. Anything good can be made bad. The fact that some people overuse depositions or stumble through them is not a general indictment. It is like food. The possibility of poor cooking or gluttony does not mean there is anything wrong with the idea of eating. Depositions in fact have many advantages, but unless you understand what they are, you cannot get the most out of them.

First, and unchallengeably most important, depositions work—not always, not cheaply, not simply, but far more often than any other discovery device. Along with document requests, only depositions bring a lawyer eye to eye with what the other party (not his lawyer) thinks or knows. (I won't waste readers' time on the well-known shortcomings of interrogatories, requests for admissions, and other discovery techniques.) *Better* than document requests, depositions ordinarily develop information in one effort. There is none of the teasing, tedious back-and-forth of document discovery: an encyclopedic request; the production of 20 documents and 50 objections; a wheedling and then threatening letter exchange; a meet-and-confer session; a further dribble of documents; a motion to compel; a hearing; the passage of time; an ambiguous ruling; dispute over the meaning of the ruling; further resort to the judge; and, finally, maybe, more documents. Compared to that, a deposition does it quickly.

Depositions are also obviously better than witness interviews, the sort of "informal discovery" often prescribed as a cure for litigation ills. You usually *can't* just interview the other party. If your opponent is a corporation, hundreds will be claimed off-limits. And depositions are compulsory; if a notice is defied, there are penalties. If the witness's oath is ignored, there is perjury. Besides, when impeachment is called for, your memory of a casual chat or even a signed statement you drafted has limitations.

The final—and, for present purposes, most significant—plus for depositions is harder to describe. Put it this way: They give you room. An opportunity to stretch out. You can experiment, even make mistakes. Though they have a certain formality and a serious purpose, depositions are blessedly more casual than many aspects of litigation. The trier of fact is not peering over your shoulder, evaluating your tie and haircut. Neither, usually, is the client. Your pauses and doubts will rarely show up on the transcript. Neither will your tone of voice. You can journey down factual side roads without fear of the confusion it may cause. You yourself can be confused but recover without fatal damage. You need not persuade or convince anyone.

Compared with a trial or motions argument, this freedom is a tonic. Part of the drudgery of many trials is caused by fear and excessive preparation. Every fact is known, every document analyzed. The proof is outlined and the jury (plus shadow jury) scrutinized. Dominating everything is the fear of making a mistake, even of falling short of perfection. Except for supremely confident courthouse veterans, there is little reliance on spontaneity or instinct.

Depositions should be different, though they too are often afflicted by a nose-to-the-outline stiffness. You must be prepared, of course, but you have freedom. And by using the freedom and flexibility of a deposition, you can do more than ask for the facts.

Remember, however, an important limit on deposition freedom: the transcript. Almost all that matters once a deposition ends (as long as videotape is not involved) is the transcript. That is the only remaining record. Whatever you do, however many levels you play on, you must know at all times how the transcript will read and look. You want it clear and coherent. You want, if possible, for each question and answer to stand on its own. A reader or judge should not be forced to leaf back seven pages to determine what the "it" or "arrangement" or "this situation" you are asking about means.

Such attention to the printed transcript will lead sometimes to stilted phraseology. You will use the same nouns and phrases over and over again. It will also lead you to jettison phrases that are not self-executing: "Strike that," "Let me start over again," and "Maybe I've asked this before" can be done away with. In addition, you must be careful about phrases that derive their sense from emphasis or tone of voice. "How can you say that?" means different things depending on whether the emphasis is on "how," "you," or "that."

The limits of a printed transcript are not especially confining, however. Tone of voice cannot give meaning to a question because it does not show in print, and that can be to your advantage. You can use a long pause between words, employ an incredulous tone of voice, or stare at the ceiling without anything appearing on the transcript. So—to begin with—remember what shows on the transcript and use what does not.

With the preliminary concepts out of the way, what contests can you plan to play in depositions while you gather information?

First is assaulting the fortress of preparation. The witness comes schooled in all the commandments of testimony: Answer only the question asked; don't guess; don't volunteer; and on and on. You want to make him violate those commandments. There are many reasons for doing this. It assists the accumulation of information. It lets you assess the witness and how he will perform at trial. And it helps you determine what witnesses and issues the other side cares about.

To break down preparation, you must be able to recognize it. Every litigator in the world knows how to prepare a witness for a deposition—or should. But what does a prepared witness look and sound like? As you ask your initial questions, look for signals like these:

- A flat, uninflected voice.
- Dead pauses between question and answer.
- A dull, serious demeanor; no sense of humor.
- Terse, dehydrated answers.
- Quibbling over questions and the meaning of words.
- And, of course, those favorite phrases of the prepared witness: I don't know (or recall); please repeat that; and can I talk to my lawyer?

In general, if the witness before you looks human but sounds like an irritable android, if she is a successful executive in a complex business but cannot remember yesterday, then what you have is an intensely prepared witness.

How do you get through this protective shield? Recall how the witness got that way. His lawyer has taught him you are the enemy and has schooled him in an unnatural discipline. For most witnesses, keeping the testimonial force field up requires concentration and memory work (How do I phrase that answer? What questions do I fear?), plus an enforced antagonism toward you. It is hard work, as all the witnesses who stray from the prepared path show.

If this is the preparation process, you might undo it by getting the witness to relax and drop his level of antagonism. There are exceptions, but many deposition interrogators go wrong by starting out intense and unfriendly. More often than not, that keeps the witness on edge, reminds him why he needs to be careful, and confirms his lawyer's warnings about the other side's hired gun.

So start friendly and apparently casual. Be solicitous of the witness's comfort. Engage in friendly banter and joke with opposing counsel during breaks. Make your questions precise, but simple and conversational, not formal. Above all do not—if you want to undercut the other side's preparation—become angry, threatening, or rude.

Often an effective aspect of "good cop" interrogation is to ask the witness's help—in explicit terms. You might ask, "Mr. So and So, I'm not an engineer, can you help explain what this patent means?" Or you might say, "Mr. Closemouth, I've been confused for weeks by the relationship between these six companies. Can you explain to me who owns what?" Questions like this are not what the defending lawyer warned about. For decent, ordinary folks, who find deposition preparation unnatural and a little silly, the human urge to help may well lead to relaxation and information.

Throughout, your goal should be to convert the deposition into something like a friendly chat between you and the witness—one in which you have careful control over what you ask, and the witness just talks.

The opposing lawyer will rarely sit, mute and inert, while you try to untune his finely strung witness. He will interject and sputter, object and prompt. He will try to pick fights with the questioner. Sometimes, the "objections" will be pretty explicit: "Objection. Mr. Lutz is just being tricky with that question. He's trying to confuse you."

These tactics may work. Like an electric prod on cattle, they may jolt the witness down the chute of preparation. All the while, this drama will tell you more than just what the answers convey. You begin to learn how the witness may perform at trial—where the cattle prods cannot be used as effectively. You gain insight into the opposing lawyer (Is she alert? Does she try to protect the witness?), and you learn, by measuring the frequency of sputters and interjections, what areas of inquiry worry the other lawyer.

Sometimes defense efforts to stiffen the witness's spine do not work. Sometimes, in fact, they help the questioner. Most litigators have conducted depositions in which the witness is more irked at his own lawyer than the questioner. Recognize the signs: an impatient look while the lawyer blathers out her objections; complete failure to get the not-so-subtle hints in those comments; requests for breaks to talk to the lawyer; answering even when the lawyer has said, "Mr. Jones can't possibly know that. . . ."

If you sense this division between lawyer and witness, exploit it. Without being coy or obsequious, turn up the charm. Stay on the relaxed-witness program. You can sometimes be direct about it, in appropriate cases. If, for example, the lawyer says, "Objection. That question is unintelligible," your response might be, "Oh, I think Mr. Jones understands the question and I'd like him to try to answer it."

In doing all this, realize that things are being learned at levels other than the responses to your questions. Knowing that a witness and her lawyer disagree or do not get along has value and may be exploited later. You may detect that they have different views of the case. Better, the particular issues or facts that cause trouble may stand out.

Sometimes, congeniality fails to compromise witness preparation. Some witnesses are better students than others. Some stay antagonistic because they are mean by nature. And some are naturally dull and laconic. For folks like that, your charm will be like a wave against a rock. You can try and try, but the preparation will still be there.

What is the approach for a hard-bitten-or-well-schooled witness? Again, hostility and tough stuff are usually not the answer. That will lead, in most cases, to the hours-long shouting matches that deposition critics rightly complain about. No information will emerge—on any level.

There are, however, other ways to undercut preparation. Again, recall what a prepared witness has gone through. After getting rules for testimony, she has been run through fake questions and answers. Probably, the facts she knows about have been reviewed in chronological order. What she has gotten is a highly structured set of do's and don'ts and a lot of memory work.

One thing to do is to surprise the witness—put her off balance. If it is feasible after a few preliminary questions, do *not* begin at the beginning. Start in the middle. Given the nature of predeposition preparation, the witness has probably begun to brace for particular questions in a particular order. Programmed to worry first about his early employment career, an unjust-discharge plaintiff may be thrown off stride if the first questions concern lost wages.

A word of caution. Do not disorder your questions if you cannot, or the case does not permit it. You must know what you are doing and be in complete command of your subject. Otherwise, the person off balance will be you. Besides, in some, maybe most, cases, your deposition strategy will depend on the patient accumulation of facts, from beginning to end.

Another unbalancing technique—which also requires skill—is to ask about *almost* the same topic at different times. The idea is not to cover the same ground twice. That would waste time and provoke legitimate objections. Instead, what you do is cover half a topic and then go on to something else. Later, come back to the second half. It might go like this:

Q: Mr. Jones, did you discuss the terms of the contract with Mr. Smith?
A: Yes.
Q: Face to face?
A: No, we talked on the phone.
Q: Did you review the contract documents before calling?
A: Yes.
Q: Which ones?
A: [A list is given.]
Q: Did you talk to your associates before calling?
A: Yes.
Q: Who and about what?
A: [Another list.]
Q: When did you call?
A: Noon on June 12.
Q: Where were you?
A: At home.
Q: How long did the call last?
A: About an hour, I guess.

—Then the shift—

Q: How long have you worked in marketing?

Twenty or thirty minutes later, the questioner will get back to the phone call.

The theory behind this is that some people can remember something well only once. The first time a topic comes up, the witness braces, ransacks his memory for the party line, gets it firmly in mind, and prepares to do battle. When you leave the topic without hitting the tough questions, the witness relaxes. He is relieved, and somewhat self-satisfied, figuring he has beaten you on the topic.

With many witnesses, an accompanying reaction is to throw preparation on the point covered in the trash can. When you return to the topic, the witness may be perplexed, and the fine edge he had the first time around may be gone.

There are other ways to pry at a witness you cannot charm. One is to seem—but only seem—like you are not paying attention. Look at him rarely. Look out the window. Act as if you do not understand or do not care about what he is saying. Such appearances—and they must be appearances only—can work wonders with egotistical witnesses. Though well prepared, such people want a stage and an attentive audience. If they are not getting it, they may try to attract attention by saying more, being cute, or acting professorial. When they do, their preparation cracks. Likely candidates for this are senior executives, Very Important People of all kinds, and those who fancy themselves superior to lawyers—experts especially.

Never underestimate the power of well-placed silence. It can interrogate better than any string of words:

Q: Did you see the accident?
A: Yes.

—a few seconds—

Q: Who was driving the red car?
A: I don't know.

—a few seconds—

Q: How far away were you?
A: About ten yards.

—a few seconds—

Q: And you didn't see the driver?
A: No.

—a longer pause; the questioner looks at the witness—

At least not very well.

Then the follow-up questions rain down.

This happens a lot. Silence makes many witnesses uncomfortable. At least when questions are being asked, they have something to think about. Silence gives witnesses no sounding board for the adequacy of their performance. Like a black hole, it sucks in nervous chatter. The beauty of this technique is that it will not show up on the transcript. Long or short, all pauses take up only a triple-spaced gap.

The value of silence can be generalized. Vary your pace. If you notice the witness is shortening the pause between question and answer that he has been coached to use, ask questions more quickly. His preparation is slipping a little, and the format should encourage the slippage. Conversely, if the witness seems bursting to tell his story, perhaps to disgorge well-practiced lines, slow down.

You might even consider standing up and walking around while you ask questions. Many lawyers act like they are required to stay glued in place while they ask deposition questions. It is true that some are; leaving the outline graven on their yellow legal pad would put them on the far side of the moon with no oxygen. Still, if you are able, consider taking a stroll. It will emphasize to the witness how confined he is—and that frustration may loosen his coaching.

In all of these things, use common sense and moderation. When I talk about silence, I do not mean a ten-minute staring match. Just pause a few beats longer than usual between questions. Walking around does not mean stalking the conference room as if you were delivering the summation in *Inherit the Wind;* merely stand up and stretch. A simple rule: If it is theatrical or obstructs the deposition, do not do it.

Witness on a Tightrope

A word on what might be called partial or concentrated preparation. In most depositions, there are three or four especially delicate spots for a witness. Testimony on these points must be gotten just right. The twin demands of truth and advocacy create a tightrope for the witness and his lawyer. What did you say at the merger negotiations? What did you mean by the phrase "we have full confidence in. . . ."? How much did you know about Fraudco's financial difficulties? In areas like these, the other side's lawyers have lavished special attention, drilling on question after question, trying to get the phrasing just right.

As you take a deposition, you can sometimes see this intensive preparation, written almost physically on the witness. An area comes up and demeanor changes. The answers come more slowly and the voice goes flat. Sometimes, the witness literally stiffens up. His lawyer starts taking notes furiously. Such signs will tell you where you must be persistent and creative to unlock the prepared script. These signs of concentrated preparation will also tell you what the other side is worried about. It is a special education when a witness goes tense in an area you thought was innocuous.

The previous paragraph refers to creative persistence in unlocking a prepared witness. The concept is worth explaining. Sometimes trying to get key information is like winning a certain kind of video game. You may have seen—or even played—such amusements: You control a tiny hero armed with sword and shield who wanders a forbidding landscape, vanquishing fearsome creatures and accumulating greater strength and colorful trinkets. At some point in the electronic quest, the little warrior comes to a dead end. You order him to try everything: sword, bombs, lasers, magic spells—but time and again you fail, and he dies. Finally, through ingenuity or dumb luck (or because your 11-year-old tips you off), you determine that a peculiar combination of actions is the answer: If your electronic alter ego stands on a magic mushroom, jumps, and throws a gold coin in the air, lights will flash, music will play, and a giant door will crash open, revealing the mysteries within.

Asking deposition questions can be like that. You ask time and again about a subject and get nothing. Then you put the same question in a slightly different way, and the treasure is revealed. This is another symptom of deposition preparation. Suppose a witness has received an absolutely devastating document. White hot. A gun pouring out smoke. It is a handwritten memorandum from the witness's boss to Mr. Jones, a coworker, with a "cc" to the witness at the bottom. It has the word "draft" on the top. It says, "I don't care what the engineers say—those extra supporting beams cost too much; we should think about taking them out." Revelation of this tidbit in a roof collapse case would—to put it mildly—not help much.

The witness's lawyer does not want the document revealed, but counseling out-and-out perjury is not his specialty. Instead, he advises the narrow view. He tells the witness to remember that the document was *not* a letter, *was* a draft, was *not* a direct communication with anyone, was *not* addressed to the deponent, was *not* a final decision, and so on. The questioning—with the witness's interior dialogue in brackets—goes like this:

Q: Did anyone tell you to change the roof design?
A: No. [Not face to face; anyhow, it was directed to Jones.]
Q: Did you ever see any letters or plans discussing a design change?
A: No. [It was a draft *memo*, after all.]

Q: Did you ever see any other documents that directed the design to be changed?

A: I don't know. [The thing was a draft; who knows what the boss really wanted to direct? He just said we should "think about" the issue.]

Q: Were you sent any documents on the subject?

A: No. [It was supposed to be sent to *Jones;* I found the thing with the *"cc"* on it later.]

Q: Do you know whether anyone wanted the design changed?

A: No. [Drafts are tentative; maybe the boss changed his mind.]

This kind of hairsplitting can go on forever. I absolutely do not commend it to anyone. Some of the responses listed drift beyond the land of careful preparation into the netherworld of sharp practice, and the wilds of misconduct are not far away.

Nonetheless, as a deposition interrogator, you must know how to deal with such witnesses, because you will meet them. The answer is to remember all the noun variations and synonyms you learned in your interrogatory drafting days. Reflect on the escape routes provided by ambiguities in certain words, such as "you," "sent," or "see." Then patiently vary the questions until you hit the right combination. In the example, if the question was, "Have you ever seen any draft documents mentioning beams in the roof?" then—absent out-and-out lying—lights would flash, whistles would wail, and the monster of preparation would be vanquished.

Strategies for dealing with close-to-the-line preparation should include techniques for handling witnesses who claim they never did anything and if they did, now remember nothing about it. Despite the honest efforts of their lawyers, some witnesses believe "I don't know" and claims of noninvolvement are answers to anything. They are not, of course, and sometimes they constitute perjury. But what is the approach with such a witness?

Not much works, but shame or implied ridicule can help. If the witness repeatedly denies responsibility for virtually anything in a company, ask her whether her job had any duties at all. Ask what duties she *did* have. Ask her whether she got performance evaluations and what they covered. If the answers are a string of "I don't knows" and "I don't remembers," ask whether the witness has memory defects. Ask why only the events connected to the lawsuit cause recollection problems. If none of this works, lock in the failed memory in as many ways and on as many details as possible. By getting a blank memory on everything, you can at least severely limit use of the witness at trial.

The notion of cracking preparation suggests another level of deposition play: witness evaluation. All the time you are listening to what the witness says, you should assess how he says it and the image he presents. Is he pompous or pleasant? Articulate or dull? Obnoxious or believable? You must try to come away from a deposition with not only what the witness knows but also who he is.

Some of the reasons for this may seem apparent but are worth stating. First, you want to get a sense of how the witness will play at trial. Will a jury or judge like this person and trust what he says? Equally important, consider whether the witness's personality makes sense in the larger context of the case. Can the meek accountant before you really have gotten into an abusive shouting match, as your client claims? Did the precise engineer being questioned really make the same subtraction error on three different occasions, as he contends? In short, does the witness, as a personality, fit the case?

Evaluating how the witness will react to trial questioning is also important. Here, care is important. You certainly do not want to run through your entire trial cross-examination (if you even know it) or engage in theatrical witness abuse. That way, the other side will learn more than you do.

The trick is to insinuate questioning variations. Pace changes have been mentioned. For a few minutes, see how the witness reacts to a fast stream of leading questions. Does she get caught in the current, as you want at trial, or (perhaps aided by incessant objections) does she keep the same measured pace? Consider also bringing a hard edge to the tone of your questions. This does not mean berating or bellowing at the witness, but, if your tone has been calm and folksy, put a bit more snap, a touch of sarcasm in three or four inquiries, and watch for the reaction. It may lead to nothing, but if you see that the witness gets peevish or is easily angered, you have learned something valuable.

Witness assessment, in fact many aspects of multilevel depositions, can be hampered by a practical problem. Every deposition questioner faces a hard task: He is being asked to do at least six things at once. He must ask questions, listen to answers, contend with objections, take notes for additional questions, keep track of documents, and remember whether he has covered everything he needs. Often this is complicated by an impending plane departure or the imminence of an afternoon hearing. Lost in the effort to keep many plates in the air without breakage is any opportunity for analysis or reflection. It sounds great to talk about evaluating the witness, but how do you have time to do it?

The answer is to bring in a second lawyer or a skilled paralegal or law clerk. Here again, my contrarian slip is showing. Many decry having more than one person at a deposition. Clients complain about overstaffing and courts sometimes refuse to award fees for an extra lawyer. The push to cut litigation costs may in this instance be shortsighted—at least for important depositions. A second set of eyes and ears needs to be there to watch reactions and demeanor. While one lawyer asks questions and evaluates answers, someone else needs to watch the match on other levels.

A final level of play is evaluation of the other side's lawyers. In many cases, this will be your first face-to-face meeting, and assessment begins immediately. Things like what issues are important to the other lawyer and his relationship with his client have been mentioned. You also soon learn whether the lawyer will conduct the suit in a professional, correct way or will maintain the enforced abrasiveness that some believe is necessary to justify a fee or retain a client.

There are other evaluative points. As with witnesses, a little gentle needling can be informative. You can also get a notion of how adroit and bright the lawyer is when she objects. Ask politely for an explanation of one or two objections. The reaction may be a refusal or only bluster; it may, however, be a careful description of the basis for the interjection. In exchanges like that, you can determine whether the lawyer knows what she is doing.

Something always interesting is who exactly the other side sends to the deposition. An experienced, adept litigator? A silver-haired senior partner who soothes the witness but has lost a step in the byplay of banter and interrogation? Or the law firm's fifth chair on the case—an associate a year out of law school? Each selection can tell you something about the opposition's view of the case and the witness.

Conducting a deposition on many levels is not easy and can be overdone. It is worth saying again: Your first goal is getting answers to appropriate inquiries. Do not let the game-playing potential of depositions—valuable though it is—dominate proceedings. This means making your questions clear and insisting on direct answers. It means remembering that the transcript can be used at trial or in motions. And it means knowing your case and what you need to discover.

If you go beyond this, and get information on other levels, care is still needed. Everything suggested here must be woven seamlessly into questions. No grandstanding. There is great freedom in the deposition process, but theatrics and extended quirkiness are not ways to use it. If the deposition is being videotaped, your tactics will be even more confined.

Part of the reason for observing such limits is that multilevel play can be conducted by both sides. The lawyer across the table is watching you. In fact, he has more time and freedom to observe you than you do to watch him. If you overplay your hand, get intense on the important points, become visibly frustrated when things do not go as you hoped, you will give to the other side what you want from them.

There are two antidotes. One is to be deadpan throughout. Become a mirror image of what the witness has been coached to be. This tactic will limit your ability to do some of the things described, but there is a second option: indirection. Seem indifferent when you are interested and intense when the topic is dull. Do not do it all the time, but throw in enough change-ups so the other side cannot get a line on what you are up to.

Do not get the impression that every deposition—or even most of them—can support an elaborate superstructure of game playing. If this article has created the impression that conducting a deposition is like running a triple agent in post-war Poland, I have overdone it. The truth is that many depositions are flat and uncomplicated. Everybody knows what is going on, and all the levels of play are mashed into one. Furthermore, playing the game may yield nothing. Still, the possibilities are usually there. You may not always play on many levels, but you must remember that you can.

This leads me to anticipate a criticism. Some readers may believe that, in its advocacy of "games," this article underscores what is wrong with litigation. Discovery, they would say, ought to be simple and straightforward; tricks and tactics are why lawsuits take so long, cost so much, and get nowhere.

On a couple of levels, I agree, but on a third—the level where we all live and work—I do not. First, as I have said, tactics can overwhelm legitimate discovery. They can be obnoxious, obstructive, and just plain wrong. In fact—and this is the second level— I agree it would be a better world if everyone came clean, witnesses did not quibble, and lawyers needed only to ask direct questions because they got only direct answers.

Unfortunately—now we are at the third level—we do not live in that better world. As often as not, the other side will coach its witnesses. Faced with that, a deposition lawyer has a choice. He can shun games, just ask questions, and go home with a bag full of "yes," "no," and "I don't know," secure in the belief that he has served a higher goal. Or, observing propriety and balance, he can represent his client effectively, engage in some gamesmanship, and maybe get some real information. I myself choose the second course, realizing it is not ideal, but without apology.

Finally, something about trial. Never lose sight of the fact that what you do in a deposition is subservient to your trial goals. You do not develop information, on any level, just as a curiosity. It all must be fit into a trial plan. That connection highlights an interesting contrast. Depositions and trials require related, but actually quite distinct, skills: In depositions, a lawyer must deal with the unknown and use his freedom creatively, keeping many lines of inquiry going and caring only a little for appearances. In trial, a lawyer must wring persuasive, emotional force from thoroughly discovered facts while confined by rigid rules and formalisms and always worrying about appearance. Unfortunately, some lawyers do not understand the difference. Many of the problems of litigation stem from depositions being conducted like trials and trials being conducted by those who have only done depositions.

CHAPTER 11

Depositions Under the New Federal Rules

Gerson A. Zweifach*

Given our almost congenital aversion to change of any kind, many litigators treated the 1993 amendments to the Federal Rules of Civil Procedure like a mad relative living in the basement. And, with all of the opting out and opting in by the local federal districts, we've been given all the opportunity we need to engage in some serious denial. Are these new rules really part of our life? If no one reads them, do they really exist? Since Congress was involved, can they really be the law? Wait a minute—is it 1999 already?

I can report the following. Unlike the controversial mandatory disclosure rules, the 1993 amendments to the Rules governing depositions are the law in most federal courts. But perhaps more surprising, these amendments make sense. In fact, we can crack open the basement door, and make these rules our friends.

1. **No more phony depositions of experts.** Expert witness discovery in the federal courts used to go something like this.

---

*Gerson A. Zweifach is with the firm of Williams & Connolly, LLP in Washington, D.C. This article originally appeared in the Winter 1997 issue of LITIGATION.

JANUARY: The plaintiff serves the defendant with an interrogatory asking the identity of the expert and the substance of the expert's opinion.

MARCH: After several rounds of ridiculous objections, the defendant finally responds by saying, "Expert? What expert? We haven't selected one yet."

SEPTEMBER: On the last day of discovery, the defendant says, "Look, I want to be fair, let me tell ya', I have a guy you'll want to depose, but he's not ready, so let's pick a date when he'll be ready." They pick a date a few weeks before trial.

OCTOBER: A subpoena duces tecum reveals that the expert was engaged as a consultant in February, but the only documents he has prepared are a series of bills. The supplemental interrogatory answer arrives. It reveals: (a) the expert's name; (b) that the expert may opine on "all subjects, including but not limited to, all subjects"; and (c) that the expert relied on (come on, you know what's coming) "everything he has learned and read in the course of his time on earth."

NOVEMBER: The deposition that follows is, of course, another charade. The examining lawyer spends his entire time pressing the expert to state his opinions, and the expert does everything he can to keep the specifics of his views under wraps for trial. The expert parries, "Opinions in what area?" Or, if the area is identified, offers, "I'm studying that issue and may have more views later." Or, he just mumbles—"expertly," of course. The examining lawyer operates under his own artificial constraints. Do too good a cross-examination, and the expert will refine his analysis after the deposition, or worse, limit his opinions to some areas rather than others. Every line of examination is cut off as soon as it begins to go anywhere.

The entire process was so cynical as to give all of us good reason to pick up a lottery ticket and hope for a quick way out of this line of work. Let us now welcome amended Rule 26, which changes the rules and the incentives in two important ways.

First, Rule 26(a)(2)(B) imposes an affirmative disclosure obligation—the expert must prepare a report that lays out the substance and bases of his opinions. And, in many districts, that report is due well before the close of discovery. If the Rule is enforced, the expert cannot hide his opinions, delay their formation, or release a few rabbits at his deposition for counsel to chase. If the expert tenders an off-the-wall opinion in his report, it will be there forever, regardless of how he scales back his trial testimony.

Second, Rule 26(b)(4) provides that the expert may be deposed after his report is issued. This means that his deposition may actually include a serious testing of his opinions. Since examining counsel does not have to spend her entire day identifying the opinions, she can actually subject them to analysis. And, since the report locks in the expert to a set of views, the examining lawyer does not have to fear that if she drives the expert off his weaker opinions, she'll lose the chance to impeach the expert.

The disclosure schedule also makes it much more difficult for a party to replace an expert who gets filleted at a deposition, although it still makes sense in some circumstances for examining counsel to hold off using every available bullet. Of course, counsel may still fear driving the weaker expert off the stand entirely, but I've had judges allow me to introduce as admissions selected excerpts from the deposition of an expert who was never brought to trial by the sponsoring party.

Do lawyers still play games under the new system? Do kids like ice cream? Of course, but it's much harder. It's abundantly clear from the Rules that the expert reports are supposed to resemble a detailed outline of the expert's direct examination. See Advisory Committee Notes, Rule 26(a)(2)(B) (the "detailed" report should "state the testimony of the expert"). All of us should insist on nothing less.

2. **No more coaching of witnesses on the record.** We've all been there. You've spent weeks studying the documents and understanding the transaction at issue; days planning your examination and setting the strategy for locking in the witness and then destroying him; and hours painstakingly executing your plan. You then move in for the kill, and ask the witness the key question.

Q: And so, following your usual practice, you read the private placement agreement before you signed it?

But before the witness can answer and you can reap the fruit of your hard work, your adversary weighs in. First, there is the "country lawyer" approach.

MR. GENTEEL: Counselor, counselor, excuse me, but can you wait just a minute? Perhaps I am confused, because when you get to my age, it happens. If you are referring to his practice in reviewing business contracts in his own line of work, where he knows what the contracts mean and what to look for, well then, I don't know how that practice could be relevant to the course he followed in this case, with an investment agreement that he could not possibly understand even if he tried to read it. But maybe you are referring to something else. I apologize most profusely, maybe it's my fault. Did I follow your question?

Q: Actually, you answered it.

THE WITNESS: And so well.

And of course, there is the "big city" approach.

MR. HARDBALL: Objection—this is just outrageous. What are we doing here, playing games? You know our position, we explained in the complaint that he did not read the document, now you are accusing this man of perjury. I thought your firm was above this kind of thing. Are you asking him whether he's changing his position? Can you at least clarify where we are?

THE WITNESS: I know one thing—I'm not changing what I said before.

Q: Why doesn't that surprise me?

We all have a right to be furious about this kind of gamesmanship. A deposition even under the unamended rules was supposed to be conducted in a manner that resembled an in-court examination. For those of us who bothered to raise a fuss and found a judge with the time and inclination to do something about coaching of witnesses, the court would occasionally take some action. *See Hall v. Clifton Precision*, 150 F.R.D. 525 (E.D. Pa. 1993) (establishing guidelines for objections made during depositions). But this went on all the time, and more needed to be done.

Speaking Objections

Meet amended Rule 30(d)(1), which expressly forbids what has been euphemistically called speaking objections. The Rule provides that objections must be stated "concisely, and in a non-argumentative and non-suggestive manner." It gives all of us a running start in dealing with adversaries and the federal court in ensuring that depositions provide us with a fair opportunity to conduct a meaningful cross-examination. At the end of the day, that not only makes law practice more fun, it makes the discovery process more productive for the people who pay our bills.

3. **(Almost) No more instructions not to answer.** To be sure, long-winded colloquies between counsel provided ample opportunity to coach the witness and get into a shouting match with your adversary, but the full arsenal of devices to block an effective examination was not complete without the instruction not to answer. Here, lawyers who felt it was too much work to make a speaking objection could step into a phone booth, emerge with robes on, and play judge. Like many diseases, this one took several forms.

   DIRECT: "No way—move on counselor. That may work in [your city], but it doesn't fly here."

   THE TWO-PART SERIES: "Would you mind telling me the relevance of that? [Of course, no answer is wanted and none would ever be satisfactory.] If you can't tell me the relevance of that, then obviously this is nothing but an effort to harass my client, and so I'm instructing the witness not to answer."

   BLAME THE CLIENT: "I'd advise the witness not to answer. On the other hand, he's free to accept or reject my advice."

   THE ECUMENICAL APPROACH: Here, all three forms are combined in a long, often sleep-inducing discourse.

This foolishness went on too long, and, over time, several federal districts adopted local rules limiting the instruction not to answer. See, e.g, Standing Rules of the United States District Court for the Eastern District of New York (1994). But there was no national rule, and no absolute restriction, even by courts that

151

frowned on the practice of instructing witnesses not to answer. *See, e.g., Eggleston v. Chicago Journeymen Plumbers*, 657 F.2d 890, 903 (7th Cir. 1981). Now there is.

Amended Rule 30(d)(1) limits instructions not to answer to three circumstances: privilege; to enforce a limitation on evidence already ordered by the court; and, to present a motion to terminate under Rule 30(d)(3). Of course, litigators will test the elasticity of these categories: someone will argue that privilege means the privilege not to lose a case; or, that a limit ordered by the court means a limit that someone thought the judge intended but just didn't get around to writing down yet. The right to seek a motion to terminate will, of course, be played for all it is worth, but the amended rule is clear that the card can only be played once—you cannot "instruct" and continue the deposition.

If you instruct, it's only to shut down the deposition, and explain your instruction to the court. That, coupled with the threat of an award of expenses under Rules 30(d)(4) and 37(a)(4), should deter the abuse of this exception.

Signing and Filing

4. **No more holding the transcript hostage.** The Old Days: As the deposition finally started to wind down, you would check your watch, try to remember what time zone you were in, search for that message slip about the flight schedule, and wonder where you left your garment bag. Maybe you'd listen to the reporter's remarks about signature, but most likely you were grateful no longer to be hearing from your adversary, and you were out the door. A few weeks later, you were back in your office, reading the transcript, and frankly admiring your handiwork in fighting through all the roadblocks that had been thrown in the way of your examination. And then, some detail-oriented colleague stops by to puncture your balloon—when is the transcript getting signed; what arrangements were made; how much time did you agree that the witness had; how are we going to make this transcript usable in court if we don't have the signed original to tender to the clerk? You look at the end of the transcript, and it contains nothing more than your adver-

sary's statement, "we'll read it and get back to you." As for your response, the transcript merely reflects, "(counsel left)."

This was a system too susceptible to abuse, or at least to enormous inefficiency as we spent time writing to deponents, calling their lawyers, and finally pleading with clerks to accept unsigned deposition transcripts. Amended Rule 30, however, comes to the rescue. Amended Rule 30's subparts (e) and (f) do not require that a deposition be signed to be deemed ready for filing with the court. Instead, Rule 30(e), (f) provide that the certification of the reporter is sufficient to permit the original to be filed by the reporter or by the lawyer who took the deposition. As for the witness, it is his burden to ask for the opportunity to read the transcript and note any changes. Even if he does so, he has only 30 days after being notified that the transcript is available for review.

What does this mean for you as you are getting ready to run for your cab? It essentially means that you will be fine as long as you remember to mumble, "the Federal Rules govern reading," or at minimum, as long as you avoid stipulating to some other procedure. Rule 29 was amended to allow parties to stipulate to just about anything regarding discovery procedures (certainly to extend the time frame for reading a deposition). Counsel or even reporters often mention the "usual stipulations" at the outset of a deposition, and they may mean anything, including that the witness has unlimited time to review the transcript. The "usual stipulations," like "regular coffee," have a different flavor in every city in the United States. Don't buy it. At the outset of the deposition, make a point of expressly disavowing any stipulations, and state that the "Federal Rules" govern everything, including review and filing of the transcript. (I'm quite serious about disavowing the stipulations; I've had reporters in New York insert a half dozen of the "usual stipulations" even when nobody mentioned stipulations at all.) This requires you to be alert at the outset of your deposition, but that's a good deal easier than remembering about a signature when you are running for your cab.

5. Let's go to the videotape! The amended rules have enhanced the value of deposition discovery not only through addition by subtraction—reducing the colloquy between counsel about objections and the like—but also by adding to the tools available to the examining lawyer. Under the 1992 Rules, videotaped depositions required consent of the party to be examined, or leave of court. Failure to respect these limitations resulted in a Rule 11 award against CBS in the Westmoreland case, when CBS moved for contempt against former CIA director Helms when he objected to having his deposition taken by videotape without notice and consent. The D.C. Circuit decided not only that Mr. Helms was right, but that CBS's effort to hold him in contempt for insisting upon his procedural rights merited Rule 11 sanctions. *See Westmoreland v. CBS,* 770 F.2d 1168 (D.C. Or. 1985).

Amended Rule 30(b)(2) provides that any deposition may be taken by videotape, subject only to notice to all counsel. The examined party can object and obtain a court order barring the use of videotape for good cause, but absent a court order, the video camera can roll.

When should you use video? Most lawyers seem to reserve its use for de bene esse examinations—to preserve testimony of witnesses unlikely to be available at trial. Some recent trial experiences tell me that this is a mistake.

Video can play an important and useful role even in depositions of witnesses who will testify live. I recently deposed a witness in a securities case (let's call her Jones), in which one of the issues was whether Jones was misled by the issuer, as opposed to being simply out of touch with facts made known to her in her position as counsel to the underwriter. When I examined Jones, I knew that she would be called by the plaintiffs at trial, and thus didn't bother to notice the examination by video. Within five minutes, the waves of regret washed over me.

I would ask a question, Jones would stare at the ceiling, look out the window, gnash her teeth, ask for a read back, think some more, and then, after a good three minutes, mumble something that was only about 25 percent responsive. If ever there was a witness whose manner of answering questions was itself important evidence for the jury to see, it was Jones in her deposition. *See NLRB v. Walton Mfg, Co.,* 369 U.S. 404, 408 (1962) ("The demeanor of a witness . . . may satisfy the tribunal not only that the witness's testimony is not true but that the truth is the opposite of his story; for the denial of one, who has a motive to deny, may be uttered with such hesitation, discomfort, arrogance or defiance, as to give assurance that he is fabricating, and that, if he is, there is no alternative but to assume the truth of what he denies.")

Frustrated Actors

Of course, the written transcript reflected none of the pauses, or head-rolling (it did reflect my periodic expressions of frustration, however, and announcements of how long the witness had taken answering the question, none of which I would read to the jury because they sounded mean-spirited). I have no doubt that, before trial, Jones will spend weeks at some witness academy, from which she will emerge glib, composed, and sounding far more competent than she was at her deposition.

What good would video have done? First, Jones probably would have tried harder to answer questions in less than three minutes each, knowing the cameras were rolling. Maybe she would have succeeded. More likely, she would have been less careful, while at the same time fumbling and mumbling. Second, at the trial—where Jones is a party—I would have played excerpts from her deposition in my case, as is my right under Rule 30 ("deposition of a party can be used for any purpose").

Video depositions are also useful in controlling the obstreperous witness or adversary (or both, as they often find each other). While many trial lawyers are frustrated actors, it seems that they long for the stage, not the small screen. There is something about the little red light on top of the video camera that seems to inhibit the most unruly adversaries from carrying on with their full act. Maybe it's the fact that you can play the tape to the judge, or even better, include a few highlights for the jury. While video is expensive, it's less expensive than spending half the deposition trying to control someone who is out of control, or running to court to try to find a magistrate judge willing to listen to you read some lawyer's objections. With a true nutcase, try turning on the camera.

Video is the best tool for preserving all aspects of a deponent's testimony. But do you want to preserve more than the words? A few years ago, three ex-employees of the defendant corporation were critical witnesses for our client, the plaintiff corporation.

We had picked up the case for trial after discovery was closed, and as trial approached, I second-guessed my predecessor for not having videotaped the ex-employees' deposition. The testimony itself was lovely, and to present it, I asked the questions, and recruited some lawyers from my local counsel's firm to play the witnesses and read the answers. I felt like the producer of a Hollywood film, particularly when I found three grey haired, silver tongued, completely credible senior-partner types—like Robert Young in *Father Knows Best*—for the plaintiff. By the time they were done, the trial judge warned defendant's counsel that he was looking at a "serious hit" in this case. And the judge proved right. But while the jury was deliberating, my adversary and I reviewed the trial over a beverage, and I learned just how fortuitous it was that my predecessor had not videotaped the depositions of the three ex-employees. They were unattractive witnesses, with 5 o'clock shadows, heavy New Jersey accents, and an inability to look anyone in the eye—in other words, they looked and sounded like they had been sent over by central casting to play "Disgruntled Ex-Employees." Instead, I got Robert Young.

Finally, don't forget that no matter how well you do with your video deposition, a resourceful witness can still find a way to undo your good work. A while ago, an enormously successful foreign film star sued a publisher in federal court. We videotaped the plaintiff's deposition. Between the odd lighting at the deposition and the actor's need for a haircut, he wasn't looking his best (still several cuts above the rest of the witnesses, but not his best).

At trial, I had planned to start his cross-examination by contrasting his videotaped testimony, in which he swore that he only gave interviews to magazines interested in "cinema" and which focused on his films, with a series of trial exhibits representing over a dozen interviews he had given to a wide range of publications, in which he spoke about a variety of what seemed to be personal subjects. I played the clips on our 51-inch TV screen in the courtroom, and then forced the movie star to authenticate the tall pile of exhibits. Before I could move on to another subject, the movie star volunteered, "I think you caught me on a bad hair day." Sure, it was a ridiculous explanation for the tension between his testimony and the exhibits, but the jury loved it—imagine a man worth millions admitting to a bad hair day; what a sport!

We mad more progress with the star later in the afternoon. One thing, however, was made clear. Video is a powerful tool. It can be turned against you by certain witnesses in a way that the cold transcript cannot. You can master a transcript in a way that you will never master the nuances of a videotape. The amended rules give you a chance to use modern technology. That doesn't mean you should.

CHAPTER 12

Taking Depositions That Stick

Steven C. Day*

Depositions serve a variety of ends. But above all else, trial lawyers take depositions to avoid the phantom that haunts them, keeps them awake at night, turns their blood cold, and makes them old before their time—surprise. A major surprise dropped into the middle of a trial can wipe out months of careful planning in one quick blow, suck the life out of a case, and leave the trial lawyer desperately gasping for a response. The result is often disaster, a lonely death before the court.

The key to preventing this type of damaging and embarrassing surprise is the skillful use of the deposition process. The deposition needs to pin down the witness. To accomplish this, however, a "discovery deposition" must do more than just give you a preview of the witness's testimony. The trial lawyer must make certain that the testimony discovered at the deposition is the only testimony he will face at trial. As we will see, there are several techniques that work well to minimize, and hopefully eliminate, surprises at a trial. But first, we should look at an all too common, wrong approach.

*Steven C. Day is with Woodard, Hernandez, Roth & Day, LLC, in Wichita, Kansas. This article originally appeared in the Winter 1998 issue of LITIGATION.

Beware: Stream of Consciousness

The stream-of-consciousness conversation can be great fun. You start off discussing fine red wines and end up talking about demolition derbies. The funny thing is, you cannot remember anyone ever changing the subject; this is how stream of consciousness works. You just drift with the tide, going wherever it takes you. Yet, while it makes for enjoyable conversation, it makes for awful depositions.

An example: Wilma Whipple has seen the cruelty of fate first-hand. Just a few short years ago, she was the happy proprietor of Whipple's Whoopees, a prosperous West Coast whoopee cushion distributorship. But that was before the Whoopee Cushion Consortium entered the novelty market. With the creation of the Consortium, everything changed. Suddenly all of Ms. Whipple's customers jumped ship, and her suppliers refused to deliver. Within three months, she was bankrupt.

If the men of the Consortium expected Ms. Whipple to pass silently into the night, however, they were in for a shock. She hired a lawyer (she knew he was a good one because he had the biggest ad in the Yellow Pages). Ms. Whipple's lawyer filed suit, alleging a conspiracy in restraint of trade in violation of the Sherman Antitrust Act. One of the defendants, Melvin Touch, is being deposed:

Q: Mr. Touch, were you present at the April 12 meeting of the Consortium?

A: Yes, I was.

Q: Who else was present?

A: Let's see, Don Bottoms, Ralph Butts, Bill Rumply, although we all call Bill "Mr. Whoopee," and . . .

Q: Really; and, why do you call Mr. Rumply that?

A: Because he's a legend in our industry—he's the one who got it all started. Before Bill, whoopee cushions were just a two-bit novelty item. He is personally responsible for creating today's multi-billion-dollar whoopee cushion industry.

Q: And how did he do that?

A: Merchandising—that man knows how to sell. For example, there was that business with Bob Dole.

Q: What was that?

A: Oh you remember, it was during the 1996 presidential election. Bill sneaked a whoopee cushion onto Dole's seat. It shocked Dole so badly he fell off the podium. Man, sales doubled.

Q: Let's get back to the April 12 meeting. What did Mr. Rumply, or "Mr. Whoopee" if you prefer, have to say during the meeting?

A: Oh, Bill's not much of a talker. Now Don Bottoms, there's a talker. You know he talked all the way through his daughter's wedding. Even during the vows, he just stood there talking to a guy in the third row.

Q: I bet that made his daughter mad?

A: Naaah, she was too drunk to notice . . .

Q: Anyway, Mr. Touch . . .

A: . . . but then, who wouldn't get drunk if they had to marry that loser half-brother Tom.

Q: She married her half-brother?

A: No, my half-brother, Tom.

Q: Oh, I'm sorry, I misunderstood.

A: What, you thought she was marrying her own half-brother? My God, man, what part of the country do you come from?

Q: Mr. Touch, if it would be possible, I would like to move this along. So please, just answer my questions.

A: Whatever you say, counselor, that's what I'm here for.

What has the deposition accomplished so far? We have learned a number of interesting things. A few of them may even be relevant. But, has the witness been pinned down as to anything? Plainly not. Mr. Touch has not even been pinned down as to who attended the fateful meeting at the heart of Ms. Whipple's case, let alone what anyone had to say. This means he will be free at trial to surprise Ms. Whipple's lawyer on any of these points.

Even if the questioning eventually covers the whole meeting, the hit-and-miss style of the deposition will make it practically useless if needed for impeachment. Assume, for instance, that Mr. Touch drops a bombshell and testifies for the first time at trial that the legendary Mr. Whoopee (since deceased in a tragic whoopee cushion–related incident) called Wilma Whipple during the April 12 meeting to invite her to join the Consortium, but that she refused. How will Ms. Whipple's lawyer use the deposition to impeach this story?

It would seem at first glance that impeachment should be easy. After all, Mr. Touch said nothing during the deposition about this supposed telephone call. The problem, of course, is that if confronted, Mr. Touch simply will respond: "But my lawyer told me just to answer your specific questions and not to volunteer things." What makes this response particularly annoying is the fact that it is almost certainly true—which will make it more than a little hard to challenge (presumably, Ms. Whipple's lawyer told her the exact same thing before her deposition). Thus, Mr. Touch's failure to volunteer the relevant information during the deposition is not a solid basis for impeachment.

Sadly, there is probably no way to effectively use the deposition transcript to impeach Mr. Touch. Nothing in the transcript is inconsistent with the trial testimony. The new testimony may well be a lie, but it is not an inconsistent lie. Perhaps they will find some other way to nail Mr. Touch, but the deposition is not going to do it.

This is the problem with a stream-of-consciousness deposition. While it may at times work reasonably well as a pure discovery device, it does nothing to pin down a witness. Since such depositions tend to wander aimlessly from subject to subject, no one subject is ever clearly closed. The witness is free to add to the testimony. This leaves trial counsel at constant risk of damaging surprise.

As we will now see, there is a better way.

Using "Bookends"

It is the third week of a five-week medical malpractice trial. Your client, Dr. White, is a renowned local obstetrician. He is accused of injuring a baby during delivery by applying too much force with obstetrical forceps. The baby's father is about to testify. After cross-examining four expert witnesses in three days, this will be a welcome break. "Thank God," you think to yourself, "I can finally take it easy." Although the father, Mr. Flexible, had been present during the delivery, he had remembered nothing of significance at the time of his deposition. He is presumably going to testify solely about damages at trial. Obviously Mr. Flexible's testimony about the child's injuries will not help your case, but, again, there is nothing to do about it. Just sit and take it (and perhaps relax for a little while).

Q: (Plaintiff's counsel) Mr. Flexible, did you see what Dr. White did with the forceps?

A: Yes, he pulled on them as hard as he could; his muscles were bulging and sweat was pouring down his face. I couldn't believe my eyes!

And on and on the testimony goes. Many emotions spring forth within you; shock turns to panic, panic turns to amazement, and finally everything turns to anger—pure overpowering rage. This guy is lying, and, by God, you will make him pay! You shuffle through your witness file and grab Mr. Flexible's deposition. "I am going to make him eat this," you think to yourself as you begin your cross-examination.

Q: Now then, Mr. Flexible, based upon your testimony on direct examination, I gather you felt that Dr. White's use of the forceps was very violent and improper, is that true?

A: Yes, it is.

Q: All right then, sir, the fact is that when I took your deposition you didn't say anything like that, did you?!

A: I don't remember everything I said during the deposition. I answered your questions to the best of my ability.

Q: Well now, sir, you didn't say anything about violent or improper use of forceps during your deposition, did you?!

(Plaintiff's Counsel) Objection, asked and answered.

(Court) Well, yes, it has been asked and answered, but I will give you some leeway.

Q: Thank you, your honor. (To witness) Well, can you answer the question?

A: Like I said before, I answered your questions the best I could. Did you even ask me about that?

Q: I most certainly did.

(Plaintiff's Counsel) I object, your honor. If counsel has something specific from the deposition he should identify it page and line.

(Court) Sustained. Stop arguing with the witness. If you have something from the deposition, let's hear it, otherwise move on.

There follows a laborious reading of 19 pages of deposition transcript, involving numerous questions and answers concerning various time frames.

Eight of the jurors are staring blankly into space; two are sleeping; one is looking in her purse for chewing gum; while another is working on his income tax return. Both alternate jurors have disappeared, never to be seen again.

Not exactly the smashing cross-examination you had in mind.

A far-fetched example? Not really. It is, in fact, remarkable how frequently a witness professes at the deposition to have little or no memory, only to later show up at trial claiming to be a virtual encyclopedia of relevant information. This is no doubt a product of human nature. After all, when the initial depositions are taken in a case, the parties (and other interested witnesses) often do not know precisely which factual issues ultimately will prove crucial to the lawsuit.

In our example Mr. Flexible certainly would have known at the time of his deposition that the case generally involved the birth of his child, but he may not have known that the manipulation of the forceps would become the key element of the case. It is not terribly surprising, therefore, that he did not stretch during the deposition to claim a specific memory on that point. By the time trial rolled around, however, Mr. Flexible had a much more specific idea of what testimony would be helpful to his cause. Human nature came into play—suddenly he remembered a great many more details.

This type of dramatic "memory restoration" presents a unique challenge to the lawyer cross-examining the witness. It is always difficult to effectively use a deposition to impeach a witness's description of an event which occurred over time. Depending upon the specific questions asked during the deposition, it is entirely possible that the trial testimony does not directly contradict any one statement made in the deposition. The inconsistency lies, instead, in the overall description of the event. Unfortunately, this overall description is woven through many pages of the transcript, making impossible a short, succinct impeachment.

Yet a short, succinct impeachment is by far the most effective. A long drawn-out impeachment loses its zap—-that "slam-bam, I've got you" quality—and it may even be completely missed by the jury. Recognizing this danger, the cross-examiner is often tempted to immediately confront the witness with the inconsistency by asking: "You didn't say that during your deposition, did you?" Unfortunately, this generally produces one of three answers: (1) "I think I *did* tell you that"; (2) "I don't think you ever asked me about that"; or (3) "I don't remember specifically what I said about that in the deposition."

Now you have a problem. You are in the position of having to prove a negative. To establish that the testimony in question appears nowhere in the transcript, it will be theoretically necessary to read the whole deposition. At a minimum, you will have to read many pages of testimony. So much for your slam-bam impeachment. In fact, since it is probably impractical to read lengthy excerpts from the deposition during cross-examination, you may have to let the witness completely off the hook.

So, how do you avoid this trap? The answer does not lie primarily in your cross-examination technique; by then, it may be too late. The time to protect your client against a witness like Mr. Flexible is during the deposition. You do this, of course, by asking deposition questions in such a way that if the witness later changes or adds to his description of a key event, he will be set up for impeachment. This is where "bookends" come into play.

Bookends are barriers established at the beginning and end of a witness's description of a particularly important part of an event. They carve out the critical area of testimony and separate it from the rest of the deposition. If the witness later tries to change this testimony at trial, the bookends will make the process of impeachment easier and more effective.

The first step is to identify the most important parts of the witness's testimony. Where could the witness hurt you the worst at trial? In our example, the answer is self-evident. While Mr. Flexible has relevant knowledge on many points, his most dangerous testimony will involve what he observed during the forceps delivery. This is the place for bookends.

The first bookend is a brief description of what you intend to cover in the next section of the deposition (and a comment about its importance):

Q: Mr. Flexible, we are now going to discuss what you observed during the actual delivery of your son. Do you understand where we are going?

A: Yes.

Q: You understand what I am looking for is a complete description of everything you saw and heard during the delivery process?

A: I understand.

Q: You recognize that what happened during the delivery is at the very heart of this case?

A: Yes, I do.

Q: And it is very important that I find out everything you observed at that time so I will not be surprised by something new when you testify at trial; does that sound fair?

A: Yes, it does.

Q: So, please try to be as complete as possible in your answers, all right?

A: I will do my best.

The first bookend has now been established. You are ready to explore the witness's version of the facts. One good way to do this is to begin with a general, all-encompassing question followed by a series of more specific inquiries.

Q: Please tell us everything you can remember seeing and hearing during the delivery process.

A: Really, I don't remember much at all. You have to understand I was doing Lamaze with my wife and I was kind of nervous and I really don't think I saw very much.

Q: Did you see Dr. White put the forceps in place?

A: No, I don't remember that.

Q: Did you see how Dr. White used the forceps once they were on?

A: No, I don't think I saw that either.

Q: Do you remember hearing anything Dr. White or the nurses said?

A: Well, I am sure they said things, but nothing I can remember.

Q: You said you were nervous?

A: Yes.

Q: Was this the first time you had ever seen a baby being delivered?

A: Right.

Q: Did Dr. White or any of the nurses do or say anything that made you think they were nervous or thought there was a problem?

A: No, nothing like that.

You are now ready for the second bookend. The second book-end, like the first, is a barrier to box in the witness.

Q: Mr. Flexible, have you now told us everything that you can remember seeing or hearing during the delivery of your son?

A: Yes, to the best of my ability.

It may not always come this easily. Sometimes the witness will try to hedge by saying: "Well, that is all I can remember right now, but I might remember more later." When this occurs, some follow-up is appropriate.

Q: Well, as we talked about, this is very important to my client, so take all the time you need to fully answer the question.

A: I have told you everything I can remember. All I'm saying is that it's possible that I could remember something else later.

Q: So, having thought about it for as long as you want, have you told us everything you can remember about the delivery?

A: Everything I can remember right now, yes.

Q: Mr. Flexible, after this deposition is typed up by the court reporter, she will send you a copy along with a correction sheet. You will then have 30 days to review it and to make any corrections. When you come to this part of the transcript, if you have remembered anything else about the delivery of your son which you have not told us about, will you please note that new information on the correction sheet?

A: Yes, I will.

It could be argued that the witness won this exchange, since he was never forced to completely give up his "I may remember something more later" escape valve. But, as a practical matter, he will not be credible to the jury if he tries to substantially change his testimony at trial. In fact, the evasive nature of the deposition testimony will likely only increase the jury's distrust.

Therefore, under either scenario—cooperative deponent or evasive deponent—bookends work. Mr. Flexible's description of the key event in the lawsuit is now firmly sandwiched between two bookends, leaving him with no room to maneuver. If he tries to expand this testimony at trial, he is set up for effective impeachment. More importantly, because the bookends clearly delineate the relevant time frame, the impeachment will be quick and to the point. You are ready to pounce when Mr. Flexible testifies at the trial.

> *Q:* Mr. Flexible, I gather from your testimony that you felt Dr. White's use of the forceps was very violent and improper, am I right?
>
> *A:* Yes, you are.
>
> *Q:* It upset you?
>
> *A:* Yes.
>
> *Q:* It frightened you?
>
> *A:* Of course it did. I was afraid he was going to kill my baby.
>
> *Q:* So it made a big impact on you?
>
> *A:* Of course.
>
> *Q:* Mr. Flexible, do you remember giving a deposition in this case on February 11 of last year?
>
> *A:* I remember.
>
> *Q:* The deposition was taken at your lawyer's office, right?
>
> *A:* Yes.
>
> *Q:* And your lawyer was present?
>
> *A:* Yes.
>
> *Q:* Do you remember that I asked you some questions at that time about what you saw during your son's birth?
>
> *A:* No, I don't remember the specific questions.
>
> *Q:* You do remember that you were placed under oath at the deposition?
>
> *A:* Yes.
>
> *Q:* The same oath you took today?
>
> *A:* Yes.
>
> *Q:* You swore to tell the truth?
>
> *A:* Yes.
>
> *Q:* And you did tell the truth, correct?

A: Yes, I did.

Q: All right, Mr. Flexible, please turn to page 43, line 7 of your deposition. . . .

At this point, you present the deposition testimony to the jury. There are two ways to do this. One technique is to read the deposition questions yourself, but to require the witness to read the answers. This has the advantage of forcing the witness himself to recreate the prior inconsistent testimony in front of the jury, hopefully turning various shades of red in the process. On the other hand, some witnesses will thwart you by reading the answers in a way that is hard to follow, or by adding non-responsive comments and explanations, reducing the impact of the impeachment. In such cases, it is often better practice for the questioner to personally read both the questions and the answers, asking the witness merely to confirm the accuracy of the reading. In either event, the jury is advised in a short and succinct fashion of the prior inconsistent testimony.

Like all successful cross-examinations, this one appears effortless. That's because it was properly set up during the deposition. By establishing bookends at the deposition, the defense attorney has left the witness with no wiggle room. Under these circumstances, Mr. Flexible has no choice but to try to escape to that last refuge of the testimonial scoundrel, and claim: "I had forgotten about the forceps when I gave the deposition. I remembered when I was thinking about the case before trial." However, he is dead in the water. Let's go back to the trial and see how the bookends help impeach Mr. Flexible:

Q: Mr. Flexible, are you one of the plaintiffs in this lawsuit?

A: Yes, I am.

Q: And when your lawyers filed this case against Dr. White did they do so at your request?

A: Yes.

Q: You sued Dr. White based upon a claim that he hurt your son during the birth process, did you not?

A: Yes, I did.

Q: So, from the very beginning you knew that what happened during the birth process was extremely important to your case?

169

A: Well, yeah, that's true, I guess.

Q: And you knew that when you gave your deposition, didn't you?

A: I guess so.

Q: But, despite the fact you knew that the events surrounding the delivery were at the very heart of your lawsuit, despite that fact, you simply forgot during your deposition that you saw Dr. White violently misuse the forceps; is that your testimony?

A: Yes, it is.

Q: It just slipped your mind?

A: Right.

Q: And that wasn't your last chance to tell us about the misuse of the forceps either, was it?

A: I don't know what you mean.

Q: Well, after your deposition was over it was typed up by the court reporter, and you were given a copy to review and sign, true?

A: Yes, that's true.

Q: And were you also sent a correction sheet by the court reporter?

A: That is probably true.

Q: You were told that if you needed to make any corrections to note them on that sheet, is that right?

A: Yes.

Q: In fact, do you remember that I specifically asked you during the deposition to be sure to note it on your correction sheet if you remembered anything new about the delivery process?

A: Yes, I think that's true.

Q: And, do you recall you were given a full 30 days to review the deposition and to make corrections before you signed it?

A: Something like that.

Q: Mr. Flexible, at the time you signed the deposition you made absolutely no corrections to your testimony about what happened in the delivery room, did you?

A: No, I didn't.

Q: You didn't say anything about Dr. White misusing the forceps, did you?

A: No, not at that time.

Q: And, when you signed the deposition, did you know that in doing so you were swearing under oath that everything in the deposition was true and accurate to the best of your knowledge?

A: Yes, I knew that.

Eight of the jurors are sitting with their mouths wide open in wonder at your brilliant cross-examination; one is making a hissing sound at the witness; while another is looking for writing paper to nominate you for the Nobel Prize in law. Both alternate jurors have left to begin planning your victory party.

Now, that's more like it!

While this may slightly overstate the jurors' likely reaction to the cross-examination, without question they will be inclined to disbelieve Mr. Flexible's new testimony. Equally important, the jurors will probably develop a bad taste in their collective mouths for Mr. Flexible and may even begin to wonder if the whole lawsuit is contrived. In short, the cross-examination could be a turning point in the trial—not primarily because of brilliant cross-examination technique, but because of competent, well-planned deposition practice which included use of the bookend technique.

In that quiet time just before going to sleep at night, a lawyer's mind may turn to courtroom glory.

Gone are the uncertainties and fears of the daylight, replaced by a nocturnal mantle of invincibility. These slumbering moments of reverie are not wasted on the mundane aspects of trial practice. It is the hour of the gladiator; the hour for cross-examination.

During this dusky time of greatness, your performance is always flawless. Even the most recalcitrant witness withers before the onslaught of your genius. It is simply no contest. Compared to your performance at that moment, Clarence Darrow's cross-examinations were painfully inadequate. Abraham Lincoln's famous cross-examination of Charles Allen during the murder trial of William "Duff" Armstrong was mediocre at best; you would have done it so much better.

In this happy half-conscious state, you have no need for depositions. In your mind's eye, you take the deposition transcripts from your briefcase and throw them onto the fire. Why bother with them? All you need is the cold steel of your intellect. To use anything else would be unsporting.

171

You are a lean, mean cross-examining machine.

Unfortunately, then something goes very wrong—the alarm clock wakes you.

"Oh no," you think, "I didn't really burn those depositions, did I?" Running to the briefcase, you arrive panting and out of breath (the briefcase, after all, is a full 15 feet from your bed). You try to open it, but it will not budge. Your heart races. Finally you realize that one of the three zeros on the briefcase combination has moved (you never got around to changing the factory's pre-set code). Quickly correcting this, you snap open the briefcase. "Thank God," you sigh, "the transcripts are still here."

Then you go to court, clutching the briefcase very tightly.

In the harsh light of day, most of us rely heavily upon deposition transcripts. A well-taken deposition constitutes an almost absolute guarantee against prejudicial surprise. It is that simple. As long as you get the witness's version of the facts pinned down, and then box in that version, you will not get burned. The witness loses freedom of movement. One of two things will then occur at trial: Usually, the witness knowing that he is pinned down by the deposition will be encouraged to give consistent testimony; on the other hand, a witness occasionally will try to change or expand upon the deposition testimony, in which case you will be well positioned to wield the hammer of strong impeachment. Either way, you come out fine.

To make this a veritable guarantee, however, the deposition must in fact "box in" the relevant testimony. We saw in the last section that "bookends" work well to achieve this goal when we recognize up front what testimony will be particularly important at trial. But trials have a tendency to take on lives of their own. Not infrequently, a fact or event which seemed unimportant at the time of deposition turns out to be critical at trial. Therefore, it is not enough to use bookends to tie down only the obviously important testimony; you need to box in all conceivably relevant testimony.

One solution would be to go through the entire litany used in placing bookends for all categories of deposition testimony—in other words, place one set of bookends after another. However, this is not a practical solution. Placing bookends involves asking a long series of questions. To do this repeatedly during a deposition would be a monumental waste of time and could damage the effectiveness of bookends where they are most appropriate.

Fortunately, there is a better solution. This involves the use of "testimonial boxes," which are similar to bookends, but are much less elaborate.

The key with testimonial boxes, as with so much else, is a good deposition plan. Before asking the first question, the examiner should map out the whole deposition. This does not mean, of course, that each individual question should be pre-written. But a basic outline is indispensable, and this outline should generally be followed. The best deposition plan in the world is worthless if its author ignores the outline and slips into a stream of consciousness.

In maintaining an organized approach, it may be helpful to view the deposition as a book broken up into chapters and paragraphs. Chapters of the deposition, like the chapters of a book, represent main divisions of the testimony—the logical dividing points in the witness's story. Paragraphs are subdivisions within the chapters and also delineate distinct points in the testimony.

Returning to our example of Wilma Whipple and her lawsuit against the Whoopee Cushion Consortium, the April 12 meeting of the Consortium was a chapter. The identity of the persons attending the meeting was the first paragraph of that chapter.

This organized approach to a deposition involves taking the testimony one chapter at a time, and one paragraph at a time. Exhaust the witness's knowledge of each paragraph of the story before moving to the next. Try to avoid drifting back and forth between paragraphs. Such digressions confuse the record, which will make use of the transcript for impeachment more difficult.

Again, in our example, Wilma Whipple's lawyer went astray when he allowed himself to be pulled into a discussion of the undeniably fascinating "Mr. Whoopee" before even finishing up on the identity of the persons attending the meeting. As will often happen, having once meandered, he never got back on track. This error was then compounded when he also failed to pin down all of the conversations that took place during the meeting, which in turn led to disaster.

What he should have done was to note the nonresponsive comment about "Mr. Whoopee" on a piece of paper for future reference. It could then have been addressed later as a separate paragraph, or even a separate chapter, but only after he had first closed out the paragraph at hand. Often during depositions, witnesses will volunteer comments that, while off topic, are nevertheless relevant. Such relevant information should not be ignored. On the other hand, there is no reason to allow such comments to drag you off your deposition plan. Instead, follow up later at a time of your choosing.

As with just about every "rule" of good advocacy, there are exceptions. For example, every now and then a witness will suddenly blurt something out of critical importance. It would be silly in such cases to blindly follow your outline. Consider a truck/car collision case:

Q: Mr. Bishop, where did you go to high school?
A: I only finished the seventh grade, so maybe I'm not that well educated. And, okay, maybe I didn't see that stop sign. But, I'm as good as anyone else, including you college boys.
Q: After you left high school, did you receive any other education?
A: Well, I went to truck driving school.
Q: Where did you attend truck driving school?

What do you think? Should the questioner have perhaps followed up immediately on the "maybe I didn't see that stop sign" comment? Plainly yes; but such situations are rare. More commonly, no harm is done by waiting.

Another exception occurs where it appears likely that a witness is making up a story—not just exaggerating, but committing out-and-out perjury. While this, fortunately, is uncommon, it does happen. For instance, every now and then someone will falsely claim to have witnessed an automobile accident. When this happens, there will often be something about the witness which just does not feel right to you. Upon further probing, the questioner will discover that the witness is a friend or family member of a party who "just happened to be there at the time." Yet his or her name appears nowhere on the accident report. A purely organized approach to the deposition may not be the best alternative for such a witness. Instead, it may be better to jump back and forth between the various parts of the story, which hopefully will increase the chances of tripping up the witness.

No doubt there are other exceptions as well. But the general rule holds—most often a well-planned and well-organized deposition will best serve your client. Most importantly, by sticking with an organized approach the questioner is able to "box in" the testimony chapter by chapter, and paragraph by paragraph. Boxing in a witness involves a simple three-step process—opening the box, filling the box, and closing the box.

"Opening a box" means placing a question at the beginning of a chapter or a paragraph of testimony that clearly defines the parameters of what is to be covered; it opens the discussion. "Filling the box" is the process of drawing out the details of the witness's knowledge of that topic; it is the substance of the discussion. Finally, "closing the box" involves placing a question at the end which confirms that the witness's knowledge has been exhausted; it closes the discussion. As one box is closed, a new one is opened. This process then continues more or less uninterrupted through the deposition. At the end, the witness's testimony is neatly divided up into little boxes, any one of which may be easily pulled up at trial if needed for impeachment.

These testimonial boxes are placed around both chapters and paragraphs. When applied to chapters, opening the box is often done through a separate question. In our Wilma Whipple example, opening the box for the chapter covering the April 12 meeting is simple:

Q: Mr. Touch, we are next going to discuss the April 12 meeting of the Consortium. Do you understand?
A: Yes.

Filling the box then occurs with specific questioning on matters like the attendees at the meeting, the agenda for the meeting, and the comments made by all present. These specific topics, of course, become the paragraphs which make up the chapter. When the April 12 meeting has been fully covered, the box is closed as follows:

Q: Have we now covered everything you can recall happening at the April 12 meeting?
A: Yes, I believe so.

In the meanwhile, however, boxes have also been placed around each paragraph within the chapter. Opening the box for a paragraph is usually not done through a separate question. Instead, the first substantive question in the paragraph is posed in a way which accomplishes this result. A very simple example involves the paragraph covering who was present at the April 12 meeting of the Consortium. Opening the box is this easy:

Q: Who was present at the April 12 meeting?
A: Let's see: Don Bottoms, Ralph Butts, Bill Rumply. . . .

Closing the box is just as easy.

Q: Is that a complete list?
A: Yes.

Any number of brief questions would serve the same purpose:

Q: Anyone else?
Q: Is that all?
Q: Have you told me everyone?
Q: Ya done, dude? (probably not the best choice)

What makes this particular paragraph so easy to box in, of course, is that the entire subject adequately can be covered with one opening question. Life is rarely so simple. Usually, more than one question is needed and, often, many are required. For example, the paragraph covering what Mr. Bottoms said during the April 12 meeting will likely require many questions (remember, he is a big talker). This in no way changes the fact that the first question needs to open the box. A good way to accomplish this is by asking a two-part question, with the first part acting as a "topic heading."

Q: Mr. Touch, I next want to cover what Mr. Bottoms said during the meeting; what is the first thing you can remember him saying?

Note that through the use of the topic heading, the question clearly defines the entire subject to be addressed, thereby opening the box. This is true even though the question itself covers only part of that topic. The rest is then covered by follow-up questions, until you are ready to close the box.

Q: Have you now told us everything you can recall Mr. Bottoms saying during the April 12 meeting?
A: Yes, I have.

Incidentally, in addition to closing the box, this last question also serves as a valuable discovery device. It is remarkable how often a witness who gives every appearance of having fully answered a question will nevertheless come up with additional valuable information when asked in follow-up if the answer was complete. The follow-up causes a witness to dig deeper. When this occurs, of course, an additional close-out question is required: "With that addition, have you now told me everything you can recall Mr. Bottoms saying at the April 12 meeting?" Believe it or not, a fairly substantial percentage of witnesses will then add even more information. Sometimes the process requires four or five close-outs before the witness finally admits to being done, thereby closing the box on the paragraph.

Pinning a witness down in a well-thought-out deposition, chock full of "bookends" and "boxes," is worth the effort. With the parameters of the witness's deposition testimony clearly set out in the transcript, you know the testimony will stick at trial. You may step into the courtroom comfortable in the knowledge that you have done everything possible to protect your client, as well as yourself, from damaging surprise.

CHAPTER 13

Taking Chances at Depositions

Laurin H. Mills*

Lawyers are as risk averse as they come. We can't help ourselves. Most of us are cautious and conservative by nature. These are admirable attributes, and they can be especially valuable in many legal disciplines. But it never ceases to amaze me how deep the caution of many litigators, especially defense counsel, runs. We seem to be living by a mantra from the medical profession: First, do no harm. The problem is, if you try too hard not to *lose,* you may forgo opportunities to *win.* All cases have warts. The only way that you can find many of the weaknesses in your opponent's case, and potentially take advantage of them, is to take some chances. Calculated risk taking, in most cases, can mean the difference between winning and losing.

Once you have identified a chance worth taking, you must ask yourself: Do I want to take this chance at trial or during the deposition? Reaching that decision requires a second risk assessment. If you are going to get a bad result, it is much better to encounter the failure at deposition than at trial. On the other hand, if the chance pays off at the deposition, you may have educated your opponent, which will allow her the opportunity to repair the damage at trial.

---

*Laurin H. Mills is a partner with Nixon Peabody LLP in Washington, D.C. This article originally appeared in the Fall 2001 issue of LITIGATION.

In most instances, there is little reason to worry about this conundrum. To me, the decision is clear. You are either unskillful or desperate if you are taking very many chances at trial. By the time trial rolls around, you should know what your own witnesses are going to say. You are running unreasonable risks at trial if you are asking hostile witnesses questions to which you do not already know the answer. That is why, if you are going to roll the dice with a witness, you ordinarily should do it in deposition.

Some litigators play the odds from the very start of the deposition. Take, for example, the technique that I call the "immediate attack." With this approach, you dispense with opening remarks, pleasantries, or background inquiries. Instead, drill immediately into the most sensitive or damaging facts, using leading questions designed to gain admissions or unnerve the witness.

Q: You are Jim Smith?

Q: Acme's CFO?

Q: I show you Exhibit 1. You wrote this document, correct?

Q: That's your signature on the bottom?

Q: You wrote this memo to your boss, Bill Baker, on December 1, 1999?

Q: In this memo you advised him that if he went ahead with his new pricing plan, Acme's new prices would be substantially below its actual costs?

Q: Acme went ahead with that new pricing plan on January 1, 2000, did it not?

Q: When you learned that Baker had disregarded your advice, you were angry?

Q: You confronted him?

Q: You told him he was exposing Acme to antitrust liability?

Q: Please look at Exhibit 2. This is an e-mail, right?

Q: You sent this to Bill Baker?

Q: Right here you say flat out, "Bill, I am concerned about our exposure." Correct?

Q: You were referring to the pricing plan, correct?

By starting this way, you will not get Mr. Smith to open up and tell you facts that you might not already know. But you will set a tone for how the deposition—and perhaps the entire case—will be litigated from that point forward. You will show that you are a serious, no-nonsense adversary. Moreover, by controlling the witness from the outset of the deposition, you will administer a kind of truth serum, preventing him from giving evasive answers for the remainder of the deposition.

An immediate attack also can be useful when you are new to a case and do not believe that your adversary took previous counsel seriously. It can serve as a wake-up call, letting your opposition know things will be different from here on out. An aggressive approach also may help when you have very good reason to believe that the witness knows only one or two facts that you care about, and you want to pin him down on those issues. A peripheral witness may not be prepared for a brutal interrogation, and sometimes you can extract much better admissions if you surprise him.

Still, the rabid-attack mode carries with it considerable risks. Most litigators lack the skills, preparation, and personal gravitas required to pull it off. Rest assured, if this direct assault fails, it will fail spectacularly. The witness will clam up from that point forward and not give you what you want, and your standing as a formidable foe will be diminished, not enhanced. For these reasons, I rarely use the frontal-assault method. It is simply not worth the risk.

Instead, I find it is safer, and usually more productive, to be friendly with witnesses—hostile or otherwise—during most if not all of a deposition. Anyone who has taken more than 10 depositions knows three things about witnesses: (1) most of them are nervous about being deposed; (2) they have faulty memories, at least to some degree, when testifying about events that occurred months or years in the past; and (3) some witnesses lie and therefore have a hard time keeping their stories straight. By encouraging a witness to open up, you can take advantage of these frailties.

As with the riskier, bulldog approach, you set the tone of a "friendly" interrogation right off the bat. Establish rapport. Appear very interested in what the person has to say. Remain polite. If he is nervous, take advantage of it. Show him how patient you are. I have found that if you can make the witness relax, you will learn more—and get more damaging admissions—than you will by using the third degree. Save the tough cross-examination for trial, after you have gotten what you need to hold him to his story.

The biggest benefit to the keep-them-talking approach—and the one that puts the witness, not the interrogator, at the greatest risk—comes when you make the witness retell the critical part of his story as many times as possible. No one remembers everything. Keep a list of everything the witness says he does not remember. Later in the deposition, circle back and go through 10 or 20 items (no matter how insignificant) the witness cannot recall. Then get the witness to retell the story he supposedly does remember. When you do this correctly, the witness will vary his testimony slightly each time. Confront him about these inconsistencies. When you use this technique, it is amazing how many times "yes" turns into "maybe" or "I'm not sure," and how many times "maybe" becomes "I really don't remember."

Persistence Pays

Many practitioners, especially less experienced attorneys, are so cowed by the deposition objection "asked and answered," and their fear of court sanctions, that they forgo the venerable technique of redundancy. It is a chance worth taking. Ignore asked and answered objections until you have accumulated at least 100 of them. I have encountered only one opposing attorney who ended a deposition early based on asked and answered objections. The court ordered him back to my office the next day, and he was nearly sanctioned. So long as you are asking slightly different questions, and your questions are directed at key issues in the case, you are on solid ground. Moreover, if you conclude the deposition within a day (as most of us do), no court will sanction you for asking questions designed to ferret out inconsistencies in the witness's story or gaps in his memory.

Even if you use the friendly approach, there will come a time in all depositions—usually toward the end—when you should ask hard questions about sometimes sensitive issues. Many lawyers I know are too polite to ask embarrassing questions of witnesses who look "respectable" unless they have a strong, good-faith basis for asking them or, in fact, already know the answers. But you can and should ask hard questions of even likable witnesses.

For example, many witnesses, especially plaintiffs, have criminal histories. Often, even their attorneys do not know about them. For this reason, I always ask about criminal convictions, and, in preparing my own witnesses for deposition, I always inquire about this topic so that we will not be blindsided in the deposition (or at trial). More than once in my career, longtime clients I thought were blemish-free told me about serious criminal convictions on the eve of trial or right before a deposition. In each case, we were able to prepare for the issue.

One of my partners relates a story about a deposition early in his career, when he took a shot at probing someone's criminal history. The main witness for the plaintiff was a burly but respectable-looking middle-aged man who just happened to be in the store when the alleged slip-and-fall occurred. At his deposition, he gave testimony about negligence that was devastating to the defendant's case. On cross-examination, my partner thought to ask about prior convictions. This is what happened:

> Q: Have you ever been convicted of or served time in prison for a crime?
> A: Yes, only once.
> Q: What was the crime?
> A: First-degree murder.
> Q: How long were you in jail?
> A: 25 years.
> Q: When did you get out?
> A: I was released six months ago.

The case settled for nuisance value. Few depositions yield such dramatic results. However, the occasional drug offense, assault charge, shoplifting plea, or fraud conviction that you may turn up will be well worth the risk of insulting the witness.

Similarly, it often is productive to do background checks on witnesses prior to deposing them. Not too many years ago, it was expensive and usually unproductive to check out witnesses prior to their depositions. That is no longer true. For less than $1,000 (often substantially less), you can now find a plethora of information about potential witnesses, including criminal convictions, bankruptcies, divorces, credit history, employment history, and educational and professional credentials. Whether you do the research on the Internet yourself or engage a private investigator, chances are you will find a useful nugget in a witness's background. You may even hit the jackpot.

I got lucky in a background check in a discrimination case I defended several years ago. The plaintiff was a real Horatio Alger. He literally had started in the mailroom and worked his way up to middle management, but his performance went into a long nosedive, and he was fired. He blamed it on discrimination and sued my client.

When we checked this gentleman out, we found his personal life was falling apart and that he was guilty of serious résumé fraud. He had recently been arrested for threatening the life of his live-in girlfriend and for the unauthorized use of her car. His finances were a wreck. Moreover, the overseas MBA he supposedly had was a complete fake: He had attended the school listed on his résumé, but he had dropped out after one semester, far short of the *magna cum laude* graduation he claimed. When we confronted him with these facts (on the eve of his deposition), the plaintiff dropped his case.

This and other cases have taught me that résumé inflation is quite widespread. So always check out purported credentials before and during depositions. These tidbits of information are priceless. Inevitably, the witnesses will lie about these issues when asked at deposition, especially if the misrepresentation is contained in an employment application or on a government form. Let them lie. Then confront them with the proof. That always forces an admission. But by that time, you will have demonstrated that they will lie on their résumés, on their employment applications, and under oath. It rarely gets any better than that.

Again, I usually prefer to spring these traps in the deposition, but some people prefer to wait until trial to prove the witness is a liar. When that works, it is a beautiful thing to behold. One of my colleagues effectively took this risk recently in a very high-stakes employment discrimination case. The plaintiff in her complaint alleged she had been forced out of her job. She testified in her deposition that, since her termination, she had been attending classes at a local university to retool her skills. My partner knew she was lying, through an investigation he conducted, but he waited until trial to confront her with this fact. When he called the university registrar as a rebuttal witness, the plaintiff turned green. It was something of a sideshow, but it blew her credibility. After just 30 minutes of deliberation, the jury found in favor of the defense on all counts.

My partner's case is a perfect example of knowing when to take risks. He could have confronted the plaintiff safely with this evidence during her deposition. Perhaps she would have had a plausible explanation, and, if so, he certainly would have saved himself from having egg on his face at trial. However, he knew the case would never settle, he was confident of his facts, and he correctly decided to risk potential embarrassment and save the bombshell for trial. The risk paid off.

Many cases involve one or more shady characters, either witnesses or parties. These are people who might be involved with drugs or tax evasion—a particularly sensitive topic with many types of small businesses—or have questionable immigration status. Even if those activities have nothing to do with the case, it is worth taking a few swings to see if you can get the witness to take the Fifth. While only a small subset of witnesses have prior criminal records, a far larger group have previously undocumented criminal problems. (Just look at what happens to presidential appointees for cabinet posts every four years.)

For example, drug use, sometimes quite recent, is frequently fertile ground with witnesses, and more so than most practitioners imagine. It is easier to get into this subject than one might suspect, as the colloquy below illustrates:

Q: When you witnessed the events in question, were you under the influence of alcohol?
A: No.
Q: Prescription drugs?
A: No.
Q: Illegal drags?
A: No.
Q: Have you ever taken illegal drugs?
A: Well, er, uh, yes.
Q: What kind of drugs have you taken?
A: I experimented with marijuana and cocaine when I was younger.
Q: Crack or regular cocaine?
A: Both.
Q: When was the last time you used crack cocaine?
A: May I talk with my attorney? (pause) I refuse to answer on the ground that the answer may tend to incriminate me.
Q: Have you ever sold anyone illegal drugs?
A: I refuse to answer . . .
Q: Did you snort the crack cocaine?
A: I refuse to answer . . .

185

Q: Did you smoke it?
A: I refuse answer . . .
Q: Did you inject it?
A: I refuse to answer . . .

You get the picture. If you get someone to take the Fifth, do not let go. Milk it for all it is worth. Recent drug use, or admissions of criminal activity of virtually any type, go to credibility. Questions going to the credibility of the witness are always admissible. It is devastating if your party opponent or a key adverse witness takes the Fifth.

Indeed, when it comes to credibility issues, nearly every venture is worth the potential gain. The vast majority of cases are won and lost on the perceived credibility of witnesses, and the credibility of the parties is particularly important. If you can damage the credibility of your party opponent, even on something that is relatively trivial or irrelevant to the case, you have gone a long way toward winning. Once credibility is lost, it can almost never be regained. For this reason, it is always wise to take chances at depositions on issues relating to credibility.

A good example of this happened several years ago in one of my cases, a libel claim we were defending. In discovery, the plaintiff produced a dozen letters that he had received immediately after the allegedly libelous article appeared, expressing outrage at the plaintiff's treatment by the defendant newspaper. The plaintiff intended to use the letters to support his derogatory interpretation of the article's language (which was quite ambiguous), as well as his damages claim.

I was very suspicious about these letters. In my experience, there are only two kinds of people—those who write personal letters and those who do not. Personal letter writing is something of a lost art. Today, it is rare to find many people under 60, especially men, who pen letters to others. My mother and her friends all wrote long, personal letters. They had attractive stationery and excellent penmanship. It was apparent that they took letter writing seriously.

By contrast, it was clear in this litigation that none of the people who wrote the letters my opponent produced was an habitual correspondent. Not one note was on personal or business stationery. All were handwritten. Most used block printing rather than cursive. The grammar was, shall we say, uneven. I did not believe that any of these people had made the decision to compose these letters on their own. In fact, I strongly suspected that the plaintiff had asked all of them to write to him. So I decided to take a chance at proving this.

The first thing I did was to ask the plaintiff at his deposition whether he solicited any or all of the letters. He categorically denied that he had. He then made a long, self-serving speech about the merits of his case and his personal integrity. The next day, I sent out 12 subpoenas to the letter writers and scheduled all the depositions to start one hour apart. On the day of the depositions, nine of the 12 showed up. During their testimony, four of the witnesses admitted that they had been asked by the plaintiff to write the letters (the others, I remain convinced, lied). Two of the four testified that they had not even read the article in question.

The plaintiff's credibility was destroyed. Soon thereafter, my client won a motion for summary judgment. Even though the origin of the letters was irrelevant to the motion—in fact, we argued and won on other grounds—we prominently featured the letters in our brief. I am sure the testimony about the genesis of the letters had an impact on the outcome of a close legal issue.

Failing to ask certain questions can be riskier than the deliberate trap laying that you breathlessly hope turns out all right. For example, while many good lawyers forget to do so, it is always worth asking the witness if she brought any documents to the deposition. This question often is so productive that seasoned practitioners routinely ask it. You are taking a big chance if you do not do so. It is simply astounding how many witnesses, sophisticated and unsophisticated, show up for depositions with a sheaf of documents in their briefcases. Often, their own attorneys have not even seen the documents. You have to remember to get them to open the briefcase. My practice is to bury this question in a series of routine background questions. I try to ask it when the witness has become comfortable with me and the opposing attorney does not appear to be paying too much attention. Almost every time, witnesses, especially nonparties, respond that, yes, they did bring documents. Some have even handed them to me before an opposing attorney could object. At least half the time, the question unearths a useful document that was not previously produced in discovery, such as a calendar, notebook, or personal file.

In one instance, I obtained the production of a document that, for all intents and purposes, won the lawsuit. The case was a Section 1983 claim in which my client, a prison inmate, alleged the use of unnecessary force by correctional officers. In most jurisdictions, whenever a law enforcement or correctional officer is involved in a skirmish, an incident report is required. These reports are very useful in corroborating dates and times, as well as some relevant facts. They are rarely a panacea for plaintiffs, however, because they are almost always written with a law-enforcement spin and in incredibly passive voice. In this case, I was very concerned; after a year of discovery, my opponent claimed that there was no incident report for my client's case because, he contended, the incident had never occurred.

The deposition was not of the defendant law enforcement officer but of his shift supervisor, who was an honest and organized fellow. Midway through the deposition, I thought to ask if he had brought any documents relating to the case with him. He did not answer. Instead, he reached into his inside breast pocket, pulled out a folded document, and handed it directly to me before opposing counsel even realized what had happened. It was the missing incident report. Moreover, it confirmed virtually every fact we alleged in our complaint, indicated that the defendant officer had been punished for his role in the offense, and even contained several great facts we had not alleged.

I am also ashamed to admit that, on just a few occasions, I have had my own witnesses show up with documents (despite my advice to the contrary). Some people simply cannot help themselves. This always results in needless angst and, in one of my cases, a trip to court in the middle of the deposition to determine whether the documents should be produced. (We ultimately did not have to produce the documents in question, but the issue easily could have gone the other way.) You are taking a big chance if you do not prepare your witnesses for this question before the deposition and confirm that they have no documents with them when they arrive to testify.

At certain times, common sense should outweigh any inclination to take risks. An incident that occurred several years ago involving one of my partners illustrates why. My partner noticed the deposition of the plaintiff in a libel case. Like many libel plaintiffs, this gentlemen was still quite angry when he showed up for his deposition. My partner exchanged pleasantries with opposing counsel and the plaintiff and began the deposition.

Midway through the background phase of the questioning, the plaintiff leaned back in his chair and unbuttoned his sport coat to reveal that he had a rather large pistol tucked in the waistband of his trousers. My partner—who is six-foot five and not easily intimidated—raised an eyebrow and asked a few more questions. At the conclusion of the background questioning, he suggested that they take a short break. At the break, he took plaintiff's counsel aside, and they both agreed that the deposition should be continued until such time as the plaintiff could be convinced to appear sans sidearm.

That is the perfect example of when *not* to take a chance. There is no reason to compromise your personal safety, or anyone else's, during civil litigation. Moreover, even if the gun had represented only the emptiest of threats, it would have been on my partner's mind throughout the deposition and undoubtedly compromised his questioning of the witness. Although this incident seems like a bizarre aberration, something like it will occur in almost everyone's career. Keep it in mind.

Sometimes it is the clients, and not their lawyers, who must decide on taking big chances in depositions. Very early in my career, the firm I joined out of law school let me take on a large pro bono case involving prisoners at a local jail. We contended that corrections officers had beaten and tear-gassed the inmates without justification. I took more than 30 depositions in that case, and it was a tremendous learning experience. One of the biggest lessons, however, involved the courage of one of my clients who risked his personal freedom to vindicate his rights.

My client was in his early 20s and was a prototypical jail inmate. He came from a broken home and crushing poverty, dropped out of school after the eighth grade, had an extensive criminal record (albeit for relatively minor crimes or drug offenses), and had never held any job for long. His older brother had been murdered. I learned much of this not from him but from reviewing his prison jacket when preparing to defend his deposition.

In reviewing that jacket, I noticed a separation order requiring that my client and another inmate be kept apart. These orders are not uncommon, especially with youthful offenders from the inner city who have been involved in gang activity. What caught my attention was my client's request for the separation order. In that request, he wrote that he wanted to be separated because he had experienced a very violent altercation with the other inmate's brother "in the street." (The actual facts here have been obscured to protect client confidences.) At first, I found this merely interesting. Then it dawned on me that my client had never been convicted of a crime of violence, only of drug offenses. Yet here he was admitting to a very serious crime of violence in a signed writing in his prison jacket.

My client had been released from jail shortly before his deposition. In prepping for his testimony, we discussed the possibility that he might be asked questions about a potential crime for which he had never been prosecuted. When he left my office I fully expected never to see him again. I honestly did not expect him to show up to testify. I even followed up the meeting with a letter reiterating the risks of proceeding. I heard nothing back from my client and could not call him because his telephone had been disconnected.

Betting on Your Client

At 9:10 A.M. on the day the deposition was scheduled, I literally had my hand on the phone to call opposing counsel to cancel. Just as I touched the handset, the phone rang. It was the receptionist telling me that my client had arrived for his deposition. I immediately took him into a vacant conference room and told him, quite candidly, that I was surprised to see him and thought that he was taking a very big risk in continuing. He looked at me with great conviction, held up my letter, and said that he and his mother had discussed this at length and he knew what he was doing. He said that the defendant prison guards had "beaten the $#%! out of me" and other inmates for no reason, and someone had to make them pay. He was prepared to take the risk. We went to the deposition, the feared subject came up, and my client handled it deftly. He received a nice settlement the day before trial.

Criminal defendants and individuals, especially those who are "frequent fliers" in the legal system, learned long ago that they must tell their attorneys everything—and that means *everything*— if they want good representation. Corporate clients, for a wide variety of psychological and institutional reasons, do not always feel that way. That is a prescription for disaster. In-house counsel run great risks if they do not tell their outside counsel everything that the witness has been involved in prior to that witness's deposition. The attorney needs to know.

One of my partners recalls an incident in the early '80s in a routine breach of contract case brought by a client's former employee. The client, so we thought, had relatively little at stake. The deposition of the corporate representative lasted all day and was routine, if not boring. But that all changed during the last half hour of questioning.

In the final moments of the deposition, opposing counsel got into a series of questions, backed up by documents, that ended up demonstrating that the corporate witness had been involved in illegal activity overseas on behalf of the company. These questions had nothing to do with the contract claims and came out of the blue. But no amount of objecting could stop the inquiry on this issue. The answers the witness gave ended up not only losing the case but also costing the client plenty more in the form of fines and negative publicity.

In that case, it is difficult to say precisely what would have been different had my colleague been forewarned. The case might have been settled quietly, and perhaps more favorably, had our opponents not first elicited the damaging testimony. But surely it teaches that clients with something to hide should not get involved in litigation. The client might have self-reported or otherwise remedied the situation. Any number of things might have happened. What did happen, however, was the worst-case scenario. It could easily have been avoided if the client had not taken an unnecessary risk by not being forthcoming with counsel.

Risk also inheres in deciding whether to videotape a deposition. Because of the cost, many clients do not lightly permit counsel to do this. In any case in which the amount of money in controversy is $1 million or more, I believe it is riskier not to videotape at least the depositions of key experts and the central witnesses for each of the parties. Because there can be a substantial lag between the time an expert is deposed and a case goes to trial, there is always a chance something can happen to the expert between the deposition and trial. Recently, a 43-year-old expert I was using in a patent case dropped dead moments after sending us his expert report. Moreover, a videotaped deposition is much more like trial testimony, and the tape can help you analyze, perhaps aided by a jury consultant or focus group, how a jury will perceive a witness. Opposing counsel typically behave better at a deposition when the camera is rolling.

The best reason, however, to take a chance on the expense of videotaped deposition (and the risk of suggesting it to cost-conscious clients) is that it captures any damaging testimony forever. Witnesses say and do remarkable things at depositions. I know that I am starting to get to witnesses as soon as their backs get rigid and they fold their arms across their chests. Juries recognize this, too. Some witnesses stop looking at either the camera or the questioner when they start lying. When that happens, you have it on tape. In addition, when you show up at trial with a television and VCR, the videotaped testimony is potent truth serum or devastating impeachment.

Taping depositions can backfire occasionally, however. A friend of mine told me that he videotaped the deposition of the plaintiff in a personal injury action. The testimony was recorded early on in the litigation. Between the deposition and the trial, the plaintiff's physical and emotional condition visibly declined, which his experts, of course, attributed to his injuries. The plaintiff's attorney used the deposition footage to drive this point home to the jury. By the time the man took the stand at trial, he appeared sallow and depressed, instead of the more nourished and communicative person on the video. The plaintiff recovered a six-figure verdict in the case, proving that there are potential downsides with all risks, even those worth taking.

At times, lawyers blow terrific opportunities during depositions by taking gratuitous chances. One of my partners told me about a dicey franchise-continuation case that had many warts. One of the concerns was that the male client, who was married, had a habit of conducting extramarital affairs. The opposition got wind of this tendency, tracked down one of the paramours who had moved 2,000 miles away after the affair ended, and convinced her to return to the East Coast to be deposed. This ex-lover had firsthand knowledge of many facts that would have been detrimental to our client's case. Everyone on our side feared the worst.

When the witness showed up for her deposition, our opposing counsel was grinning from ear to ear in anticipation. He then immediately proceeded to blow it. He called the witness, whom he had never personally met, "honey" several times before the deposition even started. The woman's demeanor toward that attorney instantly went from friendly to icy. Instead of helping our adversary, her testimony actually favored our client. The deposition turned out to be an unmitigated disaster for our opponent, who quickly settled the case for fear that this witness might actually show up for trial. My friend remains convinced that his opponent is still baffled about what went wrong.

Dealing with Experts

Trial lawyers also disagree whether to take certain depositions at all, especially when it comes to experts. A few of the most daring trial lawyers take the position that, so long as they have a reasonably comprehensive expert's report, they would prefer not to depose the expert, or to conduct only the most rudimentary deposition to size the expert up. They believe that it is unwise to educate the expert about weaknesses in her opinion and thereby give the expert time to fix them before trial. These lawyers are prepared to take the chance of not knowing everything the expert will say in the hope that she will be less prepared for their questions at trial. This technique works very well when employed by the right practitioner.

The overwhelming majority of lawyers, however, believe that it is more risky to let experts go undeposed. Most, therefore, conduct extensive expert depositions. One reason for this is paranoia: They simply cannot stand the possibility that they might be unprepared to cross-examine the expert on some topic at trial. (I personally do not think much of this reason; paranoia is not a wise litigation strategy.) Another more compelling reason for this approach is that the overwhelming majority of civil cases settle or are otherwise resolved prior to trial. Therefore, you may as well take your best shot at the expert at deposition to impact the settlement value of the case.

The key with experts is knowing when to take the chance of not deposing them. If the expert's report is relatively clear and comprehensive, you are reasonably comfortable asking good questions in this area of expertise, and you think there is a high likelihood that the case will be tried, it may be best to forgo the deposition. Or you can conduct only a rudimentary deposition. Assuming the situation is right, this allows you to meet the expert and size her up. This approach also has a psychological impact on your opposition because, when you cut the deposition short, you will leave the other side wondering what you know that they do not. Moreover, expert witness preparation is perhaps the most difficult skill in civil litigation. It is substantially more difficult for opposing trial counsel if you have not provided them with a road map of your questions during discovery.

Even though I began by lamenting how risk averse most lawyers are, I nonetheless am stunned by how few practitioners adequately prepare their witnesses, or themselves, for depositions. That is the chanciest proposition of all. Whether this failure is the result of ignorance, sloth, concern for fees, the refusal of witnesses to be prepared, the attorney's schedule, or some combination thereof, any attorney who does not adequately prepare his witnesses and himself is taking a big risk. Adequate preparation involves reviewing every non-privileged document in the case that the witness might have seen or written, and questioning the witness about every issue. Witnesses are obligated to tell the truth. But the truth always comes out better when your witness has heard a question, and thought about the answer, before he hears it at the deposition.

Very few attorneys can consistently wing it, though a high percentage think that they can. Their lack of preparation and focus drags out depositions and causes them to miss many of the most productive areas of questioning. Hoping you might stumble onto the truth is not much of a litigation strategy. In fact, it is a foolish gambit.

Litigation has been analogized to both war and the game of chess. No one remembers the cautious generals, and countless chess grand masters have never won and will never win any big chess matches. The great generals and chess masters know what risks are worth taking and when to take them. They may lose a battle or match on the way to learning these valuable lessons. Nevertheless, there is a profound difference between generals and chess masters who fight or play to win and those who seek merely not to lose. The same applies to trial lawyers. As the most famous general in French history once said: *"Attaque! Toujours l'attaque!"* (Attack! Always attack!)

PART III

Strategies

CHAPTER 14

Deposition Traps and Tactics

Thomas J. McNamara and Paul T. Sorensen*

Deposition. Many of us never heard the word before law school. Some of us did not really understand the significance of the term, even *after* the civil procedure exam. And most of us had little idea of how to take one when we got our first file to handle.

Soon after we started in practice, though, the word became part of our everyday vocabulary. With a little experience, we learned how to ask sensible, concise questions in a conference room with a witness and his lawyer across the table and a court reporter taking it all down on one of those amazing little black machines with the quiet keys. Yet many trial lawyers still have problems using deposition transcripts effectively at trial, and occasionally they face the even more disconcerting problem of having transcripts of their own depositions used against them in unforeseen and devastating ways.

It is no secret that the deposition is one of the most productive discovery devices available. What is not so commonly appreciated are the creative and effective uses to which deposition transcripts can be put at trial.

*Paul T. Sorensen is a partner in Warner, Norcross & Judd L.L.P. in Grand Rapids, Michigan. Thomas J. McNamara, now deceased, was a partner at Warner, Norcross & Judd. This article originally appeared in the Fall 1985 issue of LITIGATION.

The trick is knowing when and how to use a transcript to best advantage. The lawyer who recognizes that a "discovery" deposition can be a powerful weapon at trial will fit it into his overall strategy and take steps to stymie his opponent from later using the transcript against him.

- *A little law, like a little fasting, is good for the soul.* You cannot use depositions at all unless you follow the rules. Three of them apply: Rule 32 of the Federal Rules of Civil Procedure and Rules 801 and 804 of the Federal Rules of Evidence.

Civil Rule 32(a) sets forth the general circumstances under which a deposition may be used at trial. Impeachment of a witness's trial testimony with a prior inconsistent deposition statement is the most common. Rule 32(a)(1) also provides that a deposition may be used "for any other purpose permitted by the Federal Rules of Evidence." That language (added in 1980) vastly broadens the use of depositions as a substitute for live testimony.

Evidence Rule 801(d) provides that neither a witness's prior inconsistent deposition testimony nor a previous admission by a party or his agent is hearsay. So, if deposition testimony is either at odds with what witness says on the stand or is the testimony of a party or his agent, it may be offered *both* for impeachment and as substantive evidence.

A deposition of any witness may also be used as substantive evidence if the court finds that:

(A) the deponent is dead;

(B) the deponent is more than 100 miles from the place of trial or out of the country (unless the party offering the deposition procured the witness's absence);

(C) the deponent is unable to testify because of age, illness, infirmity, or imprisonment;

(D) the party offering the deposition has been unable to procure the deponent's attendance by subpoena; or

(E) upon application and notice, such exceptional circumstances exist as to make it desirable, in the interest of justice, to allow the deposition to be used. Fed. R. Civ. P. 32(a)(3).

While clauses (A) through (D) seem uncomplicated enough, the courts have had to answer a few lingering questions. For example, does the rule allow use of a deposition when the deponent is more than 100 miles away by the shortest land route but less than 100 miles away as the crow flies? No. *See, Hill v. Equitable Bank, N.A.,* 115 F.R.D. 184, 186 (D. Del. 1987); *SCM Corp. v. Xerox Corp.,* 76 F.R.D. 214 (D. Conn. 1977).

In *SCM,* the court also concluded that the 100-mile rule applied not only when the deposition was offered but at any time during the proponent's case when a subpoena could have been served. 77 F.R.D. 16. The distance also is measured from the courthouse where the trial takes place, not the judicial district's boundary. *See, Tatman v. Collins,* 938 F.2d 509, 511–512 (4th Cir. 1991).

If you intend to rely on clause (D), you had better introduce sworn testimony that you were unable to procure the deponent's attendance by subpoena. Bare assertions by counsel will not do. *State v. Keairns,* 9 Ohio St. 3d 228, 460 N.E. 2d 245 (1984). *See also, State v. Rowe,* 92 Ohio App. 3d 652, 637 N.E.2d 29 (1993).

The deposition's proponent bears the burden of establishing satisfaction of Rule 32(a). *Fairfield 274–278 Clarendon Trust v. Dwek,* 970 F.2d 990, 995 (1st Cir. 1992). Under Rule 804(a) an opponent must have had an opportunity to cross-examine the witness. *Hill v. Equitable Bank, N.A.,* 115 F.R.D. 184, 185 (D. Del. 1987). Failure to take advantage of the opportunity for cross-examination will not preclude admission. *Id.* at 185–186.

With the help of this judicial fine-tuning, clauses (A) through (D) have presented few problems. But what in the world does clause (E) mean? What (on application and notice) are the exceptional circumstances that also justify the use of a deposition at trial?

First, what is sufficient "application and notice"? This language probably requires that a party file a written request with the court, with copies to all counsel of record, for permission to use a deposition at trial. The application should set forth the reasons it is necessary to offer the deposition even though none of the specific conditions of Rule 32 have been satisfied.

Next, how "exceptional" do the circumstances have to be for your opponent to read to the jury the transcript of the "discovery" deposition that you blithely sat through three years earlier? The short answer is, we are not sure. The rule does not define the term "exceptional circumstances," the committee notes are unenlightening, and the courts have given few guidelines.

One court held there are exceptional circumstances if a named defendant does not appear at trial notwithstanding her lawyer's pretrial assurances that she would be there. *Huff v. Marine Tank Testing Corp.*, 631 F.2d 1140, 1142–43 (4th Cir. 1980). Another court has suggested that exceptional circumstances might exist merely because a trial is long. *SCM Corp. v. Xerox Corp.*, 76 F.R.D. 214, 216 n. 2 (D. Conn. 1977).

But prejudice—even in the form of dismissal due to the unavailability of a crucial witness—is not enough by itself to demonstrate exceptional circumstances. *Griman v. Makousky*, 76 F.3d 151, 153 (7th Cir. 1996). The proponent must also demonstrate "exceptional circumstances" that made the witness unavailable. The Seventh Circuit required the proponent to prove facts demonstrating that it was extremely difficult or impossible to make the witness available despite the use of all reasonable means to ensure attendance at trial. The court upheld the trial court's finding that the release and subsequent disappearance of a jail inmate were not an exceptional combination of events, saying that plaintiff's lawyer should have realized that jails as opposed to prisons are meant to hold persons for a short period of time and that plaintiff's lawyer had not made an effort to determine the witness's likely release date or to keep track of him upon release.

Mere hostility on the part of the witness also does not qualify as an "exceptional circumstance." *Martinez v. City of Stockton*, 12 F.3d 1107, 1993 WL 478922 (9th Cir. 1993) (unpublished opinion). Nor is a mere refusal of the witness to appear for trial without invoking the subpoena and contempt power of the court sufficient. *Angelo v. Armstrong World Industries, Inc.*, 11 F.3d 957, 963 (10th Cir. 1993). In the Sixth Circuit, the professional demands of doctors are not presumed to be sufficient to demonstrate "exceptional circumstances" even where a state statute provides otherwise. *Allgeier v. United States*, 909 F.2d 869, 876 (6th Cir. 1990). Sometimes, though, a doctor's unusually and unexpectedly busy schedule has been sufficient to satisfy the "exceptional circumstances" requirement. *See, Melore v. Great Lakes Dredge & Dock Co.*, 1996 WL 548142 (E.D. Pa. 1996) ("The court may, in the exercise of its discretion, find that a physician or other witness with an unpredictable schedule is unavailable. . . ."); *Rubel v. Eli Lilly and Company*, 160 F.R.D. 28, 29 (S.D.N.Y. 1995) (doctor required to handle practice of four physicians due to absence of the other physicians resulting from illness and maternity leave represented "exceptional circumstances" provided a videotaped deposition was conducted to give defendant a renewed opportunity for extensive cross-examination); *Reber v. General Motors Corp.*, 669 F. Supp. 717, 720–21 (E.D. Pa. 1987) (heavy surgical schedule sufficient where videotape deposition taken and both parties anticipated absence of doctor at trial); *Borchardt v. United States*, 133 F.R.D. 547 (E.D. Wis. 1991) (additional expense of having live testimony from physician ranging from $625 to $875 represented "exceptional circumstances" where entire claim was only $12,402).

The "exceptional circumstances" provision is obviously broad enough for a trial judge to justify the admission of almost *any* deposition transcript without abusing his discretion. From what we see and hear, though, there are a lot of judges out there who are as tough as Job, but not as patient. If none of the conditions of clauses (A) through (D) can be satisfied, your "exceptional circumstances" argument will have to be terse and overwhelming, as there is little precedent to hang your advocate's hat on.

Take another situation. What happens if your witness on the stand simply cannot remember the particular events about which you are questioning him? He remembered those events last year when you took his deposition.

You have the deposition transcript on the counsel table and would like to use it, but the witness is not dead, absent, old, sick, or in jail. He has simply drawn a blank, and nothing will refresh his recollection. You move for admission of the transcript under the "exceptional circumstances" clause, but the judge says the circumstances do not seem too exceptional to him, and besides, you did not make a pretrial application or give proper notice.

Even though that testimony is important to your case, you adjust the knot of your tie and move on to your next witness. Right? Not so fast.

Rule 804 of the Federal Rules of Evidence provides some additional grounds for admission of deposition testimony. The courts have recognized that Rule 804 is a proper basis, independent of Civil Rule 32, for using depositions at trial. *See Coleman v. Wilson*, 912 F. Supp. 1282, 1295–97 (E.D. Ca. 1995); *United States v. I.B.M.*, 90 F.R.D. 377, 384 (S.D.N.Y. 1981).

Rule 804 deals with hearsay exceptions if the person whose out-of-court statement you want to introduce is unavailable as a witness. In Rule 804, unavailability is defined to include not only many of the same circumstances listed in Civil Rule 32(a)(3) but also situations in which the witness (a) claims to be exempt from testimony because of a privilege, (b) refuses to testify despite a court order to do so, or (c) testifies to a lack of memory of the subject in question.

Lack of memory. There it is. Under Evidence Rule 804(b)(1), your witness is now "unavailable," and you can use his deposition as substantive evidence of the facts he cannot remember on the witness stand.

There is another way to do it that does not involve Rule 32 at all. The hearsay exception for past recollection recorded in the Federal Rules of Evidence, Rule 803(5), is broad enough to admit depositions. That is a big change from the common law, and here is how it works.

At common law, past recollection recorded required a writing made at or near the event, in addition to a failure of recollection on the witness stand. Obviously, "at or near the event" excludes all but the most unusual depositions. The result is we are not accustomed to thinking of depositions as past recollection recorded. But under Rule 803(5), the time requirement is relaxed. Now the writing need only be "shown to have been made or adopted by the witness when the matter was fresh in his memory and to reflect that knowledge correctly." Remembering accurately enough to swear to the testimony at a deposition ought to qualify as being "fresh in his memory." At least it is a good deal fresher than not remembering. And since past recollection recorded under the federal rules is only read to the jury (just as a deposition would be), it seems to fit depositions just fine.

If there is any basis for using deposition testimony at trial, then any party may use the transcript, not just the party who took the deposition. There is, however, one important ground for using a deposition transcript at trial that will, in the opening gambit at least, necessarily be available to one side but not the other.

Civil Procedure Rule 32(a)(2) permits *an adverse party* to use, for any purpose, the deposition of another party or of anyone who at the time of taking the deposition was an officer, director, or managing agent of a party. Either a plaintiff or a defendant, therefore, may introduce the deposition testimony of his opponent *even though that opponent is present at trial and has testified orally.* But, co-plaintiffs or co-defendants may not use each other's deposition, unless they have adverse interests by reason of cross-claims or the deposition testimony is admissible on some other ground.

One final point about the rules. Say that you have satisfied one of the requirements for using a deposition transcript at trial but have no desire to offer the whole thing. You know that Rule 32 allows you to use all or part of a deposition, so you plan to offer only that portion of the testimony where your remarkably incisive interrogation got the deponent to concede a critical point.

After you introduce those crucial few pages, be ready for opposing counsel to demand that you also read, at the same time, "any other part which ought in fairness to be considered with the part introduced." That is what Federal Procedure Rule 32(a)(4) and Federal Evidence Rule 106 both require.

Be alert to the possibility that your opponent's heavy-handed selection may bog down your neatly paced presentation and transport the jury to the state of judicial narcolepsy we all know and dread. "Long" is a great virtue in cigars and sailboats. It is no asset at trial.

- *The strategy of depositions: I'd rather see a sermon than hear one.* What good are rules without a contest? When you are sitting in your office hatching prediscovery strategy, the rules give no help in deciding how, when, or even whether to use the depositions that will mushroom during the course of discovery.

First, we will deal with pretrial strategy; then we will move on to the art of using deposition testimony at trial.

Interesting tactical problems arise during depositions. Sometimes lawyers forget that "discovery" depositions might well resurface as evidence at trial.

Unless a lawyer takes care to make a clean record at a deposition, the transcript will be unimpressive at trial. Asking imprecise questions, suffering harassing objections, and tolerating rambling answers can make the deposition virtually useless at trial, either for impeachment or as substantive evidence. But those problems can be minimized, if not avoided. *See* P. Kolczynski, "Depositions as Evidence," 9 LITIGATION, No. 2 at 25 (Winter 1983).

It is important at the start of any deposition to make a record that the deponent understands what a deposition is and what you will be doing. Something like this works well:

Q: Mr. Jones, my name is Paul Sorensen. I am the lawyer for the Essex Company in the lawsuit that Robert Emmett has brought against Essex. This deposition is an opportunity for the lawyers to ask you questions to learn more about what really happened. Do you understand that everything said in this room will be taken down by the court reporter?

A: Yes.

Q: If you do not hear one of my questions, please tell me and I will be glad to repeat it. If you do not understand one of my questions, let me know and I will rephrase it. Fair enough?

A: Fair enough.

Q: Do you understand that you have given an oath to tell the truth and that you should answer the questions here just as if you were sitting in court in front of a judge and jury?

A: I sure do.

Q: After we finish with the deposition, the court reporter will transcribe it, and you will have a chance to read it and correct any errors. You will then sign the transcript and return it to the reporter for filing with the court. Your signature means that the transcript, as corrected by you, accurately reflects your testimony today. Do you understand that?

A: Yes.

Why bother with this introduction? Because it makes the deposition a more potent weapon for impeachment.

When a witness at trial contradicts his deposition testimony, it is difficult for him to explain away the inconsistency if you remind him that (1) he said he understood the rules when he testified at the deposition, (2) he later had a chance to review and correct the transcript, and (3) he signed the transcript, confirming its accuracy. So go through the introduction. And do not waive reading and signing by the deponent, except for a very good reason.

The introduction is a useful way to reinforce impeachment. But what if there is no one to impeach because the witness does not appear at trial?

Instead, your opponent offers *your* "discovery" deposition against you at trial. Have you sharpened your sword only to sit on it inadvertently?

Say that your adversary can satisfy one of the conditions of Rule 32(a)(3), so the deposition can be used as substantive evidence. Now you have a problem. When you took the deposition, you assumed that it was just discovery. But, unless you are in a state where the rules specifically recognize the distinction, the courts have consistently concluded that discovery depositions (even if only exploratory in nature) can be used at trial if the requirements of Rule 32 or Rule 804 are satisfied.

In *Gill v. Westinghouse Electric Corp.*, 714 F.2d 1105, 1107 (11th Cir. 1983), for example, the plaintiff's lawyer had taken the discovery deposition of the defendant's expert. The expert died before trial.

The defendant, now short an expert, offered the deposition transcript at trial. Plaintiff's counsel objected on the grounds that he had taken the deposition only to discover what the expert had to say, not to challenge his opinions. Both the trial court and the court of appeals rejected that argument. In light of the witness's death, the requirements of both Rules 32 and 804 were met, and the deposition was admitted into evidence.

Early in the case, lawyers usually focus on uncovering the facts, not conducting a cross-examination to use at trial. But that "discovery" deposition you took a month after you got the complaint can come back to haunt you at trial. It is like the old Missouri proverb about appearances: "When a fellah make a show of puttin' all his cards on the table, he probably ain't playing cards."

There are some circumstances to watch for. If the witness is:

- more than 100 miles from the courthouse or likely to be at the time of trial;
- beyond the subpoena power of the court or intending to be by the time of trial;
- elderly or very ill, you should be aware that your opponent could wind up using the deposition transcript against you at trial.

Then your standard discovery deposition technique should give way to a more structured, formal interrogation designed not only to elicit facts but also to score points as you would at trial. In this situation, you should consider taking the deposition later in the discovery period, after you have armed yourself with the facts and documents you need to cross-examine rather than just explore with the witness.

It is equally important to stay on the alert when your opponent notices the deposition of your elderly, infirm, foreign, or fleet-footed witness. If it is likely that either you will be unable to produce the witness at trial or that you will need the witness's testimony but might choose not to call him live, you should consider questioning him thoroughly at deposition. Your examination serves two purposes: to defuse any unfavorable testimony that your opponent elicits and to develop a coherent record to introduce as evidence at trial.

Sometimes your own interrogation can save your case. If the deponent is the only witness to key facts, conducting a thorough examination at the end of your opponent's discovery deposition will preserve the testimony for trial.

When you question your own client, there are few risks—if both of you are well prepared. If you take the time to get your client ready for the possibility that you may want to slam the door on a few points made by your artful opponent, the client will hardly ever surprise you with his testimony.

Remember: if, by answering a few additional questions, your client clears up some apparently damaging admission, you will be in a position to fight off your adversary's use of the deposition at trial. You will be able to read into the record those passages that take the sting out of the answers your adversary picks out, thus reminding the trier of fact that your adversary is selectively editing the transcript.

It is a different story if you are defending the deposition of an uncommitted, nonparty witness. Consider this scene: Your opponent has just questioned the witness. The lawyer has elicited a few facts that help his case, but nothing really devastating to your client. Because you know that the deposition transcript could show up at trial, you decide to ask a few questions to repair the damage done on direct.

As the witness answers your first question, you realize that you have made a big mistake. The witness is guessing, opining, and exaggerating, and you are to blame. You feel like someone explaining alternate-side parking to a cranberry.

You try to stop the debacle, but it is too late. What began as a harmless discovery deposition has ended in disaster. The moral? There are just two reasons for cross-examining in this situation:

abysmal innocence and bottomless desperation. Neither is a sufficient justification for what inevitably follows.

The instinct to control the damage done on direct is a good one. But to avoid making a mess like the one in the example (if your unwholesome curiosity once again exceeds your self-control), you must prepare thoroughly beforehand. Be as ready for that deposition as you would be if you had to cross-examine the witness at trial without the benefit of a deposition.

Learn ahead of time what the witness knows. That information will dictate what questions (if any) you should ask. Without that kind of preparation, never assume that neutral witness will help your case on cross simply because he did not devastate it on direct. Some witnesses listen very carefully to the questions, and maybe your opponent just asked the wrong ones.

- *Experts: the elegant lie sometimes prevails over the unintelligible truth.* Experts' depositions present unique problems. Because experts are scattered across the country, often their depositions are admissible at trial on the grounds that the witness lives more than 100 miles from the courthouse.

A lawyer deposing his opponent's expert faces some tough decisions. Certainly, he wants to discover the expert's opinion and the basis for it. But the last thing he wants is to set the stage for a replay of *Gill v. Westinghouse,* where the transcript of a foraging, nonconfrontational discovery deposition was introduced against the questioner.

Does all this mean that, when deposing an expert, you have to conduct a complete cross-examination right after you find out for the first time what his opinion is? That is an unappealing prospect.

It would be extremely difficult, if not impossible, to prepare adequately for a penetrating cross-examination without knowing in advance a lot about the expert's opinion. Even if you could prepare a good cross-examination, you might hesitate to pull out all the stops at the deposition because, if you did, you would reveal more than you cared to about your own strategy. If the expert later appeared at trial, he would be ready for every one of your questions.

There are several possible outs. For example, expert testimony will not be admitted at trial, either in person or by deposition, unless the expert's qualifications appear in the record. So when you take that discovery deposition of your opponent's expert, you do nothing but harm to your own case if you ask the typical series of questions about the witness's background and expertise. The answers often tell you little that you really need to know. Usually you already have the expert's curriculum vitae or can get it later. But your questions can do a nice job of qualifying the expert on the record.

Skip those questions. Move right into the meat of the deposition. If you do not qualify the witness, you will minimize the risk that the deposition will come back to bite you at trial. You will be able to discover what the expert has to say without having to cross-examine him at the same time.

Before you start to feel too smug, you should realize that your opponent can spoil your strategy. He can qualify the expert himself after you have completed your examination.

If this happens, then reserve the right to return and "complete" the expert's deposition another day, unless your opponent stipulates that he will not offer the deposition transcript as evidence at trial. If you have a co-party whose lawyer has not yet questioned the witness, urge him to make the same reservation. Alternatively, you could proceed to cross-examine the witness on the spot under the "innocence or desperation" rule discussed earlier, but you would probably regret it.

This quandary is as real as your opponent's willingness to dispense with the expert's live testimony at trial. You can make him show his hand if you skip a review of the expert's credentials. If he then fills in those credentials, you will have a better chance of avoiding the *Gill* trap if you have developed a contingency plan in advance.

Judges usually require lawyers to disclose at the final pretrial conference whether they intend to introduce depositions at trial. If so, transcripts must be reviewed and edited for reading to the jury.

The cleanup is not some sort of illicit editing. Its sole purpose is to make the deposition brief and comprehensible to the listener.

If you made objections during the deposition, decide whether to present them to the judge for decision. Cross out those that are carping or otherwise unmeritorious. The remaining objections should then be presented to the judge, together with any additional objections that were not made during the deposition but that are nonetheless preserved.

If the judge sustains an objection, the objection, question, and answer should be crossed out. Otherwise, the question and answer remain, but the objection is eliminated.

Follow the same process to eliminate motions to strike, colloquy, and extraneous remarks of counsel. In most cases, the deposition as read at trial will contain only the lawyers' questions and the witness's answers.

If you do not intend to introduce the entire transcript, you will have to designate which portions you are going to offer. Your opponent should then have an opportunity to identify any other portions that he believes you must, in fairness, also read. It is far better for both sides to resolve this issue before trial.

The lawyer against whose client the deposition is offered certainly wants a fair reading in context. The lawyer introducing a portion of a deposition wants to be as credible as possible to the jury, while avoiding an extended dramatic reading. His credibility would be undercut if he just read the favorable part of a deposition, only to have his opponent then stand up and demand: "Counsel, kindly also read pages 100 through 105, where the witness stated that he had misunderstood your previous question and then fully explained his answer."

Usually, it is not quite so obvious that some additional portion of the transcript should be introduced. If your opponent thinks you should read other passages along with the ones you have designated, and you disagree, get a ruling in advance. The risk of waiting until trial is far too great. If the jurors are convinced that you are trying to hide the "bad stuff" from them, they will ignore only two things about the rest of your presentation: the style and the content.

- *Using depositions: If you've only got one trick, you haven't got any tricks.* Some trial lawyers seem to assume that offering deposition testimony at trial runs a close second in captivating interest to reading the tax regulations.

You can tell it is not their favorite part of the trial from the way they announce it: "Your Honor, at this time I would like to read Mr. Smith's deposition into the record." And that is all they do—read it into the record. No persuasion. No pizzazz. Like a hunter with bad aim, they take whatever falls. And little does, except the jurors' eyelids.

Using depositions at trial does not have to be this grim. Sure, you miss the spontaneity of live interrogation, but there is still hope.

When you know that you are going to offer deposition testimony at trial, the first step is to let the jury in on it during voir dire. Something like this would work:

> Ladies and gentlemen, during the trial, you will hear the testimony of John Smith. But Mr. Smith will not be here in the courtroom. Because he lives halfway across the country, Mr. Smith's testimony was taken in his hometown at a deposition, and that is what you will be hearing. Very briefly, a deposition is an official proceeding at which the witness and the lawyers for both sides appear. A court reporter gives the witness an oath to tell the truth, just like the one given in the courtroom. The lawyers then ask questions, and the witness answers. Either lawyer can object to questions just as he can here. The court reporter records the entire thing, word for word. Will any of you tend to give Mr. Smith's testimony less weight because he is not here in person? Can you commit to me that you will consider Mr. Smith's testimony the same as if he had testified from the witness stand?

This short piece of voir dire (whether done adroitly by you or less so by a time-conscious judge) accomplishes three things. First, it alerts the jurors that the deposition is coming and lets them know why it is being used. Second, it assures the jurors that the deposition process is just as serious as what they are about to see in court. Third, it gets as much of a commitment as possible that the jurors *will listen* to the testimony.

Listening. That is what you want. What else can you do to keep the jurors as interested in the deposition testimony as they are in the live witnesses?

You can turn the deposition into a live witness. Do not read the transcript all by yourself. Save the monologues for opening and closing. Get someone up on the witness stand to read the answers.

Make the exercise as realistic as possible. You want the jurors to look at the person on the witness stand and *believe* they are seeing the witness whose testimony they are hearing. You also want the jury to believe that witness's testimony. If the judge will let you select your reader, pick the most interesting, sincere person you can find—one who oozes credibility.

This "witness" must prepare before he appears at trial. The last thing you want him to do on the stand is stumble through because he is unfamiliar with the deponent's terminology or syntax. The witness should review the entire transcript carefully in advance. Bring him into your office as often as necessary before trial to rehearse, so he knows exactly how you intend to offer the testimony in the courtroom.

Some judges will not permit the lawyers to bring in a "ringer" to read the deponent's answers at trial. But most will allow you to use a colleague or a legal assistant. The same rules about preparation apply. Obviously, you should find out in advance what your particular judge's practice is.

The lawyer reading the questions should also review the transcript ahead of time. If you are going to introduce deposition testimony, know the questions well so that in court you do not sound as if you are reading. It is important for you to do the same things you would do if the deponent were testifying in person: modulate your voice, change the pace of your delivery, and show interest in the answers.

So much for using the deposition of an unavailable witness. How do you handle depositions of parties?

One of the most effective ways is to introduce the helpful admissions as part of your own case-in-chief. The tactic is particularly persuasive for a plaintiff, because he can fit the defendant's admissions into his case before the defendant has even had a chance to take the stand. By introducing the favorable deposition testimony as part of your own case, not only do you give the jury a longer time to think about it, but you also incorporate it neatly into your own presentation. Finally, if the defendant testifies differently later, then the plaintiff's lawyer can impeach him with the same deposition.

CHAPTER 15

Preparing for Rule 612

John S. Applegate*

Cases so often settle that many lawyers find the climax of litigation—the moment of greatest anticipation and anxiety—is their client's deposition. Perry Mason has moved from the courtroom to the conference room. And, because defending a deposition is usually an exercise in silence punctuated by occasional objections, the real work for a latter-day Perry Mason takes place earlier, in another conference room—the one where the witness is prepared. Even though such preparation occurs long before trial, in the midst of discovery, it requires a careful understanding of a courtroom evidence rule—Rule 612 of the Federal Rules of Evidence (or its state counterparts), which governs the use of writings to refresh recollection.

Suppose you are sitting at a client's deposition. The client is the plaintiff in a breach of contract case. The testimony *must* go well, and so you have spent hours preparing him for the rigorous questioning to come. Now the pleasantries are over. After a sanctimonious opening speech and the routine name, age, and address questions, opposing counsel asks, "What did you do to prepare for this deposition?"

---

*John S. Applegate is the Executive Associate Dean for Academic Affairs and Walter W. Foskett Professor of Law at Indiana University School of Law, Bloomington, IN. This article originally appeared in the Spring 1993 issue of LITIGATION.

You have anticipated this. You have explained to your client that witness preparation is an ordinary, ethical, and necessary part of litigation. He responds, "I met with my lawyer to discuss the case, and we reviewed a number of documents together."

"What documents did you review?"

"I don't remember exactly. There were a lot of documents from my company's files and from your files. There were some notes my lawyer asked me to make and some charts she made. And we looked over our own correspondence."

"Why did you do all that?"

"I suppose so that I would remember what happened as accurately as possible for this deposition."

So far, so good—but now the problem question: "Counsel, please give me a copy of every document reviewed by the witness in preparation for this deposition."

This is not what you had planned. Questions about witness preparation? How can that be? Preparation involves your strategy, your thought processes, your work product. It also involves communications with your client. It is private—it has to be, you think. You therefore decline the request on the grounds of the attorney-client privilege and the work product privilege.

Your opponent is ready for that: "Under Federal Rule of Evidence 612, I am entitled to see any writing this witness used to refresh his memory during *or before* his testimony, and I can question him about it. You've waived any privilege you had. You'll get a motion to compel."

Looking back over the wreckage of the day, you realize that opposing counsel may have a point. Your training has taught you—or at least implanted the instinct—that conversations with your client and trial preparation materials are protected. Your experience has been that lawyers respect that privacy and do not probe deeply into each other's preparation. Still, you can understand why your opponent would be concerned about the documents you used in preparation. She surely has an interest in how they may have affected your client's testimony. It may be, for example, that what your client claims to remember is not a memory at all, but the creation of document review. From that point of view, your opponent has every reason to want to use those documents to test your client's recollection—and that is what Rule 612 is all about.

After that passing moment of weakness, however, something occurs to you: Rule 612 is a rule of *evidence*. It governs admissibility and availability of evidence at *trial*. This is *discovery*. Maybe opposing counsel was just blustering, and maybe Rule 612 doesn't apply at all.

Actually reading the rule—something your concern has led you to put off—provides some comfort. "If a witness uses a writing to refresh memory for the purpose of testifying," it says, "an adverse party is entitled to have the writing produced at the hearing, to inspect it, to cross-examine the witness thereon, and to introduce in evidence" pertinent parts of the document. The drafters of Rule 612 obviously had trials, and not depositions, in mind.

The strongest support for this idea is the rule's requirement of document disclosure "at the hearing." It seems inappropriate to call a deposition a "hearing"; among other things, a presiding officer is almost never present at a deposition, and Rule 612(2) expressly requires such an officer to exercise discretion in ordering disclosure (more on that later). This certainly suggests that your opponent has no right to the documents, at least not now.

Unfortunately, only one court has directly faced up to the poor fit between Rule 612 and discovery: *Omaha Public Power Dist v. Foster-Wheeler Corp.*, 109 F.R.D. 615 (D. Neb. 1986) concludes that Rule 612 applies only to "the presentation of evidence before a judge or magistrate." That conclusion is unique, however. Every other court to consider Rule 612's application to depositions has ignored the "hearing" issue as well as the clear command that disclosure occur *at that time*. Instead, such courts have mechanically applied Federal Rule of Civil Procedure 30(c), which states that depositions generally are subject to the Federal Rules of Evidence. In short, you still have a problem.

Because it is unlikely you can avoid Rule 612 completely, you decide more study is needed. Here is what you learn:

First, private consultation with witnesses in advance of a deposition or trial is an entirely appropriate activity in the context of the adversary system, and it may well be part of a lawyer's ethical duty of adequate preparation. *See, e.g.,* James M. Altman, "Witness Preparation Conflicts," 22 *Litigation*, No. 1 at 38 (Fall 1995); Richard C. Wydick, "The Ethics of Witness Coaching," 17 *Cardozo L. Rev.* 1 (1995); John S. Applegate, "Witness Preparation," 68 *Tex. L. Rev.* 277 (1989).

However, the law governing the use of privileged materials in witness preparation reflects the collision of two powerful principles: (1) privacy in trial preparation and (2) the need to cross-examine. As a result, the use of such documents to prepare a witness for a deposition is governed by rules of privilege, discovery, *and* evidence. Their application depends on, among other things, the type of witness, the type of material used, and the circumstances of their use. *See* Applegate, "Witness Preparation," *supra.* Given the many forces at play, courts have tended to adopt an *ad hoc* approach to disclosure of such materials. It is therefore important that lawyers preparing witnesses recognize the risks involved *before* they are brought home in a motion to compel. By that time it is often too late, and you cannot be sure of the outcome.

Some basics: To begin with, we are concerned with documentary, not oral, preparation. Your instinct was correct that most witness preparation is protected from discovery. The other side may ask whether a witness has discussed the case with his lawyer, but judges have shown little patience with elaborate questioning concerning the content of preparatory discussions—unless there is reason to suspect that real improprieties have occurred. *See, e.g., Ford v. Phillips Elec. Instruments Co.,* 82 F.R.D. 359, 360 (E.D. Pa. 1979).

Documents used in preparation, however, stand on a different footing. Being tangible, they are more easily produced than memories of conversations, and may be separable from a lawyer's mental impressions. More important, both the definition of work product in Rule 26(b)(3) and the text in Rule 612 itself apply to documents and not to oral preparation. Because those rules give written expression to the need to conduct meaningful cross-examination and discovery, they provide the strongest grounds for the discovery of preparation materials.

The preparation documents that are most likely to become the subject of litigation fall into four categories according to their privileged status:

(1) Correspondence between client and lawyer. Such materials can be an excellent source of summarized information about complex events or key documents. A lawyer is often involved from the earliest stages of a dispute, and lawyer and client share information and views as events unfold. Even if the lawyer is only involved after the fact, the correspondence may record rec-

ollections that are considerably fresher than at the time of deposition. To the extent that these materials constitute or reflect confidential communications between client and lawyer regarding the subject of representation, they are covered by the attorney-client privilege.

(2) Work product materials—documents prepared by or at the direction of a lawyer in anticipation of litigation. These, too, are sometimes used to prepare witnesses. Such materials fall into two categories: ordinary (or fact) work product, and core (or opinion) work product. Under Rule 26(b)(3), ordinary work product is protected from disclosure except upon the opposing party's showing of "substantial need" and an inability to obtain the information elsewhere. Ordinary work product might include a client's own notes of events (if prepared at counsel's request). This can be an excellent tool for assisting a witness during deposition preparation. The work of accountants or investigators—also ordinary work product—might also be used to clarify issues in preparation.

(3) Core work product—"the mental impressions, conclusions, opinions, or legal theories of a lawyer or other representative of a party concerning the litigation," and Rule 26(b)(3) says the court "shall protect" it from disclosure. It may be used in preparation, but it must be treated differently. For example, to prepare herself for a case, a lawyer may compile a chronology of events, based on review of many documents and interviews or depositions of witnesses. Such a document could reflect the lawyer's sense of what is important in the case; its utility in preparing a witness is obvious. Other core work product—like annotated deposition transcripts, notes of interviews, opinion letters, position papers, and unsigned affidavits or statements—can also be used to focus the witness's attention on what others have said and how his recollection compares.

(4) Collections of relevant, nonprivileged documents selected by the lawyer and reviewed with witnesses. Perhaps this is the most important category of witness preparation materials. Where discovery has uncovered a mass of paper of varying importance and relevance, a major part of a lawyer's job is reviewing and evaluating that material, culling out the most important to be reviewed with witnesses. Each document in the collection is not, by itself, privileged; in fact, it may have been obtained from the opposing party, or produced to the other side.

However, courts have recognized that the particular *collection* of documents—that is, the identity of the documents actually selected by the lawyer—is core work product, reflecting mental impressions and evaluations of the case. *Stone Container Corp. v. Arkwright Mutual Ins. Co.*, 1995 WL 88902, *2–4 (N.D. Ill. 1995); *Schwarzkopf Corp. v. Ingersoll Cutting Tool Co.*, 142 F.R.D. 420, 423 (D. Del. 1992); *Sporck v. Peil*, 759 F.2d 312, 315–16 (3d Cir. 1985); *Berkey Photo v. Eastman Kodak*, 74 F.R.D. 613, 616 n.8 (S.D.N.Y. 1977).

Knowing why courts sometimes order production of such documents will help guide your witness preparation—or so it would seem. Unfortunately, Rule 612 does not apply to privileged witness preparation material directly and of its own force. Instead, courts treat the issue as one of "implied waiver."

You already know the general rules on waiver of privileged material: Virtually any disclosure of confidential lawyer-client communications outside that relationship waives the privilege. The work product privilege is more forgiving, but any disclosure "inconsistent with the privilege" (for example, to an opponent) is considered a waiver. In addition, unfair use of either type of privileged material, such as partial disclosures, strategically timed disclosures, or placing privileged matters into issue, may be deemed waiver. *See* Richard L. Marcus, *The Perils of Privilege: Waiver and the Litigator*, 84 Mich. L. Rev. 1605 (1986); Note, *Developments in the Law—Privileged Communications*, 98 Harv. L. Rev. 1450 (1985).

But what does all of that have to do with witness preparation materials? The whole point of resisting their production is so that the privileged information—what you wrote your client, your own chronology, the documents you picked—will *not* be revealed. How can it be waiver to show your client a privileged document that you sent to him, and him alone, in the first place?

The "implied waiver" theory under Rule 612 is as follows: The use of writings to prepare a witness is deemed to be equivalent to, or to entail, refreshing that witness's memory. Under Rule 612, writings used to refresh a witness's memory are subject to disclosure to opposing counsel. Therefore, the argument goes, because the use of documents in witness preparation could result in their disclosure, such use is inconsistent with the confidentiality required to preserve their privileged status.

This reasoning is fairly attenuated, which means that a lawyer preparing a witness cannot focus simply on one rule—Rule 612 or Rule 26(b)(3) or the issue of waiver—but must cope with the interaction of a number of rules. As a first step, it makes sense to sort out the situations where the effects of waiver and of Rule 612 are clear.

One of the surest points is that merely testifying about facts that are also contained in privileged documents does not constitute waiver as to the documents. *United States v. Nobles*, 422 U.S. 225, 239–40, n.14 (1975); *Bogosian v. Gulf Oil Corp.*, 738 F.2d 587, 593 (3d Cir. 1984). If a witness testifies at his deposition about the circumstances that provoked an employee's termination, the mere fact that those events are also described in correspondence with the witness's lawyer or analyzed in the lawyer's notes does not constitute waiver of the privilege in the correspondence or notes. The idea is almost self-evident, and it is rarely the subject of contention.

It is equally clear that using a document to refresh recollection *during* testimony *does* require production upon demand. That result, required by Rule 612, is a matter of simple fairness. It is obviously unfair for a witness to be able to make "testimonial" use of a privileged writing and not to give the questioner a chance to examine it. *See Eckert v. Fitzgerald*, 119 F.R.D. 297, 299 (D.D.C. 1988). The Supreme Court has reasoned that such unilateral use denies the opportunity for effective cross-examination of the witness. *U.S. v. Nobles*, 422 U.S. 225 (1975). (This may also be thought of in terms of waiver, since testimony immediately following refreshment is likely to reflect the contents of the document, thereby disclosing the privileged material. *R.J. Herely & Son Co. v. Stotler & Co.*, 87 F.R.D. 358, 359 (N.D. Ill. 1980)). If waiver is involved, however, it is usually a restricted one: Instead of applying the usual rule that disclosure of part of a privileged document results in disclosure of all of it, some courts have taken a narrow view under Rule 612 that only disclosure of the parts of the document actually used during testimony is necessary, *S & A Painting Co. v. O.W.B. Corp.*, 103 F.R.D. 407, 409 (W.D. Pa. 1984); and that disclosure of one document does not require disclosure of others. *Marshall v. U.S. Postal Serv.*, 88 F.R.D. 348, 350–51 (D.D.C. 1980). *But see Audiotext Communications Network, Inc. v. US Telecom, Inc.*, 164 F.R.D. 250, 254 (D. Kan.

1996) (allowing access to entire notebook even though only a few documents established as having influenced testimony).

Materials used to prepare experts for their testimony also tend to be an easy case for disclosure. Experts in most lawsuits have little knowledge of the facts other than that provided by lawyers, and so a questioner cannot effectively learn the basis of the expert's opinion without knowing what the expert has read. In fact, Federal Rule of Civil Procedure 26(b)(4) and Federal Rule of Evidence 705 both provide a firm basis for an adverse party's access to these materials, quite apart from Rule 612 and implied waiver. The new Rule 26(a)(2) and revised Rule 26(b)(4), relating to experts' statements, remove any doubt that full disclosure is required. *See Karn v. Ingersoll Rand*, 168 F.R.D. 633 (N.D. Ind. 1996).

An Arbitrary Distinction

The use of privileged documents to refresh the recollection of a lay witness *before* testifying—classic witness preparation—is different from the situations just described. The thinking behind the implied waiver argument under these circumstances is that use of a privileged document *necessarily* will result in its disclosure under Rule 612. As you have discovered, that may be true of use *during* testimony, but Rule 612 applies differently to preparation. The case law prior to Rule 612 sharply distinguished between memory refreshment during and before testimony; it routinely allowed the questioner full access to the former but rarely to the latter. (Similarly, while courts have shown little willingness to explore oral preparation, as noted above, they have little reluctance to explore conversations with counsel *during* testimony, for example, at breaks in a deposition or trial. *See, e.g., Geders v. United States*, 425 U.S. 80, 89–90 (1976).) The drafters of Rule 612 saw this distinction as arbitrary and unrelated to the real issue of how much the documents actually influenced testimony. They therefore permitted access to both. However, the common law distinction survives in that disclosure is automatic for writings used *during* testimony, Fed. R. Evid. 612(1), but disclosure of *prior* use is allowed only "if the court in its discretion determines it is necessary in the interests of justice." Fed. R. Evid. 612(2).

The background of Rule 612 may help illuminate the "interests of justice" standard. The legislative history of the rule shows that it was not meant as a no-holds-barred discovery device. The

House Report warns against use of Rule 612(2) to conduct "fishing expeditions among a multitude of papers which a witness may have used in preparing for trial." H.R. Rep. No. 650, 93d Cong., 1st Sess. 13 (1973), *reprinted in* 1974 U.S. Code Cong. & Admin. News 7075, 7086. Even more pointedly: "The Committee intends that nothing in the Rule be construed as barring the assertion of a privilege with respect to writings used by a witness to refresh his memory." *Id.* Moreover, application of Rule 612(2) in the discovery context is extremely awkward. Rule 612 always requires that the questioner lay a foundation of loss of memory, use of the writing to refresh that memory, actual refreshment of the witness's memory, and the witness's use of the material for the purpose of testifying. *See* Weinstein & Berger, *Weinstein's Evidence* at ¶ 612[01]. The lawyers at a deposition are hardly the people to decide whether these requirements have been met. The further requirement in Rule 612(2) that "the court" determine "in its discretion" that disclosure would be in the interests of justice—an ad hoc balancing test—is not susceptible to extrajudicial resolution, as in a deposition.

As a result, courts have had to wrestle with a rule that is ill-suited to the circumstances and offers little guidance. "Assertion of a privilege" is permitted, but how should it be weighed? The Rule does not permit "fishing expeditions," but how much discovery or disclosure *does* it permit? It is as if the Advisory Committee had said to judges: "Think about privilege, waiver, and fairness, and figure it out yourself—but don't allow fishing expeditions." This is difficult for a judge at an actual hearing; it is impossible for the participants in a deposition.

One of the first cases to consider the problem was *Berkey Photo v. Eastman Kodak,* 74 F.R.D. 613 (S.D.N.Y. 1977). In *Berkey,* counsel for Kodak had provided his expert witnesses with notebooks containing his selection of important, non-privileged background documents. Judge Frankel found that the selection of documents was core work product, but held that Rule 612 nevertheless required disclosure of the notebooks. "[I]t is disquieting to posit that a lawyer may 'aid' a witness with items of work product and then prevent totally the access that might reveal and counteract the effects of such assistance." 74 F.R.D. at 616.

Berkey's pro-disclosure reading of Rule 612 has shortcomings. Most significantly, the *Berkey* court never mentioned the fact that the case involved expert witnesses, who were presumably subject to the broad disclosure requirements of Rules 26(b) and 705 (and now 26(a)(2) as well) wholly apart from Rule 612. In addition, the opinion placed little weight on the availability of the underlying documents to Berkey through discovery. It gave only passing attention to the legislative history. And it did not take into account the "interests of justice" language of Rule 612(2).

Despite these problems, *Berkey* was followed by several courts in opinions that remain part of a standard string citation for those seeking disclosure of witness preparation materials. *See, e.g., Audiotext Communications, supra,* 164 F.R.D. at 253; *Redvanly v. NYNEX Corp.,* 152 F.R.D. 460, 470 (S.D.N.Y. 1993); *James Julian, Inc. v. Raytheon Co.,* 93 F.R.D. 138,144–46 (D. Del. 1982); *Wheeling-Pittsburgh Steel Corp. v. Underwriters Laboratories, Inc.,* 81 F.R.D. 8, 9–10 (N.D. Ill. 1978).

Other courts, however, resisted using this rule of evidence to justify extensive discovery. They expressed concern that Rule 612 not bear more weight as a waiver and discovery rule than its drafters intended. *Aguinaga v. John Morrell & Co.,* 112 F.R.D. 671, 683 (D. Kan. 1986); *Barrer v. Women's National Bank,* 96 F.R.D. 202, 203 (D.D.C. 1982) (noting that Rule 26(b)(1), which defines the scope of discovery, limits itself to "matters, not privileged"). The *Berkey* approach, these courts reasoned, threatens to invade the confidentiality of proper witness preparation without considering the value of such preparation.

Courts taking this more cautious approach insisted on a showing of actual reliance on the privileged documents (*Berkey* simply presumed it), and they emphasized the court's discretion under the "interests of justice" language. *In re Comair Air Disaster Litigation,* 100 F.R.D. 350, 353 (E.D. Ky. 1983); *Barrer, supra,* at 19–20. Core work product materials have been protected, if at all possible. *See Al-Rowaishan Establishment Universal Trading & Agencies, Ltd. v. Beatrice Foods Co.,* 92 F.R.D. 779, 780–81 (S.D.N.Y. 1982).

These competing considerations were carefully analyzed in *Sporck v. Peil,* 759 F.2d 312 (1985), which is now firmly established as the leading case in the area. *Sporck* involved a collection of otherwise discoverable documents. Like *Berkey,* the court recognized that such collections are core work product. However, instead of looking at the problem in terms of implied waiver, it focused on the language of Rule 612. The Third Circuit concluded that, as long as the foundational requirements of Rule

612(2) were strictly applied, there would be no conflict with the work product and trial preparation protections in Rule 26(b)(3).

The key to avoiding this conflict, the court held, is found in the Advisory Committee's note on the rule. The note cautions that Rule 612 cannot be a "pretext for wholesale exploration of an opposing party's files" and should be applied so as to "insure that access is limited only to those writings which may fairly be said in fact to have an impact upon the testimony of the witness." Following this guidance, *Sporck* requires that a questioner establish as to each document for which disclosure is sought (1) actual use of the specific document to refresh memory, (2) the witness's use of the document for the purpose of testifying, and (3) that disclosure would be in the interests of justice. 759 F.2d at 317–19. This approach has been followed in more recent cases. *Stone Container Corp. v. Arkwright Mutual Ins. Co., supra; Arkwright Mutual Ins. Co. v. National Union Fire Ins. Co.,* 1994 WL 510043 (S.D.N.Y. 1994); *Omaha Pub. Power Dist v. Foster Wheeler Corp.,* 109 F.R.D. 615, 617 (D. Neb. 1986).

Some cases since *Sporck* have placed even greater emphasis on the discretionary balancing test in Rule 612(2). *In re Joint Eastern & Southern Dist. Asbestos Litigation,* 119 F.R.D. 4, 5–6 (E.D. & S.D.N.Y. 1988); *Parry v. Highlight Indus.,* 125 F.R.D. 449, 452 (W.D. Mich. 1989); *Baker v. CNA Ins. Co.,* 123 F.R.D. 322, 327–28 (D. Mont. 1988); *Bloch v. Smithkline Beckman Corp.,* 1987 WL 9279, *2–3 (E.D. Pa. 1987). In particular, the Rule's "interests of justice" language has provided the occasion to consider the following factors: whether improper coaching may have occurred; whether the material represents core work product; and whether the questioner's request for disclosure represents a fishing expedition. The issue, in other words, comes down to a fairness test, balancing the propriety of each party's actions and the importance of confidentiality.

Sporck is not without its critics, however, and a number of courts have sought to limit its scope. The most common reason given for applying *Sporck* narrowly is that the material in question is either not work product at all or is merely ordinary work product. This obviously alters the balancing under Rules 26(b)(3) and 612(2) substantially. Perhaps the most thoughtful of these opinions is *Washington Bancorporation v. Said,* 145 F.R.D. 274 (D.D.C. 1992), which emphasized the "selectivity that was central" to

Sporck's finding of lawyers' mental processes in document collections. Not finding it, the court ordered disclosure. *See also In re San Juan Dupont Plaza Hotel Fire Litigation,* 859 F.2d 1007, 1017–18 (1st Cir. 1988); *In re Minebea Co.,* 143 F.R.D. 494, 499–500 (S.D.N.Y. 1992). Other courts have simply placed a higher value on disclosure than *Sporck* did, and so have exercised their discretion in favor of the questioner. *See e.g., Audiotext Communications, supra,* 164 F.R.D. at 254; *Redvanly, supra,* 152 F.R.D. at 468–69.

It is too much to say that these cases are part of a trend to limit or supersede *Sporck*. Even its strongest critics recognize *Sporck* as the standard to be applied—and to be distinguished if disclosure is appropriate. Moreover, by undertaking a detailed examination of foundational requirements and balancing of interests, the current judicial attitude toward Rule 612(2) clearly reflects *Sporck's* appreciation of the importance of confidential witness preparation. How that attitude will affect any given case is impossible to say, however, given the individualized balancing test mandated by the Rule. Courts have considered a whole range of facts to be important, including

- What exactly are the materials involved?
- Do the materials really reflect a lawyer's evaluative mental processes, or are they just a mechanical compilation, *e.g.,* in response to a document request?
- Are they available under other rules (Rule 26(b)(4) for example)?
- Will the compilation be revealed soon anyway?
- How much did the refreshed testimony reveal privileged information?
- Was it a waiver of privilege to show the document to the witness during preparation?
- Have the documents been revealed elsewhere—in settlement discussions for example?
- Did the document plant the memory and not just refresh it?
- Is the document available elsewhere?
- How much will non-disclosure hamper cross-examination or discovery questioning?

Your journey through the cases has left you better informed but not much more certain. Even properly applied, the "interests of justice" balancing test is unpredictable. And, whatever the

224

final result, your current battle will require a costly hearing and in all likelihood in camera review of documents by the court. Faced with all that, you begin to reflect on what you could have done to avoid this problem.

For the defender of the deposition, the job begins early: Careful attention must be given to how a witness is prepared. It is absolutely essential for a lawyer preparing a witness with privileged documents to clarify for herself (and later for a court) certain key facts. What type of witness (expert or fact) is involved? What is the claim of privilege (lawyer-client, core, or ordinary work product)? And when were the documents used (during or before testimony)?

Confusion on these basic points is common. A lawyer can unnecessarily lose a protection by accepting the application of the wrong legal standard. For example, *Berkey* is routinely cited in all kinds of cases for its automatic waiver rule, but *Berkey* on its facts applies only to experts. If you have a non-expert witness, don't accept the *Berkey* standard. Likewise, cases that apply an automatic waiver rule to the use of privileged documents during testimony should not be applied to the very different situation of use in preparation. Conversely, one case involving memory refreshment *during* testimony erroneously applied a balancing rather than the Rule 612(1) per se test. *See Auto Owners Ins. Co. v. Totaltape, Inc.*, 135 F.R.D. 199, 202 (M.D. Fla. 1990).

Such legal variation should alert a lawyer to the risk involved in using privileged documents for witness preparation. Ideally, she should avoid the use of privileged materials altogether. Where correspondence and similar lawyer-client communications are merely a shortcut or a convenience, it is probably wiser to take the longer route and show the witness only nonprivileged documents created during the events in issue. In fact, there is often no real need to use written lawyer-client communications or core work product written by a lawyer, because the lawyer's views are not in themselves relevant to the case.

Where the use of privileged documents cannot be avoided, a lawyer preparing a witness should take special care to minimize the risk of disclosure of lawyer insights and advice. A chronology, for example, can be very helpful to a witness; if it is simple and based on well-known facts, its production would be no great loss—even if it was drafted by a lawyer. Another technique, if truly privileged documents are used for preparation, is redaction. If you have written a letter to your client summarizing events and offering a candid assessment of the case's strengths and weaknesses, delete the assessment before using the document in preparation.

Showing important, nonprivileged documents to a witness, on the other hand, is a preparation technique that cannot be eliminated. The element of selection is, of course, inevitable and reflects core work product; if production is ordered under Rule 612, the work product will be revealed. There are, however, ways to reduce the chance that production will be required, or to blunt the effect if it is. The best way to convince a court not to order production under Rule 612(2) is to be sure that everything used in preparation has already been produced or made available in discovery. If you are not hiding anything behind a privilege, fairness concerns like those articulated in *Berkey* evaporate. The court is likely to conclude that the "interests of justice" favor protection of your strategy over the production of documents that have already been produced.

To support this claim, you might take care to ensure that your witness's testimony reflects certain characteristics of the documents. Most lawyers number stamp the documents they produce. If you prepare a witness with documents already given to the other side, point out those numbers. When the preparation questions come up in a deposition, the witness will be ready to say, "I looked at a lot of documents, and I remember they all had numbers stamped in the lower right-hand corner." Such testimony will help make your record for the judge.

Remember also that refreshment of recollection is a predicate to Rule 612's production obligation. The truth is that documents are usually *not* shown to a witness to remind him of forgotten past events, but to clarify timing or to talk about particular phrasing in the document. It may be just to re-familiarize the witness with particular pieces of paper, or to advise him on answering questions on documents in general. A lawyer preparing a witness, therefore, might consider asking the witness whether she remembers events a document covers before revealing the document. If she does, give her the document; it arguably will have refreshed nothing. If she does not remember, reconsider whether you need to discuss the document at all; you have no obligation to bring back lost memories before a deposition. (In some cases, of course, you may want to do so, and in those circumstances fairness may require that your opponent be able to explore the refreshment process.)

There are also ways to avoid disclosing your thinking if preparation documents must be produced. One is to give the witness many documents. Some you can rush by in preparation. Some you can emphasize. If you must produce the whole lot, it won't reveal much about which ones you think are important. A court almost certainly will not require you to reveal what you *said* while reviewing documents in the preparation session. The real danger in this tactic, though, is that you may confuse your own witness.

What do you do if you are the questioning lawyer? How can you do unto others what has been done to you? How do you create a record that will help to persuade a court that you as questioner are entitled to preparation documents? The job is easy to describe, but difficult to perform in practice.

As a first step, a questioner must make some effort at the deposition—it need not be time-consuming—to determine what sort of witness preparation occurred and what kinds of documents were used. Then she should attempt to establish three things on the record. First, she should lay the basic foundation for Rule 612: loss of memory, actual reliance on the writing to refresh that memory, actual refreshment of the witness's memory, and the witness's use of the material for the purpose of testifying. It is important to try to direct inquiries to specific documents, since *Sporck* and the more recent cases demand an individualized showing of waiver.

Second, the questioner should try to determine the precise identity of any important documents that the witness can recall. Ask who prepared them, why, and how they were used with the witness. The witness's counsel may supply some of this information in making the claim of privilege—he may say, for instance, that some of the documents were work product, or that the selection of documents in itself is privileged. If the nature of the claimed privilege and its supposed basis can be determined, a questioner will be in a much better position to argue that the privilege does not exist or was waived, or to determine whether the privileged portions are separable.

Unfortunately, the reality of what happens in deposition can complicate such efforts. Anyone who has actually gotten into a dispute like this knows that very few foundation-laying questions about individual documents will be voluntarily answered in a deposition. *Sporck* and other cases may suggest that document-specific questions are the order of the day, but defending lawyers are likely to instruct their witnesses not to answer. If a privilege arguably prevents disclosure of the documents used, they will argue, how can it be proper for a questioner to ask about the details of those documents? And they will argue even more vigorously that the way the documents were used and how the preparation session was conducted are also privileged. In short, a lawyer can ask these questions, but she may need judicial assistance to get them answered.

Even if foundational questions are not objected to, never underestimate the ability of a fuzzy memory to act as a roadblock. A witness may admit he saw documents. He may concede that they revived his memory. But when asked who prepared the document, or which particular pieces of paper helped him remember, his likely response will probably be the most common phrase in all depositions: "I don't know."

A questioner's best strategy to avoid early instructions not to answer and convenient memory loss is to proceed by indirection. Do not reveal why you are asking foundational questions before you absolutely must. You might, for example, establish the general preparation process as part of introductory, non-substantive questioning. Then drop the subject and return to it in the course of a specific discussion of a specific point. Under these circumstances, the witness may answer the necessary questions before their significance is apparent. Or he may have demonstrated sufficient knowledge to make a later "I don't know" incredible.

Finally, the questioner should be aware of "interests of justice" factors and explore them where possible. She must be able to argue that the documents have been used, not to refresh a memory, but to alter or embellish it. Documents shown to the witness may eliminate genuine doubts or ambiguities on issues of importance, but do so in a partisan direction. They may shade or slant the testimony by suggesting choice of words or by indicating the "right" answers to questions. Showing a witness only selected documents, or selected portions of documents, may have the same distorting effect. Finally, documents may educate a witness with information he never knew in the first place.

Memory and Suggestion

As to all these questions, a questioner can argue that she needs to be able (in Weinstein and Berger's words) to "separate memory from suggestion." But, as with most Rule 612 fights, the resolution will be neither simple nor predictable. Given the many factors Rule 612 calls into play—plus the uncertain impact of judicial discretion in determining the "interests of justice"—no strategy (other than avoiding *all* privileged materials) can assure a particular result. In fact, courts increasingly take matters into their own hands by ordering in camera inspection. *See, e.g., Butler Mfg. Co. v. Americold Corp.*, 148 F.R.D. 275, 278 (D. Kan. 1993); *Parry, supra*, 125 F.R.D. at 451. A lawyer preparing a witness simply cannot be certain of maintaining the confidentiality of documents used in preparation. Still, a clear understanding of the dangers and opportunities that Rule 612 presents will help litigators structure their preparation—and their questioning—as effectively as possible.

CHAPTER 16

Using and Utilizing Depositions

Christopher T. Lutz*

This article is about depositions—but first, a diatribe about word choice.

The word in question is "utilize." Those three syllables typify much of what is wrong with legal writing. "Utilize" is fancy-sounding junk. It is a term that attorneys say and stick in briefs even though a better, shorter alternative—the word "use"—is always at hand.

Something odd must happen in the brain when a writer chooses "This Honorable Court utilized a Restatement analysis" instead of "The court used the Restatement." Maybe some think "utilize" sounds academic or smart. Maybe the word makes them feel grown up—the way that wearing their parents' shoes did when they were three. The motivation may remain a mystery, but the rule is simple: Don't utilize "utilize." Use "use."

Actually, "utilize" has a meaning distinct from "use." Or, it *had* such meaning: Years ago, Fowler's *Modern English Usage* said the distinction had "disappeared beyond recall" (it also said that

*Christopher T. Lutz, a former Editor-In-Chief of LITIGATION, is a partner with Steptoe & Johnson, LLP in Washington, D.C. This article originally appeared in the Summer 1997 issue of LITIGATION.

"utilize" was "an example of the pretentious diction that prefers the long word"). Still, the difference is worth mentioning—if only because it provides a way to move from a linguistic pet peeve to the actual subject of this article.

What "utilize" means, according to Fowler, is this: "make good use of, especially something that was not intended for the purpose, but will serve." Thus, you use a shovel to dig a hole, but you can utilize a spoon to do the same thing, just as you can utilize copies of law reviews as door stops.

It is the same with depositions. The Rules say lawyers can use a deposition to conduct discovery. But how can you utilize a deposition? In other words, to what good purpose can you put a deposition other than the one for which it was designed? To make it simpler: What can you do with a deposition?

Answers to that question separate experienced litigators from the rest of the pack. Recent graduates would give an orthodox but limited answer. They would say depositions are meant to discover facts through sworn testimony. The same response might be expected from those who have practiced in the calmer counseling and advice side of the profession.

For those who have smelled the smoke of litigation, a satisfactory answer would be more elusive. Asked whether depositions are for discovery, they might answer "partly." Or "not always." Or "it depends." A simple answer would be hard, because depositions do not involve only discovery.

Of course, depositions *are* discovery devices. The Rules say so. Depositions are listed in Rule 30. They form the expensive, time-consuming spine of most lawsuits. They can be, and usually are, *used* to uncover facts. But depositions can be *utilized* for more than that.

This is not true of other discovery techniques: Serve a document request, and sometimes, after objections and phone calls and negotiations and motions, you get paper. Ask interrogatory questions, and the answers that struggle through objections are what might be expected from a prisoner of war: terse, elliptical, calculated to convey as little as necessary while seeming to say something. Serve requests for admissions and you learn that, even weeks before trial, your opponent professes not to know much about core elements of the case. All these approaches can reveal some facts, but not much more.

Depositions have other uses. It is important to understand why. A deposition is a face-to-face, back-and-forth, person-to-person encounter. At a deposition, even the most hostile session with the most taciturn witness, there is constant dialogue. Questions are asked and answered. Reactions are assessed, and mid-course corrections are made. This personal, eye-to-eye quality has no equivalent elsewhere in the discovery rules. It is what makes depositions so good for the discovery of facts. It is also what gives depositions so many other uses.

For present purposes, there is little reason to linger over the predominant purpose of depositions: the discovery of facts through testimony about the perceptions, opinions, and even speculations of a witness. There are scores of books and articles on the subject. Find and read them. Right now, simply remember two things: (1) A lawyer who takes a deposition without some conventional discovery in prospect is abusing the system. (2) A lawyer who takes a deposition only for discovery has a lot to learn.

One common nondiscovery function of depositions is *sizing up important witnesses*. This ought to be obvious. Many lawyers do it instinctively, but some forget, and others do it poorly.

In a deposition, a living, breathing human being sits in front of the questioner. Giving answers, reacting to all that is happening, she is on her own. Her lawyer may try to fashion a screen of predeposition preparation and intradeposition objections, but no one can really run interference for a deposition witness. Such personal immediacy provides a chance to evaluate a number of important points: how the witness will appear in court, whether she seems honest, and whether what she says seems consistent with what your client tells you.

These points will be taken in reverse order. First, the witness and your client. In taking a deposition, you will not only learn what the witness knows, you will also compare the witness's testimony and presence to what you have heard from your client.

Trust Your Instincts

Time and again, the first major deposition in a lawsuit is an education. Until then, lawyers on both sides have an abstracted, abridged version of the case. They know what their clients say, but that is often slanted—by rationalization, tunnel vision, delusion, ignorance, embarrassment, self-interest, or outright lying.

Lawyers also know what the other side says in writing, but that is so terse, edited, and partisan that most dismiss it out of hand. Even informal discovery and private investigators may not give a full picture: They only look at what they are ordered to examine, and, in the quiet of your conference room, your client always has an explanation for inconvenient facts that may turn up. Still, from such limited sources, and from reading documents (not just what they say, but their tone and style too), a lawyer develops an expectation about the upcoming witness.

Reality—in the form of a deposition—can be sobering. The supervisor you have been told is a tyrant may seem the mildest of souls. The accountant your client accuses of gross inattention may appear precise and methodical. The other side's story of contract negotiations, which your client has assured you is an invention, may be the witness's unshakable conviction.

In such situations, the deposition helps establish not just what the witnesses know, but who they are: Does their demeanor, approach, and apparent character fit the picture you had before questioning began? An aspect of this sizing-up process is considering how the witness will play in court. Is he pleasant and charming, or vain and shifty? Is she straightforward or evasive? Will the jury like him? Trust her? Sympathize with him?

Such judgments are critical. Unfortunately, no one can write a manual on how to make them. A deposition questioner must trust her instincts based on her talent and honed by experience. Some people are simply better at such evaluations than others. Most get better the more they do it. Rules on how to make such judgments would be claptrap. There are, however, useful points to keep in mind about witness appraisal.

Remember that a deposition room is not a courtroom. It is more casual and less imposing. A trial is more formal and public than three hours of inquiry in the firm conference room. No one referees a deposition. Fewer sets of eyes peer at the witness. While deposition testimony counts, it usually does not matter as much as actual trial testimony. These differences exist even where the lawyers are aggressive and nasty.

As a consequence, many witnesses are worse, or at least different, in court than in a deposition. There are exceptions, of course: If the witness you are questioning has never before testified and is the central figure in a high-pressure lawsuit—the allegedly offending manager in a sex harassment case, for example—the

234

deposition may well be one of the most frightening events of his life. If he gets past it with his self-possession and story intact, his trial performance may be better.

When evaluating a witness during a deposition, remember that you would not be a typical juror. What you find impressive or implausible a juror might not. What is self-assured and confident to big-firm lawyers may seem cocky and condescending to a juror whose usual lunch is beef jerky and a Big Gulp. What seems precise and careful to you may look prissy and picky to him. Remember, your jury will prefer salted snack foods to white wine.

There are two ways to fight this handicap. One is talent: Some attorneys are just plain good at sizing up witnesses in depositions. The other aid is to have another set of eyes and ears at the deposition. This conflicts with much that is now faddish in case management. Clients and bill auditors abhor having two people participate where one can just barely manage to do the job. If you want assurance in judging a witness, especially if the witness is important, fight this tendency. Bring along a new lawyer, one not too badly bent by years of dispiriting practice. Have a paralegal help you at the deposition. Then listen to what they say about the witness after the session is over.

Finally, remember that the witness may be trying to trick you. Just as his lawyer told him to keep his answers terse, he may also have advised a neutral, controlled demeanor. The dull, plodding witness across the table may turn into an eloquent, charming champion of his own cause when the curtain goes up, the lights go on, and court is in session. This is hard to do well; usually, deceptive self-control at a deposition will crack or the courtroom histrionics will come across as forced and shrill. But it happens: All you can do is to be aware of this possibility and compare the witness's deposition demeanor with his reputation, his apparent role in the case, and what the documents say.

Depositions also help in *sizing up the other lawyers*. In small towns, the trial lawyers know one another. They understand who can try a lawsuit and who cannot. They can anticipate their opponent's tactics and personality. To a lesser extent, this is true of courthouse regulars in big cities. For many, however, looking at the name on the precipe or the complaint is a step into uncertainty: Who is this person? What does she know about libel law? Is he a screamer? Can he be intimidated? Where did she go to law school? Will every request for an extension be a battle?

The basic resources for answering these questions are Martindale-Hubbell and other lawyers in the office. The first is accurate, but limited; Martindale usually only gives age and whether your adversary graduated from a fancier school than you did. The second source—the law firm or e-mail grapevine—sometimes helps; more often, it is a dry hole, or a thicket of outmoded, opinionated, third-hand speculations, guesses, and rumors. From both sources, you rarely learn much.

Inflicting Pain on the Witness

Things change with the first deposition. Then you learn whether the suit will be civil or obnoxious. From the lawyer's responses to questions, you may learn whether the months ahead will be filled with picky, pointless bickering. And you can tell how well your opponent understands her case: Does she become attentive when key events are the subject of questioning? Can she keep up with the kind of banter that characterizes deposition breaks? Can she converse in the citation and concept shorthand used by lawyers who know an area of the law?

Besides the stories that casual conversation tells, there is another way to appraise your opponent's quality. Does he focus on the essentials or waste time on trivia? Good, experienced lawyers know what is necessary and what is not. They know that a position can be preserved by just stating it and that a two-minute speech is unnecessary. They know that technical objections likely forgotten in a month are better off not uttered in the first place. It is the difference between being a lawyer and playing lawyer. In depositions, you see that distinction first.

A small word of warning: Lawyers, like witnesses, sometimes play dumb or affect silence. They may act a little slow, ask for questions to be repeated, seem to have trouble following what you are saying. They want to throw you off. More commonly, the other side's lawyer may say nothing. One of the best plaintiff's employment lawyers I know does almost nothing when his client testifies other than inscribing intricate doodles on the back of a legal pad.

Are there ways to see through such subterfuge? Yes and no. Lawyers playing possum rarely say harmfully dumb things. They may act confused. They may be wrong when it doesn't matter. But they rarely make unnecessary concessions or damaging admissions. In addition, good lawyers, whether they are being coy or not, will come to the aid of their clients if the questioning becomes unfair or objectionable. Still, some lawyers are skillful actors; they may prepare witnesses so well that rescue efforts are not needed. Most of the time, fake and genuine ignorance can be separated—but not always.

Depositions are not merely ways to study your opponent. They can also provide *a way to show the other side a thing or two.*

For example, depositions of parties and key witnesses can be a good time to show that litigation is not a tea party. For some misguided lawyers, this is the only reason for a deposition. They think that berating a witness is always appropriate. These ranters and screamers are wrong, but uncomfortable deposition questions can be valuable and proper. To be blunt, sometimes lawyers can properly inflict pain on the road to discovery of facts. They want to impress the witness that litigation is hard, full of searching questions and people with sharp elbows.

It is important to be careful here. We now live with litigation reform and civility codes. Nasty, abusive lawyering is out of favor, and always should have been. But in some quarters, merely aggressive, or even merely thorough, advocacy is disdained. The notion is not just that we must be civil, but that we should be kind, pleasant, and nice.

The truth is that some unpleasantness is inherent in litigation. A lawsuit is, after all, a disagreement that could not be resolved more sensibly. And it is a serious enough disagreement that one side decided to spend time and money pursuing it. Conflict, division, and unhappiness are inescapable. It is not necessarily wrong to make a deposition witness confront the jagged, painful edges of a lawsuit. If the questions have a legitimate purpose, if the questioner stays within bounds of decency and propriety, then tough, hard interrogation is fine, even if the witness is uncomfortable and feels oppressed—*and* even if the questioner wants just that reaction.

Remember also that legitimate, hard questions are challenging not because of the volume, tone of voice, or flamboyant verbiage they involve. They are hard because, in substance, they hit weak or embarrassing points. Thoroughness, persistence, making the witness confront inconsistencies, or making him admit that a claim has no support is what can make a deposition uncomfortable. Tone, pace, and phrasing can enhance the effect, but without actual substantive challenge, such things are just yapping.

As with most advice, there is a contrary view. Some adept lawyers do not want to let the witness hear hard questioning in discovery. They want the deposition to be as dull as possible, boringly securing admissions and locking in positions. Such lawyers do not want the witness to have any hint of the onslaught he will face in court. The deposition is the sheep suit from which the wolf will emerge.

Neither approach is always right. What you do depends on many factors: Is the witness important? Is the case really going to go to trial? Are you that good a cross-examiner in court? Think about your case and decide.

Sometimes a deposition is not taken to uncover unknown facts, but *to reveal facts to the other side*. This is an inversion of the normal role of depositions. The most common way to do this is to ask the witness questions that start "Did you know that _____?" or "Were you aware that _____?" Such inquiries inevitably trigger a cloud of objections. In fact, almost any question that can provoke that most senseless of deposition objections—"assumes a fact not in evidence" (as if any fact is "in evidence" during discovery)—can serve this purpose. Thus, in a products liability case, a question like "Why didn't the company make changes after receiving the Research Department report on design flaws?" indicates that the questioner knows something the witness would prefer he not know.

Usually, besides objections, questions like this will lead to answers like "No," "I didn't know," or "Nonsense." No matter. The point is not to get answers. It is to show off what you know.

Why would any self-respecting lawyer use a deposition this way? The orthodoxy is to hold high cards close to the vest. Only ask and never tell unless necessary or until trial. Sometimes, however, showing off can help end the case—usually by promoting settlement.

You may want to show you know the key facts the other side hoped to suppress. You may want to acquaint a senior decision-maker witness with realities you think his counsel is not telling him. In a way, the deposition becomes like a minitrial. The idea is that you can use questions to break through the smokescreen of cheerleading and wishful thinking that the other side's attorneys have laid down. This might be done with questions such as:

Did you know, Mr. Big, that your company's entire engineering team advised against changing the design of the steering gear that broke in Mr. Torted's car?

Were you aware, Mr. Gutman, that we have a tape recording of your chief purchasing manager agreeing with another company on carpet prices?

Ms. Tycoon, what did you know about your personnel director's statement that he wanted to "dump the old guys" from the sales force?

Are you familiar, Mr. Midas, with the study by our expert that shows your company may owe the class $90 million?

Doing this can have a number of benefits: It may, as you hope, stun the witness into asking his lawyers (after the deposition is over) "What the hell is going on in this case?" If the witness provides substantive answers (a rare occurrence with questions like these), you will know the other side's response to your good points. However, if the witness claims ignorance, or objections get in the way, you will have a record of the most senior person in the company repeatedly ignorant of key facts (a very useful thing if all the lapses are spliced together on videotape).

There are two other somewhat less provocative reasons to use a deposition to show what you know.

The first is to preserve or lock in facts you already know. The point is almost self-evident. Through prior discovery—earlier depositions or the review of documents—many facts will become clear. In fact, in most cases, most facts are clear and indisputable. Near the end of discovery, when you take the depositions of key witnesses—the people likely to testify at trial—you want them tied to the facts you now know are true, and know they cannot deny. For this part of such depositions, leading questions are the order of the day.

The last way to show off what you know in a deposition comes when you do dry runs of trial questions. Every lawyer dreams of having an advance picture of how key witnesses might respond to various questioning strategies. That can be achieved to some degree in a deposition, but care is essential. Too much of a preview will simply tip the witness off to your thinking. To avoid that, perhaps you can test some of the style of your trial questions, but not their substance. The reason for that approach lies in the differences between trial and deposition questioning.

Trial interrogation usually is faster-paced and more aggressive. The idea is to push, nudge, pressure, and confront the witness with facts that help you and hurt him. Lines of questioning in court are usually more focused and prepared than deposition inquiry. Of course, a lawyer must respond in court, on the spur of the moment, to what the witness says, but trial examination is not the open-ended exercise common in a deposition. Instead, questions in court often include carefully constructed and concealed snares. They seek to wrap the witness in an ever-tighter-fitting blanket. First, he agrees to obvious facts. Then, he is asked to accept what appear to be the logical consequences of those initial concessions, and then there is another round, and another, and another. By the end of the drainpipe, the witness has no choice, you hope, but to come out where you want him. It requires skill, care, and preparation.

It also requires surprise. If the witness has a detailed idea of what you will ask, he can spike the snares and refuse to enter the drainpipe. For this reason, the orthodox view on deposition questions is that they should never give away what will be done at trial.

For the *substance* of trial questions, that advice is often sound. But sometimes the pace and tenor of trial questions can be tested in a deposition. Try leading questions, and see whether the witness starts agreeing or fights. Sound a bit hostile, and see if the hostility is returned. Make accusations. Flatter the witness. Learn whether he responds to changes in expression or tone of voice. None of this should be overdone, nor should it dominate the deposition. Simply scatter a few inquiries with a different tone and you will have a better idea of what you may face when it really counts.

Sometimes, a deposition is more than a preview of trial testimony. Sometimes, it *is* trial testimony. This happens in two situations. The first is where a witness lives outside the jurisdiction, is not subject to the trial subpoena power of the court, and will not travel to attend the trial. (This is often referred to as a "trial" or "*de bene esse*" deposition.) The second involves deposition witnesses who you think will show up, but later do not. They may have died, gotten ill, or moved away.

In the first case, you must approach a *de bene esse* deposition differently than you would an exercise in pure discovery. If what the witness knows is important to your affirmative case, you must be certain that your questions are clear and coherent. If read back later, they must make sense. No false starts and no jumping around. If what the witness may say could hurt, be aware that the deposition is your cross-examination. If you do not undercut the testimony, you may find yourself faced at trial with someone who only provides direct testimony. Or, to put it another way, you will have waived cross.

Besides less discursive questioning, the *de bene esse* deposition will involve atmospheric differences. The witness's lawyer will be more attentive and will object more frequently. Calls to the judge to resolve differences over questions—something that should be avoided like typhoid in an ordinary discovery deposition—become more common.

Taking a deposition for use at trial is difficult. Even though the judge can be called, it is harder to control the witness and her lawyer. The setting—conference room and not courtroom—is less intimidating for the witness. And sometimes, such depositions must be taken before discovery is complete. All the facts may not be out on the table, which means that your basis for formulating coherent, trial-like questions may be uncertain.

Unfortunately, the problem is bigger than that. Many times, witnesses who say they will show up at trial do not; people die, move out of the jurisdiction, or evade service. This means that *the possibility of a deposition being trial testimony is always there.* What looked like just another discovery exercise can become more than that. The conflict is inescapable: To discover facts you do not yet know, a casual, informal, disjointed questioning style, one festooned with objectionable questions, may be best. But information learned that way may be awkward or unsatisfactory to read into evidence if the witness flees to Peru.

So what is the answer? There isn't one—at least not one that offers a clear plan of action and works in all cases. All you usually can do is simply remember that the problem may crop up. There is not an easy answer for everything in litigation. If you went to law school because you hoped to make a good living,

241

you should have considered that no one pays big bucks for an easy job.

One of the duller things to do with a deposition is to *create a foundation for the authentication and admission of documents*. This simple, often boring job is important. The goal is to ensure that there are no surprises when a document is offered into evidence in court. More commonly these days, deposition testimony is used as a basis for a pretrial stipulation that streamlines the trial uses of documents. How do you do this? There are two subjects to consider: authenticity and the hearsay rules.

Establishing that a document is authentic can be an odd process. What does "authentic" mean? Federal Rule of Evidence 901 says that something is authentic if it "is what it is claimed to be" by the party seeking to use it. Put another, less precise, way, a document is authentic if it is not a fake. It is not a forgery, and the photocopy is accurate.

How is this established in deposition? Giving a witness a piece of paper and asking "Is this what it purports to be?" is likely to produce a blank stare. In theory, the way to do it is easy. The witness is shown a document. When asked if he has seen it and knows what it is, he says something like "Yes, I got this letter in May 1976; this is an exact Xerox copy of it."

In real life, that rarely happens. Witnesses often do not have a clear memory of documents. They will not deny receiving a memorandum, but have no recollection of reading it either. Few will have an opinion on the accuracy of the copy. The usual exchange goes like this:

Q: Mr. Witness, I show you a document dated "5/12/81." It is stamped with production number 243. It says "Memorandum" at the top and, just below, says "To: John Q. Witness." Can you tell me what this is?

A: It seems to be a memo dated May 12, 1981.

Q: Whom is it directed to?

A: Me.

Q: Did you receive this document?

A: I don't remember it. I don't deny that I got it, but I just don't remember.

Q: Did you read it when you got it?

A: I said I don't remember anything about it. It's been over twenty years.

Q: Do you have reason to think you didn't get it?

A: No.

Q: Do you think you got it?

A: I don't know. I assume so. [It is astonishing how many witnesses, even those told not to guess or speculate, will say this when shown a document addressed to them.]

Q: In the normal course of business at your company in 1981, did you receive documents addressed to you?

A: I suppose so.

Q: Do you have any reason to think the copy has been changed [and/or the memo has been altered]?

A: No.

This can go on and on. Such answers do not quite establish what the Rule 901 requires, but many witnesses will not give you want you want on that score. Usually, such an exchange is enough to force the other side into an authenticity stipulation.

Remember also the hearsay rule and its many exceptions. Other than contracts and wills, most documents will be hearsay when you offer them at trial—at least, if you are trying to get them in for the substance of what they say. For each such document, consider what exception or nonhearsay definition might apply. Ask questions guided by the details of the rules of evidence or evidence law. This will usually involve establishing the circumstances of a document's creation: Is it a business record? Present recollection recorded? An admission of a party opponent?

A deposition also can show what someone does *not* know. This stands usual deposition practice on its head. The basic concept of a deposition is that it is a series of questions about what a witness knows. The questioner comes to the session with a general idea of the subject's role in the case—his job title or where he was standing when the bus careened through the intersection. Document review may provide other hints and theories about what the witness knows. Often, deposition questions are meant to test these general theories and to determine if the witness has unanticipated beliefs and perceptions.

Sometimes, however, a deposition has almost an opposite purpose: to establish what the witness does not or cannot know. What I am taking about is not the usual, almost accidental, determination of absent knowledge. In other words, this use of a deposition does not involve open-ended questions genuinely

243

designed to discover facts that just happen to be answered (as are so many): "I don't know."

Instead, this effort to establish that the witness does not know something is intentional and focused from the start. The questioner begins the deposition with the firm belief that the witness knows nothing about various categories of facts and tries to establish that ignorance conclusively.

Know Your Case

Knowing how to do this requires an understanding of the purpose of the exercise. This use of depositions is really another aspect of trial testimony. Rather than fishing for facts, this application of deposition questioning is designed to limit the witness's usefulness in court. The inquiry is meant to define chunks of the case as to which the witness will be a cipher at trial.

To do this, a lawyer needs to know her case. She needs to have a clear idea who the other side's witnesses are, what they may say, and what they are likely to know. This generally means that witness nullification depositions occur late in the discovery period.

Here is the kind of situation where depositions can be used to establish lack of knowledge. A chemical company must defend the way it disposed of wastes at the testing laboratory of a former plant. There have been two lab directors. From 1962 to 1977, the director was a gruff, overweight, somewhat embittered man who opposed environmental regulation as a matter of principle. From 1977 to 1982 (when the plant closed) the director was a poised, articulate, charming woman with a degree in environmental engineering who has, since plant closure, opened her own pollution-testing business and even does work for the regulators.

The company wants to use the second lab director as its trial witness on disposal practices. She will talk engagingly about what she did at the lab, and the company will try to steer her around hearsay problems by having her testify about her training, which will be characterized as an explanation of how "the plant has always done things." They will also use her to authenticate old lab documents (she's the records custodian) that are self-serving compliments to the cleanliness of the lab (the "ancient document" exception to the hearsay rule will let most of this stuff in; maybe it's my age, but does a memo authored in 1983 seem "ancient" to you? When I learned about this exception in law school, I thought about moldy paper and crumbling parchment, not a memo from the Reagan administration).

Building a Deposition Record

The second lab director's charm offensive testimony could be a big problem for you. One way to dent it is to build a deposition record full of admissions that she knows nothing about the company before 1976. For example:

Q: You were hired in 1977?
A: Yes.
Q: You had no dealings with Sludgco before then, correct?
A: Right.
Q: You can't tell us from your own observation what was happening in the lab before 1977, can you?
A: No. Only what I read in the records.
Q: But others wrote those, correct?
A: Yes.
Q: The lab operated for 20 years, true?
A: Yes.
Q: You only worked there five years, isn't that right?
A: True.
Q: So you don't know anything about laboratory waste disposal for 75 percent of the history of the lab, do you?
A: No, I don't.
Q: So if I told you the lab injected cyanide into the groundwater in 1967, you wouldn't have a firsthand basis to disagree, would you?
A: No, but it would surprise me very much.
Q: But you don't know, do you?
A: No.
Q: In 1967, you were a senior in high school in Akron, Ohio, isn't that right?
A: Yes.
Q: Thousands of miles and a decade away from the Sludgco plant, true?
A: Yes.

Such questions can go on for quite some time, making the point more and more decisively. Finally, the witness's lawyer may sputter out an "asked and answered" or a "harassing the witness" objection, and the fun will eventually end.

Note that leading questions work well when you are trying to tie down a lack of knowledge. Note also that this is one area where tipping off trial questions is not much of a risk. If the witness truly lacks knowledge, advance warning and clever witness preparation cannot create something that is not there.

A lawyer showing what a witness does not know in a deposition should leave no room for doubt or change. You wouldn't want the lab director to say, at trial, "You know, Mr. Lutz, I've been thinking hard since my deposition, and it occurred to me that my high school science club took a field trip to the Sludgco plant." Once a witness has said "I don't know," consider the following questions, even though they may seem somewhat theatrical:

Are you sure? Think hard.

Do you have even a faint memory of anything covered by my question?

Why don't we take a five-minute break so you can think more about your answer.

If you think of something later in this deposition, please let me know.

Slightly more risky, but usually worth asking, are:

Is there anything that you could do or look at that would help you remember more?

Do you have any notes [diaries, calendars, memos, etc.] that would be helpful to review?

Setting Outer Limits

Establishing that the witness's mind holds absolutely nothing on a subject is not the only purpose of such tactics. You can also show that a witness has just so much knowledge—and no more. This is important for putting an outer limit on parts of a case. You want to know the number of claims in a case, how many reasons the witness cites for her actions, and how many times particular conduct occurred. You also want to establish that there is nothing more. The technique is simple. Get all the claims, reasons, events, observations, and the like on the record. Then say "Is that all?" and "Are you positive?" Then nail the end point down with the kinds of questions described earlier.

Depositions can do many other things—some appropriate and some less so—but I am running out of space and enthusiasm for the subject. A brief listing will suffice.

A deposition can set up (or help fend off) a summary judgment motion. This usually comes late in a party's discovery. The lawyers have a good sense of the facts, and they know the legal standards for the arguments they want to put in a dispositive motion. The deposition becomes an effort to confirm what you believe to be true and—this is the important part—to do it so that the witness's testimony matches the way in which legal standards are phrased. The trick is to insinuate the needed word formulas without being too obvious.

From summary judgment–related questioning, we descend to more dubious deposition uses. One is to mislead, or at least confuse, the other side. This was mentioned earlier. Lawyers always want to know what their opponents are thinking, what they will argue, and what they know. If a lawyer is *very* clever, she can seem ill-informed in a deposition. She can appear to emphasize subjects that eventually will not be prominent. She can salt in questions about unimportant people, places, or events simply to get the other side thinking.

All I can say about deposition disinformation is: Be careful. Do not do it often. Unless you are adroit, the effort may be ineffective or comical. Worse yet, the dramatic flourishes required can so preoccupy the questioner that something genuinely important is lost.

A further descent into the deposition depths leads to the use of a deposition to impress a client. Every lawyer has had a client who, at the start, wants to inflict pain: Serve the papers on Christmas Eve! Ask for a TRO just before a holiday weekend. Schedule a deposition on the witness's birthday.

Some lawyers want a fee more than they want independence or self-respect. Some sell themselves as pain inflictors. In addition, some lawyers see a deposition as a way of showing their client, usually a new client (whom they drag along), how tough or impassioned they can be. They are hostile. They ask aggressive, accusatory questions. They give speeches. Usually such posturing is pointless—or worse. It gets in the way of legitimate discovery. It embitters more than it intimidates the other side. If you are inclined to show off in a deposition, try to do so simply by being professional and effective and not by putting on a show. Remember also that histrionics and deposition carpet bombing are inefficient and expensive. Many an aggressive client loses his combativeness when the first month's bill arrives.

Only to Harass

Finally, the lowest circle of deposition Hell: Depositions as pure engines of harassment.

Taking a deposition only to harass the other side is wrong. It cannot be justified. Yet it happens. Witnesses are browbeaten. One day of questions lasts two weeks, though the growing presence of presumptive time limits in the rules has put a damper on that. Sessions are scheduled on Fridays and questioning is extended late into the evening. A small problem with this subject is that "harassment" can be a matter of degree and perspective. An objective observer might see only good tough questioning in what the witness believes is oppressive. An embarrassing, difficult question, if relevant, is not harassment.

Still, some depositions are meant to do nothing but irritate and confound. That is not proper. Depositions should not be used that way. In fact, they should not even be utilized that way.

CHAPTER 17

Deposition Essentials: New Basics for Old Masters

Diana S. Donaldson*

It has been a few years. As a senior partner, you meet with clients, oversee settlement talks, and try a few major trials. You have taken hundreds—maybe even thousands—of depositions in your career, but none since your youngest, now a college senior, was starting school. After a long hiatus, you are slated to take one in your latest big case.

How hard could it be? Taking depositions is like riding a bike—once learned, never forgotten. But the rules of the road change.

Deposition practice today differs dramatically from what it was 20 years ago—even five or 10 years ago, for that matter. Lawyers—rookies and veterans alike—need to learn some new basics.

---

*Diana S. Donaldson is with the Philadelphia, Pennsylvania, office of Schnader Harrison Segal & Lewis LLP. This article originally appeared in the Summer 2000 issue of LITIGATION.

The changes result from judicial decisions, amendments to the Federal Rules of Civil Procedure (and some states' rules), and widespread criticism of certain deposition tactics under the old regime. The wisdom of at least a few of these changes remains in dispute, but there is no question that they have had a real impact on how lawyers conduct themselves at depositions.

The trouble starts before you even begin. The deponent walks in with his boss, who is next week's witness. The boss wants to sit in. You remember that when you last did this under Rule 30(c) of the Federal Rules of Civil Procedure, the Federal Rules of Evidence governed depositions. Extraneous witnesses who wanted to attend depositions could then be sequestered under Federal Rule of Evidence 615. Corporate representatives had to be so designated in advance. You ask the boss to leave.

The callow youth who is your opponent (about the same age as your middle child) stops fiddling with his laptop and flashes the revised Federal Rules of Civil Procedure. Federal Rule of Evidence 615 no longer applies. In fact, revised Rule 30(c) expressly exempts depositions from the operation of two Federal Rules of Evidence: Rule 103 (Rulings on Evidence) and Rule 615 (Exclusion of Witnesses). The 1993 Comments to Rule 30 advise the interrogator to anticipate any problems concerning sequestration and apply to the court in advance for a protective order excluding the attendance of other witnesses under Rule 26(c)(5). The Comments also suggest that while you are at it, you might consider expanding your request so that future witnesses are prohibited from reading the transcript or being informed about the testimony.

The new rules require lawyers to anticipate the possible presence of unannounced spectators at depositions. Little can be done after you walk into the conference room on the day of the deposition and find someone you did not expect to be there. Of course, the questioning lawyer can still seek sequestration by pressing the issue with the adversary in discussions, threatening to adjourn the deposition, and, if necessary, getting a ruling from the court. But that approach may have minuses as well as pluses.

Whatever position you take, make sure you consider and discuss with your opponent the consequences for future depositions. If you successfully insist on exclusion of the witness—whether by negotiating with the adversary or obtaining a ruling from a judge or magistrate—you will likely have to live with the same rule when your opponent takes a deposition.

Local court rules may also affect your analysis. For example, in the Eastern District of New York, a local rule permits any party to attend a deposition and provides that a witness or "potential witness" may attend a deposition unless the court orders otherwise.

Faced with the incontrovertible language of the rule, you reluctantly agree not to fight about who will be in the room. But the trouble continues. Not wanting to hassle with court orders, you have arranged simply for a stenographer, not a videographer, to record the deposition. Counsel for one of your client's co-defendants also served a deposition notice for this witness and mentioned videotaping in her notice, but she never sought a court order. You therefore expect that the deposition will not be videotaped.

Wrong again. Videotaping has come of age. The interrogator may now choose videotaping without seeking permission; the deposition notice merely has to state "the method by which the testimony shall be recorded." Rule 30(b)(2). Any other party may designate videotaping if the interrogator does not. Rule 30(b)(3). (Not all state rules are equivalent.) Videotaping by ambush is still prohibited. The deposition notice or designation by another party must actually give notice of the intent to videotape. But that is all that is required. (You would have worn a different suit had you known.)

With the attendees in place, you are ready to proclaim the rules that will govern the deposition. In the days before you had a PC on your desk, you used to sit down and announce the three magic words that would control: "the usual stipulations." But what are the usual stipulations for your latte-sipping opponent?

The rules governing the usual stipulations have not changed a great deal in recent years. Yet the area remains a surprisingly tricky part of taking and defending depositions.

Do the usual stipulations mean that the defending lawyer never has to object—that all objections are preserved for trial? Can the witness consult with the defending lawyer at any time? Do the stipulations waive the deponent's right to correct the transcript?

Counsel often agree on the usual stipulations at the start of the deposition without stating them on the record and without knowing exactly what they are. That is dangerous. If you do not specify them on the record, court reporters sometimes put their own version of the stipulations at the beginning of the transcript. The list may include stipulations to which you never meant to agree (for example, the stipulations may call for signing in front of a notary, when you intended to waive all requirements for signing). Learn what the usual stipulations are in the locale where you are conducting the deposition. If you agree to stipulations, list them for the record or ask the reporter what he will list at the start of the transcript.

Absent specific agreement otherwise, the usual stipulations often provide that certification, sealing, and filing are waived and all objections, except as to the form of the question, are reserved until the time of trial. Sometimes, the usual stipulations also provide for waiver of the signing of the transcript by the witness.

Many lawyers will agree to most of the usual stipulations but still reserve the witness's right to read and sign, to ensure that the deponent can review the transcript and make corrections. That is a good idea, even if you should later decide that you do not want to give an extra imprimatur to the deposition by having the witness sign it. If it makes strategic sense, the witness can simply let the opportunity lapse later on. Note that the deponent or party must request he opportunity to sign before the completion of the deposition under Rule 30(e).

"Certification, sealing, and filing" waives the rather outmoded procedure that Rule 30(f)(1) requires of the reporter: certifying that the witness was duly sworn and that the deposition is a true record of the testimony, placing the transcript in an envelope labeled with the name of the deponent, and filling it with the court. Although the last two requirements are generally eliminated by local rule, you may want to consider declining to waive the certification requirement. If a witness attempts to deviate from his deposition testimony at trial, the formality of a certification enhances the transcript in the eyes of the jury.

Reserving objections except as to form is the trickiest part of the usual stipulations. Some lawyers believe that this stipulation merely conforms to what is already in the Federal Rules (or analogous state rules). They are wrong. Rule 32(d) provides that objections "to the competency, relevancy, or materiality of testimony are not waived by failure to make them before or during the taking of the deposition, *unless the ground of the objection is one which might have been obviated or removed if presented at that time."* Rule 32(d)(3)(A) (emphasis added). That exclusion is not the same as an objection to form.

The best example is a foundation objection. An objection based on foundation is an objection to the competency of testimony. It is also an objection that might be "obviated or removed" if made at the time of the deposition. But it is not an objection as to form. Unless you stipulate that such an objection is reserved until the time of trial, you will waive it if you do not raise it.

Suppose you question the witness about a handwritten document that is very helpful to your case. You ask the witness if he can identify the handwriting. The witness says that he can and proceeds to identify the writer. You do not establish foundation—that is, how the witness knows whose writing it is. Believing that only objections to the form of questions must be made at the deposition, your opponent does not object based on lack of foundation.

Fast forward to trial: You move to introduce the document into evidence based on the deposition testimony. Your arrogant opponent smugly objects on the ground of authentication or identification under Fed. R. Evid. 901, claiming that the handwriting has not been identified. But you triumphantly brandish the deposition transcript in which the witness identified the writer. Your opponent, brandishing the same transcript, counters that the identification testimony lacked foundation. There is not a shred of evidence to show the basis of the witness's knowledge of the source of the handwriting. He is sure he has vanquished the master.

You now play the trump card: At the deposition, your opponent—showing his inexperience—failed to object based on the lack of foundation. If the deposition was taken under Rule 32(d), the foundation objection had to be made at the time of the deposition because it was a ground that might have been "obviated or removed" if presented at the time of the deposition. By not making it, he waived it. The judge overrules the objection. Only if the deposition was taken under the usual stipulations—providing that the only objections the defender had to make at the time of the deposition were those on the basis of "form"—should the judge sustain the objection.

An objection based on lack of foundation can frequently play an important role at depositions. The interrogator may question a witness, for example, about the components of a product or the details of an event and never ask whether the witness has firsthand knowledge. In defending a deposition under the usual stipulations, requiring only objections as to form, you can let the interrogator sloppily pursue that line of questioning without prompting him to find out how the witness obtained the information at issue. Under Rule 32(d), on the other hand, you might be compelled to object based on lack of foundation or risk waiving the objection. Forcing the interrogator to ask the witness the basis of her knowledge may reveal that the witness learned the information only from talking with another employee. The interrogator will then be tipped off to take the deposition of someone else, someone with firsthand knowledge. Your adversary will be better prepared for trial and will be alerted that he cannot safely rely on the admissibility of the first deponent's testimony.

Leave nothing to chance. Agree in advance about which objections will be waived if not raised and which will be preserved. And always follow the litigator's first rule: When in doubt, object.

The defender is often more inclined to enter into the usual stipulations regarding objections. That way, there is less risk that objections will be waived, and less information will be revealed to the other side. The interrogator faces a judgment call. The usual stipulations make her job riskier in the long run. The defender is under no obligation to object based on the lack of foundation, thus calling the issue to the questioner's attention. The failure to elicit foundation testimony could prove irremediable at trial. But agreeing to the usual stipulations may cut down on the number of objections during the deposition, allowing for a freer exchange with the witness.

For the experienced lawyer in the role of interrogator, the best advice is usually to refrain from entering into the usual stipulations regarding objections. That way, you know where you stand. You will then have a chance to cure objectionable questions and to ferret out problems with the testimony and the witness.

Shortly into the deposition, your opponent appears to be implementing a time-honored tactic: trying to make you hurry. The deponent has to catch a plane early in the afternoon. Your opponent keeps interrupting the deposition to make telephone calls but nonetheless presses you to finish the deposition that day.

As a veteran, you refuse to be stampeded. You calmly note the interruptions and threaten unilaterally to schedule another day of depositions.

Not so fast.

The revised Federal Rules have modified the interrogator's options. They have limited the time for discovery, including depositions, making it harder for interrogators to schedule a second day of depositions even for intransigent witnesses and obstreperous opponents. No witness may be deposed for more than one seven-hour day without leave of court or written stipulation of the parties under Rule 30(d)(2). The rules also limit the number of witnesses who can be deposed. No side in a case may depose more than 10 witnesses, except by leave of court, under Rule 30(a)(2)(A).

District courts can set their own limits on the number and length of depositions. Many have done so. The District Court for the Middle District of Pennsylvania, for example, has restricted depositions to six hours unless a longer period is authorized by the court. The Alaska District Court limits depositions to six hours for parties, experts, and treating physicians and three hours for all other deponents.

State courts can be even more restrictive. The Illinois rules, for example, generally limit depositions to three hours, except by stipulation of all parties or by court order upon a showing of good cause. Before beginning depositions in a case, every attorney should become thoroughly familiar with the local rules and with any standing orders of that court and of the individual judge to whom the case is assigned.

Despite your years of experience in fending off adversaries who try to hurry your deposition, you may not be able to schedule a second day of depositions without leave of court. It may be time to change tactics.

If your opponent deliberately is going to deny you sufficient time to complete the deposition of a key witness, you must document it. Make certain that all unnecessary breaks and other delays are put on the record, and have the reporter note the times when the deposition stopped and resumed. Caution your opponent that you will have no choice but to apply to the court to resume the deposition for a second day if the conduct continues.

The written rules may be more restrictive, but courts have remained willing to permit further questioning when appropriate. In fact, courts have readily permitted the scheduling of additional days of deposition and have even awarded counsel fees for wasted first days when defending counsel and deponents have been uncooperative.

The warnings and documentation of the record likely will stop the stall tactics. If not, you can use your record to apply to the court for more time. But never ignore the tactics by assuming more time automatically will be available.

The delay game stops, but your troubles continue. Your questions are pointed. The witness is squirming. Yet, in a maddening Pavlovian response, your opponent interrupts whenever damaging information is about to come out. He notes that he is seeking "just to clarify the question" or provides a detailed explanation of what is wrong with the question, just in case the witness had not gotten the point.

> **Interrogator:** Didn't you know as early as 1995 that your breathing difficulty might be related to asbestosis?

> **Defender:** Objection. Asked and answered. The witness has already testified that he was first told six months ago by his doctor that he has asbestosis.

Your temper flares, and you object to the speech in no uncertain terms. Your opponent's temper flares, and he responds in kind. The deponent sags in his chair, superfluous to the process.

If no judge is present, why the little speech? The defending attorney plainly felt that the witness needed to be reminded of his prior answer. Maybe he gave that answer earlier in the day when he was fresher and more able to stay on script. Inconsistent testimony about his first discovery of his cause of action would jeopardize the lawsuit.

Your latte-drinking opponent's other favorite tactic is to chirp "if you know" after particularly probing questions. His practice may be a well-motivated reminder to the witness not to feel obliged to answer every question and not to guess at answers. Or it may be less innocent—a thinly disguised instruction to the witness to respond with, "I don't know." Whatever the lawyer's motivation, many witnesses will follow the lead by professing ignorance.

The 1993 revisions to Rule 30(d) were aimed at correcting the abuse of speaking objections by the defending lawyer. The rule now provides that "any objection to evidence during a deposition shall be stated concisely and in a non-argumentative and non-suggestive manner." The rule presents quite a challenge. Litigators are expected to monitor the deposition of their clients and other critical witnesses without acting like advocates.

Six months before the revised Federal Rules took effect, a judge in the Eastern District of Pennsylvania put the goal this way: "The witness comes to the deposition to testify, not to indulge in a parody of Charlie McCarthy, with lawyers coaching or bending the witness's words to mold a legally convenient record." *Hall v. Clifton Precision*, 150 F.R.D. 525, 528 (E.D. Pa. 1993). *Hall* has been cited by courts around the country on deposition misconduct, and some of its guidelines have been implemented widely.

Perhaps the fault for speaking objections rests not only with your uppity adversary. As a veteran, perhaps you have participated in the abuse by using objectionable questioning to elicit inaccurate and inconsistent testimony. Perhaps you have tried to—dare we say it—trick the witness. You may be staving off summary judgment when the record really should be far clearer, or you may be building a record of arguably inaccurate testimony to bully the timid witness at trial.

Perhaps the young whippersnapper on the other side of the table really does need to do more than make a concise, non-argumentative, non-suggestive objection to protect the deponent and the record. After all, testifying under oath in a legal proceeding can be unsettling and upsetting. It is not realistic to assume that deponents can cope on their own with unfair crafty questions. Objections preserved until trial may not correct all the damage that is done.

A Contrary View

Recognizing the other side of this problem, a Pennsylvania state court judge disagreed with the *Hall* opinion and, by implication, with the 1993 revisions. *Acri v. Golden Triangle Management Acceptance Co.*, 142 *Pitt. Leg. J.* 225 (1994). The judge refused to relegate defending counsel to what he termed a "fly on the wall." He pointed out that in preparing the witness, the defending lawyer has a duty to tell the witness that he must tell the truth, even if unfavorable. And, as a quid pro quo, that lawyer must be able to assure the witness that she will be there to intervene if unfair, tricky, or embarrassing questions are asked.

The *Acri* court lamented that sometimes witnesses guess at an answer to a deposition question. Unfair questions sometimes call for a guess, and that guess can later be used as an admission. For example, suppose that a witness guesses incorrectly about the time he left the office on a given day, when the appropriate response would be to admit not knowing. The witness is then shown a copy of a police report of the subsequent car accident, which states the time of the collision. The guess about the seemingly unimportant detail can then be used to secure a critical admission—or to make a convincing argument—about the speed at which the witness must have traveled if he left the office when he said he did.

Perhaps you have purposely asked the witness an ambiguous question, hoping that he will not detect the ambiguity. For example, you know that there were two requests for extra work, one of which the witness approved and the other of which he rejected; but you ask simply whether he approved the extra work. With his lawyer limited to fly-on-the-wall status, the witness answers yes. His affirmative answer is an inadvertent—and erroneous—admission.

Revised Federal Rule 30(d), by its terms and strictly enforced, would bar the defender in either example from saying enough in an objection to be helpful to the witness. That cannot be what the rule contemplates.

There must be room for compromise. Object. Without testifying, say enough to provide some indication of the threatened unfairness.

Consider this example. The deponent is the head of quality control for a division of a large corporation. She testifies to that at the beginning of her deposition. Then, some 50 pages later, the questioner returns to the theme:

Interrogator: So, is it fair to say that you were in charge of quality control for the corporation?

Earlier in your career, you might have objected this way:

Defender: Objection. Your question mischaracterizes the previous testimony. The witness testified that she was head

258

of quality control for the plastics division, not for the entire corporation.

Under the revised rules, because the error is in the form of the question, you still must object. But your objection should sound like this:

Defender: Objection. Your question mischaracterizes the previous testimony.

If you say more, your objection might be labeled argumentative or suggestive. But if you say less, a judge at trial might rule that it was insufficient to permit the interrogator to obviate or remove the error and that you waived the objection.

The permissible objection still may do little to help the deponent deal with the potential problem. She might still inadvertently concede that, yes, indeed, she was in charge of quality control for the entire corporation.

You have some consolation that she testified differently—and accurately—earlier in her testimony. But the record now will contain a discrepancy—a discrepancy that may prevent summary judgment for your side if the extent of this witness's quality control role is a material fact. You can clarify the witness's job responsibilities again when it is your turn to examine the deponent, but that will only create another piece of contradictory testimony. So when you ask questions to clarify the testimony, try at least to resurrect the record:

Defender: Earlier, when you testified in response to Ms. Interrogator's question that you were in charge of quality control for the corporation, did you mean the entire corporation or a division of the corporation?

You will undoubtedly get an objection, but the answer might at least partly undo the damage done by your inability to guide your witness with more explanatory objections during your opponent's interrogation.

Perhaps the best defense against an unfair interrogator is a well-prepared witness. Teach your witness to listen to your objections. The witness should be told that when you object that a question mischaracterizes previous testimony, she should ask to have the question repeated. The witness should consider how the question differs from her assumptions. Practice this routine with your witness in preparing for the deposition.

Lacking the ability to interpose a speaking objection, what other weapons do you have against the unscrupulous interrogator? You could correct the transcript later, changing the "yes" to a "no" or adding an explanation. But beware! Some states (for example, Illinois) do not permit substantive changes to deposition transcripts. You could go off the record and talk to the questioner to try to solve the problem without as much posturing. (This may be a good tactic to use on an unruly defending lawyer as well.)

If going off the record several times does not reduce the level of tension or trickery—or if your obstreperous adversary refuses to go off the record to discuss issues—then provide several warnings on the record before closing down the deposition and applying for sanctions and perhaps a protective order for future depositions. But before you close a deposition, be sure that you cannot be tagged with having contributed to the misbehavior, or the judge will simply punish all the kids in the sandbox. And remember that the limits you impose will come back to bind you as well.

Calling the Court

In *Hall*, the judge reminded lawyers that they are acting as officers of the court in a deposition and that the judge is "but a phone call away." That may be true in some courts, but it is not true in all of them. Commenting on *Hall*, one state court judge said that the caseload in his court was so heavy, lawyers could make the call but no one would answer the phone.

The Delaware Supreme Court issued warnings against unprofessional deposition conduct in *Paramount Communications Inc. v. QVC Network, Inc.*, 637 A.2d 34, 51–57 (Del. 1994), another opinion that has sparked substantial discussion by state and federal courts around the country. The court was horrified at the behavior of two out-of-state lawyers, revealed in a deposition transcript attached as an appendix to the record on appeal. Without any motion, the court issued an addendum to its opinion on the merits and addressed the deposition misconduct, quoting liberally the worst examples from the transcript. The court stressed that it would not tolerate such unprofessional conduct from any Delaware lawyer, that every Delaware lawyer or lawyer admitted *pro hac vice* in Delaware was an officer of the court and had a duty to curb such behavior in other lawyers, and that the court was considering taking into account deposition misconduct by out-of-state lawyers when they seek admission *pro hac vice* in Delaware.

As your deposition continues, you mind your P's and Q's. You want to get into sensitive areas, but you fear that the defending attorney will instruct his witness not to answer. Earlier in your career, you instructed witnesses not to answer questions about their divorce or child support arrears or questions that were asked repeatedly earlier in the deposition. Can your opponent get away with a direction not to answer these days?

Revised Rule 30 limits the situations in which a defender can instruct a witness not to answer. Now, a lawyer can direct his client not to answer only when the lawyer is asserting a privilege, enforcing a court order, or preparing to make a motion for a protective order. A motion for a protective order might be contemplated for intrusive, personal questions about the deponent's divorce and child support, but not for a question that has already been asked and answered.

An instruction not to answer is also likely to be appropriate with respect to questions calling for an impermissible conclusion of law or constituting harassment. For example, the witness should not be forced to state the appropriate measure of damages for the breach of a contract. Likewise, in a case involving a lease dispute, the witness should not be required to describe the product liability claims that the company's European subsidiary faced during the past 20 years. Yet if you instruct the witness in either of these situations not to answer, Rule 30 requires you to be prepared to file a motion for a protective order or proceed at your peril. (As a practical matter, your opponent may back off after your instruction if the question is clearly inappropriate, and you will never have to file your motion.)

You ask the witness which documents he reviewed with his lawyer during preparation for the deposition. Defending counsel instructs the witness not to answer on the ground of work-product privilege, arguing that the information discloses his thought processes in selecting the documents with which to prepare the witness. You respond that you are entitled to learn what documents the witness used to refresh his recollection in preparing to testify. Who is right?

Maybe both of you. That is because there is a tension between protection for work product and Federal Rule of Evidence 612, which provides for access to documents used to refresh the recollection of a witness. Ordinarily, the work product privilege trumps the rule, and the identity of documents generally reviewed with counsel are usually protected. But if the interrogator first asks questions about a particular subject and then establishes that the witness's responses were refreshed by a review of the documents, the interrogator can usually gain access to the particular documents reviewed on the specific subject.

The opponent's deposition ends, and your thoughts turn to stage two: defending your client's deposition. Having been around for years, you know how to coach a witness as well as any of the masters. Is coaching still allowed? It depends upon whom you ask.

The *Hall* case is somewhat famous for its treatment of private conferences between the witness and counsel. The court ruled that counsel could not confer off the record with their witness-clients during deposition breaks or recesses, including overnight recesses, except to determine whether to assert a privilege. But that extreme prohibition against conferences remains the exception. The revised Federal Rules do not mention conferences.

Nevertheless, a few district courts have taken advantage of their authority under Rule 26 to control deposition practices and have codified restrictions on conferences as part of their local rules. *E.g.*, D. Colo. Local Rule 30.1C. A.2; M.D.N.C. Local Rule 26.1(b)(2)(iii); S.C. Civil Rule 30.04(E). The Delaware Rules of Civil Procedure, which generally follow the Federal Rules of Civil Procedure, incorporated the *Hall* guidelines after the *Paramount Communications* case and prohibited conferences between attorneys and their witness-clients during depositions, including recesses and continuances. Del. Super. Ct. Civ. R. 30(d)(1). Most of those jurisdictions also permit opposing counsel to inquire into any conferences that are not for the purpose of determining privilege.

Even if you are in a jurisdiction where conferences are generally permitted, you probably are not allowed to confer with your witness while a question is pending. Local rules often prohibit such conduct; even if there is no local rule, the practice is generally discouraged. In fact, conferring while a question is pending could well lead to sanctions because such misconduct so fundamentally interferes with the question-and-answer process of a deposition. As one court put it, "It is too late once the ball has been snapped for the coach to send in a different play." *Eggleston v. Chicago Journeymen Plumbers' Local No. 130*, 657 F.2d 890, 902 (7th Cir. 1981), *cert. denied*, 455 U.S. 1017 (1982).

Document Review

In *Hall*, the defending counsel wanted to consult with his client about a document before the interrogator started his questioning. But counsel defending a deposition generally cannot interrupt the questioning to confer with the witness about a document that she neglected to review in the preparation session. In some jurisdictions, the local rules spell this out. *E.g.*, M.D.N.C. Local Rule 26.1(b)(2)(iv). Other objections provide variations on the theme. In South Carolina (which prohibits off-the-record conferences), for example, if the interrogator does not provide copies of all deposition exhibits to opposing counsel at least two business days before the deposition, then the deponent and counsel may privately confer about an undisclosed document before the interrogator questions the deponent about it.

The new restrictions on objections, instructions not to answer, and conferences make witness preparation more important than ever. The witness needs to be equipped to handle the interrogator with much less intervention by the defending lawyer.

Prepare your witnesses to be alert to your few concise objections. Remind them to listen carefully to suggestive mischaracterizations of testimony. Tell witnesses that the words "Would it be fair to say" or "Isn't it true that" at the beginning of questions often mean the opposite and should be resisted.

Although witness preparation takes place in private, the Model Rules of Professional Conduct have a lot to say about it. You may not counsel or assist a client in conduct you know is "criminal or fraudulent." Model Rule 1.2(d). You may not knowingly offer false evidence. Model Rule 3.3(a)(4). You may not "falsify evidence, counsel or assist a witness to testify falsely." Model Rule 3.4(b). Be prepared, but be truthful.

Tell your witnesses not to rely on hairsplitting when they answer deposition questions. Although literally true answers should not constitute perjury, *see Bronston v. United States*, 409 U.S. 352, 361 (1973), keep in mind the disciplinary committee of the Arkansas Supreme Court initiated disbarment proceedings (later reduced to a five-year suspension and a $25,000 fine) against then-President Clinton for his deposition testimony, which he

263

claimed was literally truthful under the definition of sexual relations approved by the judge in the *Paula Jones* case.

When all is said and done, the instincts that you started to develop before any of your children were born will serve you well as you re-enter the deposition arena. But it does not hurt to revisit the rules that will govern the exercise of those instincts. Those rules have changed and will continue to change throughout your career. Experienced or not, knowing the rules will make your job a lot easier—and your representation of your client a lot more effective.

CHAPTER 18

Effective Use
of Depositions
at Trial

Jeffrey J. Kroll*

People grasp ideas best when they are conveyed through images as well as words. At trial, one of the best multimedia tools for any advocate is the deposition. Run the tape, please.

Most depositions are taken for discovery purposes, because depositions are the ultimate fact-finding discovery tool. Done well, they can obtain evidence—most notably admissions—for use at trial or to defeat an opponent's summary judgment motion. But attorneys often go into a deposition thinking it will never be used at trial. They view the deposition as a mere discovery tool, not as packaged evidence. When a deposing attorney walks into a deposition expecting it to serve as a simple exercise in fact finding, the lawyer is ignoring the potential uses of the deposition at trial. I think this is a grave mistake.

The purpose of a deposition shapes the manner in which it is taken. Thus, before taking the deposition, the examining attorney must first consider the deposition's ultimate purpose or purposes. Even the examining attorney who expects to conduct only a discovery deposition should realize that it potentially could be useful at trial.

*Jeffrey J. Kroll is a partner with Clifford Law Offices, P.C., in Chicago. This article originally appeared in the Fall 2003 issue of LITIGATION.

A deposed witness may offer an important part of the whole picture, like a piece of a puzzle. Before inquiring at a deposition, you must understand how the testimony might be used. The value of testimony can increase or decrease during the course of litigation, depending on where the case takes you. Going into a deposition with the thought that the witness may have testimony that can be used at trial represents a positive thought process. It makes the questioning attorney more aggressive and forces him or her to think about the potential uses of the testimony for trial. Typically, you have but one shot at a key witness. You cannot count on being able to reopen a deposition to obtain trial testimony when you missed important information the first time. In other words, you must believe that the deposition will be used at trial.

True, most depositions are sought primarily for discovery purposes. The main object of discovery depositions is to elicit all information from the deponent concerning the facts of the case. Typically you are bringing out any information that can be damaging to the examiner's case, as well as any helpful information. But in addition to seeking a broad range of information, a discovery deposition can have other purposes. For example, a discovery deposition can lock a deponent into his or her story of the case. This allows the attorney to prepare counter-testimony or evidence. If the deponent tells a different story or veers from the testimony offered at trial, the deposition can be used to impeach the deponent. A discovery deposition also can be used to assess a deponent's credibility and demeanor. This may be critical when the deponent is the opposing party or a crucial witness.

Federal Rule of Civil Procedure 32 governs the use of depositions at trial and in other courtroom proceedings. Rule 32 permits the use of depositions at hearings on motions. Although subsection (a)(3)(E) indicates a strong preference for live testimony in lieu of deposition testimony, depositions may be introduced as evidence in certain situations and with proper procedural safeguards in place.

In the absence of a stipulation or court order, use of deposition at trial is contingent on the witness's being "unavailable." Rule 32(a)(3). The term "unavailable" is somewhat expansive. Rule 32 allows the use of a deposition at trial for any purpose under the following circumstances:

- The witness is deceased (Rule 32(a)(3)(A));
- The witness is located more than 100 miles from the place of trial (Rule 32(a)(3)(B));
- The age, illness, or imprisonment of the witness prohibits live testimony of that witness (Rule 32(a)(3)(C));
- The party offering the deposition was unable to subpoena the witness (Rule 32(a)(3)(D));
- Other exceptional circumstances exist that make unavailability desirable, in the interest of justice and with due regard to the importance of the testimony (Rule 32(a)(3)(E)).

How do you use a deposition at trial for the unavailable, nonparty witness? If a nonparty deponent is unavailable, testimony can be used for any purpose, including substantive evidence at trial, provided there are no preserved evidentiary objections. Typically, the witness will be "unavailable" when she is more than 100 miles from place of trial, outside the United States, incapacitated, or outside the reach of a subpoena. Of course, the death of an individual renders the witness unavailable for purposes of Rule 32.

An available nonparty deposition at trial can be used at trial for the "available" witness, as either substantive evidence or non-substantive evidence. With respect to substantive evidence, the deposition can be used at trial as a prior inconsistent statement. It can be used as a prior consistent statement where the statement is challenged by either the witness or opposing counsel. It can be used as an admission by a party opponent even if made by an agent of the corporation.

The deposition of a nonparty witness who is available at trial also can be used to impeach a witness. It can be used to contradict trial testimony or to refresh the recollection of a witness. And it can be used as a prior consistent statement when the testimony was not shown to that witness during the cross-examination of opposing counsel.

Can a prior deposition be used for your own party? The answer is yes. It can be used to impeach your party's own trial testimony or to contradict his or her own testimony. Unfortunately, it may be a needed tool. Also, the attorney may introduce the deposition as substantive evidence if the party is unavailable due to infirmity, distance, or death.

Some depositions are taken primarily so they may be introduced in evidence at trial. This may be the case with both friendly and opposing witnesses. For example, when a witness whose testimony will support the case has a serious illness, it is best to depose this witness and preserve the testimony, in case the witness dies or is hospitalized and unable to testify at trial.

Can a deposition be used at trial as substantive evidence against the adverse party? Generally deposition testimony introduced substantively at trial against a party falls under the adverse or unavailable witness provisions. Of course this is subject to evidentiary objections. Most states will permit a substantive use of deposition testimony in lieu of live testimony where the adverse party is involved. Depositions also may be used for non-substantive purposes, such as to impeach the witness or to refresh the recollection of the party.

Whenever you ask yourself whether to videotape a deposition, consider several reasons for answering yes.

Our society has become very visual during the past decade. We have become visually dependent on information because of the increased use of televisions and the Internet. Many people shop via the Internet and communicate with loved ones through e-mail. For years we have been conditioned to expect and understand short bursts of information broken up by frequent intermissions, ordinary commercials, or pop-up ads. According to one study, the average person's attention span lasts no longer than a few minutes. When you consider how we have been conditioned, it makes sense. The average television news item takes roughly 90 seconds to cover a story: The first 30 seconds set the stage, the next 30 seconds provide the details, and the final 30 seconds wrap up the story.

The use of videotape in trial is almost expected these days. Society relies on visuals for gathering information, whether from television, the Internet, or even cell phones with tiny picture screens. One trial consulting firm estimated that the average graduating high school student has watched more than 15,000 hours of television. Therefore, listening to a talking head for hours at a time is boring to the average juror. The prudent lawyer must think of ways to spice up a boring topic or, worse yet, a boring witness. The logical deduction that can be reached is that videotapes offer a familiar and convenient method for a juror to receive information.

A witness schedule may conflict with an obligation to testify at a trial. In that situation, a videotaped evidence deposition should be strongly considered. Typically, this is done by agreement. If not, that party should file the appropriate motion with the court.

Unavailability is not the sole reason to opt for a videotaped deposition in lieu of in-court testimony. A strategic trial attorney can introduce a videotaped evidence deposition of a witness when he or she fears a damaging cross-examination in the presence of a jury or is wary of the in-court demeanor of the witness. Not too long ago, I took a case to trial against an excellent lawyer, renowned for parading around the courtroom during cross-examination and for giving essentially closing arguments during examination. All eyes in the courtroom would be focused on the cross-examiner, as they should be—so I opted to videotape several witnesses in lieu of live testimony to minimize the grandstanding of the cross-examiner. This strategy worked.

A videotaped evidence deposition also can be effective when opposing counsel is not quite up to speed on all the issues in the case. In many cases the associate works up the case and the partner waits in the wings for the trial. Electing to videotape a witness may catch your opponent off guard and not yet in trial mode. In short, the videotaped evidence deposition is a tool that litigators can use for convenience and/or strategic planning.

More and more attorneys are videotaping witnesses during the discovery phase of the case, not only for trial. Today's society understands video impeachment. Many individuals can recall quite vividly when President Clinton proclaimed, "I did not have sexual relations with that woman." Of course, he was talking about Monica Lewinsky. We know how that statement came back and impacted his credibility. Similarly, a video can be used at trial to impeach a witness who is being less than candid. Once the witness veers from the discovery deposition, you have the option of impeaching the witness with the videotaped testimony. This permits the jury to view the inconsistent testimony as they hear it, thus providing a more powerful impeachment.

Another reason for videotaping a deposition for use at trial is that the witness typically is not dressed up at the deposition but at trial may wear a suit and tie and look like a true professional. For example, in a trucking accident case I had a few years ago, it was alleged that the truck was traveling too fast for conditions and violated several Federal Motor Carrier Safety Regulations. At the discovery deposition, the defendant wore a dirty flannel shirt and a baseball hat that partially hid his shoulder-length hair and was badly in need of a shave. The witness made several inconsistent statements during his discovery deposition. At trial he appeared in court wearing a sport coat and bifocals, with a haircut and no facial hair. He was impeached with the videotape at trial, and the jurors could not even recognize the deponent. During closing argument, I argued that you can "dress up a pig all you want, but the fact of the matter is . . . it is still a pig." The jury came back with a favorable verdict and found that the driver was the sole cause of the collision.

Many trial lawyers routinely videotape depositions of key liability and damage witnesses to guarantee that the jury will be able to observe the witness at trial if that witness is unavailable. There are additional factors that favor using videotaped evidence depositions. Unlike a transcribed record, a videotaped deposition captures the mannerisms, demeanor, and gestures of a witness—all the factors that make up the credibility of a witness. A pause that may not be included on a written page can seriously impact the credibility of a struggling witness. Many times it is not what a witness says but how he or she says it.

If a video deposition will be shown to the jury, most judges will want to rule on objections in advance, so the videotape can be edited by a video technician to delete objections or questions the court rules objectionable. Setting up the viewing of a video deposition is equally important within the courtroom. There should be at least one large monitor or two smaller monitors for the jurors, located so they can easily see the scene; the judge and attorneys should have separate monitors. The reporters hired to perform the videotaping are usually experts on the mechanics and can provide the necessary equipment at trial.

A video impeachment follows certain steps. First you must decide which deposition testimony you will designate for trial. Rely on your trial strategy in light of the nature of the case. Obviously, strategy and instinct should be your guides, but keep the following points in mind in designating videotaped evidence deposition testimony:

1. Err on the side of designating too much rather than too little information. When in doubt, designate the testimony you may use at trial. It is that simple.

2. Of course, anything you intend to use to impeach a witness at trial must be admissible in evidence. Lay the necessary foundation to include any of this information into evidence.

3. If you are using a videotaped deposition, the designation process involves editing and counter-editing the videotape. It is going to involve large amounts of time and preparation.

The designation process should begin well in advance of trial. I also think it is important to retain the full question/answer for the video impeachment. For example, do not delete the pauses between question and answer. Often, lapses in time and demeanor of the witness are your most effective areas of cross-examination.

The designation process often involves give and take between parties. Your adversaries will designate other portions of the videotape they intend to use at trial. Of course, if you are the only one with a videotape, that may be difficult. Consider well in advance of trial whether or not the parties will cooperate or whether only the party taking the deposition will be able to use the videotape to impeach that witness.

It is important to vary how you use deposition testimony. Use video depositions when appropriate. If you are going to read into the record the deposition testimony of a witness, you run the risk of boring the jury to death. Read a deposition only when it is absolutely necessary for the case. Depending on the jurisdiction, you may want to consider hiring an actor to read the deposition at trial.

Rule 32(c) indicates that a party offering deposition testimony pursuant to the rule may offer it in stenographic or non-stenographic form. If the deposition testimony is offered in non-stenographic form, however, the party must provide the court with a transcript of the portion it will offer. Any party in a case tried before a jury may request that deposition testimony offered other than for impeachment purposes be presented in non-stenographic form, if available, unless the court for some good cause orders otherwise. Therefore, if the proceeding at which the deposition is presented is a jury trial, parties must present depositions used other than for impeachment purposes in a non-stenographic form, if one is available, unless the court allows otherwise. Subsection (c) supplements Rule 26(a)(3)(B), which requires a party expecting to present deposition testimony in a non-stenographic form as substantive evidence to provide the other parties with a transcript of the pertinent portions of the deposition. A note of caution: A videotaped evidence deposition must be properly noticed as such. For example, in Illinois, Supreme Court Rule 202 states that if discovery and evidence depositions are to be taken, they must be taken separately unless the parties stipulate otherwise or the court orders otherwise upon notice of motion.

The procedure for videotaping depositions varies from jurisdiction to jurisdiction. Illinois Supreme Court Rule 206(g) sets forth the requirements for procuring a videotaped deposition. The operator will take custody of the videotape and will determine the exact length of time of the deposition. The videotape of a deposition for purposes of discovery will be returned only to the attorney for the party for whom the deposition was videotaped. The attorney is responsible for safeguarding the videotape. If it is an evidence deposition, it should be securely sealed by the operator in an envelope containing the title and number of the action, and promptly filed or sent by certified mail to the clerk of the court for filing. The videotape may be used in lieu of reading a transcribed record.

Federal Rule 30(b)(4) dictates the general requirements for noticing up depositions in a "non-traditional fashion." The party taking the deposition has the choice of the medium for recording the testimony and must pay the cost of the recording. Generally, permission from the court or opposing parties to take depositions other than by stenographic means is not required. If a party desires to take a deposition by telephone or by other remote electronic means, Rule 30(b)(7) states that permission of court or stipulation of the opposing party is required.

If videotape or audiotape is used as the sole means of recording the deposition testimony, the party taking the deposition must arrange for a transcription of the tape. If audiotape, videotape, or another non-stenographic medium is used to record a deposition, the deposition must begin with a statement of record of the office of the court reporter's name and business address, date, time and location of the deposition, and name of the deponent. These items must be repeated whenever a new tape or unit of recording is used. It is important to note that if a deposition is taken by videotape, the appearance or demeanor of the deponent cannot be distorted through camera or sound-recording techniques.

Choosing a qualified and capable videographer is an important decision to be made by the attorney. Do not cut corners to save costs. Ensure that both audio and video are high quality and do not detract from the presentation of evidence. Determine whether the witness will use a table or lavalier microphone. If exhibits will be used by the deponent, a lavalier microphone is preferred.

Also, look at the size of the room before you plan a video-taped deposition. If you are going to be using exhibits, you may need a larger room. Will you introduce any type of videotape through the deponent? If so, a television and VCR monitor will be required. This, too, will impact the decision on the size of the room.

Today, many depositions are taken via video teleconferencing. Teleconferencing centers now exist in most major cities throughout the country. Teleconferencing enables individuals at various locations to communicate both verbally and visually. A camera at each conference center allows the parties to observe each other while verbal communication takes place. Is it expensive? Yes. It is effective? Absolutely. Of course, there are potential problems with video teleconferencing. Make sure each witness and each party has all pre-marked exhibits well in advance of the deposition.

Federal Rule 32(a)(4) governs using excerpts of a deposition and admitting it into evidence by a party. If a party offers into evidence only part of a deposition, subsection (a)(4) allows an opposing party to require the party offering the deposition as evidence to introduce any *other* part of the deposition that should in fairness be considered with the part introduced. All parties have the right to introduce any other part of the deposition originally offered as well. The distinction between the first provision of Section 32(a)(4) and the second provision is that an adverse party seeking to have portions of the deposition considered relevant to that offered by the original party does *not* have to introduce those portions itself. This actually could require the offering party to introduce portions of the deposition originally omitted.

Similarly, substitution of parties does not affect the right to use depositions previously taken. FRCP 32(a). All depositions lawfully taken and duly filed in a previous action may be used in the current action as if the deposition originally was taken in the current matter. Therefore, when an action has been brought

273

in any court of the United States or any other state involving the same subject matter, these depositions can be used. The depositions also can be used for non-substantive purposes. The Federal Rules of Evidence (FRE) permit non-substantive use of prior depositions for refreshing recollection (Rule 612), for statements against interest (Rule 804(b)(3)), or for impeachment by prior inconsistent statements (Rule 613).

Under the evidence rules, depositions taken in other proceedings can be used as substantive evidence. Rule 804(b) provides that former testimony is not covered by the hearsay rule excluding such testimony. To use a deposition, it must be testimony: under oath, recorded, and in accordance with procedural requirements. The deposition must have been taken in the course of a proceeding. The party against whom the deposition is offered must have had an opportunity and similar motive to develop the testimony by either direct, cross, or redirect examination. If you have a deposition taken in another proceeding you need to use in your case-in-chief, and you are concerned about its admissibility, treat the deposition as a written or verbal statement and apply the FRE or the local rules of that particular state to gain admissibility.

Deposition excerpts may be read into the record or played during various portions of the trial, depending on strategy. I personally believe that an attorney is entitled to present excerpts of a videotaped deposition in closing arguments, as long as it conveys a credible and honest impression to the jury. In closing arguments, an excerpt from a videotaped deposition can be helpful as well as persuasive. Crucial deposition testimony serves a strategic purpose as a reminder to the jury of key points brought out during the trial. Because a deposition is legally equivalent to any other admitted piece of evidence, an attorney should be able to use any portions of the videotaped deposition that were properly admitted into evidence. Imagine the impact where a defendant doctor testifies in his videotaped discovery deposition that he did not perform a certain test but changes his testimony at trial. This video impeachment can be devastating. Highlighting that impeachment and showing the jury the inconsistent testimony one last time before deliberations can be a powerful way to close your case. Of course, when using depositions as substantive evidence, counsel must remember to move the transcript or videotapes into evidence. This type of reminder should be included in the trial notebook or checklist.

Not only is variety the spice of life, it is a way to keep a jury's attention. Incorporate modern technology with traditional methods of presenting demonstrative evidence and arguing damages. For example, depending on the case, a combination of photographs and videotapes may be the best way to present the plaintiff's condition to a jury. The prudent attorney must take into account that in some situations, photographs may be the sole means of presenting the plaintiff's condition to the jury. Similarly, day-in-the-life videotapes may be the only way to convey the plaintiff's pain and suffering throughout grueling physical therapy sessions. Although there is no one correct way to demonstrate damages to the jury, certain exhibits may be better suited to depicting the plaintiff's physical, mental, and emotional condition at various stages of the recovery process.

Keep your presentation simple. For example, in a medical malpractice case, I successfully employed a colored poster board representation of the human circulatory system as a piping system. The pipes running toward the heart were labeled veins and those away from the heart were labeled arteries. The jury clearly understood the analogy, which distilled complicated human anatomy into an understandable concept that allowed jurors to comfortably return a verdict in favor of the plaintiff.

It is time to embrace technology. When deciding how to present evidence, consider that the old standby exhibits like graphs, charts, and anatomical models may not be enough anymore. The prudent attorney must look at all the effective ways of getting points across. This often means a multimedia trial. From a plaintiff's attorney's perspective, the multimedia trial allows jurors to see, hear, feel, and understand the evidence. Videotaped depositions are a potent tool for driving home your point to the jury. Use them at trial, and you can empower a jury to return a favorable verdict.

CHAPTER 19

Showing Your Hand: A Counter-Intuitive Strategy for Deposition Defense

Steven Lubet*

Anyone who litigates "by the book" is familiar with the standard advice for defending depositions: Do everything you can to limit the information given to the other side. After all, a deposition is a discovery device used in preparation for trial. When the other side takes a deposition, they are, by definition, seeking information that might be used to bolster their case. Because the

*Steven Lubet is professor of law and director, Bartlit Center for Trial Strategy, Northwestern University School of Law, in Chicago. This article is adapted from Lawyers' Poker: 52 Lessons that Lawyers Can Learn from Card Players (Oxford University Press, 2006)

goal of defending a deposition is to minimize the other side's benefit, the presumptive strategy is to withhold as much as possible, within the confines of the rules. As one leading handbook puts it, "[t]here is no sense sharing information with the other side when there is no requirement of doing so." David Malone and Peter Hoffman, *The Effective Deposition* 198 (2d ed. 1996).

There is a compelling logic to this approach. Information that may eventually become evidence is the currency of a trial. Whoever has the most information is at a substantial advantage. Consequently, lawyers should want to find out everything the opposition knows, while keeping all of their knowledge (or as much as possible) to themselves. Information is viewed almost as a zero-sum commodity. Because the objective of a successful deposition is to obtain information, the objective of a successful defense must be to deny it. By unnecessarily sharing knowledge, a lawyer loses the advantage of having it.

To be sure, no ethical lawyer would simply disobey or flout discovery rules. But the rules are subject to considerable interpretation and are often ambiguous and flexible. Even more to the point, deposition responses depend on the particular questions asked, with no general duty to volunteer or expand— hence the lawyer's usual admonition that the witness provide only the shortest possible answers, without explanation or elaboration. If opposing counsel wants more information, it's their job to make further inquiry.

Questioned about this assumption, most attorneys will respond that their strategy is to surprise the other side at trial. Why allow the opposition to prepare its cross-examinations, or set up impeachment, or search out other witnesses, or otherwise patch up the holes in their case? These objections to disclosure and others like them would be persuasive if a substantial number of cases actually went to trial. In a practice environment where trials are predictably frequent, there would be great reason to design one's pretrial strategy primarily on the basis of anticipated trial tactics. Today, however, actual trials in civil litigation are few and far between. Although it is debatable whether this is good or bad from the perspective of social policy, it is an inescapable reality.

According to the National Center for State Courts, less than 3 percent of civil cases are tried to verdict. Settlement is far and away the most common result in litigation, with as many as 30 cases settled for every trial. National Center for State Courts, *Examining the Work of State Courts,* at 10 (1996), cited in Thomas Koenig, "The Shadow Effect of Punitive Damages on Settlements," 1998 *Wisc. L. Rev.* 169, 171 (1998). Although no competent lawyer could neglect trial preparation—if only because better preparation leads to stronger negotiating positions—it is surely the case that depositions are most likely to be used as negotiating tools rather than trial bombshells. This, in turn, should lead to at least a partial re-evaluation of "by the book" deposition tactics.

Negotiation theory posits that the strength of one's position is a (or perhaps *the*) major determinant of the outcome. The acronym for this concept is BATNA: best alternative to a negotiated agreement. Roger Fisher, et al., *Getting to Yes* 97 (2d ed. 1991). The better your perceived BATNA, the better your negotiated result. Of course, the opposing party cannot be intimidated by your BATNA unless they know about it. Thus, a good deal of any negotiation must be devoted to a detailed description of your powerful case (without details, it would just be unpersuasive bragging). And what is it that makes your case so compelling? One factor would certainly have to be the strength of your witnesses and the quality of their expected testimony, leading to the likelihood that you will prevail at trial.

Negotiation theory indicates that you would want the other side to know about your witnesses well in advance of the trial, the better to influence their settlement posture. And what better way to educate the opposition than by showcasing your witnesses at their own depositions? Don't prepare your witnesses to give short, unrevealing answers; encourage them to tell what they know, explaining why you represent the winning side.

This proposition is discordant. Lawyers have been conditioned to stash information, not give it away. Secrecy, not disclosure, is the animating principle. Moreover, there are some good reasons to ask witnesses to keep their answers short. As Malone and Hoffman point out, short answers can "simplify the witness's job," thereby reducing the burden of the deposition. Freed from the need to be thorough or explanatory, the witness can concentrate exclusively on accuracy.

The "shortest answers" approach is no doubt essential with some witnesses—those who are anxious, undependable, or ill-prepared. With others, however, thorough preparation may be

279

sufficient to create an adequate comfort level with the process. After all, they will have to be prepared for direct and cross-examination if the case goes to trial. Recognizing that the deposition may well function as a substitute trial, it may make sense to engage in that preparation sooner rather than later. True, that might take slightly more time than simply drilling the witness to give short, correct answers, but a substantial payoff could come from the settlement value of the case.

This proposal rests on two related premises. First, concealing information (okay, protecting information) is less valuable than most lawyers believe. Second, it is often advantageous to inform the opposition about the evidentiary strengths of your case. Each premise is somewhat counterintuitive and therefore subject to some obvious questions.

What about the smoking gun? The first premise is that lawyers exaggerate the importance of concealing information from the opposing side. But isn't there some information that truly needs to be protected—the case-breaking fact or factoid that must be shielded if at all possible?

In fact, smoking guns are rare indeed. Very few cases turn on a single fact or set of facts. And absolutely critical information is usually so important that both sides have sufficient incentive to ferret it out, notwithstanding evasive tactics in deposition defense. Thus, the likelihood of effectively hiding bad facts may well be outweighed by the disadvantage of turning your own witness into a recalcitrant clam. How much positive persuasion must you forgo in an often-futile attempt to suppress a potentially prejudicial fact?

Of course, in an extremely small percentage of cases, there actually is a devastating smoking gun, the revelation of which will make the case unwinnable, or nearly so. But in those cases, it is astoundingly risky to expose the witness to deposition in the first place. What sort of lawyer allows an entire case to hang on her ability to thwart a determined adversary's interrogation? Certainly, you can never confidently expect both witness and opposing counsel to cooperate in preventing certain information from emerging at the deposition.

The better approach would be to avoid such cases if possible, or to settle them before they ever get to the deposition stage. Allowing a case to go forward to the point of deposition, in the hope of evading inquiry into salient-but-devastating territory, is a risky strategy indeed. In fact, it isn't a strategy at all—it's gambling.

In most cases, however, there are no such killer facts to worry about. There are simply positive facts and negative facts—the latter being subdivided into more refined categories such as contradictory, inconvenient, hard-to-accommodate, and embarrassing. But whatever the classification, very few items of information are the exclusive knowledge of a single witness. Consequently, even successful efforts to divert one deposition will not ensure that the information is ultimately suppressed. Moreover, most such efforts merely delay rather than blunt the inquiries. Malone and Hoffman, for example, provide numerous effective techniques for dogged interrogators determined to pursue each line of questioning. Against this array of methods—open questions, follow-ups, clarification, closing-off, exhaustion, summaries, and theory testing, to name a few—one real result of short answers becomes simply to perforate the witness's own story rather than to conceal any important part of it.

There actually may be a cost to concealing even dangerous facts. If a topic is never broached in the deposition, the witness will never have a chance to rebut, explain, or accommodate the potentially damaging information. Of course, the rebuttal or explanation could always come at trial—in the exceptionally unlikely event that there is a trial. Otherwise, opposing counsel will never have to reckon with the fact that the seemingly bad facts might be neutralized or discredited by your witness's well-organized, persuasive response. And the settlement will not reflect the witness's well-prepared clarity and probity.

Can the other side really be influenced? It is one thing to show that conventional wisdom exaggerates the value of withholding information during depositions. It is another matter to show that reversing that strategy can actually bring about better results in negotiation.

Lawyers are creatures of habit. As a profession, we tend to respond positively to the familiar while discounting anything novel or innovative—at least for a while. Consider, for example, the rote insistence on using "magic words" in evidentiary foundations. Though any number of formulations would be acceptable under the rules of evidence, the use of a familiar incantation will usually forestall an objection.

In deposition practice, lawyers have come to expect a certain level of recalcitrance from a well-prepared deponent. Indeed, a standoffish disposition is probably taken as the very hallmark of a tough witness—providing as little ammunition as possible for future cross-examination. Measured against such expectations, would a surprisingly cooperative or unusually voluble witness be seen as a pushover, thus negating the supposed settlement value of the forthcoming testimony? In fact, this possibility cannot be denied, though it can be overstated.

Most deposition books recognize that witness evaluation is a crucial aspect of the deposition process. Malone and Hoffman put it this way:

> The face-to-face confrontation of a deposition permits each side to evaluate the witness being deposed and make judgments about the credibility of the witness and how the judge or jury will perceive the testimony. When the witness comes across as particularly believable or unbelievable, it will affect the settlement value of the case. In addition, each side will also make judgments about the abilities of opposing counsel that will influence the amount at which a case will settle.
>
> Malone and Hoffman, at 25.

The witness's performance is recognized as crucial. It certainly must follow that the *content* of the witness's testimony is as important as perceived credibility. Why would it affect settlement value for a witness to be credible about trivia? If opposing counsel is, in fact, evaluating the witness's potential future testimony, why not present that testimony in a manner comparable to the anticipated direct examination at trial?

We all know lawyers who habitually bluster about the quality of their cases—we all know too many—whether or not they have the actual goods to back up the bragging. In negotiation, it is important to separate bluff from strength. It is not difficult to imagine that counsel's willingness to let a deponent speak might quickly be recognized as a sign of confidence. Thus, revealing information could eventually be recognized for the assertive, perhaps even aggressive, tactic that it is.

The effectiveness of intentional disclosure can be illustrated with a legendary, but true, story from the annals of professional poker. (Poker, especially at the highest level, has much in common with litigation: Both involve strategy in the face of uncertainty, bluffs and raises, and an eventual showdown over "the facts.")

Jack "Treetop" Straus is one of the great professional poker players, winner of the 1982 World Series of Poker. His most famous successful bluff came in a round of Texas Hold 'Em, a challenging game in which each player must make the best possible five-card hand by using any combination of each player's two "hole" cards (not shown to the other players) and another five communal cards that are dealt face up for use by everyone. The hole cards are dealt first. After a round of betting, three communal cards are dealt face up (the "flop"); this is followed by another betting round. Next, a single communal card (the "turn") is dealt, then betting, then the last face-up card (the "river"), then the last betting round.

In this particular game, Straus was initially dealt the worst possible hole cards—a deuce and seven of different suits (the deuce and seven are the two lowest cards that cannot be combined into a five-card sequential straight). Ordinarily, a good player would fold such a hand, but Straus kept playing. The three-card flop consisted of one seven and two threes, giving Straus two pair (sevens and threes), but also giving everyone else a pair of threes to work with. Anyone with a big pair in the hole (higher than sevens) would beat Straus's hand. That appeared to be the case when another player raised aggressively, indicating a very good hand. Straus nonetheless called, even though he was virtually certain that he was up against a better hand (in fact, the other player was holding jacks and threes). The next face-up card (the turn) was a deuce—that gave Straus three pairs, though it did not improve his hand because only five cards can be used.

At that point, Straus bet $18,000, more than triple the amount of any previous bet in the game. The other player, who had been betting aggressively, suddenly paused. How could a deuce have helped Straus so much? While the other player was thinking it over, Straus leaned over the table, smiling. "I'll tell you what," he said. "You give me one of those little old $25 chips of yours and you can see either one of my hole cards, whichever one you choose." The other player hesitated, then tossed Straus a chip as he pointed to one of the hole cards. Straus turned it over, revealing a deuce. The conclusion seemed obvious. Straus must have a pair of deuces in the hole (why else would he offer to show either card?), giving him a full house, deuces over threes. His opponent folded, and Straus won the pot with an inferior hand. (Note that he would have achieved the same outcome had his opponent selected the other card, a seven, which would have indicated that Straus was holding a full house—sevens over threes.)

The point of this story, in case it isn't obvious to non–card players, is that Jack Straus won the hand (and became a poker legend) by voluntarily revealing information, not by concealing it. Showing his hole card was an aggressive show of strength that forced the other player out of the game. But there was even more to his strategy. Good players seldom show their hole cards, so why didn't the other player recognize Straus's move as a bluff? That was due to another masterful bit of reverse psychology. The opposing player reasoned that Straus wanted him to think he was bluffing, in order to get him to dump another $18,000 into the pot. "If Straus wants me to think he's bluffing," the loser's thinking went, "then he must really have the cards." Folding, therefore, was the only rational decision. (This story comes from A. Alvarez, *Poker: Bets, Bluffs, and Bad Beats* 83 (2002).)

In other words, good things can happen when you show your hand.

As most trial advocacy texts explain, direct examination is usually far more important than cross-examination. Direct is the very fulcrum of the trial, the heart of the case, the opportunity for counsel to present the theory and tell the story. Far more cases are won by powerful direct examinations than are lost by witnesses who are damaged on cross.

Why, then, do we routinely attempt to conceal our witnesses' forthcoming answers from opposing counsel? Standard deposition defense strategy has turned the discovery process into a guessing game or treasure hunt, when it might more profitably resemble a preview of direct examination. To be sure, there is no one-size-fits-all deposition tactic for every situation; sometimes, though less often than conventional wisdom presumes, there are compelling reasons for withholding information. Nonetheless, it is simply an empirical error to treat deposition defense as though its primary purpose is to prepare for trial. Instead, the deposition should be recognized as a critical stage of an ongoing negotiation. In that context, there is only one question: What good are your strengths if you keep them hidden?

PART IV

Special Cases

CHAPTER 20

Preparing a Witness to Testify in a Commercial Case

Briscoe R. Smith and Edward D. Cavanagh*

It is remarkable that the same lawyers who take great care with their own arguments to the court and jury can be oblivious to the care and feeding of the players who will largely determine whose client wins a case—the fact witnesses.

Often a lawyer will rely on a quick meeting with a witness in the adversary's waiting room before a deposition, expecting to control damage during the deposition by a barrage of speaking objections, directions not to answer, off-the-record conferences, and other diversions. Even with the doubtful assumption that as a result the witness will survive the deposition without wounds, this approach excludes an opportunity for counseling and advocacy of a most important kind.

---

*Briscoe R. Smith is of counsel to the Atlantic Legal Foundation in New York City, and Edward D. Cavanagh is professor of law at St. John's University School of Law and of counsel to Morgan, Lewis & Bockius in New York City. This article originally appeared in the Summer 1992 issue of LITIGATION.

By working carefully with a witness before a deposition and trial, you can guide a layperson through some bumpy terrain that may be confusing and even threatening. So concentrate on thoughtful preparation designed to give the witness confidence. Show that witness that lawyers know how to grapple with facts while respecting the vagaries of the truth. We here assume that the client expects thorough preparation, even if it is time-consuming.

The battleground of commercial litigation increasingly has moved from the courtroom to the conference room and depositions. There, facts are nailed down; those facts to be decided at trial—and the attendant risks—take shape; and settlement opportunities come into sharper focus. In most cases, deposition practice substitutes for the trial itself. While lawyers understand this, for the witness the deposition most likely will be a new experience. The witness will testify under oath about facts, but the lines separating fact, opinion, and speculation are not easily drawn. "The truth and nothing but the truth" is not in generous supply in the marketplace.

Just as the distinct phases of a trial can be easily identified, so can the separate aspects of deposition preparation. First, investigate the witness and study the relevant documents; second, interview the witness to cover all the areas that may be raised by the examiner; and third, discuss the guidelines to be followed in responding to the questioning. Each phase deserves attention.

Know Your Witness

Before meeting with any witness, find out the witness's background and pertinent responsibilities and know the reason the testimony is sought. You then can pinpoint the issues and documents that will be significant for that witness and, just as important, determine whether others can be covered quickly or ignored.

Learn about the physical surroundings in which the witness works. The assistant controller who sits behind a metal desk in a glass cubicle will probably see a document differently than will the senior executive in a fancy office who reads reports showing the performance of underlings. Much can be learned from a witness's office trappings—or their absence. Ask to meet with the witness at the office and take in as much of the surroundings as you can. Chances are you will discover a good deal about the witness's style of doing business and personal habits, among other things.

Some businesses are run by the distribution of formal memoranda; others run on meetings, often recorded only by slides and other visuals. In still others, a handwritten buck slip passed between two executives means more than a 15-page analysis over which someone has labored for days. The point is obvious: The more you know about how witnesses function in their business environments, the better you can help them explain the documents, sort out the facts, and put their decisions in the right context.

The chain of command is something else to keep in mind. Employees have a natural tendency to adopt the party line—usually set by an immediate superior's view of the problem at hand. Often a witness's view of events will change after a transfer to new responsibilities or the arrival of a new boss. These influences are sometimes apparent when the witness has been fired or has resigned abruptly.

Collect the relevant documents, recording the source of each and segregating privileged material. Follow this procedure for each key witness. Read everything, and when you understand the issues and dynamics of the case, determine whether further coding and organizing will be useful.

Make certain the witness has produced to you everything remotely relevant. Do not overlook personal computer databases. Remember that executive secretaries have been known to keep detailed records unknown to their bosses. Some witnesses show up just before a deposition or even trial sheepishly bearing "confidential" or "personal" files that they somehow overlooked and did not produce earlier. Your adversary then has a field day, and you must report this turn of events—and its ramifications—to your client.

The document search must be handled diplomatically because unspoken client opposition often comes into play. You may have to ask for some personal material—appointment calendars and personnel records, for example—and that will make people nervous. Responding to requests for routine documents, moreover, takes time and distracts people from their other responsibilities. A paralegal or junior lawyer may not have enough clout to gain access to such records. It will work wonders, though, if the general counsel or chief executive officer sends a brief memorandum urging cooperation.

Give special attention to documents containing trade secrets and other competitively significant material. You and the client should consider a stipulation covering disclosure of sensitive documents and then negotiate it with the opposition. Without it, you may need to make a motion before discovery begins.

Provide the witness with the relevant documents before your first interview—with a few days' lead time so that the witness can schedule this "homework." Flag important passages. You may also want to give the witness a bare-bones chronology of the significant events. It is often helpful to ask the witness to review before the interview a summary of the principal claims and defenses in the case. Even before you meet, the witness should understand that the deposition must be taken seriously and that you want to conserve time, concentrating on those fact issues about which the witness may be able to testify.

Keep in mind that anything you show the witness to refresh recollection may be discoverable (Rule 612 of the Federal Rules of Evidence); unless you are careful, you may waive the protected status of work product and lawyer-client communications. Show the witness only those documents that will be produced or are fact neutral.

Ask your adversary to have exhibits premarked for identification to save time at the deposition.

If your adversary tries to use discovery to gain an advantage outside the litigation—for example, by deposing a valued customer of your client—make a motion to block the deposition or, even better, negotiate in such a way as to force your adversary to move to compel the deposition. The December 1993 amendments to the Federal Rules of Civil Procedure minimize the opportunities for this type of gamesmanship. Rule 30 as amended establishes a presumptive limit of ten depositions per side in each case. Courts may limit the number of depositions to fewer than ten if it can be shown that as many as ten depositions would serve only to create unnecessary cost and delay. The Committee on Rules of Practice and Procedure of the Judicial Conference of the United States rejected a more far-reaching proposal to limit each deposition to six hours. Some courts, however, have imposed time limits on depositions pursuant to their inherent powers to manage the pretrial phase of a case.

In addition, the 1993 amendments to Rule 26 seek further to reduce gamesmanship by requiring parties to disclose, without prior request from the adversary, certain core information, including the names of witnesses and the identity of documents relevant to disputed facts alleged with particularity. Rule 26 also permits district courts by local rule to opt out of these disclosure requirements, and about half of the 94 districts have in fact opted out. Nevertheless, some opt-out courts have imposed similar disclosure requirements by local rule or pursuant to Civil Justice Expense and Delay Reduction plans under the Civil Justice Reform Act of 1990.

When a deposition date has been set, try to convince your adversary to conclude the examination without interruption. Block out two or more days if necessary. Your adversary will be forced to prepare fully, knowing there is a limited period within which to get what is needed (and only one shot at the witness). An adversary who needs yet another session will be forced to make a motion; even if you lose, you probably can secure an order limiting the subjects of additional questioning.

Encourage Cooperation

Before meeting with the witness, consider whether the attorney-client privilege will protect your interview. Of course, you can assist the witness even if the privilege does not attach.

Sometimes you must make clear to the witness—especially a client's employee—that you are not the witness's lawyer, that you do not represent the witness but nonetheless can assist and counsel. New York's Code of Professional Responsibility (DR5-109), for example, requires this disclosure if the lawyer represents an organization and the organization's interests may differ from those of the witness. The announcement that you do not represent the witness is bound to confuse because few witnesses know the lawyer's responsibilities in the lawyer-client relationship. Sometimes you must advise the witness to retain another lawyer, especially if your facts suggest criminal problems and a Fifth Amendment privilege. In this murky area the only general rule to follow is that the lawyer must not by design or neglect mislead the witness into thinking that the lawyer-client relationship is in place if it is not.

If your adversary notices the deposition of a witness who is not your client's employee, seek an interview. The witness may be more expansive and unguarded before taking the oath and going on the record. Follow the same rules with a disinterested witness before the deposition as you would with a client's employee.

Consider also whether the witness is especially friendly to you or will be just as cooperative with your adversary, perhaps revealing the witness's impression of your efforts to develop facts favoring your client. Whatever situation you believe you have encountered, do not risk a claim that you were tampering with recollection or coloring a witness's understanding of the facts. That can torpedo your own case—and career. The fictional assistant district attorney in Tom Wolfe's *Bonfire of the Vanities* learns that lesson when Maria Ruskin's taped conversation with Sherman McCoy is played for the criminal court judge: "He practically drew me a map. These were the correct stories, and these were the ones you concocted. I'm supposed to agree with the correct stories."

Sometimes, a prospective witness has no interest in the controversy, is hostile to your client, or is just uncooperative. Then the problem is gaining access to the witness.

Assuming there's no ethical impediment to your interviewing the witness (a point to consider carefully), ask for a meeting, requesting a time and place convenient for the witness. If your client or some other intermediary is on good terms with the witness and can enlist cooperation, by all means seek her help. If there is resistance, emphasize that a meeting will save the witness time at the deposition. If you suspect that the witness has been cooperating with your adversary, ask for a level playing field. Suggest that lack of cooperation will be costly to the parties. Press for the interview politely but persistently, using all the arguments you can muster to show how a meeting will benefit the witness. Often the reluctance will melt, particularly if your request is made on your own behalf and not on behalf of the client.

Paying the Witness

Some witnesses are perfectly willing to cooperate—provided they are paid for their efforts. Some interesting questions surface. The New York Code of Professional Responsibility (DR7-109) permits the payment to a witness of expenses "reasonably incurred." Unless you put a teenager in the best suite in town with unlimited room service, there should be no difficulty. The problem arises in determining what is reasonable compensation for the loss of time in attending or testifying—expenses that may also be paid under the rule. You can safely agree to reimburse a witness for pay actually lost in preparing for and attending a deposition. But what if the witness is not compensated by an hourly rate or loses no pay while preparing to testify? What is the time of a retired bank president worth? What if the witness is a retired purchasing agent?

The question of payment must be raised initially by the witness, not by the lawyer. If the witness sets the amount, particularly if the witness uses the amount routinely—say, as a consulting fee—the lawyer is less likely to be criticized. Your own good sense will tell you what is reasonable and what looks suspicious. One test is to determine what the fee would be on an annual basis.

The real problem in paying a witness is that your adversary will argue that the testimony has been bought. It is best to tell the witness who wants payment that any arrangement may well have to be revealed to the opposition, fueling the argument that the witness's credibility is in doubt. Try to defer agreeing on the amount of the fee until the testimony has been taken. When you do discuss the amount of compensation, make certain the witness knows about your ethical proscription. You cannot be a party to an arrangement that would not be regarded as reasonable in your community.

Interviewing the Witness

Even if you have known the witness for years in a different setting, make it clear that your work together is to be structured carefully and separated from your other dealings. Should your witness be a captain of industry whose time and patience are in short supply, naturally, tailor your approach.

The witness must be prepared by one or more lawyers who are equipped to discuss all aspects of the witness's knowledge of relevant issues. Every line of inquiry must be anticipated. Nevertheless, a witness should never be prepared by a committee of lawyers. Rarely can the necessary rapport be developed in a group. Just as important, it is wasteful to have more than two people working with a witness at the same time; try not to give the impression that the case is not staffed efficiently. If personnel must be changed, explain that this is necessary to save the witness's time and your client's money.

At the outset of your meeting, explain that you want to begin by talking generally about the case and the witness's role. Emphasize that you need to know the whole picture and that preparation for the deposition will come later. Early in the interview, describe your client's principal contentions as well as those of the other side. Encourage the witness to discuss your theory of the case in broad terms but avoid specifics at this point, particularly details about which the witness will have to testify. Use everyday words that can be understood without sending the witness to the dictionary. At all cost, avoid legalese. Show that you have done your own homework without coming across as a know-it-all.

Witnesses should understand that you want to put their conduct and decisions in the best possible light. But to protect the witness, as well as the client, you must know all the facts—even the distasteful ones. You must know the blemishes and soft spots to anticipate and meet them fairly during the deposition and at trial. The witness will realize that the point of the interview is to chase out the facts so that you can use them effectively.

Let the witness talk. You may learn of concerns not revealed by the documents or your interviews with others. Listen, then probe for weaknesses or strengths in your client's position. Seek out troublesome areas and talk them over. But wait until the end of the session to discuss the areas most sensitive for this witness; by then she will be confident in your ability to develop the facts while looking after her interests.

Many lawyers take no notes during the initial phases of the interview because they do not want to put the witness on guard. Some witnesses have the impression that something said off the record somehow does not count. Conversely, something written down is "on the record." A lawyer's notes of an interview somehow freeze the record. If you begin in an unstructured way, the witness is less likely to become prematurely locked into a position that she may wish to change as the interview progresses. You want to encourage candor.

Review the important documents carefully. If there are apparent inconsistencies, resolve them, or if there are irreconcilable problems, point them out. Identify the smoking guns so that the witness understands what your adversary will want to make of them.

Before a witness addresses an unfriendly document or allegation, it is useful to explain how others have reacted to the same evidence. Another technique is to ask what the witness would have done if your adversary's allegations about the witness's conduct were true. It may help to set up a series of hypothetical alternatives, with the witness determining which one most closely portrays the witness's behavior. Again, the witness must not be led to believe that by using these techniques you are attempting to shape the testimony. Witnesses who think that they *can* or, worse, *should* play with facts—parroting the party line at the lawyer's seductive urging—may well do so, exposing themselves to impeachment or other weapons of cross-examination. The witness is not bound by ethical rules, but the lawyer is. It is far easier to cope with a witness whose testimony does not fit neatly into your theory of the case than with one who is inventive and will be exposed at trial as a liar. The truth almost always can be explained.

Warn the witness that the examiner may ask what was discussed during your meeting. The witness should not be rattled by this challenge. Rarely will an examiner take much time to develop in detail what was discussed in predeposition interviews or preparation sessions.

After the interview, prepare a summary memorandum. Not all the areas discussed in the interview will be brought out in the deposition, and the memorandum may be useful in your trial preparation. Write with care; your record may wind up in the hands of your adversary. Control the memorandum's distribution. Sometimes you may wish to ask the witness to review your memorandum for accuracy. If you do, however, it is more likely that the memorandum will be discoverable as a nonparty statement subject to Federal Rule 26(b)(3).

At times it may be tempting to tape-record an interview. Bear in mind, however, that the tape is probably discoverable, and the fact of recording may cause a witness to freeze.

Horseshed the Witness

Schedule the interview several working days before the deposition to give you and the witness time to check facts with others and to locate additional documents. Even if the deposition preparation immediately follows the interview, make sure that the witness understands that the two sessions are very different.

Tell the witness that you are now preparing for the deposition. Explain that to this point you have encouraged her to discuss past events freely, without regard to her personal knowledge, and to put all the facts, good and not so good, on the table. Emphasize the distinctly different approach required in answering deposition questioning. The witness must understand that testifying involves a level of concentration and meticulous communication foreign to most business and social conversation.

A surprising number of executives have never been deposed and, apart from television, theater, and novels, have no idea about testifying, much less about testifying at a deposition. Explain the ground rules with care. Even seasoned witnesses need to be reminded that deposition testimony is serious. By all means, "horseshed" every witness; never neglect to do it.

It may be appropriate to tell the witness the identities of the other deponents—past and future—and describe their handling of the examination. You may want to let the witness read portions of other witnesses' depositions—bearing in mind that the examiner may ask about this kind of preparation and use it to suggest that the witness has been tailoring the testimony and not testifying truthfully. Sketch for the witness the background of the examiner. Describe the deposition's physical setting and the kind of questioning to expect: disjointed and confused, methodical reconstruction of details, or rapid and aggressive cross-examination.

One way to counsel the witness before a deposition is to establish first the heavy adversarial climate—the good guys against the bad. *They* want to twist the facts to fit contrived theories and will try to put words in the witness's mouth. Against this background, the litany of accepted "rules" follows logically: Answer only the question asked; do not volunteer; do not guess; testify only about what you know firsthand; do not let the examiner testify; and, above all, do not worry if you have no recollection, because a deposition is not a memory test. It is even better if the witness has no knowledge at all. These rules are fine; but, without more, this kind of preparation may leave the witness with the impression that a deposition is a license to stonewall. Understandably, this would not create a positive opinion of lawyers generally or of your own integrity.

There is another, more appealing, way to counsel the witness. Emphasize that the witness is under oath and must tell the truth. Therefore, questions must be answered with a precision not expected in usual business or social dealings. A few examples selected to fit the witness will bring the point home: "But, officer, I came to a full stop"; "You're looking great"; "The junior high musical was marvelous."

The witness should realize that your aim is to encourage precise statements of fact under oath, not to slant facts or to stonewall. The focus must be on the oath and the separation of sworn testimony from guesswork, hearsay, general impressions, rumor, and talk to fill the vacuum after a question is asked.

Point out that the examiner is not under oath, nor were the witness's business associates who made statements at meetings or who prepared routine documents that could have been designed to motivate or shock the reader. But the witness is sworn to tell the truth. The guidelines for answering deposition questions stem from that fundamental premise. With some witnesses, you may want to refer to Rule 602 of the Federal Rules of Evidence and its emphasis on the witness's personal knowledge of the matter.

Make certain that the witness understands what it means to have a refreshed recollection. Whether a document refreshes a recollection is, of course, different from whether the witness prepared or received the document. Keep in mind that if you use a document to refresh a recollection, you may be required to turn it over under Rule 612 of the Federal Rules of Evidence.

The "talker" requires particular attention. This witness—often a junior executive or clerical employee—seems driven to talk rather than risk that silence will be taken for incompetence. Talkers' depositions have been handled in any of a number of unsatisfactory ways: for example, talkers have been advised to count silently five seconds before answering any question, no matter how simple, or to face the court reporter and pretend to dictate the answer. There probably are other devices. This breed of witness has no concept of facts; you cannot change that. In emphasizing the significance of the oath (and conducting a fair number of practice question-and-answer sessions), you can only hope to control the flights of fancy.

Some witnesses like to be challenged by a mock cross-examination before they are deposed, particularly if the examiner has an aggressive style. Consider with the witness whether that kind of exercise would be helpful. If so, do not get carried away. You want to build, not undermine, the witness's comfort level.

Convey the sense that you are there to protect the witness's interests. Say that you will object to form if the question is vague or otherwise objectionable and that you may direct the witness not to answer. Provided no question is pending, the witness can confer off the record with you. And short breaks can be taken at the witness's request. A deposition is not an endurance contest. Let the witness know that you can ask questions on direct if something needs to be straightened out. If a substantive error is made, have the witness correct it on the spot (even over the examiner's objection) or on redirect, with the witness explaining the error. Although the witness can correct the transcript before it is signed, substantive after-the-fact changes look suspicious and, if consequential, can lead to the reopening of the deposition. Emphasize that changes in testimony cannot be made effectively after the deposition is concluded.

The Abusive Examiner

If you have conducted the interview and the preparation session well, the witness should handle the deposition comfortably. You need not fall back on tactics that once were well-worn tools in the litigator's kit: speaking objections, obvious coaching—for example, "You can answer if you know"—and directions not to answer. Nevertheless, do not hesitate to object if the examiner strays from legitimate questioning or is abusive. And the witness will want your interruption if the testimony becomes casual or confused or if the examiner starts to draw blood.

The rules are stacked against a lawyer defending a deposition. The custom in most courts and the practice under the federal rules is to preserve for trial all objections except those that could have been obviated by promptly calling them to the examiner's attention at the time the question was propounded. Thus, the witness is permitted to testify on deposition with respect to information that is hearsay or irrelevant. This is not to say that counsel defending a deposition is without recourse. The ultimate defense weapon in a deposition is the direction not to answer. For years, directions not to answer were among the grayest of gray areas in deposition practice. Prior to 1993, the federal rules did not address this practice, but courts generally recognized a limited right to instruct a witness not to answer in a deposition, though not without some criticism. *E.g., Nutmeg Insurance Co. v. Atwell Vogel & Sterling,* 120 F.R.D. 504, 508 (W.D. La. 1988). The 1993 amendments to the federal rules codified the practice in limited circumstances. Rule 30(d)(1) authorizes directions not to answer (1) where necessary to preserve a privilege; (2) to enforce a court-ordered limitation on discovery; and (3) where the deposition is being conducted in bad faith.

You should not hesitate to instruct a witness not to answer when the examiner inquires in a privileged area. Otherwise, the privilege may be deemed to have been waived. Even so, this tactic should be employed sparingly. Repeated use of instructions not to answer is symptomatic that the deposition is not proceeding as it should. But that may be the fault of an inexperienced or abusive examiner and not necessarily the fault of the lawyer giving the direction not to answer.

Protect the witness against sloppy questioning by objecting regarding form. For example, the question may be confusing because it is compound or indefinite as to time. Other, more substantive, objections include relevance, the assumption of facts not in the record (the foundation objection), the eliciting of opinions and speculation rather than facts, abusiveness, and repetitiveness ("asked and answered").

Objections to form as well as foundation objections are waived unless made immediately. These objections should encourage the examiner to ask clear questions. Do not be timid. Your objections will be welcome if your adversary reads the deposition at trial.

Merely stating an objection may not be enough, particularly if the examining lawyer is abusive. If you cannot divert your adversary into other areas, you have two options: direct the witness not to answer or adjourn to seek a protective order. The two differ in burden and expense.

The route you choose is dictated by the dynamics of the case. If the atmosphere is heated, you may opt to adjourn and move for a protective order to defuse a volatile situation. This step is typically unnecessary, however; you can protect the witness by simply directing her not to answer. Your adversary then has to decide whether the information sought is important enough and the objection weak enough to justify the expense of a motion.

Courts understandably take a dim view of directions not to answer unless they are grounded in a recognized privilege.

Questions that wander far afield, assume facts not in evidence, are repetitive, or call for opinions are annoying, time-consuming, and often confusing. Responding (to the extent possible), however, rarely causes any real harm or prejudice comparable to the result of the requirement that witnesses divulge privileged information.

There are two risks in directing a witness not to answer: First, the court may get the impression that you are not mindful of the liberal sweep of discovery—or, worse, that the well-guarded ground contains gold. Second, the court may impose sanctions (which some lawyers now request routinely whenever a discovery motion is made).

There are several ways to keep the confidence of the court and to reduce exposure to sanctions in a deposition. The key is to be reasonable even to the point of appearing helpful by doing the following:

- Explain to your adversary the basis of your objection. If you assert privilege, give the details.
- Offer nonobjectionable ways to develop the facts.
- If your direction not to answer involves a nonprivileged area, do not immediately impose the instruction not to answer. Object, but offer some leeway.
- Do not direct a witness not to answer for reasons you will not be able to justify when you are responding to a motion.

No matter how abusive the examiner is, help the witness maintain poise. And although you will want to show that you, too, can dish it out, your objections should be made in a calm, deliberate manner. Avoid sarcastic comments—particularly those aimed at the examiner.

Insist on short breaks every hour or so. The court reporter will be grateful. As the session wears on, the witness will tend to become bored, sloppy, impatient, argumentative, or all of the above. A few private moments will let you remind the witness about the importance of precision or enable you to say how well the deposition is going. Witnesses like to be told they are doing well, and a compliment will underscore the fact that a deposition is serious business and not a chatty, social affair. Again, keep in mind that heavy coaching during a break can be explored by your adversary when the deposition resumes.

Sometimes the examiner overlooks—or intentionally avoids—topics about which your witness may have information helpful to your case. You may be tempted to let the incomplete record stand, reasoning that you do not want to expose a strong point so that your adversary is forewarned. Or, you may simply want to see the examination terminated, thinking that you can tell your side of the story at trial.

Think carefully about holding your fire for trial. The witness may not be within subpoena range and may choose not to attend trial voluntarily. Even if the witness agrees to testify at trial, memories fade and emotions calm over time. Moreover, deposition testimony strongly supporting your trial strategy can be used in drafting requests for admission and pretrial motions and can be powerful in settlement negotiations. Finally, under Rule 32(a)(4) of the Federal Rules of Civil Procedure, your adversary may be required at trial to bring out important elements of your case by reading those parts of the deposition "which ought in fairness to be considered with the part introduced." If the deposition has abundant evidence favorable to your client, your adversary may think better of offering it at all.

If you do examine the witness, make sure you avoid leading questions. You may not be permitted to lead the witness at trial, and the evidence you so carefully preserved may be useless.

Unless the witness has testified to purely formal or inconsequential matters, make sure the witness reads and signs the deposition, making all appropriate corrections. You will want to discuss any changes of substance with the witness before the deposition is filed. This step may be critical if a key witness wants to make important changes.

At bottom, defending a deposition successfully depends on your grasp of the facts and your ability to focus the witness's attention on the importance of the exercise. Chances are that you and the witness will know each other better when the questioning is completed.

Trial Testimony

If you have done your job well before the deposition, preparing the witness for trial should not be complicated, because you will follow mechanical steps similar to those involved in preparing for the deposition. Let the witness know well in advance that testimony is required. Send her a copy of the deposition transcript and key exhibits, pointing out any material that is no longer relevant.

Before appearance at trial, bring the witness up-to-date about developments after the deposition. Again, give her a chance to express personal views and concerns. Explain how her testimony will fit into the larger picture. Identify the witnesses who have already testified, the topics covered, and the topics anticipated. Explain how direct, cross, and redirect are conducted and how objections are handled. Again emphasize the importance of the oath and the need for precision. Unless the testimony is to purely formal matters, convey the sense that each witness's testimony is important to a successful outcome and that each witness's efforts are appreciated.

Explain the basic difference between direct and cross-examination. For direct testimony, the examining lawyer should have a detailed outline of facts and exhibits to be covered. A practice session or two will help ensure that the witness will bring out the key details without leading questions or will tell you how much help she will need. Asking the witness to identify and testify regarding documents is often an effective way not to overlook details. The risk is that the overly conscientious witness's testimony may seem contrived and unbelievable.

Anticipate lines of attack the cross-examiner might use. The witness must not be surprised by any document or line of questioning. If circumstances permit and if a difficult cross is expected, practice a cross—or better, have someone else familiar with the case play the heavy—before the witness testifies.

There are not many ways to protect a witness from a skillful cross-examiner. Thorough preparation for direct testimony, however, can avoid some of the traps that can be sprung. Obviously, the witness who stays closest to objective facts is the least vulnerable. The witness who is prone to exaggeration, self-serving asides, or role-playing is likely to get into trouble. Even worse is the witness who turns hostile on cross or whose memory suddenly fades.

A courteous and respectful witness will offer fewer opportunities for the cross-examiner than will the arrogant proponent of one side of the case. At bottom, the witness who is prepared properly for direct, with the strictures of sworn testimony in mind, should be able to withstand a rigorous cross, even gaining credibility in the process.

It is often wise to ask the witness to arrive at court an hour or so before taking the stand. That provides a chance to absorb the style of the lawyers and to see how objections and sidebars are handled. If the rule of exclusion has been invoked, describe the layout of the courtroom and the basic mechanics so that the witness does not come into a wholly foreign setting.

After being excused, the witness should leave the courtroom immediately and—if the testimony has been lengthy or especially critical—should not return as a spectator.

When it is all over, write the witness a brief note of thanks, avoiding any characterization of the substance of the testimony. Even if the outcome was not what you wanted, let the witness know how the case was decided.

* * * *

Preparing a witness to testify in an important case is a daunting challenge to your personal and professional abilities. Frequently, you must act as the witness's conscience, as well as coach, referee, and advocate. The job is often difficult, but if you do it right, it wins cases, as well as the confidence and even the gratitude of clients.

CHAPTER 21

Strategies in Expert Depositions

Peter L. Winik*

An "expert" is:

"One who knows more and more about less and less."

—*Ambrose Bierce*

"One who knows too much about one subject."

—*Leonard L. Levinson*

Webster's New World Dictionary of Quotable Definitions, 2nd Ed.

Experts have been the brains behind the growth in injury lawsuits since the 1960s. Over the years, they have become ubiquitous in court, indispensable in many suits and a flourishing industry in their own right. For a fee, experts will do most anything, or so it seems. . . .

—*Wall Street Journal*, "Who Is An Expert? In Some Courtrooms, The Answer is Nobody," June 17, 1997

*Peter L. Winik is a partner is the Washington, D.C., office of Latham & Watkins LLP. He gratefully acknowledges assistance on this article from Cynthia Cwik, a partner in the firm's San Diego office. This article originally appeared in the Spring 1998 issue of LITIGATION.

In high-stakes litigation—whether commercial or tort—expert testimony typically can determine the outcome of the case. Although the United States Supreme Court, in its landmark decision in *Daubert v. Merrell Dow Pharmaceuticals, Inc.*, 509 U.S. 579 (1993), acted to put some sensible brakes on the use—or, rather, the overuse—of experts, handling an expert properly can still mean the difference between winning or losing. Furthermore, dealing with an adverse expert is a singular experience. In most cases you should take the rules that you would normally follow in handling fact witnesses and throw them out the window.

Tearing down the adverse expert also can be hard work. That person can be confident, self-assured, and very knowledgeable, and juries often are predisposed to believe experts who establish a threshold of credibility. In fact, according to survey data compiled by Hale Starr, a jury consultant with whom I and a number of my colleagues have worked, 96 percent of a sample group responded that it was "likely" or "very likely" that they "would believe testimony given in a court of law by an expert witness. . . ." Moreover, when asked to react to the proposition that "expert witnesses are nothing more than 'hired guns' who will testify to anything that helps the side that is paying them," 41 percent agreed and 58 percent disagreed. In short, you've got your work cut out for you in trying to dim the aura of credibility an expert brings to the witness stand.

This article is not intended to be a discourse on "the law." There are thousands of cases that deal with the subject area of experts. This is not the time to discuss them. Instead, we will take a brief look at the key federal rules (most states' rules dovetail the federal rules), then delve into personal perspectives on how best to take advantage of the occasion of taking an expert's deposition.

The Rules

Rule 26(a)(2) of the Federal Rules of Civil Procedure provides the basis for expert discovery. Rule 26(a)(2)(A) requires a party to "disclose to the other parties the identity of any person who may be used at trial to present evidence under Rules 702, 703, or 705 of the Federal Rules of Evidence." In addition to disclosing names, Rule 26(a)(2)(B) mandates that this disclosure shall "be accompanied by a written report prepared and signed by the witness." The report must contain:

... a complete statement of all opinions to be expressed and the basis and reasons therefor; the data or other information considered by the witness in forming the opinions; any exhibits to be used as a summary of or support for the opinions; the qualifications of the witness, including a list of all publications authored by the witness within the preceding ten years; the compensation to be paid for the study and testimony; and a listing of any other cases in which the witness has testified as an expert at trial or by deposition within the preceding four years.

Note that this requirement may be modified by the parties' agreement or by order of the court. Most modifications are made in the area of depositions. The Rules do not specifically provide for depositions of experts. However, parties ordinarily agree to a deposition procedure that applies to all experts. Additionally, the Rule does not preclude documentary discovery from experts; typically, parties agree to such an exchange (or, it can be handled by subpoena, document request, or case management order).

Fed. R. Civ. P. 26 deals with matters of procedure. The substantive basis for expert testimony resides in the Federal Rules of Evidence. Rule 702—hardly a model of clarity—lays out the bedrock principle of admissibility:

If scientific, technical, or other specialized knowledge will assist the trier-of-fact to understand the evidence or to determine a fact in issue, a witness qualified as an expert by knowledge, skill, experience, training, or education, may testify thereto in the form of an opinion or otherwise.

The Supreme Court, in *Daubert*, interpreted Rule 702 in the context of *scientific* expert testimony. The Court interpreted "scientific knowledge" as being "derived by the scientific method." *Daubert, supra.*, 509 U.S. at 590. The Court also said that the testimony must have a "valid scientific connection to the pertinent inquiry as a precondition to admissibility." *Id.* at 591–2. The Court properly recognized that it was creating a "gatekeeping role for the judge," *id.* at 597, at least in cases involving "scientific" testimony. Later courts have split on the question of whether *Daubert's* tests also must be applied in cases of expert testimony concerning "technical, or other specialized knowledge."

Rule 703 allows, among other things, for the use of hearsay by an expert:

The facts or data in the particular case upon which an expert bases an opinion or inference may be those perceived by or made known to the expert at or before the hearing. If of a type reasonably relied upon by experts in the particular field in forming opinions or inferences upon the subject, the facts or data need not be admissible in evidence.

Rule 704(a)—the "opinion on ultimate issue" rule—provides another important guidepost for the civil litigator. It provides that "testimony in the form of an opinion or inference otherwise admissible is not objectionable because it embraces an ultimate issue to be decided by the trier-of-fact."

Finally, Rule 705, entitled "Disclosure of Facts or Data Underlying Expert Opinion," provides:

The expert may testify in terms of opinion or inference and give reasons therefor without first testifying to the underlying facts or data, unless the court requires otherwise. The expert may in any event be required to disclose the underlying facts or data on cross-examination.

While the Rules themselves are not models of clarity, and case law interpreting them abounds, a working knowledge of the Rules is essential as you prepare to depose the other side's expert.

Preparing for the Expert Deposition

You have the other side's Rule 26 statement and the opposing expert's documents. You have read the Rules. Now it's time to get ready to take her deposition. Of course, this assumes that you have agreed with the other side to take each other's experts' depositions. In my view, this typically makes sense. It is possible, however, that in a particular case you may decide you have more to lose than gain by allowing depositions, and you may therefore seek to rest on the Rule 26 statements alone and forego the depositions.

Assuming you have decided to proceed with depositions, you should accomplish a number of things before going into the deposition room. First, you must know the expert *cold*. Find out everything you reasonably can about him. That entails:

- Reading thoroughly the Rule 26 statement, as well as any documents that you may have obtained.

- Searching online databases for references to the expert in published decisions. I am living proof that this can sometimes pay off. A number of years ago, before deposing a plaintiff's expert in a products liability case, I found a case in which the court had refused to qualify the expert to testify. After the deadline for naming experts had passed—and therefore it was too late for the plaintiff to make a substitution—I questioned the expert about this case at his deposition. My opponent either had not known about the expert's other case or did not anticipate that I would find it. His discomfort was palpable (and fun to watch).
- Searching databases for news stories or articles mentioning the expert.
- Gathering and reviewing all of the expert's writings. In looking for the expert's writings, your firm's librarian (or someone else with knowledge of available data bases) can be of invaluable assistance.
- Gathering and reviewing all of the expert's prior testimony. If the expert has not produced to you transcripts of her prior testimony, you may have to dig some to find them. Find the name of the case and the identity of the expert's opposing counsel in the case, and contact that person directly. Most litigators, as a courtesy, will share information about experiences with a given expert.
- Conducting independent research into the expert's background and credentials. Do not assume that the expert's resume is fully truthful or accurate. My partner Cynthia Cwik, someone with substantial experience deposing experts in the scientific and medical arena, recalls a toxic tort case in which she called the university from which the opposing side's immunologist supposedly received his degree—only to learn that the degree was from the college's *veterinary school!*
- Consulting closely with your own expert.
- In general, becoming as knowledgeable as any expert in the particular field of endeavor. Become as much of an expert as the expert herself by the time you are ready to take depositions.

Once you have fully armed yourself, you're ready to take the deposition.

One initial question you will face is how to record the expert's deposition. My own preference is generally to videotape it, if your client's budget will allow it. When used properly, impeachment at trial with videotape can be far more effective than a simple, two-dimensional transcript. There is no right answer for all situations, however, Cynthia Cwik sometimes prefers *not* to videotape the other side's expert. She reasons that the other side's expert may be more guarded with the cameras rolling, and she also points out that it will typically mean your opponent will insist on videotaping your expert in exchange. Obviously, you should carefully consider whether to videotape, taking into account the case's particular merits and drawbacks.

A second threshold question is when to take the deposition. My practice is to take the experts' depositions after fact discovery has closed, preferably close to trial. Waiting until that point maximizes the odds that the expert will have completed her analysis, and, accordingly, minimizes the chances that the expert will change her mind, or perform additional work, after the deposition. If instead you opt to take the deposition early, and a significant amount of time passes from the deposition to the trial, you may want to re-depose the expert. The question of "who goes first" can also be a significant one. Typically, it makes sense for the expert for the party with the burden of proof to be deposed first.

Regardless of how or when the deposition is recorded, keep the following principles in mind as you take the deposition of an expert.

Sizing Up the Expert

One of the primary reasons to take an expert's deposition is that it provides a marvelous opportunity to size the person up. How does the expert appear? Is he humble or pompous? Verbose or succinct? Precise and careful, or a hipshooter? Having the opportunity to take the expert's measure before trial can be of incalculable benefit as you prepare your trial plan. Armed with this knowledge, you can determine the best way to combat the expert at trial.

My partner Everett Johnson has a theory about confronting experts at trial that has lessons for the expert's deposition. His view is that at trial, you must have a single theme as to why the expert should be disbelieved. He says that you should pick your focus, whether it is to show that the expert is dishonest, or is careless, or is simply relying on wrong facts. "Have a single cohesive theory," he counsels. Your best chance to decide on a theory to pursue will come in the deposition, when the expert is before you and where you can test, probe, and experiment. Remember that, unlike a fact-witness's deposition, the expert's deposition most likely will not be introduced into evidence by your adversary. The expert will testify live, unless the matter is being handled by affidavit in a nonjury setting. Therefore, you can take more risks than in a fact deposition, because you know the answers in all likelihood will not be introduced against you.

If attacking the expert directly won't do the job, another way to neutralize him is through other witnesses. In a jury trial several years ago, I saw my co-counsel, Tom Green—a partner at Sidley & Austin and a veteran trial lawyer—do a very effective job at discrediting an expert in a rather unconventional way. A key issue in the case was whether the majority of the board of directors of a small, family owned corporation breached its fiduciary duties when it took a certain, challenged action. The plaintiff put its expert—we'll call him "Professor Adams"—on the stand. He had unimpeachable credentials: a professor at a major school, a leading commentator on corporate governance issues, and a member of several corporate boards. If there was a flaw in the expert's armor, it became clear at the deposition (and later was confirmed at trial) that the witness had a pompous, haughty demeanor. Rather than spending a great deal of time challenging Professor Adams head-on, Green let the expert profess his self-importance and waited until plaintiff had put someone else on the stand, a securities lawyer testifying as a fact witness. Toward the end of cross-examination, after it was obvious that the lawyer was very experienced in corporate-governance matters, Green asked him, seemingly as an innocent aside: "By the way, have you ever heard of Professor Adams?" When the witness answered, unwittingly, "No, I haven't," Green muttered: "I'm sure he'll be sorry to hear that." The jury and courtroom erupted into laughter, in the process deflating the professor's self-important testimony. That one (albeit risky) exchange did more to negate the plaintiff's expert than any attempts at frontal assault on the professor himself.

The importance of coming to know the other side's expert cannot be overstated. You cannot accomplish this goal if you follow a strict script, or if you rush from one question to the next. Give the expert time to talk. Let her reveal her true colors.

A second goal for the deposition is to learn as much as you can from the expert. This is your chance to be educated by him. Being a good listener is much more important than being a sharp questioner. Try adopting a conversational, nonconfrontational tone. Have good eye contact with the witness. Draw him out fully on such things as:

- His education and work experience in the field of expertise.
- His past writings and speeches concerning the topic(s) at hand.
- Past work as an expert. But don't limit yourself to past testimony. Include affidavits and expert reports/opinions that have been exchanged.
- What he has done to date on the case.
- What, if anything, he thinks remains to be done.
- The basis for his opinions in the case. (Recall that Rule 705 provides that the expert may be "required to disclose the underlying facts or data on cross-examination.")
- Everything that he has been shown, or that he has considered, in forming his opinions.
- Anything that he has requested but not been provided, or not been allowed to explore.

This should take time. With an experienced and somewhat talkative expert, the discussion could yield several hundred pages of transcript. You are carefully and painstakingly, though perhaps not dramatically, laying the foundation for ultimate success at trial.

Determining the Expert's Critical Variables

Part of learning all you can from the expert involves discovering the variable factors on which the expert's opinion is based. Thus, once you have eliminated all the areas of agreement between the expert and your own expert, focus on whether any areas of difference depend on facts or assumptions that, if changed, could lead to opinions that are consistent with you own expert's opinions. This can be an extremely important exercise, because at trial you can demonstrate that the assumed facts or variables actually are wrong, and that the adverse expert's opinions therefore are wrong as well. Even better, you may be able to show that, in reality, the opposing expert would agree with your own expert if the key fact or variable were changed.

In addition to all of these points—which might strike many as obvious or basic, but which often are not covered in sufficient depth at an expert deposition—Everett Johnson emphasizes another often-overlooked proposition that should be equally obvious: make certain to try to narrow the areas of disagreement between the opposing expert and your own expert.

You don't accomplish this by quickly asking a single, all-encompassing question such as: "What are your views on Dr. Jones's opinion in this case?" Instead, patiently ask many less ambitious questions aimed at finding as much common ground as possible. For example, assuming you are deposing an economist ("Dr. Smith") in a valuation case (in which your expert is "Dr. Jones"), you might ask questions such as:

- You believe that Dr. Jones is an honest person, don't you, Dr. Smith?
- You don't believe that he is lying here, do you?
- You don't believe that he is tailoring his opinion to fit what the other side wants to hear any more than you are, Dr. Smith?
- You and he have come up with different answers here, but you're not challenging his integrity, are you?
- Would you agree that Dr. Jones's degree is from a first-rate university?
- Would you agree that his degree in economics is relevant to the opinions that both of you are expressing in this case?
- His work at Acme Corporation was in the very same field that both of you are opining in, correct?
- He has honors from the XYZ Council—that's a reputable organization, is it not?
- You and Dr. Jones both agree that it is appropriate to apply the principles of economics to this case, correct?
- You both think it's appropriate to examine past property sales in arriving at your opinion, right?
- You both think it's appropriate to look at economic trends in arriving at your opinion, correct?
- Among the trends that you both look at are interest rates, employment, and new home starts, correct?

You get the point. You would be amazed at how many areas of common ground you can establish between the two sides' experts. Establishing that the other side's expert agrees with many of your own expert's views, and agrees that your own expert has good qualifications, should help you focus the jury on the key areas of difference between the two experts. Everett Johnson recently used this tactic to good advantage in a bench trial in the U.S. Court of Federal Claims. He managed to narrow the difference between competing valuation experts to one critical variable: the adverse expert's analysis depended on a number of subjectively derived data points, while Johnson's expert depended solely on objective data. Pursuing his strategy of limiting the attack to one key theme, he prevailed at trial by convincing the court that his expert's analysis was the more reliable one because it was more objective than the other side's analysis.

Once you have elicited at the deposition all information that is in the expert's brain, you should resist the urge to cross-examine and "destroy" the expert. All you are doing is educating him, and his counsel, as to the flaws in the analysis. At trial, you will face a better-prepared foe who will be grateful that you exposed his weaknesses beforehand, while he still had time to make corrections.

Instead, your paramount goal should be to lock the expert into his testimony and seal off all means of escape. This is particularly crucial if you are able to determine in the course of the deposition that your best angle of attack at trial is to highlight the errors in the opposing expert's analysis. Once you have totally locked the expert into his analysis through effective deposition questioning, if your opponent figures out after the deposition that his theories are flawed, he will realize that he is trapped. What are the techniques required to lock the expert in and close all routes of escape?

- When finding out whether you have been told all facts (or opinions or theories), keep asking "Have you now told me everything, Dr. Smith?" or "Is that all?" until you elicit an affirmative answer. If he keeps adding more information, wear him down until he conclusively says, "That's it."
- Exhaustively explore the areas of weakness. Make the expert repeat his errors time and time again. If you do this, the expert's attempt at trial to change his testimony

by saying he didn't understand a question simply will not be believed.

- Make certain to ascertain whether there is anything else that the expert feels he needs to do before trial. Keep asking until you have a full and complete list. As to each point he raises, ask why that task needs to be done. This will expose the flaws in the expert's current analysis. And, if the expert never performs the additional work, you can prove at trial—with his own words—that his work is flawed. Note that depending on the answers, you may need to re-depose the expert closer to trial (or bring a motion in limine to preclude testimony based on work performed after the deposition).

Painting the other side's expert into a corner at the deposition freezes the validity of his analysis in time. It also gives you the powerful ammunition you'll want for cross-examination at trial if he tries to enhance, qualify, or augment what he told you in deposition.

Even before the Supreme Court's decision in *Daubert*, an important objective in any expert's deposition was to learn if fair grounds existed to seek to disqualify the expert. Other than the obvious grounds for disqualification—that the expert lacks sufficient credentials to qualify as an "expert" under Rule 702—I would (and still do) frequently try to establish that the proposed testimony or area of "expertise" is not appropriate for expert testimony, because it does not pertain to an issue as to which the trier-of-fact needs assistance "to understand the evidence or to determine a fact in issue." Fed. R. Evid. 702. Testimony is most frequently excluded on these grounds because it is offered on a subject that is within the average juror's common knowledge, or because it leans too far toward telling the jury the law and, thus, invades the province of the court. Furthermore, testimony may be excluded on these grounds because it simply tells the jury how to decide the case. True, Rule 704 does not automatically preclude expert testimony simply because it concerns the "ultimate issue" in the case. But that does not mean the court must allow all expert testimony that purports to tell the jury how to decide the case. The commentary to Rule 704 makes clear that "opinions which would merely tell the jury what result to reach" can still be excluded, among other reasons, because they would not be helpful to the jury.

It may not be obvious, from the expert report alone, that there are strong grounds for excluding an expert's testimony. Make certain to draw the expert out fully in her deposition concerning all areas of testimony you expect him to give, and especially those aspects you believe invade the jury's province. You want to leave the deposition with an adequate record for your motion to disqualify.

Yet another ground for disqualification that should not be overlooked is whether the adversary's expert has a conflict of interest by reason of prior work for your client, or is otherwise tainted by access to confidential information from your client. Make certain to ask sufficient background questions to determine if this is a fruitful area of inquiry.

The testimony that you elicit from the expert in her deposition can be pivotal to the success of your disqualification motion (or to a motion in limine). Therefore, it is important to decide before the deposition—generally, based on the expert's written report—whether you plan to make a stab at disqualification or limitation. If so, your questioning should focus on attempting to make the best record possible for later use.

Dealing with *Daubert*

As discussed above, the 1993 Supreme Court decision in *Daubert v. Merrell Dow Pharmaceuticals, Inc.*, has had a dramatic impact on the way in which we approach and present experts. The Court in *Daubert* held that trial judges must play a strong gatekeeping role in determining whether to allow expert testimony, at least in cases involving "scientific" matters; essentially, the task for the courts is to weed out "junk science." In order to accomplish this end, the Supreme Court held that the previously prevailing test of determining whether evidence was "generally accepted" in the relevant scientific community had been superseded by the 1975 adoption of the Federal Rules of Evidence. The Court directed that under the Rules, judges must take into account a number of factors in determining whether to admit a scientific opinion, including: (1) whether the theory or technique has been tested; (2) whether it has been subjected to peer review and publication; (3) its known or potential error rate; (4) the existence of standards controlling its operation; and, (5) the degree to which it has been accepted in the relevant scientific community. The Supreme Court stressed that this threshold inquiry should be a flexible one that seeks to ascertain the scientific validity of the expert opinion's underlying principles as a way of determining reliability. *See Daubert, supra,* 509 U.S. at 592–5.

Much already has been written on the application of *Daubert* by the lower courts. While the courts have split on the question of whether *Daubert* applies beyond the realm of "scientific" evidence, some courts have held that it applies directly to all expert testimony. Others—while rejecting the direct application of *Daubert*—nonetheless have engaged in far more rigorous scrutiny of the admissibility of nonscientific expert testimony than in the pre-*Daubert* days. Thus, regardless of the type of case in which you are involved, the *Daubert* decision has profound implications for any litigator preparing to depose the adverse expert.

Cynthia Cwik observes that some experts (at least those that spend a significant amount of time as testifying experts) are, at this point, as savvy about *Daubert* as the lawyers. She recalls recently deposing an expert whose report "spent pages" explaining why his opinions should be qualified under the *Daubert* standards. She counsels that you should assume the opposing expert will be very well prepared to posture his opinions in order to maximize the likelihood that he will be allowed to express them.

If you believe the *Daubert* filter will be applied to expert testimony in your case, anticipate the possibility of an evidentiary hearing, before trial, on the question of whether the opposing expert will be allowed to testify. Make maximum use of the deposition opportunity, and map out your strategy in advance of the deposition most likely in close coordination with your own expert on how best to attack the expert's opinions under *Daubert*.

Do not overlook a final line of inquiry that arises from Rule 703. The Rule allows an expert to base an opinion on facts that are not admissible into evidence if they are of a type "reasonably relied upon by experts in the particular field in forming opinions or inferences upon the subject." Many lawyers assume that experts can rely on hearsay and fail to remember that a threshold showing must be made, before the opinion may be admitted, that the hearsay evidence is of a type "reasonably relied upon" by experts in the field. If you think the opposing expert may be vulnerable on this point, make sure to question her at the deposition about this threshold standard. As with the *Daubert* analysis, this issue is one where you may also obtain or present evidence from third parties (e.g., other experts in the field) that bears on the admissibility questions.

Even taking into account the influence of *Daubert* in limiting the range of expertise recognized by courts, expert testimony will continue to have a powerful impact on the outcome of litigation. The deposition of your adversary's expert can derail or even destroy a strong case.

Work hard, learn all you can, prepare thoroughly, and explore each weakness. A favorable settlement, trial win, or even outright dismissal might result.

CHAPTER 22

Playing Hardball in Expert Witness Depositions

Steven C. Day*

Cross-examining an expert witness is one of the great challenges of trial practice. At its worst, it can be the ultimate humiliation—you strut up to the podium full of vim and vigor and launch into an attack, only to watch the expert effortlessly bat your questions aside. Like the emperor without his clothes, you stand there exposed and helpless. You know that you lack the right stuff, and you know that the jury knows it, too.

But at its best, cross-examining an expert witness can be a classic confrontation—in the baseball tradition of the pitcher throwing heat while the home-run king stands at the plate. It can be the stuff of legend. Nothing is more satisfying than deflating the ego of a professional expert witness, reducing it from the size of a large planet to that of a small moon.

Your initial confrontation with the expert usually happens outside the courtroom, in a deposition. That confrontation will set the stage for what is to follow. In fact, the method you choose for deposing the expert may well determine whether the expert whiffs or hits the long ball at trial.

---

*Steven C. Day is with Woodard, Hernandez, Roth & Day, LLC, in Wichita, Kansas. This article originally appeared in the Summer 2000 issue of LITIGATION.

There are two distinct styles commonly used in taking the depositions of adverse expert witnesses. These styles are based on different views concerning the substantive purpose of the deposition. The first style is a softball approach—a pure discovery deposition without any effort to challenge the expert's opinions. Gathering information is the whole purpose of such a deposition. The second style is a hardball deposition, in which the questioner goes beyond pure discovery and tries to throw strikes. Gathering information is only one objective of a hardball deposition; other goals may include setting up a motion for summary judgment, achieving a favorable settlement, convincing an adverse party to dismiss a minor defendant, or gaining concessions from the expert for use in trial cross-examination.

Not every expert deposition is a good candidate for a hardball approach. Deciding on the best approach for each deposition requires careful thought. The right answer will vary from case to case, witness to witness, and lawyer to lawyer. In fact, there is nothing wrong with avoiding all hardball questioning in expert depositions, and trial advocacy publications tend to endorse the softball expert deposition. A recent article in Litigation, for example, cautioned that "[o]nce you have elicited at the deposition all information that is in the expert's brain, you should resist the urge to cross-examine and 'destroy' the expert." Winik, "Strategies in Expert Depositions," Vol. 24, No. 3 Litigation at 17 (Spring 1998). Similar sentiments have been voiced by other authors, including the venerable Professor James McElhaney. *See* "Exposing Fatal Flaws," 83 *ABA Journal* at 78 (April 1997).

Given this weight of authority, one might expect to find nearly complete conformity among trial lawyers. But the opposite is true. Most trial lawyers reject a pure softball approach during the expert's deposition. Indeed, it is the rare litigator who does not at least occasionally throw a hardball question at an expert during a deposition. Many do so in most depositions. In reality, expert depositions tend to reflect more the rough-and-tumble clash of a trial cross-examination than the gentle waltz of a pure discovery deposition.

Critics of the hardball approach say that cross-examining an expert at his deposition risks educating the expert and opposing counsel, making them better prepared at trial. Although this is a legitimate concern, it can be overstated. After all, once the expert has answered a question, to a very great degree she is stuck with the answer. Certainly, she can try to change it at trial or, more often, try to explain it away. But this carries a significant price. Credibility is an expert witness's stock in trade; anything that damages that credibility diminishes the expert's effectiveness.

In my view, there is much to be gained from an effective hardball deposition. Taking on a polished expert witness for the first time at trial, in front of a jury, is scary business. After all, the witness is the expert. In a very real sense, the lawyer is playing on the witness's home field. The successful hardball deposition gives the lawyer a safe place to start. If the witness has already answered a question during the deposition, the lawyer will know how even a slick professional expert witness will answer the question at trial. This is probably the principal reason why lawyers take hardball depositions of opposing experts—to set up cross-examination at trial.

There are at least four things a lawyer must do to be fully prepared to take the deposition of an expert witness: First, learn the facts of the case in detail; second, learn at least a little something about the witness; third, learn the science of the case; fourth, create a deposition plan.

Of the four, learning the facts may be the most important. This is the one place where you have a natural advantage over the expert. While you have lived, breathed, and eaten the case for months or even years, the expert's factual understanding often will have come from a few hours spent reviewing records and talking to your opposing counsel. If you take the time to freshen up your knowledge by reviewing the key documents and transcripts, you should start the deposition knowing the factual details much better than the expert. This gives you a hidden power: the ability to be inscrutable to the witness. By using this power artfully, you can win concessions without the witness's knowing she has given them.

Learning about an expert's background and personality serves a different purpose: It can help you to prepare intelligently by giving you an idea of what to expect from the witness. Is the witness a know-it-all who will stretch her opinions beyond what is credible? Will she admit her limitations and concede what she truly believes must be conceded? Will she give straight answers to straight questions? Or will she fight tooth and nail every step of the way?

A good way to start learning about the expert is by checking her out with your own expert. It also helps to speak with lawyers who have deposed the expert before. Sometimes, a wheelbarrow full of information will fall into your lap merely by checking with the lawyer next door.

By far the best resource for studying up on an expert witness comes literally from the expert's own mouth: This refers to collecting and reviewing testimony she has given in other cases. Transcripts can be pure gold; nothing will give a lawyer a better feel for a witness. Also, because expert witnesses tend to travel down the same testimonial highway in case after case, there is a very good chance that you will find a transcript in which she has previously testified about some of the very same issues presented in your case. The value of such a transcript is self-evident, especially if the expert testified for the other side in an earlier case.

Read everything the expert has written on the relevant topic. If possible, read everything the expert has written, period. You never know where something helpful will turn up.

Occasionally, an Internet search will produce something interesting, although you may have to paw through a lot of junk to find it. A better computer resource may be running a search of the expert's name through a commercial legal research service. This can lead to other cases where the witness has testified and perhaps other transcripts. And you may even get lucky and discover that the expert's testimony was previously rejected under *Daubert*.

Another essential step in your preparation is learning the science of the case—the expert's area of expertise. Cross-examining an expert on the science can be an intimidating task, and no wonder. Here, the natural advantage is entirely with the witness. She has likely spent decades learning everything in her field of expertise; you, on the other hand, are lucky if you have two days to get ready for the deposition. Realistically, there is no way to completely neutralize this advantage.

So face up to it: If you are taking the deposition of a design engineer, she will inevitably show up at the deposition knowing a lot more about design engineering than you can hope to learn—and certainly more than your client can afford to pay you to learn. That is the bad news. The good news is that your case is not about the whole field of design engineering; it is about only the one product that your client claims was defective. Focus on this limited area, and you actually may be able to out-study the witness.

There is no way to make this sound glamorous. Learning the science of a case is just plain hard work. It means reading, research, and study. It involves looking up words you have never heard before and obsessing over subjects that would normally bore you. It is eye strain and headaches. Sometimes it requires climbing on top of a building, touring a factory, or watching a surgeon take out a gallbladder. At other times, it means sorting through ponderous industry codes and uninterpretable governmental regulations. It can include using the Internet, but learning the science of a case is usually more about libraries than about cyberspace. And library work can range from blowing the dust off the yellowed pages of an ancient text to trying to get an advance copy of an article not yet in print. In short, learning the science of a case means doing whatever you have to do to make certain that the expert cannot hide from you in a fog of hyper-technical industry jargon.

The final step in preparation is taking the information that you learned in the earlier steps and using it to create a deposition plan. This is a very individual process, the fruit of which depends upon the skills, experiences, and tactical judgments of the particular lawyer. For most lawyers, a central feature of the plan involves building a chain of logic. But the plan should be more strategic than logical; it should be designed to accomplish what you need to accomplish, not just to get through the deposition in some organized way.

Even the hardest of hardball depositions should generally include a lot of softball discovery. Never underestimate the power of information. Depositions occur so commonly in the life of a trial lawyer that it is easy to forget just what powerful engines they are for generating information. Where else in life can one human being force another to answer any question that happens to come to mind (as long as it is reasonably calculated to lead to the discovery of something admissible)?

So armed, a lawyer is free to ask an expert witness detailed questions about a wide range of subjects, including the expert's professional background. Just what is it that makes the expert an expert? This includes questions covering the witness's education, employment history, publications, presentations, professional successes and failures, research interests, academic appointments, previous testimony, approximate earnings from testifying, history of professional discipline, and anything else that might bear on the witness's qualifications or bias.

Another indispensable goal of softball questioning is learning everything the expert has done in reaching her opinions. What files and records has she reviewed? Did she ask for any others? Has she read any of the depositions taken in the case? What books and articles has she reviewed? Did she do any experiments or research? Has she discussed the case with anyone? Has she seen everything necessary to give her final opinions? If not, what else does she need to see? When does she expect to see it? If she changes her opinions or forms new ones, will she let your opposing counsel know so that he can tell the other parties?

Softball is also the perfect approach for identifying resources that you can use to prepare your trial cross-examination. Who are the top authorities in the expert's field? What have they published and in which journals? Which authors have written the best material on the specific issues in this case? Which journals have the best articles on these subjects? Are there any industry standards, professional protocols and guidelines, or government regulations relevant to the case? If so, how would one go about getting a copy of the pertinent documents? Does the expert believe that her opinions are universally accepted? If not, who are the experts who disagree with her?

It is usually a good idea to maintain a cordial demeanor during the softball phase of questioning. People open up more in a comfortable atmosphere than in a hostile one, and in softball discovery, getting the witness to open up is a primary goal. In fact, conducting an effective softball examination means doing almost the exact opposite from what is needed for effective hardball questioning. It involves asking non-leading questions, asking questions without knowing the answers, and asking broad, open-ended questions. In other words, you want the witness—not you—to do the talking. Your turn will come later, when you get out the old hardball.

One of the secrets in cross-examining an expert witness is not to get to the point too quickly. Experts are usually smart, educated, and savvy advocates. Often, they have sizeable egos. You will make their day if you probe their opinions and fail to discredit them. And if they can find a way to thwart your attempts to diminish the effectiveness of their testimony, they will do so.

A Chain of Logic

So try not to lead with your chin. If you want to knock out an expert, you need to set up your punch first. One good way of doing this is by building a chain of logic.

A chain of logic is a carefully planned series of questions—first very broad and general, later becoming narrow and more specific—that in theory should lead inexorably to the conclusion you desire. The idea is to begin by getting the witness to acknowledge helpful broad principles. If those principles include the unassailable basis of the expert's area of expertise, this usually can be done quite easily. Then, the later questions, while growing out of these same principles, gradually become more and more case-specific. Each individual question, when viewed separately, is a no-brainer, leaving the witness with little choice but to agree. Yet when taken together, these answers assume considerable power. Even before the specific facts of your case have been mentioned, the witness begins to lose freedom of movement. When a chain of logic works well, it closes on the expert like a vise, so slowly as to be almost imperceptible. With each successive question and answer, the testimonial options narrow.

In building a chain of logic, each question should move the witness only a small step beyond the previous answer. Larger leaps may spook the witness and should therefore be avoided. In fact, this is one of the advantages to introducing a chain of logic at the expert's deposition rather than saving it for trial. Depositions permit a measure of leisure often not practical at trial. You can safely take the time you reasonably need to set up the chain without worrying about angering the judge or boring the jury. Then, having pinned down the witness at her deposition, you can abbreviate your questioning at trial so as to give the cross-examination a more rock'em-sock'em style.

For example, imagine that you are defending a lawyer in a legal malpractice case. You believe that one of your strongest arguments is the so-called professional judgment defense, and you intend to pursue this issue during the deposition of plaintiff's expert witness. If you start off by asking the expert directly if he thinks that your client acted reasonably in exercising his professional judgment, you probably will not like the answer. Better to ease into it:

Q: Mr. Expert, does practicing law involve using judgment?
A: Of course.
Q: And is interpreting the law one of the places where judgment comes into play?
A: Yes.
Q: Are there times when the law on a particular point is unsettled?
A: Yes, that can be true.
Q: Even with hundreds of volumes of published decisions, there are still a lot of legal questions that remain undecided in this state, true?
A: True.
Q: And when there is an unsettled legal issue in a case, is it often unclear how that issue ultimately will be decided?
A: That is often true.
Q: Do you agree that an attorney faced with an unsettled legal issue should use his or her best professional judgment in deciding how to proceed?
A: Yes. I think every lawyer has that prerogative.
Q: Incidentally, in your own practice do you at times have to make decisions in the face of unsettled legal questions?
A: Yes, that happens.
Q: When that happens, are you always correct in your predictions as to how the court will rule?
A: Usually, but not always.
Q: On those occasions when you were wrong, do you think that you were also negligent?
A: No, I don't.
Q: So the fact that a lawyer concludes that the law on an unsettled point is probably one way, but a court later decides it in another way, does not necessarily mean the lawyer was negligent, does it?
A: I think that would be correct.
Q: None of us has a crystal ball, do we?
A: True.
Q: Do you agree then that in judging a lawyer's actions, we need to look at the state of the law at the time the lawyer acted?
A: Agreed.

Q: And we should not judge him on the basis of decisions that came down later?

A: Right.

Now, suppose the specific issue involves a claim that your client made a procedural error of some sort. At the underlying trial, your client won the case, and the court of appeals affirmed. But the Supreme Court held that your client committed a fatal procedural error and reversed. That reversal led to the pending lawsuit. In deposition, the plaintiff's expert witness concedes that your client's actions were not faulted by any court before the Supreme Court's ruling. So far, so good. You continue:

Q: The Supreme Court reversed the court of appeals because it came to a different interpretation of the law, isn't that right?

A: Yes.

Q: Are both the Supreme Court and the court of appeals well-respected courts in this state?

A: I certainly believe they are.

Q: Given the fact that these two well-respected courts disagreed as to what the law required in this situation, would you agree that before the Supreme Court's decision, the law was unsettled?

A: It would seem logical that the law was at least somewhat unsettled.

Q: And since the law was unsettled, my client had the right, as an attorney, to use his best judgment in deciding how to proceed, true?

A: Yes. I have no problem with that. My concern is whether he used good judgment, which I question.

Q: So this case ultimately comes down to the question of whether a reasonable lawyer, using good judgment, could have reached the conclusion reached by my client?

A: I believe that states the question quite well.

Q: Because if a reasonable lawyer, using good judgment, could have reached that conclusion, then it wasn't negligence, was it?

A: Assuming that all those factors were present, I would agree.

At some point, after you score early concessions in your chain of logic questioning, a faint voice may whisper in your ear, warning you to be careful. Things have gone well so far, and perhaps you should not press your luck. What you probably are hearing is the echo of Irving Younger's famous commandment to shut up, sit down, and avoid asking one question too many during cross-examination. But remember that Younger was talking about cross-examination at trial. A hardball deposition is like a dress rehearsal. No jury has heard you speak yet, nor has the last word been spoken in the deposition. Remember, the other lawyer still gets to ask deposition questions, not to mention the questions he will pose at trial. He will try to undo any damage you have done, and his witness will try to help him.

This means that even though the deposition has already accomplished a great deal, you may want to push the chain of logic all the way through to its conclusion. True, you may not like the witness's answers. But you will almost certainly not like the answers he will give when your adversary covers the same ground. So you press on:

Q: Do you know the three court of appeals judges who were on the panel in this matter?

A: No, I don't know them.

Q: Do you know their reputations?

A: Not really.

Q: But you believe the court is well respected?

A: Oh, certainly.

Q: Would you expect then that court of appeals judges are reasonable, competent, and intelligent people?

A: Yes, I would.

Q: And that they have reasonably good judgment?

A: Certainly.

Q: And, as we have discussed, they basically agreed with my client's interpretation of the law, true?

A: Yes, we covered that.

Q: So apparently a reasonable, competent, and intelligent lawyer, using good judgment, could reach the same conclusion my client reached, would you agree?

A: I would think that's right.

That went pretty well. Heck, why not come right out and say it: it was terrific.

Can a hardball deposition really be that successful? The answer is yes, once in a while. Those are the days that a litigator lives for. But you cannot count on it; it is a rare blessing. Most of the time the witness will fight you off long before making any fatal concessions; sometimes the witness will get the better of you early in the process.

When that happens, you may leave the deposition feeling dejected, bruised, and defeated. You may ask yourself why you became a lawyer. You may wonder whether there are any openings in taxidermy school. Take a deep breath. Later, when you review the transcript, you may well find some gold nuggets. A chain of logic does not have to stretch unbroken all the way to the end to have value. Even if the expert has agreed with only some very general propositions, at least he is pinned down somewhere. That is often all you need to set up a strong trial cross-examination.

In cross-examining an expert witness at trial, momentum is critical. Early in the questioning, someone—maybe you, maybe the witness—will become the dominant figure. The dominant figure is the one whose story will be told to the jury. Of course, the witness has already had a chance during direct examination to tell his story. Make cross-examination your turn—the time to tell your story, to use your own words to make your own points.

If you can begin your cross-examination with a series of questions that produce the answer "yes," you will go a long way toward assuming the dominant role. One way to do this is to begin your cross by asking questions that seek confirmation of what the witness said at his deposition. The expert must be consistent or face impeachment. In fact, if the expert does stray from the deposition testimony, so much the better. In the fight for dominance, nothing is more effective than a couple of quick, solid shots of impeachment from the deposition transcript. When this happens, the expert becomes more circumspect; in fact, he becomes gun-shy. This, in turn, sets the tone for the rest of the examination.

Sometimes, a hardball deposition can do even more than set up an effective cross at trial. On rare occasions, one will actually win the case for you outright—for example, by setting up a successful motion for summary judgment.

Now, let us be honest: Trial lawyers tend to have an ambivalent attitude toward summary judgment. Somehow, it feels like cheating—as though we are afraid to go to trial. If John Wayne had played a lawyer in a movie, his character would not likely have done anything as sissified as filing a motion for summary judgment. No, he would have slugged it out at trial.

What a summary judgment lacks in theatrical drama, it more than makes up for in service to the client. Avoiding the expense and trauma of trial can be a benefit of incalculable value. Although most lawsuits are unsuitable candidates for summary judgment, you should be ready to pursue the prospect vigorously when a good opportunity arises.

Occasionally, a good opportunity for summary judgment presents itself to you on a silver platter. But that is rare. More often, you have to work for it. This begins early in the case, when a good lawyer probes the opposing side's case, looking for a weakness. If a potentially fatal flaw is found, the deposition process will often become a key battlefield in the summary judgment war. Indeed, if you are going to obtain a concession from an expert that can lead to summary judgment, it must come during the deposition.

This is not to suggest that you should expect to beat up the expert during the deposition and make him cry uncle. That will not happen. But that is not the only road to summary judgment; in fact, summary judgment is very rarely won through a head-to-head battle over the main points of an expert's disclosed opinions. More often, it follows a path that cuts along the edges of the expert's opinions, trimming away a critical element of the other side's case.

Imagine that you are defending a hospital against a claim made by the parents of a profoundly brain-damaged infant. Your client performed a routine non-stress test on the mother; although the test came back as non-reactive, the treating physician was not unduly alarmed. Following his usual practice, he sent the mother home for the night and told her to come back for retesting the next morning. When she returned, the test results showed that the fetus had become critically compromised.

The parents sued both the doctor and the hospital. Their theory against the hospital was that it violated the Emergency Medical Treatment and Active Labor Act (EMTALA) by discharging the woman at a time when she was suffering from an emergency medical condition.

In defending the hospital, you believe that you have a good chance at summary judgment because the treating doctor did not believe that the situation was an emergency when he sent the mother home. Under EMTALA, a hospital is not liable for discharging a patient with an unstabilized emergency condition unless the caregivers have actual knowledge of the emergency; a negligent failure to diagnose an emergency is not actionable under the Act.

There is, however, a fly in the ointment: One of the plaintiff's expert witnesses has submitted a report that suggests that a non-reactive non-stress test, standing by itself, is well recognized as a medical emergency. Before moving for summary judgment, you need to take his deposition on this point.

Q: Dr. Expert, what percentage of non-reactive non-stress tests prove to be false alarms?

A: More than half, at least.

Q: Would it surprise you if the statistic were 90 percent?

A: Not at all.

Q: A non-stress test is an initial screening examination, right?

A: Yes.

Q: It doesn't give you a final diagnosis?

A: No, it doesn't.

Q: And, if the test is reactive, that is considered a good sign that the fetus will probably be all right in utero a while longer?

A: Yes.

Q: On the other hand, if the test is non-reactive, that means you need to do some follow-up testing, correct?

A: Exactly.

Q: Doctor, do you believe that when a non-stress test is non-reactive, the physician should act under the assumption that there is an emergency present?

A: Yes, until proven otherwise.

Q: But in most cases, it will turn out that there really is no emergency with the fetus?

A: Exactly.

Q: Doctor, based upon your review of the records, would you agree that the medical personnel in this case were acting under the assumption, inappropriately in your view, that there was no medical emergency?

A: It would appear so.

Now you can file your motion for summary judgment without worrying that it will be torpedoed by the opposing expert.

Note that the critical concessions in the deposition came on points that the witness himself viewed as unimportant. There may have been good grounds to challenge the expert's fundamental opinion that it was improper to send the woman home after a non-reactive test, but that was not the road to summary judgment. The expert never would have conceded that point. Instead, the road to summary judgment followed a path that did not directly challenge the expert's most basic opinions.

One of the biggest tactical dilemmas in taking a hardball deposition is deciding which pitches to throw in the deposition and which ones to save for trial. Although it is often wise to wait, there can be a number of good reasons why a lawyer may want to throw at least some of her best pitches at the deposition stage. Although every case must be prepared with an eye toward trial, the vast majority of cases are resolved short of trial. Scoring points during depositions may lead to a better settlement for the client—and it may even lead to complete capitulation by your opponent.

The chance of this happening is greatest when you represent a minor player in a multi-party lawsuit. Minor defendants are frequently the beneficiaries of the earlier hardball questioning by lawyers representing major defendants. The lawyer for a minor defendant is allowed to ask his questions when the expert is already tired, irritated, and not much interested in small fry.

To give yourself the advantage of this situation, do not volunteer to take the lead in the deposition of a liability or causation expert. Let one of the big boys soften up the expert first. Then, when it is your turn, jump in with a brief and carefully planned examination. Use a hardball approach in the sense of leading questions, but keep a soft touch by using a non-confrontational manner. With a little luck, your client may end up out of the case.

Hardball expert depositions are not for everyone or for every case. But sometimes it makes sense to throw your best pitches before trial. Whether you are going for an early win or simply want to set up a more effective cross at trial, a fastball or two at the deposition can be just the right stuff.

CHAPTER 23

Your Client's Employee Is Being Deposed: Are You Ethically Prepared?

Lawrence J. Fox*

It happens so often, we don't even think about it. We are representing an organization, typically a corporation in a litigation matter. Discovery is proceeding apace. The other side notices the depositions of any number of corporate officers and employees. We spend hours or days preparing the witnesses. We sit next to them at the deposition. We object to questions on the ground of the form, or privilege, or relevance (to the extent we are still allowed to play a meaningful or, as some would say, disruptive role). We direct the witness not to answer. We try to sneak in speaking objections without incurring the wrath or scorn of the

*Lawrence J. Fox, former chair of the ABA Section of Litigation, is with Drinker Biddle & Reath, LLP, in Philadelphia, Pennsylvania. This article is based on a presentation at a South Texas Law Review symposium, and originally appeared in the Summer 2003 issue of LITIGATION.

other side. We resist the temptation to kick the witness under the table. We call for well-timed breaks. We worry that the witness might lie and how we will handle our duty of candor to the tribunal if that occurs. We have lunch and, perhaps, even dinner with the witness and review the day's events and prepare for the next. We tell the witness how well he is doing.

We complete the deposition, bid the witness adieu, put what we have learned into our database for the trial we know is unlikely ever to occur, and, perhaps, chat with the witness one more time when we remind him to read his deposition, make corrections, and send it back to us. And we do this without giving any real thought to what has occurred. Yet, if we do think about it—as I hope this article will help you to do—we realize that we have negotiated an ethical minefield, we hope, with no real damage but with an opportunity for a number of untoward consequences.

Rule 1.13 Generally

Starting from first principles, we know that when a lawyer represents a corporation, the lawyer does not, as a result, represent any constituent—shareholders, directors, trustees, or employees—of the organization. *See* Model Rules of Prof'l Conduct (Model Rules) R. 1.13, cmt. [1]; Model Rule 1.13. Indeed, as tempting as it would be for some purposes—particularly the protection of our organizational client—to be able to tell the other side that we represent all the constituents of the organization and therefore none of them may be contacted under Model Rule 4.2's interdiction of contacts with represented persons, we recognize that were a lawyer representing a corporation deemed to represent all of the corporation's constituents, the conflicts that situation would create could be totally disabling.

Simply think of how many issues there are on which employees have interests that diverge dramatically from those of the organization. Examples include the interests of employees in higher wages, of salespeople in higher commissions, or of a dissident director in liquidating the organization. This entire article, indeed, is a demonstration of this point. Thus, in the normal case, the lawyer representing a corporation will deal with and through many employees but will not, by that fact alone, form a lawyer-client relationship with any of them. As Comment 2 to Model Rule 1.13 observes:

Thus, by way of example, if an organizational client requests its lawyer to investigate allegations of wrongdoing, interviews made in the course of that investigation between the lawyer and the client's employees or other constituents are covered by Rule 1.6. This does not mean, however, that constituents of an organizational client are the clients of the lawyer.

Rather, as conscientious lawyers, we will go out of our way to remind employees, who might be misled into thinking that the company lawyer represents the employees, that that is not the case. *See* Model Rule 1.13(d).

This means that, absent an affirmative decision to the contrary, the lawyers representing Company A must deal with Company A's employees as unrepresented persons. This status carries enormous implications. The lawyer must avoid confusion as to whom the lawyer represents, *see, e.g., W. T. Grant Co.* v. *Haines,* 531 F.2d 671, 674 (2d Cir. 1976); Restatement (Third) of the Law Governing Lawyers § 103, cmt. e; where the lawyer's loyalties lie, *id.;* and what the lawyer is required to do with information, even personally embarrassing information, the lawyer learns from the employee: "The constituent's expression of a belief that the lawyer will keep the conversation confidential from others with decision-making authority in the organization . . . would normally require a warning by the lawyer." *Id.* The result is even worse if the mistake is induced by the lawyer's statements, and it can lead to discipline as well as other relief. *See Id.* § 103 cmt. f. It also means the lawyer must avoid providing any legal advice to the employees other than the advice to get separate legal representation when such advice appears warranted. *See* Model Rule 4.3; Model Rule 1.13 cmt. [7].

Does that change when the company employees and officers are going to be deposed? Can the lawyer for the company continue to treat these employees as unrepresented? Before lawyers may ask themselves that question, they must recognize that the decision on how to treat these employees is not solely theirs. Rather, any view the lawyer may have on this topic is subject to the decision of the organizational client; it is also subject to the decision of the organizational employee. As a result, as we consider the decisions each interested party must make, we must remember that the decisions of who is represented by whom are subject, in effect, to being trumped by another decision maker.

Thus, the lawyer for the company has an ethical obligation to decide what representations the lawyer is able to undertake. Model Rule 1.7 requires the lawyer to identify any conflicts and, if any are found, to make a determination whether the conflict is one as to which the lawyer may seek a waiver. The test is whether the lawyer "reasonably believes that the lawyer will be able to provide competent and diligent representation to each affected client." Model Rule 1.7(b)(1).

But even if the lawyer is willing to undertake a joint represen-tation of the company and company employees, the company obviously must decide, regardless of the lawyer's lack of ethical concern, whether it wishes to be jointly represented. Similarly, the individual employee must decide—even if both lawyer and company are content with the joint representation—whether he or she wishes to be represented separately. Thus, as we consider decisions that might fall to the lawyer to make in this context, the autonomy of the other players must always be kept in mind.

The Unrepresented Employee Analysis

Assume the lawyer's organizational client wishes the lawyer to treat the employee client as unrepresented. How will that affect the conduct of the lawyer? The lawyer who embarks on prepar-ing an unrepresented employee of an organizational client for a deposition has a heightened duty—compared to the lawyer who simply is dealing with organizational employees on day-to-day matters—to precede any substantive work with a very long speech regarding the lawyer's role. This speech must make it clear whom the lawyer does (and does not) represent; the obliga-tion of the lawyer to report all information learned to the organi-zational client (i.e., this person's boss); and the fact that the lawyer will not provide legal advice to the individual, other than the advice to get separate counsel. Comment [1] to Model Rule 4.3 provides:

> An unrepresented person, particularly one not experienced in dealing with legal matters, might assume that a lawyer is disinterested in loyalties or is a disinterested authority on the law even when the lawyer represents a client. In order to avoid a misunderstanding, a lawyer will typically need to identify the lawyer's client and, where necessary, explain that the client has interests opposed to those of the unrepre-sented person. For misunderstandings that sometimes arise

when a lawyer for an organization deals with an unrepresented constituent, *see* Model Rule 1.13(d).

Absent such a speech (preferably confirmed in writing when given), the lawyer runs the risk that the employee client will believe that the lawyer was representing him. After all, their conversations, to be effective—no matter how hard the lawyer tries to act like he or she is dealing with an unrepresented person—will look very much like lawyer-client discussions. As a result, there is a real risk that the employee's after-the-fact assertion that he perceived he was represented by a lawyer may prevail over any assertion by the lawyer that the lawyer was representing just the company. *See E. F. Hutton & Co. v. Brown*, 305 F. Supp. 371 (S.D. Tex. 1969) (company employee deemed to be represented by company lawyer despite lack of formalities); *Cooke v. Laidlaw Adams & Peck, Inc.*, 510 N.Y.S.2d 597 (N.Y. App. Div. 1987); *Wick v. Eismann*, 838 P.2d 301 (Idaho 1992) (lawyer did not make role clear to shareholder of corporate client); Restatement (Third) of the Law Governing Lawyers § 14 cmt. f:

> Under Subsection (1)(b), a lawyer's failure to clarify whom the lawyer represents in circumstances calling for such a result might lead a lawyer to have entered into client-lawyer representations not intended by the lawyer. Hence, the lawyer must clarify whom the lawyer intends to represent when the lawyer knows or reasonably should know that, contrary to the lawyer's own intention, a person, individually, or agents of an entity, on behalf of the entity, reasonably rely on the lawyer to provide legal services to that person or entity.

And if the lawyer in fact has treated the client as unrepresented yet the employee can later make a colorable argument to having thought he or she was represented by the lawyer, the opportunities for the lawyer to be alleged and, in fact, found to have engaged in malpractice vis-à-vis this other "client" can be quite high. Think of the employee client's later claiming the lawyer should have told the client not to testify as just one of myriad examples. Indeed, the lawyer could be in trouble simply for failing to take all the steps outlined in this article to undertake a joint representation.

One issue that does not turn on whether the employee is treated as a client is the ability of the lawyer to keep the witness preparation confidential and subject to the testimonial privilege. Even if the employee is not a client, *Upjohn Co. v. United States*, 449 U.S. 383 (1981) teaches us that so long as this is work in furtherance of the representation of the corporate client, regardless of the employee's status in the organization, the conversations in preparation for the deposition should be privileged and subject to the attorney work-product doctrine as well.

In the conduct of the deposition itself, however, the lawyer's role will turn quite challenging. The lawyer will have to avoid giving personal advice to the deponent and be sure to serve only the interests of the organizational client, and may be barred, for example, from directing the witness not to answer. Although the lawyer should be able to direct the witness not to answer to protect the organizational client's privilege, typically when that direction is given, the lawyer taking the deposition asks whether the client "will follow counsel's advice." If the deponent, in fact, is unrepresented, the awkwardness in this situation is self-evident, as may be any other instructions to the witness that could be misconstrued as giving legal advice to an unrepresented person.

Moreover, in dealing with employees who are unrepresented, the lawyer will have to determine, based on what the lawyer learns during those dealings, whether the employee should have separate representation. A review of Model Rules 1.13(d) and 4.3 does not find, *in haec verba*, a requirement that the lawyer so inform the unrepresented person. Rather, the lawyer is simply limited, if the lawyer chooses to give any advice, to advise only that the individual should seek separate representation. Under these particular circumstances, however, where the lawyer is dealing with an unrepresented person who is an employee of the client, the lawyer for the corporation, in my view, should treat this advice as mandatory rather than simply a best practice. I say so because if the lawyer fails to provide that advice, and it turns out that the client's employee is in serious trouble, the lawyer's silence could have serious repercussions, even if the lawyer escapes liability for failure to act. *See* Restatement (Third) of the Law Governing Lawyers § 51(3). Giving that advice guarantees that the employee does not mistakenly assume the lawyer is representing the employee.

A warning to get separate counsel might be quite unsettling to the employee, a result that could affect the lawyer's representation of the organization. To ameliorate that effect, the lawyer's "speech" to the individual can be as benign as an explanation that under the professional rules, it is not at all unusual that the same lawyer cannot represent the company and its employees; that this matter presents one of these situations; and that the interests of the employee would be best served by having his or her own lawyer. And if this speech must be given, it will then be up to the lawyer's organizational client to decide whether the company is required by state law or its bylaws to advance the fees for that representation or, if not required but nonetheless permitted to do so, whether it will undertake to make such advances.

In sum, if these employees remain unrepresented, then the company's lawyers have to be especially circumspect in their dealings with these employees both before and at the deposition. Negotiating the path among (a) engaging in activity that the lawyer hopes will advance the interests of the organizational client, (b) avoiding giving advice to an unrepresented person, and (c) not being deemed the lawyer for the deponent is an exercise that must be approached with great care.

It should be noted that it would be the rare situation in which a lawyer would attend a deposition with an employee of a company that the lawyer represents and would treat this individual as unrepresented. Looking at the situation from that point of view, however, does highlight some of the important issues lawyers confront in this area.

The "accommodation" client. Some would assert that the corporate employee who is represented by the corporation's lawyer at a deposition is simply an accommodation client. They would argue that in order to solve the ethical problems outlined above, it is enough to provide this individual with this second-class quasi-client status. *See* Restatement (Third) of the Law Governing Lawyers § 132, cmt. i.

There are two problems with this informal approach to the issue. First, our rules simply do not reflect such a construct. An individual is either a client or an unrepresented person. The person either is being advised, or the providing of advice is consciously avoided. A conversation is subject to the attorney-client privilege or it is not. Airlines are free to offer business class as a compromise between first class and steerage, but that middle ground has no doctrinal support in the law governing lawyers, and thus there is no place for the lawyer to look to determine how the accommodation client may be treated.

Second, the accommodation client "solution" solves the problem—admittedly applicable to 99.9 percent of such events—only when everything goes smoothly. Yet, if lawyers posited their obligations on everything's going smoothly, none of us would need malpractice insurance. What lawyers need is a framework for dealing with the one-in-a-thousand problem—which, given the number of depositions of corporate employees that take place each day, means in absolute terms we are dealing with a very serious problem. What we must do is approach these matters in an analytically rigorous manner to deal with the rare—yet I would posit certain—event that will require the lawyer to be able to explain with precision how the lawyer addressed the matter. The assertion that the deponent was treated as an accommodation client answers no relevant question that I can imagine would ever be posed.

The Represented Employee Analysis

The difficulty of treating the employee deponent as unrepresented, and the failure of the accommodation client construct to answer the really important questions, leaves the lawyer with only one real alternative: to treat the employee deponent as represented by the lawyer for the organization. But, as will be seen, although this may be the best solution to the problem, it creates as many issues for the ethical lawyer as it solves. Recognizing that the lawyer is representing this individual requires the lawyer to demonstrate an ethical and diplomatic sensitivity that will challenge even the most conscientious counsel.

The ethical analysis of treating the deponent as client begins from first principles. The lawyer now is about to have two clients: the company and the individual. It thus will become a joint representation and, as a result, the lawyer who is considering taking on this joint representation must determine at the outset whether any conflicts might be created by the lawyer's representation of parties whose interests may diverge.

In every situation like this, of course, one fact of life is that the company is likely the longtime and, in any event, the far more important client. Although lawyers often talk about "important" clients—by which they mean those whom their losing might hurt their pocketbooks in a dramatic way—we must be ever mindful that our rules do not differentiate between the ethical duties we owe "important" clients and those we owe "less important" clients. Importance aside, one client is being represented for all purposes; on the other hand, one would expect the representation of the individual to be "for this day and trip only," i.e., for the preparation and the taking of the deposition. Nonetheless, the lawyer can usually proceed in this manner because the lawyer normally can view the corporate client's interests and the interests of its individual representatives as aligned. The individual corporate representative usually wants to help support the defense of his or her employer, and the corporate client is usually prepared to defend the individual's conduct on its behalf. Thus, in the great majority of cases, counsel for a corporation does not give a second thought to representing its individual employees and officers at depositions. Indeed, this is undoubtedly why few lawyers ever are forced to take the time to think analytically about what they are doing—engaging in a joint representation of the corporation and its employee—before they proceed without incident and without ethical transgressions (other than, perhaps, on the disclosure side) to undertake the engagement.

Nonetheless, the ethical lawyer will certainly want to consider whether the lawyer's relationship with the longtime powerful client creates a material limitation on the ability of the lawyer to represent the individual employee. Typically, that will not be the case at the beginning of the representation of the individual. On the other hand, the lawyer will want to recognize that the Model Rule 1.7(b) analysis—does the representation of the organization place a material limitation on the lawyer's ability to represent the employee—must be made not only at the outset of the representation but also as the representation proceeds.

Even if the conscientious lawyer determines that he or she is perfectly or sufficiently comfortable with taking on the second representation, the lawyer still must determine whether there are any other conflicts between the organizational client and its employee. One cannot assume that no conflict (other than the longtime client conflict) exists. The ethical problem is that the lawyer may need to make a significant inquiry into the factual circumstances of the employee to make this determination. Just knowing the employee's name, rank, and serial number is not enough; the lawyer will have to engage in some investigation of the employee's status, role, and concerns before the conflict decision can be made.

In doing so the lawyer will be dealing with the employee as a prospective client, a status that carries its own pitfalls. A prospective client is entitled to the protection of confidentiality. Model Rule 1.18 makes explicit in the rules the duties a lawyer has long owed to prospective clients. *See* Restatement (Third) of the Law Governing Lawyers § 15(1). And although in a normal joint representation in which the clients come to the lawyer at the same time, the lawyer can set ground rules for the treatment of confidential information (must it be shared or shall it be kept a secret from the other client?), here there already is one client. In chatting with the second, the lawyer could easily learn information that requires the lawyer to turn down the representation of the employee and, more critically, could require the lawyer to withdraw from representing the corporate client as well. *See, e.g., Bridge Products Inc. v. Quantum Chemical Corp.*, No. 88 C 10734, 1990 WL 70857 (S.D. Ill. Apr. 27, 1990). Thus, the ethical lawyer will want to warn the organizational client of this risk before even exploring the propriety of undertaking the joint representation.

Assuming the lawyer conducts an initial investigation that reveals no conflict between the corporate client and the employee, the lawyer must then address the issues that arise in any joint representation. First, the normal rule is that if a conflict develops between jointly represented clients, the lawyer is supposed to withdraw from both representations. *See, e.g., In re Corn Derivatives Antitrust Litigation*, 748 F.2d 157 (3d Cir. 1984), *cert. denied,* 472 U.S. 1008 (1985); *Brennan's Inc. v. Brennan's Restaurants*, 590 F.2d 168 (5th Cir. 1979). That "rule" can be avoided if two preconditions are met. First, both clients have to agree that if a conflict develops, the lawyer may represent one of them designated in advance. Second, at the time the conflict develops, the client losing the continuing representation has the right, regardless of any earlier agreement, to revisit the issue. This is necessary because the original agreement was, in effect, a prospective waiver given at a time when the facts and circumstances of the future joint representation were not yet known; confidential information from both clients was not yet revealed; and the basis for the conflict that later developed was, by definition, unidentified. As a result, when the conflict develops, the lawyer, notwithstanding any prior agreement, will still have to consider whether the basis of the conflict prevents the lawyer from continuing with either representation. *See* Restatement (Third) of the Law Governing Lawyers § 122, cmt. d.

Of course, the dropped client has a chance to revisit the prospective waiver based on the facts and circumstances that are now known. What is the nature of the conflict? Are the two clients now directly adverse? If not, how critical is the material limitation that has arisen? What confidential information has been shared with counsel since the representation began? In short, the dropped client must consider whether he or she can live with the former lawyer's continuing to represent the employer. Needless to say, the lawyer for the corporation will have to warn the corporate client of this possibility as well, even before the joint representation is considered.

Another issue the conscientious lawyer will want to address with both clients before the joint representation is undertaken is the effect of the joint attorney-client privilege that arises by virtue of a joint representation. Under this doctrine the lawyer is bound to keep privileged from the outside world everything the lawyer learns from either client. *See* Restatement (Third) of the Law Governing Lawyers § 75. Although the clients will likely embrace this protection when the matter is broached at the beginning of a joint representation, they must be reminded how often it becomes advisable for a party to waive the privilege at some later date. Think of parties who decide they want to "cooperate" with the SEC or of new management's taking over an enterprise—in bankruptcy or otherwise—and seeing some advantage in dropping claims of privilege. If the client has been part of a joint representation, this option—waiving the privilege—may not be available unless both clients agree to waive their rights. Although there is some dispute as to what one co-client can waive without the express consent of all others, at most, a co-client can waive only as to a "communication [that] relates *only* to the communicating and waiving client." *Id*. cmt. e (emphasis added); *see id*. rep. n. cmt. e.

Third, on a related topic, the lawyer must establish ground rules for dealing with confidential information. Is all information from each client shared with the other? Is none? Is it left to the lawyer's discretion? The attitudes of two clients—when one is the corporate employer and the other, the corporate employee—may differ substantially on any of these matters.

Possible Conflicts

It is helpful for the lawyer to recognize the conflicts that might develop between the long-term organizational client and the individual organizational employee. Many might come simply from some revelation by the client-employee unrelated to the reason for the underlying lawsuit. There are, in addition, at least three, and probably far more, conflicts that could arise from the representation itself.

First, the witness corporate employee may have engaged in conduct that could expose the employee to personal civil or criminal liability. For example, the employee may have shared inside information with a family member or friend or may have destroyed documents. Under those circumstances, the individual needs counsel to evaluate any potential exposure and attendant risks, as well as help to prepare a defense to any allegations that might arise. Although this may be something that the organization's lawyers are also fully capable of undertaking, there is a problem: Even at this early juncture, it is possible to identify, without much effort, the fact that these individuals are entitled to a lawyer who is free to advise them to (a) refuse to testify and (b) take some action to protect themselves (e.g., to seek immunity or file a qui tam action)—actions that may not be in the employer-client's best interests or, even more debilitating, may be directly adverse to them. In short, it is possible to envision with little effort that such matters could result in a conflict between the company and these employees regarding the terms of their future employment and responsibility for their conduct.

Second, the witness corporate employee may have engaged in conduct that the company would like to disavow. Although the conduct may not be illegal, the company may want to distance itself from, for example, the investment banker employee's helping the investment bank's client to structure off-balance sheet financing. Under these circumstances the employee may want to assert that the company (a) knew what the employee was doing, (b) encouraged such creativity, or (c) told the employee to behave in a way that would permit the company to maintain deniability. Again, under these circumstances, it can be seen that the employee is entitled to a lawyer who is free to advise the employee to argue that the conduct was (a) explicitly authorized, (b) tacitly approved, or (c) in the best interests of the company's clients and bottom line. Because such arguments may well be contrary to the best interests of the company, they may create a conflict of interest for the lawyer who is embarked on a joint representation.

Third, the employee may have engaged in conduct that violated company policy. Imagine an employee directing allocations of initial public offering shares in the go-go '90s to CEOs of important investment banking clients rather than to important brokerage clients. If the company is willing to overlook the conduct in a way that is binding, no conflict results. But if that conduct could result in the corporate client's threatening the individual employee with the loss of employment or otherwise creating a conflict because the employer is likely to sanction the employee for violating company policy, then a conflict exists. Under the circumstances the employee clearly needs a lawyer who can advise the employee how to retain the employment or otherwise reduce the negative consequences of the employee's activities—advice that a lawyer with loyalty to the company (whose best interests might involve termination of the employee) cannot provide.

If any of these circumstances arise, it is apparent that the lawyers for the company, in undertaking this joint representation, will be operating under a disabling conflict of interest under Rule 1.7(a)(2), in that their representation of the employer creates a material limitation on the advice they can give the individuals. When the lawyer is foreclosed from providing certain advice to one client because of the lawyer's duties to another client, an ethically significant conflict of interest clearly exists. *See* Annotated Model Rules of Prof'l Conduct, at 129 (5th ed. 2003). Moreover, the lawyer can recognize that there may come a time when the fallout between the company and its employees over the latter's conduct may become pronounced and the conflict of interest between them, substantially more open and acute.

Waiving the Conflict

Having identified the conflict, it then becomes necessary to determine whether the conflict is waiveable. The rules provide that a lawyer should not even seek the waiver of a conflict in a situation in which no reasonable lawyer would seek a waiver. In the terms of the latest revision to the Model Rules, the lawyer must "reasonably believe[ ] that the lawyer will be able to provide

345

competent and diligent representation to each affected client"
Model Rule 1.7(b)(1).

It would be difficult to conclude that any of these three representations would be waiveable. Simply consider the "speech" the lawyer seeking a waiver would have to deliver. This is not simply one of those conflicts where the lawyer confidently informs the client that the lawyer can represent the client vigorously in this matter adverse to the plaintiff despite the fact that other lawyers in another office of the lawyer's firm represent the plaintiff on some totally unrelated matter. Rather, the lawyer would, in effect, need to say, "I could represent you in preparation for this deposition, but if it turns out you have potential criminal liability by virtue of your conduct, there is a whole range of advice an unconflicted lawyer would be free to give you that, unfortunately, I cannot." "And what would that be?" asks the potential client. "Sorry, I cannot tell you that," answers the ethically compromised lawyer.

Even if the lawyers could get over the hurdle with respect to non-waiveability, the process of seeking a waiver itself raises serious ethical concerns. Here, the lawyers are representing the company—their long-term client, and one that is separately represented by worldly, wise in-house counsel. Gaining the organization's consent to the joint representation raises little in the way of concerns. The company is sophisticated, it has its own counsel, and it is not being asked to accept circumscribed advice.

On the other hand, dealing with the individual raises all kinds of power imbalance issues. The individual is highly unlikely to have counsel and is being asked to agree to be solely represented by his or her employer's lawyer. It is also unlikely that the individual has anything approaching the sophistication the organizational client possesses in matters of this type. Moreover, the individual is the one being asked to accept a cramped representation, an acceptance that may be alleged—if events turn sour—to have been motivated in part to save some money and, not coincidentally, to maintain some measure of control over the litigation for the company's benefit. Finally, as has been pointed out by others, the individual's need for effective representation is even greater than his or her employer's because, between them, only the individual might face incarceration. *See E.F. Hutton & Co. v. Brown*, 305 F. Supp. at 389–90.

Few lawyers, after identifying the issue, would conclude that they could fairly seek a waiver of the conflict of interest between the organizational client and the employee in these circumstances.

The lawyer facing this joint representation issue might ask whether this is a potential future conflict that may never eventuate and, therefore, not one with which the lawyers must presently grapple. The fact is that virtually all conflict-recognition problems deal in varying degrees of likelihood rather than certainties. The question that is asked is not whether there is a problem that at the moment must be addressed but, rather, whether there is a "substantial risk that [in the future] the lawyer's representation of the client would be materially and adversely affected" by the conflict. Restatement (Third) of the Law Governing Lawyers § 121. As one set of commentators has observed:

> In the modem view, a conflict of interest exists whenever the attorney-client relationship or the quality of the representation is 'at risk,' *even if no substantive impropriety—such as a breach of confidentiality or less than zealous representation—in fact eventuates.* The law of lawyering then proceeds by assessing the risk and providing an appropriate response.

Geoffrey C. Hazard, Jr. & W. William Hodes, *The Law of Lawyering* § 10.4, at 10–11 (3d ed. 2003) (citations omitted). Given that standard, it is clear that the analysis here presents a conflict sufficiently likely to arise in the future that the lawyer must decline the dual representation.

How Many Lawyers Must Be Hired?

If the conclusion is reached that the company's lawyers cannot represent individual employees who, on the basis of known facts, present an existing conflict or the reasonably foreseeable likelihood of a future conflict, the question arises whether a second lawyer or law firm could undertake the representation of all of these individual representations. This is not, of course, a question the company or its lawyers would have the right to decide. Rather, the lawyer asked to represent the first of these individuals will have to consider in each case whether the next proffered representation can be undertaken; moreover, any individual who, at that point, has retained the lawyer will also have to consent to being represented as part of a different joint representation.

In any event, an intensive factual inquiry will have to be conducted about any given individual to determine whether multiple individuals can be represented by the same lawyer. Obviously, to the extent the employees tend to be similarly situated and do not have conflicts among themselves, it may be possible for one lawyer to represent many of these individuals, at least until the time some proceeding against the individuals is threatened or brought.

If, consistent with the foregoing, it is concluded that some of the company's individual employees require separate counsel, that separate representation will not necessarily result in a change in the way the litigation looks from the perspective of the opposing party or parties. Although these individuals will be consulting different counsel, once that consultation occurs, the company's counsel is then free to urge the individuals' counsel to permit the company's counsel to "represent" these individuals at the depositions under whatever reasonable guidelines their respective lawyers may specify. Indeed, counsel for the individuals likely will consider that approach as well, because he or she will not want to raise any suspicions in the minds of plaintiffs' counsel as to why there might be a need for separate representation. But that decision will occur in a context in which each individual will be counseled, not by the company or its lawyers, but by the individual's own counsel, regarding all of the ramifications of the individual's conduct, the opportunity to refuse to testify, the possibility of "cutting a deal," the best chance to retain employment, and stock options—by someone not inhibited by a conflict yet presumably, in most cases, as motivated as the employer's counsel to want to avoid having a bull's-eye painted on the individual's forehead.

Depositions Involving Company Lawyer and Independently Represented Employee

How should company counsel conduct any deposition in which an otherwise independently represented employee seeks to be "represented," solely for purposes of the deposition, by company counsel? It is my view that company counsel can now undertake this very limited joint representation. Though a conflict triggered the need to hire separate counsel for the individual, that conflict has been significantly ameliorated by the fact that the individual is now separately represented for virtually all purposes. And the conflict is now clearly waiveable because the individual will be separately represented in assessing the risks of being represented at the deposition by company counsel.

As for how, returning to first principles, we must recall that part of the reason this employee was referred to independent counsel was a perceived need for the individual to receive advice, inter alia, whether to invoke the Fifth Amendment. Thus, when the individual's counsel decides that, for purposes of the deposition, it would be in the individual's best interest to be represented by company counsel, company counsel must assume that (a) all of the issues relating to whether this person should testify at all have been explored with independent counsel and (b) two decisions have been made. The first is that the individual will testify and the second, that it is in the individual's best interest to be represented by company counsel at the deposition (provided, of course, that company counsel and the company are agreeable to that approach).

The other first principles one must recognize are those relating to what a lawyer may do at a deposition. Other than advising a client to invoke the Fifth Amendment, directing a client not to answer questions on the grounds of privilege, or objecting to the form of the questions, counsel at a deposition has virtually no decisions to make. Therefore, representation of this individual by company counsel at a deposition is practically circumscribed in any event. It is also possible, however, that counsel at the deposition will be confronted with a lying witness and believe that he or she has some obligation to act under Model Rule 3.3. In that unlikely event, however, the lawyer will not have to act at the deposition and will have to act thereafter only if the witness and the witness's lawyer fail to take appropriate remedial action.

Nonetheless, what happens if, based on how the questioning is going, company counsel concludes that the individual should be advised to invoke the privilege against self-incrimination? In this situation, company counsel must realize that this is the very issue for which the individual was referred to independent counsel; it is not up to company counsel to second-guess the decision the individual and his or her personal counsel reached. Nor does company counsel want to take any steps in the deposition—such as taking a sudden break—that could create any special suspicion about the individual's testimony. In short, company counsel does not have an ethical duty, in my view, to give the individual advice relating to this question during the deposition. The lawyer must assume that the subject was already addressed by individual counsel and that the decision to appear at the deposition without individual counsel was made by the individual after consultation with individual counsel. It is not for company counsel to seek to "influence" that decision mid-deposition.

That having been said, if at appropriate junctures company counsel wishes or makes advance arrangements to consult with the individual's counsel about how the deposition is going and even to share company counsel's view that the privilege against self-incrimination should be invoked, company counsel is certainly free to do that as long as it is understood that company counsel has no obligation to do so. Company counsel must recognize that all decisions in this regard must be made by the individual employee in consultation with his or her individual counsel, not by or in consultation with company counsel.

* * * *

Attending a deposition with the employee of a client seems simple enough. It is an act that is repeated hundreds of times every day. But it is fraught with ethical considerations that I hope will be recognized and considered in a thoughtful way as a result of the approach suggested in this article.

CHAPTER 24

Deposing Corporations and Other Fictive Persons: Some Thoughts on Rule 30(b)(6)

Sidney I. Schenkier*

The law entertains the fiction that corporations are "persons." Consistent with that fiction, the law affords corporations many of the same rights and obligations it gives real persons. For example, corporations may enter into contracts just like real people may, and corporations have the obligation to pay taxes just as real people do.

Similarly, just as a human being may be subject to the deposition process, under Federal Rule of Civil Procedure 30(b)(6) [thereinafter FRCP], so is a corporation, partnership, association,

---

Sidney I. Schenkier is a U.S. Magistrate Judge for the Northern District of Illinois. This article originally appeared in the Winter 2003 issue of LITIGATION.

351

or governmental agency. Rule 30(b)(6) is of relatively recent origin. It was not part of the Rules when they were adopted in 1937. It was not until the 1970 Amendments that it was thought "advantageous to both sides as well as an improvement in the deposition process" to include a provision for taking the deposition of a corporation. FRCP 30(b)(6), advisory committee's note. The Rule, which has remained unchanged for 33 years, provides:

> A party may in the party's notice and in a subpoena name as the deponent a public or private corporation or a partnership or association or governmental agency and describe with reasonable particularity the matters on which examination is requested. In that event, the organization so named shall designate one or more officers, directors, or managing agents, or other persons who consent to testify on its behalf, and may set forth for each person designated, the matters on which the person will testify. A subpoena shall advise a non-party organization of its duty to make such a designation. The persons so designated shall testify as to matters known or reasonably available to the organization.

Although most civil practitioners are familiar with taking and defending depositions of individuals, many are relatively unfamiliar with the additional considerations that come into play when taking or defending a Rule 30(b)(6) deposition.

In propounding a Rule 30(b)(6) deposition notice, the requesting party must consider, among other things, at what stage in discovery to use the Rule 30(b)(6) deposition; the subject matters on which to seek a Rule 30(b)(6) witness; how to draft the Rule 30(b)(6) notice; and how to conduct the deposition when the corporation's designated witness is presented in one session for both a Rule 30(b)(6) and an individual capacity deposition. The responding entity has significant issues to consider as well, such as: whether to object to the Rule 30(b)(6) notice; whom to select as the corporation's designee for the 30(b)(6) deposition; whether to use different individuals to address different Rule 30(b)(6) categories (or to divide a specific Rule 30(b)(6) category among two or more witnesses); and how to prepare the Rule 30(b)(6) witnesses who are designated to fulfill their responsibility to "testify as to matters known or reasonably available to the organization" without compromising attorney-client privilege communications or work product. And both the requesting and the responding parties must consider the effect of an answer (or non-answer) by the corporation's designee: in particular, whether the corporation can offer evidence at trial that contradicts the testimony of its Rule 30(b)(6) witness. These considerations are the subject of this article.

Purposes of the Rule

From the perspective of the deposing party, the rule reduces the range of disputes over whether a person is a "managing agent" of a corporate defendant, who can be deposed by notice rather than subpoena and whose testimony—under Federal Rule of Evidence (FRE) 801(d)(2)—may be an admission of the corporation. The advisory committee's notes also explain that the Rule 30(b)(6) deposition was intended to "curb the 'bandying' by which officers or managing agents of a corporation are deposed in turn but each disclaims knowledge of facts that are clearly known to persons in the organization and thereby to it." Consider, for example, the party that serves an interrogatory asking for the persons with knowledge of a decision made by the corporation to fire an employee. The corporation answers by providing a list of 15 people, some of whom likely have only very limited or indirect knowledge. The requesting party then begins deposing these people; if it is unlucky in whom it chooses first (or second, third, and so on), a number of depositions may be taken that reveal no meaningful information, delay the progress of discovery, and increase the costs. Rule 30(b)(6) seeks to obviate this problem by allowing the requesting party to identify the matters that it wants to discover from the corporation through a deposition, and then requiring the corporation to select the person or persons who are able to provide that information.

As a corollary to this scenario, the corporation may moan that the requesting party is methodically—and mindlessly—trying to depose each and every person who may have some knowledge, however indirect or limited. Rule 30(b)(6) is intended to aid the corporation by providing the means to avoid that spectacle as well. You may be thinking that reasonable parties could avoid these problems without the need for a rule, possibly by using more artfully drafted interrogatories or informal discussions wherein the corporation's lawyer tells the requesting party which of 15 people really are the most knowledgeable—and the requesting party's attorney believes that the corporation's attorney is shooting straight. You are right, that is how it should work, but it often does not, which is one reason why we have rules.

The drafters of Rule 30(b)(6) rejected the objection that a corporation should not be burdened with having to figure out which person should appear to testify about a particular subject, reasoning that "[t]his burden is not essentially different from that of answering interrogatories under Rule 33, and is in any case lighter than keeping an examining party ignorant of who in the corporation has knowledge." You might be fairly skeptical about the former proposition: The time needed to assemble information to answer an interrogatory, which requires only a written narrative answer without cross-examination, generally is far less than the time necessary to prepare a witness to testify during the give and take of a deposition. However, the latter proposition is certainly true: It generally is far easier and more efficient for the corporation to figure out who can best testify to particular subjects than it is for the opposing party to play "20 Questions" (or, worse, 20 depositions) to identify the person or persons who can do so.

With that historical perspective in mind, we turn to a discussion of some issues parties might wish to consider in taking and defending Rule 30(b)(6) depositions.

Requesting Party Issues

Is a Rule 30(b)(6) deposition appropriate? The types of issues suitable for Rule 30(b)(6) depositions include the obvious example of an action by the corporation that involved many individuals, but it is unclear what role each played. Consider, for example, a sexual harassment case in which the corporation asserts as a defense that it promptly conducted a thorough investigation of the charges of sexual harassment and found no action was necessary. The plaintiff serves interrogatories seeking to learn who has knowledge of the investigation and receives a list of 10 names, ranging from the plaintiff's supervisor, to employees in the human relations department, to the vice president of the company, all the way up to the president. But it is unclear who knows what. A Rule 30(b)(6) deposition provides an efficient way to find out details about the investigation and learn who had the kind of involvement that might warrant further exploration through individual depositions. Keep in mind that pursuing a Rule 30(b)(6) "does not preclude taking a deposition by any other procedure authorized in the rules." Indeed, this is the paradigm that gave rise to the addition of Rule 30(b)(6) to the civil discovery rules in the first place.

A Rule 3(b)(6) deposition also may be useful when a party is interested in finding out about conduct that took place years earlier and involved people who may no longer be with the corporation. For example, let's say that a patent infringement suit asserts that the defendant corporation infringed a patent issued years earlier. The defendant claims the plaintiff obtained the patent by failing to disclose relevant prior art to the Patent and Trademark Office (PTO). The defendant seeks to learn about the prior art search the plaintiff made before filing the patent application and the criteria the plaintiff used to decide what prior art to disclose to the PTO. But some employees involved in those decisions may no longer be with the plaintiff, and the remaining employees do not have sufficient direct knowledge. A Rule 30(b)(6) notice provides a mechanism by which the defendant can force the plaintiff to produce a witness to testify both to the facts known to the corporation and those "reasonably available" to it about the prior investigation.

Another example of a Rule 30(b)(6) deposition put to good use is with a document request in a large case that yields voluminous indecipherable information. A Rule 30(b)(6) notice that attaches the documents and asks for a witness (or witnesses) able to testify about them is an efficient way to get answers and determine which documents may be useful in the case.

The common thread connecting these situations is the inability of the requesting party to identify witnesses who can clearly testify about the particular activity or documents. There is little point to seeking a Rule 30(b)(6) deposition of a witness able to testify about the company's decision to fire an individual if that decision was made by a sole individual. There also is little point to it in a breach-of-contract case for testimony about why the plaintiff claims the goods it received did not conform to the contractual requirement. Because you already know whom to depose for the information you want, there is little to be gained from a Rule 30(b)(6) deposition.

Timing of Rule 30(b)(6) requests. You may have questions about when the request be should made. The short answer is, the sooner the better. Consider again the underlying purpose of Rule 30(b)(6): to give a requesting party the means to obtain testimony efficiently from the corporation when the requesting party does not know who the appropriate witnesses are, or when one witness may not be able to provide the desired information. The interests of the requesting party are rarely advanced by being kept in the dark about this information until the end of discovery. Obtaining the Rule 30(b)(6) testimony as early in the discovery process as is reasonably possible allows more time to consider what use to make of documents that are identified and explained at the deposition, or to take the depositions of individuals identified during the Rule 30(b)(6) deposition whose testimony may truly be important.

A Rule 30(b)(6) notice is not a repository to be used at the end of the case for all discovery requests that could have been pursued earlier but were not. Nonetheless, it is not uncommon to see Rule 30(b)(6) notices sent out at the eleventh hour (or later), or for a party who waited until the very end of discovery to take a Rule 30(b)(6) deposition to ask for an extension of time to follow up with further discovery based on the Rule 30(b)(6) deposition. The requesting party's ability to pursue this additional discovery is left up to the discretion of the judge—which might not be the most friendly position to be in, depending on the age of the case, how long discovery has lasted, how often it has been extended, the expansiveness of topics called out by the Rule 30(b)(6) notice, and the reason for waiting so long to serve it. Unless there is a good reason for a late notice, the requested discovery might well be denied as untimely.

Considerations in crafting the Rule 30(b)(6) notice. The requesting party should give careful thought to how it describes the subjects to be covered in the Rule 30(b)(6) deposition. First, Rule 30(b)(6) requires the subject matter on which testimony is being sought to be described "with reasonable particularity." *See generally Mitsui & Co. (U.S.A.) v. P.R. Water Res. Auth.*, 93 F.R.D. 62, 66 (D.P.R. 1981) (notice is sufficient if it informs corporation "of the matters which will be inquired into at the deposition" so corporation can "determine the identity and number of persons whose presence will be necessary"). Although reasonableness often is in the eye of the beholder, in this context reasonableness should relate to the underlying purpose of the rule: to shift the burden of determining who is able to provide information from the requesting party to the corporation concerning the matter in issue. In order for the burden shifting to work, the requesting party must describe the information being sought in a way that fairly allows the corporation to identify the person or persons able to provide the information and to prepare them adequately to do so. *Compare, e.g., Steil v. Humana Kansas City, Inc.,* 197 F.R.D. 442, 444 (D. Kan. 2000) (notice seeking testimony regarding specific group health insurance policy issued to plaintiff identified subject matter with reasonable particularity); *Marker v. Union Fld. Life Ins. Co.,* 125 F.R.D. 121, 125–26 (M.D.N.C. 1989) (notice seeking testimony about claims processing, claim records, general file keeping, storage, and retrieval systems was specific and understandable) *with Reed v. Nellcor Puritan et al.,* 193 F.R.D. 689, 692 (D. Kan. 2000) (notice stating "the area of inquiry will 'include, but not [be] limited to,' the areas specifically enumerated" was overbroad because listed areas of inquiry were not exclusive); *Operative Plasterers' & Cement Masons' Int'l Ass'n v. Benjamin,* 144 F.R.D. 87, 89–90 (N.D. Ind. 1992) (finding notice was defective because it did not describe the subject matter of the proposed examination).

In considering whether your notice meets this test of reasonableness, this Golden Rule works as well in litigation as it does in life: If you would think the request was unfair if you received it, then your opponents will probably think it is unfair if you serve it on them.

Second, the obligation of the responding corporation is to present a witness able to testify about matters "known or reasonably available to the organization." Going back to the patent case example described above, the defendant may be very interested in what the patent examiner thought about the listing of prior art set forth in the patent application. However, although the corporation can reasonably be expected to know what the examiner said to its representatives about this, the examiner's private thoughts or private conversations within the PTO are neither known to the organization nor reasonably available to it. Thus, a Rule 30(b)(6) notice that describes the subjective beliefs of the patent examiner as a subject matter of the Rule 30(b)(6) inquiry likely will not yield the requesting party very much beyond a discovery dispute.

Third, consider how many separate Rule 30(b)(6) categories you wish to designate in a notice. The more categories listed, the more likely the requesting party will buy itself a discovery dispute on the ground that the request is unduly burdensome. Rule

30(b)(6) has no numeric limit on categories that may be contained in a notice (unlike, for example, Rule 33, which limits to 25 the number of interrogatories that can be served without leave of court). But Rule 30(b)(6), like other discovery rules, is subject to the discretion of the court to limit discovery under Rule 26(b)(2), based on factors such as the burden imposed by the request, the likely benefits of the requested discovery, and other means available for obtaining the information. *See, e.g., Insituform Tech., Inc. v. Cat Contracting, Inc.*, 914 F. Supp. 286, 287 (N.D. Ill. 1996). It will be the rare case in which scores of Rule 30(b)(6) categories are appropriate. The more listed categories, and the more preparation for producing corporate witnesses required, the better the case for the responding party that the discovery should be denied (or limited) because its burden outweighs its likely benefit.

To quote those illustrious modern philosophers the Rolling Stones, "You can't always get what you want, but if you try sometimes, you just might find you get what you need." There is no harm in drafting an all-encompassing wish list of Rule 30(b)(6) topics. But the key is to then review that list with a critical eye to reduce the categories to those truly likely to obtain useful information in the case.

Fourth, one of the most common errors in Rule 30(b)(6) notices is the demand that the corporation produce the person or persons "most knowledgeable" about the matter in issue. You can search high and low in Rule 30(b)(6), and you will not find a requirement that the corporation produce the "most knowledgeable" witness. The requirement is that the persons offered by the corporation as the Rule 30(b)(6) designee "shall testify as to matters known or reasonably available to the organization." The person offered by the corporation may be the "most knowledgeable," in the sense of having the most direct knowledge of the subject—but not always. Sometimes the "most knowledgeable" person has left the corporation. So if you draft a request that demands production of the "most knowledgeable witness," do not come to court complaining—you will be fighting a losing battle.

Fifth, while focusing on the issues unique to a Rule 30(b)(6) notice, do not forget that the general requirements for noticing up a deposition also apply to Rule 30(b)(6) depositions. For example, there must be reasonable advance notice under Rule

30(b)(1) (and what is reasonable will depend on the scope of the subjects listed in the notice); if you want the deposition to be videotaped, you must specify that in the notice, as required by Rule 30(b)(2). You may seek production of documents in the deposition notice, as permitted by Rule 30(b)(5); further, if you are pursuing a Rule 30(b)(6) deposition of a non-party corporation, make sure you satisfy the requirements of FRCP Rule 45.

Responding Party Issues

We now look at the responding corporation's side of the equation. Here are some considerations to keep in mind:

Objections to the notice. As counsel for the corporation, you receive a Rule 30(b)(6) notice and—reflexively—cringe. You canvass the requests to see whether the corporation may have legitimate objections. Perhaps one or more of the topics identified seems to you to be overly broad or difficult to interpret; if so, you may have an argument that the requests do not describe the topics with "reasonable particularity." Maybe there are so many requests that the notice should be limited under Rule 26(b)(2) because it would be too burdensome to satisfy. Keep in mind that these type of objections often are easier to articulate than substantiate. But if you believe you have a good objection, your first step should be to raise it with the requesting party. A conference with a party is required by Rule 37 before any motion practice can commence, but who knows? You just might be able to work it out—or be persuaded that motion practice would be futile.

One objection to Rule 30(b)(6) notice that in most, but not all, cases is unlikely to go very far is that no facts are known or reasonably available to the corporation concerning the subject matter of the request. But what about the situation in which the corporation normally would be expected to know, or be able to obtain, facts about a subject matter but legitimately pleads ignorance? The corporation still must do the best it can to get the information and provide a witness. *See, eg., Jakob v. Champion Int'l Corp.*, No. 01 C 0497, 2001 U.S. Dist. LEXIS 19010, at *3 (N.D. Ill. Nov. 14, 2001) (corporation must designate representative even if no employee with actual knowledge of events currently exists); *Canal Barge Co. v. Commonwealth Edison Co.*, No. 98 C 0509, 2001 WL 817853 (N.D. Ill. July 19, 2001); *United States v. Taylor*, 166 F.R.D. 356, 359, 361 (M.D.N.C 1996) (corporation is not relieved of duty to produce representative when matters are reasonably available through documents, past employees, or other sources): *Mitsui & Co. (U.S.A.), Inc.*, 93 F.R.D. at 67 ("[t]he general rule is that a claimed lack of knowledge does not provide sufficient grounds for a protective order"). Of course, reasonable attorneys should be able to craft a stipulation that would obviate the need for a Rule 30(b)(6) deposition. But if they cannot, the requesting party might well be able to force the corporation to present a witness to testify to the corporation's lack of knowledge.

Identity of the Rule 30(b)(6) witness. A critical consideration in responding to a Rule 30(b)(6) notice is whom to designate as the corporate representative. The rule describes what the witness must be able to do: testify to "matters known or reasonably available" to the corporation in connection with the designated topic. Although the rule does not require the person designated to be the individual "most knowledgeable" about the subject matter, there is nothing to prohibit the corporation from designating that person. There are certain advantages to doing so. For example, the more the individual knows about the subject, the less difficult the task of preparing the witness to testify. And the more the witness actually knows, the less the chance that the witness will say something at the deposition the corporation may wish to take back at trial—which, as we shall see later, is not an easy thing to do.

Rule 30(b)(6) does not require the witness designated by the corporation to be one of its employees. The rule indicates that in addition to officers, directors, or managing agents, a corporation may designate "other persons who consent to testify on its behalf." This can include a person not employed by the company. *See, e.g., J.M. Taylor*, 166 F.R.D. at 362 (corporation with knowledge must designate officer, employee, agent "or other" individual to present company's position); *Dravo Corp. v. Liberty Mut. Ins. Co.*, 164 F.R.D. 70, 75 (D. Neb. 1995) (if no current employee has knowledge of requested information, corporation must prepare other witnesses to give "complete, knowledgeable and binding answers on behalf of the corporation"). There may be instances where it is advantageous to the corporation to reach out to a former employee to act as the Rule 30(b)(6) witness on a particular topic.

Let's go back to the example of the sexual harassment case and the request for a witness to testify about the corporation's investigation of the plaintiff's harassment complaint. It may be that the human resources manager at the time was central in directing the investigation, assembling the results, and discussing with upper management what action to take. The corporation may want that person to be the designee to testify about the investigation even though the individual no longer is employed by the corporation. Having the former employee act as the Rule 30(b)(6) witness may be to the corporation's advantage, because it would eliminate the possibility that another designee might testify to certain actions in the investigation and then be contradicted if the former employee were subpoenaed by the plaintiff to testify at trial. A former employee on good terms with the corporation well may consent to act as the Rule 30(b)(6) witness.

Sometimes the person most knowledgeable is not available; the witness may be deceased or may have left the corporation under circumstances that do not make that person willing to be a Rule 30(b)(6) witness—and the rule expressly states that without consent, the person cannot be offered as the corporate witness. Even when a person who might be most knowledgeable is available, the corporation may decide that this individual is not the best witness to tell the corporation's story and designate someone less knowledgeable to be the corporate designee.

The party responding to a Rule 30(b)(6) notice also must decide how many witnesses to designate to cover the proposed subjects. In this respect, the designating party must keep in mind the advisory committee's note to Rule 30(d)(2) concerning the limit of one seven-hour day per deposition and that "the deposition of each person designated under Rule 30(b)(6) should be considered a separate deposition." Thus, if a responding party to a notice designates two people to cover one subject, the result would be 14 hours of deposition rather than seven, and a significant increase in expenditures of time and effort, to prepare the witnesses.

Preparing the Rule 30(b)(6) witness. Although the corporation need not offer the most knowledgeable person, the designee must be able to testify as to matters "known or reasonably available to the organization." This requires the corporation to prepare its designee(s) to testify fully about the subject matter. The corporation cannot designate a person without any knowledge to stonewall legitimate discovery requests by repeatedly saying "I don't know" in response to questions about the designated subjects when in fact the information is known or reasonably available to the corporation. Such a tactic would undermine the purpose of Rule 30(b)(6) and is sanctionable. *See*, e.g., *Reilly* v. *Natwest Mkts. Group, Inc.*, 181 F.3d 253, 268–69 (2d Cir. 1999) (affirming district court's sanction precluding certain witnesses from testifying at trial); *Resolution Trust Corp. v. S. Union Co.*, 985 F.2d 196, 197 (5th Cir. 1995) (affirmed award of sanctions where the corporation designated two witnesses, neither of whom had knowledge of noticed topics); *Marker*, 125 F.R.D. at 126–27 (sanctions imposed under Rule 37(a)(4) for failure to provide Rule 30(b)(6) witness prepared to give "complete, knowledgeable and binding answers on behalf of the corporation").

The less direct knowledge the corporate designee has about the subject matter of the Rule 30(b)(6) topic, the more the corporation's lawyer will have to do in order to prepare the witness to testify to what is "known or reasonably available" to the corporation. The question of how to prepare a witness would be a fit subject for an article unto itself, and so here we limit ourselves to one obvious, yet critical, consideration: In preparing the witness, you must take care that privileged documents and other privileged information are not used by the witness to obtain knowledge about the subject.

Let's go back to the patent infringement case for a moment and consider a situation in which the corporation's Rule 30(b)(6) witness familiarizes himself with the prior art search that was done by reviewing a memorandum, prepared by the person who conducted the search to the patent counsel, setting forth the search and asking for legal advice as to whether it was adequate. The corporation declined to produce that document during discovery on the basis of privilege but identified the document on a privilege log. At the outset of the deposition, the Rule 30(b)(6) witness is asked, quite properly, which documents were reviewed to prepare for the deposition. The witness responds that he reviewed a privileged, non-produced memorandum. Under FRE 612, that may lead to the unhappy (for the responding corporation) and unintended result that the privilege in the document is deemed waived and the document must be produced. The corporation runs a similar risk if the sole source for the information used by the witness is what counsel told him during preparation. Simply issuing a Rule 30(b)(6) notice cannot create a right to obtain such privileged information. But it is quite another matter if the corporation injects privileged material into the case by using it to prepare the corporate designee. Thus, when preparing the witness, make sure that the witness does not review privileged documents and that the sole source of his or her information is not facts related by counsel.

The capacity in which the witness testifies. It is important to clarify, on the record, the capacity in which the witness testifies. Remember that Rule 30(b)(6) states that proceeding with a corporate representative deposition "does not preclude taking a deposition by any other procedure authorized in these rules." Frequently, the witness offered up by the corporation as its representative to testify about a Rule 30(b)(6) topic is a person whom the requesting party also wants to depose in an individual capacity. And, in the case of small, closely held corporations, there may be no difference between the knowledge of the entity and the knowledge of the principals. *A.I.A. Holdings v. Lehman Brothers*, 2002 W.L. 1041356 (S.D.N.Y. May 23, 2002). As a matter of convenience and efficiency, the parties frequently will agree that the witness can be deposed in one sitting, as both a corporate representative and an individual witness.

When this occurs, take care to make it abundantly clear in which capacity the witness is answering certain questions. It would be prudent for the party taking the deposition to begin by deposing the witness in that witness's individual capacity and then to make a clear break in the record to indicate that the deposition is now questioning the witness in the witness's 30(b)(6) capacity. However, the nature of the subject matter may not always permit completing the deposition in one capacity before embarking on the deposition in the other capacity. If this is the case, the questioning attorney, at a minimum, should clearly state on the record when the questioning switches from one capacity to the other.

This is essential because a witness testifying in an individual capacity is testifying to what the witness *personally* knows, or said, or heard, or did. But a witness testifying as a corporate representative is testifying not to the information that he or she personally knows but to what the *corporation* knows. Using the patent case hypothetical, if the president of the corporation testifies in his individual capacity that he does not know what prior art search was done before the patent application was filed, that is of debatable significance. Depending on the other evidence in the case, one might infer that the president's professed lack of knowledge is not credible; or that it is credible but not particularly flattering because it shows that the president is asleep at the helm: or that it is credible and perfectly understandable because these kind of details would be handled by subordinates. But if the president of the corporation gives that testimony as a Rule 30(b)(6) witness, that testimony takes on an entirely different level of significance because it asserts that the corporation has no knowledge about the investigation. And it is difficult to spin that kind of testimony in a way favorable to the corporation.

Disputes during the deposition. Two types of disputes never come up in a personal-capacity deposition but frequently arise during the course of a Rule 30(b)(6) deposition. One dispute concerns whether a particular question is properly within the scope of the matter designated in the Rule 30(b)(6) notice; the other, related complaint is that the witness did not do what is necessary to prepare to testify fairly about the information known or reasonably available to the corporation. These complaints are related because they both have root in the way the Rule 30(b)(6) notice is drafted. At the specificity of the notice increases, so does the possibility that during the ebb and flow of the deposition, the deposing attorney will draw the objection that a particular question exceeds the scope of the notice. *Compare King v. Pratt & Whitney*, 161 F.R.D. 475, 476 (S.D. Fla. 1995) (examining party allowed to ask questions beyond three specific areas listed in notice, but limits in notice "define a corporation's obligations regarding whom they are obligated to produce for such a deposition and what that witness is obligated to be able to answer"), *aff'd*, 213 F.3d 646 (11th Cir. 2000), *with Paparelli v. Prudential Ins. Co.*, 108 F.R.D. 727, 730 (D. Mass. 1985) (holding that party "must confine the examination to the matters" in the notice, reasoning that "a limitation on the scope of the deposition to the matters specified in the notice is implied in the rule"). At the same time, the possibility decreases that the witness can credibly assert he or she did not know what information the requesting party was looking for.

On the other hand, as the generality of the Rule 30(b)(6) topic increases, the likelihood of an objection that a particular question exceeds the scope of that general notice decreases—but so does the likelihood that a witness is going to answer that he or she did not know that the questioning attorney was looking for that particular detail and thus did not obtain that information. This tension underscores the importance of drafting the Rule

30(b)(6) notice with care to seek a balance between a notice that is both general enough to cover the topics the requesting attorney wants to learn about (without getting so broad as to be unduly burdensome), yet specific enough to give the corporation enough direction to be able to prepare a witness to provide the information that the requesting attorney really wants.

What does the lawyer representing the corporation do if he or she believes a question has been asked that exceeds the scope of the Rule 30(b)(6) notice? *Must* the corporation's attorney object, or waive the point? Perhaps not: Under FRCP 32(d)(3)(A) and (B), objections to the competency of a witness or to errors or irregularities occurring during the oral examination are waived if not made at the deposition, but only if the ground of the objection is one that could have been avoided or cured at the time of the deposition. Rule 32(d)(3) seeks to avoid the questioning attorney's being sandbagged by having the defending attorney hold an objection that could have been cured at the deposition and spring it when it is too late to be cured. If a question truly exceeds the scope of the notice, that likely is an objection that cannot be cured at the taking of the deposition: failure to raise that objection likely would not be a waiver.

Nonetheless, *should* the defending attorney raise the objection on the record? The prudent answer may be yes, for two reasons. First, making the objection obviates any risk that if the matter is later litigated, the presiding judge will find that the objection was waived. Second, raising the objection may allow the defending attorney to hear why the opposing attorney thinks the question is within the scope of the Rule 30(b)(6) notice, which will either give the defending attorney more confidence in his or her position or cause the defending attorney to reconsider its wisdom.

However, even if the defending attorney believes the question is beyond the scope of the Rule 30(b)(6) notice, the defending attorney must think twice—and then think again—before instructing the witness not to answer. Rule 30(d)(1) allows an instruction not to answer only when "necessary to preserve a privilege, to enforce a limitation directed by the court, or to present a motion under Rule 30(d)(4)" for protective order on the ground that the questioning was being conducted in bad faith or to harass. It is generally better to note the objection and have the witness testify subject to the objection—which, if the defending attorney's objection is meritorious, will result in the testimony's being that of the individual and not of the corporation. *See generally Detoy v. City & County of San Francisco,* 196 F.R.D. 362, 367 (N.D. Cal. 2000) (If corporation objects to questioning beyond scope noticed, corporation may request jury instructions to explain that answers of deponent were answers or opinions of individual and not admissions of corporation): *King;* 161 F.R.D. at 476 (S.D. Fla. 1995) (answers to questions outside those noticed will be governed by general deposition rules); *but see Paparelli,* 108 F.R.D. at 730 (party must confine examination to matters stated in Rule 30(b)(6) notice).

What does the deposing attorney do when the response to a question within the scope of a Rule 30(b)(6) request is "I don't know"—which, within the context of a Rule 30(b)(6) deposition, means that the corporation doesn't know? As with most things, it depends on the circumstances. Suppose the witness clearly prepared thoroughly for the deposition and has generally been forthcoming, but simply cannot recall or failed to look into certain details. The deposing attorney could ask, and the defending attorney likely would agree, to have the witness try to obtain that information during a break and then testify to it during the deposition session. If the information will take longer to obtain; the parties might agree that additional information could be supplied in a stipulation or added when the witness reviews and signs the deposition as required by Rule 30(c). But keep in mind that if the additional information is significant enough, the Rule 30(b)(6) deposition may need to be reconvened—perhaps with a new witness. *See, e.g., Resolution Trust Corp.,* 985 F.2d at 197 (5th Cir. 1995) (corporation must designate another witness knowledgeable about relevant facts when it is realized that witness originally designated is not sufficient); *Marker,* 125 F.R.D. at 126 (even if corporation is good faith believed designee was knowledgeable, corporation "had a duty to substitute another person once the deficiency . . . became apparent during the course of the deposition").

On the other hand, suppose the initial questioning of the witness establishes that the corporation selected as its representative someone who had no significant knowledge about the relevant subject matter and who did nothing to obtain the information, so that questioning leads to a litany of "I don't know" responses. The questioning attorney might fairly suspect a tactical gambit was afoot: Perhaps the corporation presented a know-nothing witness in order to smoke out specific questions the requesting party would ask, so the corporation could later assemble the information through this or another witness (thereby converting an oral deposition under Rule 30 into something more akin to a deposition of written questions under Rule 31); perhaps the corporation presented a know-nothing witness simply to stonewall. Either way, the requesting party could fairly claim an abuse of the Rule 30(b)(6) process and seek sanctions.

Rule 37(a)(2) authorizes sanctions when a deponent "fails to answer a question propounded or submitted under Rules 30 or 31, or a corporation or other entity fails to make a designation under Rule 30(b)(6) or 31(a)." Rule 37(a)(3) further provides that an "evasive or incomplete disclosure, answer or response is to be treated as a failure to disclose, answer or respond." These sanctions include an order compelling the corporation to produce a Rule 30(b)(6) witness who can testify fairly to the subject matter, and an award of fees incurred by the requesting party as a result of the corporation's conduct. If that order is then violated, the full panoply of sanctions under Rule 37(b)(2) is available—ranging from ordering certain facts established to a default or dismissal.

None of those sanctions would be pleasant for the corporation. But perhaps no less dangerous for the corporation is the possibility that the requesting party might decide to forgo a motion for sanctions, accept the litany of "I don't know" answers, and then use them at trial.

Using Rule 30(b)(6) testimony at trial. Rule 32(a)(2) provides that a Rule 30(b)(6) deposition of a party corporation "may be used by an adverse party for any purpose," without respect to witness availability. The right to use a Rule 30(b)(6) deposition is, of course, subject to the rules of evidence, except hearsay rules, which of necessity operate in a more limited scope (because the whole point of the Rule 30(b)(6) deposition is that the corporate representative will be testifying to things the *corporation* knows, irrespective of the witness's personal knowledge of them).

If the adverse party uses the Rule 30(b)(6) deposition testimony at trial, can the corporation offer other evidence or testimony to contradict it—and impeach what its Rule 30(b)(6) witness said during discovery? Two schools of thought exist on this point.

One approach treats Rule 30(b)(6) testimony as "binding on the corporation" and prohibits a corporation from offering contrary evidence at trial. *See, e.g., Rainey v. Am. Forest & Paper*

Assoc., 26 F. Supp. 2d 82, 94–95 (D.D.C. 1998) ("Rule 30(b)(6) preclud[es] defendant from adducing from [plaintiff] a theory of facts that differs from that articulated by the designated representatives"). The rationale for this approach is that the underlying purpose of Rule 30(b)(6) is to "prevent a corporate defendant from thwarting inquiries during discovery, then staging an ambush during a later phase of the case." *Rainey*, 26 F. Supp. 2d at 95. This approach in effect treats Rule 30(b)(6) testimony the same as admissions made in response to a Rule 36 request to admit: The matter admitted is "conclusively established."

This approach creates great risk for the corporation whose Rule 30(b)(6) witness testifies incorrectly or says "I don't know" on an important matter the corporation should know. Rule 30(b)(6) testimony can be reviewed and changed by the witness for 30 days after the transcript becomes available (*see* Rule 30(e)), thus giving the corporation a short window to revise the testimony. However, a corporation cannot use Rule 26(e) to amend the deposition because the duty (and right) of supplementation extends to materially incomplete or incorrect responses to interrogatories, requests for production, or requests for admission—not to depositions.

Pursuant to Rule 36(b) a court may permit "withdrawal or amendment of an admission" under appropriate circumstances. Thus, the cases that treat Rule 30(b)(6) testimony like a binding Rule 36 admission would allow the corporation to escape from the preclusive effect of Rule 30(b)(6) testimony. *See, e.g., Rainey*, 26 F. Supp. 2d at 95 (designee testimony may not bind corporation if corporation can show information contradicting designee was not "reasonably available" at time of deposition); *J.M. Taylor*, 166 F.R.D. at 362 ("if a party states it has no knowledge or position as to a set of alleged facts or area of inquiry at a Rule 30(b)(6) deposition, it cannot argue for a contrary position at trial without introducing evidence explaining the reasons for the change"). But the "appropriate circumstances" exception would be limited and could not be counted on to provide the corporation with a safe haven.

Another school of thought is that Rule 30(b)(6) deposition testimony has no more preclusive effect than any other deposition testimony. *See, e.g., A.I. Credit Corp. v. Legion Ins. Co.*, 265 F.3d 630, 637 (7th Cir. 2001) (Rule 30(b)(6) deposition does not bind corporation as judicial admission and can be contradicted at trial); *see also R&B Appliance Parts, Inc. v. Amana Co.*, 258 F.3d 783, 786 (8th Cir. 2001) (designee "is no more bound than any witness is by his or her prior deposition testimony" and may testify differently at trial). Under this line of authority, a corporation may offer testimony or other evidence to contradict its Rule 30(b)(6) testimony, leaving it to the jury to make what it will of the contradiction. Although certainly not as extreme as treating the Rule 30(b)(6) testimony as preclusive, this approach can present serious complications to the corporation that tries to explain why its trial witnesses are contradicting the sworn testimony of a person designated by the corporation as able to testify as to the corporation's knowledge.

Skillfully used, the Rule 30(b)(6) deposition is a valuable litigation tool that can significantly streamline the discovery process. If treated carelessly, however, the Rule 30(b)(6) deposition will engender needless discovery disputes that only will increase the cost of litigation and may come back to haunt the corporation at trial. In either event, the message is clear. A Rule 30(b)(6) notice is not something to treat lightly.

ABOUT THE EDITORS AND CONTRIBUTORS

Priscilla Anne Schwab is a Senior Attorney-Advisor of the Administrative Review Board of the U.S. Department of Labor in Washington, D.C.

Lawrence J. Vilardo, a past editor-in-chief of LITIGATION, is a partner in Connors & Vilardo, LLP, in Buffalo, New York.

John S. Applegate is the Executive Associate Dean for Academic Affairs and Walter W. Foskett Professor of Law at Indiana University School of Law, Bloomington, Indiana.

Arthur H. Aufses III is a partner with Kramer, Levin, Naftalis & Frankel in New York City.

David M. Balabanian is a member of Bingham McCutchen LLP in San Francisco.

Kenneth R. Berman is a partner in Nutter McClennen & Fish LLP, Boston, Massachusetts.

Edward D. Cavanagh is Professor of Law at St. John's University School of Law and of counsel to Morgan, Lewis & Bockius in New York City.

Steven C. Day is with Woodard, Hernandez, Roth & Day, LLC, in Wichita, Kansas.

Diana S. Donaldson is a partner in the Philadelphia office of Schnader Harrison Segal & Lewis LLP.

Jerome P. Facher is a senior partner in the Boston firm of Wilmer Cutler Pickering Hale & Dorr LLP and a lecturer in trial practice at Harvard Law School.

Lawrence J. Fox, former chair of the ABA Section of Litigation, is with Drinker Biddle & Reath, LLP in Philadelphia, Pennsylvania.

Stuart M. Israel is a partner with Martens, Ice, Klass, Legghio & Israel, P.C. in Royal Oak, Michigan.

Janeen Kerper taught ethics and trial advocacy at California Western School of Law in San Diego.

Jeffrey J. Kroll is a partner with Clifford Law Offices, P.C., in Chicago.

Steven Lubet is Professor of Law and Director, Bartlit Center for Trial Strategy, Northwestern University School of Law, in Chicago.

Christopher T. Lutz, a former editor-in-chief of LITIGATION, is a partner with Steptoe & Johnson L.L.P. in Washington, D. C.

David M. Malone is the founding partner of Trial Run Inc., a trial consulting and advocacy training firm.

Thomas J. McNamara, now deceased, was a partner at Warner, Norcross & Judd L.L.P. in Grand Rapids, Michigan.

Laurin H. Mills is a partner with Nixon Peabody LLP in Washington, D.C.

Sidney I. Schenkier is a U.S. Magistrate Judge for the Northern District of Illinois.

Briscoe R. Smith is of counsel to the Atlantic Legal Foundation in New York City.

Paul T. Sorensen is a partner in Warner, Norcross & Judd L.L.P. in Grand Rapids, Michigan.

Stuart A. Summit is a member of the New York City firm of Phillips Nizer L.L.P.

Dennis R. Suplee is a partner in the Philadelphia office of Schnader Harrison Segal & Lewis LLP.

Peter L. Winik is a partner is the Washington, D.C., office of Latham & Watkins LLP.

Gerson A. Zweifach is with the firm of Williams & Connolly, LLP in Washington, D.C.